PRAISE FOR
The Lives of the Muses

"A stylish assessment of nine very different women who appear to have made the alchemy of art possible.... [Prose] has braided these lives together closely and nimbly, so that the whole is even more resonant than the sum of its vibrant parts."
—STACY SCHIFF, *New York Times Book Review*

"Rollicking.... Almost too much fun to read."
—MAUREEN CORRIGAN, NPR's *Fresh Air*

"Wry, deeply intelligent, and beautifully written, *The Lives of the Muses* illuminates the complex partnerships of creativity. The struggles and occasional triumphs of these women are fascinating."
—ANDREA BARRETT, author of *Voyage of the Narwhal* and *Servants of the Map*

"Juicy reading.... A thoroughly researched, highly opinionated series of fascinating double biographies."   —*Los Angeles Times*

"The book's achievement is its quiet reevaluation of the received notion that genius is solitary in nature.... A complicated vision of the necessary contradictions of artistic life."   —*The New Yorker*

"Francine Prose humanizes nine women who, in some cases, have been idealized beyond recognition. Hurrah for *real* women."
—*San Francisco Chronicle*

"Wonderfully learned and witty. *The Lives of the Muses* teaches us that the role of muse is more of a care than a consolation, and also that we should all have one, even though they are rather demanding possessions. Poor Yoko Ono! Hats off to the understanding Mrs. Thrale. It's a delight."   —DIANE JOHNSON, author of *Le Divorce* and *Le Mariage*

"You should read [*The Lives of the Muses*] for the newly eloquent force these stories acquire when resituated and refocused by Prose, who ... strives to reveal the enabling, essential presence of love at the core of any artistic creation."   —*Houston Chronicle*

"Francine Prose's *Lives of the Muses* is an addictive delight—one enthralling story after another told with luminous intelligence and wit."
—JEAN STROUSE, author of *Alice James* and *J. P. Morgan*

"Sharp and funny. . . . The eleven stories [Prose] unfolds are studded with details that showcase the author's deftness for drawing character."
—*Chicago Tribune*

"A supple work of cultural history." —*Time*

"Prose expertly analyzes the conflicts between romance and dependence, sacrifice and exploitation, passion and genius that generate the volatile chemistry between muse and artist, thus deepening our insights into human behavior and art, the ridiculous and the sublime."
—*Booklist* (starred review)

"Politically incorrect or not, the muses, as Prose presents them, genuinely 'illumine and deepen the mysteries of Eros and creativity, as each Muse redraws the border between the human and the divine.' . . . Prose makes a remarkable case for the exceptionality of these women in their own right." —*Publishers Weekly* (starred review)

"A remarkable book. . . . Piquant, intelligent, provocative—and sometimes haunting." —*Minneapolis Star Tribune*

"Exceptionally well researched. . . . An elegant study." —*Book Forum*

"*The Lives of the Muses* is a daringly conceived renovation of current and historical notions of what drives the creative process."
—*New York Observer*

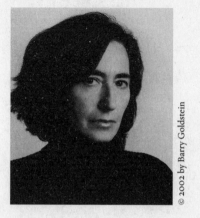

About the Author

FRANCINE PROSE's books include *Bigfoot Dreams, Household Saints* (which was made into a film by Nancy Savoca), *Hunters and Gatherers, Women and Children First, Primitive People, Guided Tours of Hell,* and *Blue Angel,* a Finalist for the National Book Award. Her fiction and nonfiction have been published in *The New Yorker, The Atlantic, GQ, The Paris Review, Harper's,* the *New York Times, Elle,* and many other publications. She writes regularly on art for the *Wall Street Journal.*

THE LIVES OF THE MUSES

THE LIVES OF THE MUSES

Nine Women and the Artists They Inspired

FRANCINE PROSE

Perennial

An Imprint of HarperCollins*Publishers*

First Perennial edition published 2003.

Designed by Elliott Beard

The Library of Congress has catalogued the hardcover edition as follows:

Prose, Francine.
     The lives of the muses : nine women and the artists they
        inspired / Francine Prose.—1st ed.
          p. cm.
     Includes bibliographical references and index.
     ISBN 0-06-019672-6
        1. Creation (Literary, artistic, etc.). 2. Man-woman relationships.
     3. Artistic collaboration. I. Title.

NX160 .P765 2002
700′.92′2—dc21
[B]
                                                        2002024682

ISBN 0-06-055525-4 (pbk.)

03 04 05 06 07 ❖/RRD 10 9 8 7 6 5 4 3 2 1

For Robert Jones
Editor, Friend, Muse Supreme

CONTENTS

List of Illustrations ix

Acknowledgments xi

Introduction 1

Hester Thrale 25

Alice Liddell 57

Elizabeth Siddal 99

Lou Andreas-Salomé 137

Gala Dalí 187

Lee Miller 227

Charis Weston 269

Suzanne Farrell 297

Yoko Ono 327

Afterword 369

Endnotes 375

Bibliography 399

Index 405

ILLUSTRATIONS

Mrs. Thrale and Her Daughter Hester (Queeney).
   (Sir Joshua Reynolds)   26

Portrait of Alice Liddell as the Beggar Child.
   (Charles Dodgson)   66

How They Met Themselves. *(Dante Gabriel Rossetti)*   121

Beata Beatrix. *(Dante Gabriel Rossetti)*   134

Lou Andreas-Salomé, 1897.   138

Lou von Salomé, Paul Rée, Friedrich Nietzsche, 1882.   146

Salvador and Gala Dalí. *(Brassaï)*   188

Self-Portrait, New York, 1932. *(Lee Miller)*   228

Lee with her father, Paris, January 1931. *(Man Ray)*   232

"Nonconformist Chapel," Camden Town.
   From *Grim Glory,* 1940. *(Lee Miller)*   250

Charis Weston, 1935. *(Edward Weston)*   274

My Little Gray Home in the West, 1943.
   (Edward Weston)   295

Movements for Piano and Orchestra. Jacques d'Amboise watches
  as Balanchine, working with Suzanne Farrell,
  shows him how his part should go. (*Martha Swope*)   307

Yoko Ono and John Lennon. (*Lilo Raymond*)   328

ACKNOWLEDGMENTS

THIS BOOK MIGHT never have been written if not for the New York Public Library's Center for Scholars and Writers, if Dorothy and Lewis Cullman had not so generously funded the Center, and if Peter Gay had not decided, solely on the evidence of my fiction, that I should be given a year to work in the library, with its great collections at my disposal—and picked me to be one of the Center's first Director's Fellows. My thanks to them, and to everyone connected with the Center, to Paula Baxter in the art library, to Rodney Phillips, who—in what was surely the most magical moment in my writing of this book—brought to the Center, fresh from restoration, the original presentation photograph of *Portait of Alice Liddell as the Begger Child*, the actual print that Charles Dodgson hand-tinted and framed as a present for Alice.

My colleagues at the Center helped me in every way, from translating Nietzsche's letters to venturing medical opinions on Lizzie

Siddal's substance-abuse problems. I want to thank, especially, Kathleen Cleaver, Andrew Delbanco, Greg Dreicer, Anthony Holden, Ada Louise Huxtable, Marian Kaplan, Allen Kurzweil, Howard Markel, Harvey Sachs—all of whom provided and continue to provide ideas, information, help, encouragement, conversation, entertainment, and enduring friendship. My thanks to Paul LeClerc and to Pamela Leo and Rachel Afrikissen for countless practical matters.

I would also like to thank Mark Strand for coming up with the book's title, and for doing so in the garden of the former Polish-American Restaurant, the sort of a place in which he would never normally find himself. Thanks to Deborah Eisenberg, Richard Howard, and Connie Brothers for adding their attentive, sympathetic, and knowledgeable readings of the manuscript to the countless indispensable benefits of their friendship and love.

Thanks, as always, to Howie Michels, for literally everything; to Bruno Michels for his humor, his steady support and understanding, and to Leon Michels for suggesting Yoko Ono. Thanks to Denise Shannon, for her unfailing energy, resourcefulness, good cheer, common sense, and enthusiasm. Thanks to Kamy Wicoff and to the Mellon Foundation, which enabled her to be my hardworking, resourceful assistant; to Arlene Phalon; and to Nico Baumbach for his attention to the details that make the rest possible. Thanks to everyone connected with the American Academy in Rome, and especially with its library, where, thousands of miles from home, I was able to find the books I needed to finish the chapters on Charis Weston and Hester Thrale.

My gratitude to Terry Karten, for the intelligence, spirit, tact, and, above all, grace with which she took on the editing of this book. The people at HarperCollins—Jane Friedman, Cathy Hemming, Susan Weinberg, Jane Beirn, Susan Friedland, Andrew Proctor, Alison Callahan—could not have been more sympathetic, patient, and fully human when it was most needed. Thank you.

THE LIVES OF THE MUSES

INTRODUCTION

IN THE SPRING OF 1932, at the age of eighty, Alice Pleasance Liddell Hargreaves sailed into New York Harbor to collect an honorary Ph.D. from Columbia University for having inspired, for having *been*, Alice in Wonderland. Her doctorate in musedom, possibly the only one in academic history, was conferred on the elegant, faintly imperious, and still rather pretty old woman to honor the hundredth anniversary of the birth of Lewis Carroll, whom she knew as Charles Dodgson, and whom she had seen only rarely since she was eleven, when her parents abruptly ended her friendship with the thirty-one-year-old mathematician.

The ceremony—held in the rotunda of Low Library, decorated for the occasion with masses of white flowers—got off to an unfortunate start when university president Nicholas Murray Butler sat on the flowered throne intended for Alice, who remained standing as the enthroned president summarized her doctoral qualifications:

"Awakening with her girlhood's charm the ingenious fancy of a mathematician . . . you as the moving cause—Aristotle's 'final cause'—of this truly noteworthy contribution to English literature."

Lewis Carroll's muse wore a smart brown suit and a corsage of rosebuds and lilies of the valley. In her acceptance speech, she spoke of her old friend, dead for more than forty years, as if he were still alive. She confidently expressed her faith that "Mr. Dodgson knows and rejoices with me in the honor you are doing him." And the audience applauded this incarnation of the goddess: what remained of the little girl who had caused a genius to flower on a golden summer afternoon beneath a haystack beside a river.

THE DESIRE TO EXPLAIN the mystery of inspiration, to determine who or what is the "moving cause" of art, resembles the impulse to find out a magician's secrets. It's a childish, suspect desire; we fear the truth will spoil the fun. Doesn't the mystery add to our delight? Still, it's human nature to want to see through the sides of the box in which the magician's assistant is being sawed in half, or into the mind of the poet at the instant when the sonnet appears in all its neonatal glory. During Alice Liddell's stay in New York, reporters asked her to tell, once again, how she begged Mr. Dodgson for a story—as if it were a small, obvious step from that bright summer afternoon to the incandescence of Wonderland.

One difference between magic and art is that magic can be explained. Were he willing, Houdini could have told his fans how he escaped from the chains and straitjacket, suspended under water. But the artist can never fully account for the alchemical process that turns anatomical knowledge and fresco technique into the Sistine Chapel. To create *anything* is to undergo the humbling and strange experience—like a mystical visitation or spirit possession—of making something and *not knowing where it comes from*. It's as if the magician had no idea how the rabbit got into his hat.

But we find that hard to accept, and so we look around for some myth to help explain, or at least surround, the genesis of art. The logical solution to the mystery of creation is divine intervention—a simple enough explanation, except for the dizzying speed with which our ideas about divinity change from era to era, from culture to culture. The Greeks assumed that a deity had to be involved. Significantly, they picked goddesses—nine of them—and had the common sense to make these celestial sisters more abstract, private, and distant than their heavenly colleagues, with their juicy soap operas of betrayal, jealousy, mortal lovers metamorphosed into animals and plants. Perhaps the Greeks intuited that the muses' important, elusive work was beyond the limited reach of anecdote and gossip.

In fact, we know remarkably little about the origin of the muses. Were the nine goddesses born in sequence or in a litter like puppies? Were they the result of one act of love or of a nine-night affair between the amorous Zeus and Mnemosyne, the goddess of memory? The muses' birth order may be unclear, but their lineage is inspired. Mate the life force with a sense of the past, and what you get is a culture. In Hesiod's poem, *Theogeny*, the nine muses appear to the poet and his fellow shepherds as they tend their flocks in the fields and tell them that without art and history, men are, essentially, bellies.

Mortals have yet to agree on the origin of the word *muse*. Some trace it back to the term for *ardor*, others to the same root as *mind*, or *memory*, or *mountain*. And which mountain *did* the muses inhabit: Helicon, Parnassus, or Olympus? After centuries of debate, some consensus has emerged, at least about their number, their names, and their dominions: Thalia inspired comedy, Melpomene tragedy, Euterpe lyric poetry, Erato love poetry, Terpsichore dance, Calliope epic poetry, Urania astronomy, Polyhymnia sacred poetry, Clio history. We know what props they carried (Erato is customarily shown with a bunch of wild grapes, Euterpe with a flute) when, led by Apollo, they arrived to entertain at the wedding of Cadmus and Harmonia, and the funeral of Patroclus.

They loved water and played in sacred founts; the swan was their holy bird. Pegasus belonged to them, a present from Athena. They showed Echo how to sing and play, taught the Sphinx her riddle. A few had half-mortal children who suffered hideous fates. Clio's son, Hyacinthus, was accidentally killed by Apollo in a discus-throwing game. Urania's son, Linus, was slain for inviting Apollo to take part in a music contest.

The muses could be nasty to those who challenged them or their leader. When Marsyas boasted that he was a better musician than Apollo, the muses sentenced the flute-playing satyr to be tied to a tree and skinned. The daughters of Pierus—would-be rival muses— were transformed into birds. The nine goddesses blinded the Thracian bard Thamyris for claiming that his power was greater than theirs, and plucked the Sirens' feathers for similar offenses. Sadly, as is so often the case, art failed to make the muses *nicer*. And yet their blessing could inspire and cheer the poet and his audience. "Happy he whomsoever the Muses shall have loved," wrote Hesiod. "Sweet is the sound that flows from his mouth." And when one "pines away troubled at heart, yet if a minstrel, servant of the Muses, shall have chaunted the glories of men of yore . . . quickly does he forget his melancholy, nor does he at all remember his cares."

Whether or not we share Hesiod's exalted estimation of the psychotherapeutic benefits of poetry, these verses from *Theogeny* demonstrate a faith in the muses' direct involvement in artistic creation. Or at least that's what the Greeks concluded about the source of the art, when the gods (with their Olympian omnipotence and wide range of lower impulses) still permitted a smooth conjoining of the holy and the profane. But once the gods stopped descending to earth to lecture shepherds and have sex with mortals, the culture needed an alternate explanation for the ways in which the life force expressed itself in culture.

In severing Eros from Agape, Christianity dug a chasm between religious and secular art. A vision of Jesus on the cross could inspire a great painting of the Crucifixion, but might put a bit of a damper on the erotic poet. There *were* no deities to oversee the lyric, the love song, the dance. Another source was needed, an alternate explanation for creativity—for what cannot be summoned at will and seems beyond the artist's control. Since a reversion to paganism was clearly out of the question, there was nowhere to go but down— from the divine to the mortal. And since falling in love is the closest that most people come to transcendence, to the feeling of being inhabited by unwilled, unruly forces, passion became the model for understanding inspiration. Why does the artist write or paint? The artist must be in love. And so the troubadour's lady, the ideal unattainable object of courtly love, became the compromise candidate, positioned somewhere between the Virgin and an actual flesh-and-blood woman.

Telescoped by the passage of time, this progression from the ethereal to the corporeal has come to seem so seamless and inevitable that when Homer asks the goddess to sing through him, or when Dante tells us how each poem in *Vita Nuova* reflects a delicate shift in his feelings for Beatrice, modern readers naturally understand that both poets mean the muse. We recognize that the heavenly muse invoked by Milton and Spenser belongs to a purer, loftier, and more attractive branch of the same family as Gala Dalí, the shamelessly earthy muse of her husband, Salvador. When a Surrealist artist was working well, he was said to be in love with Gala, much as an eloquent Attic bard was believed to have been visited by Calliope. Is God speaking through them, or the God of Love? It hardly seems to matter.

But of course it matters. To state one obvious fact: You can know more about a woman than you can about a goddess. Homer's muse is ageless. But Dante reminds us that when he first saw Beatrice, in Florence, in 1274, both were children of nine—a figure (the number of the circles of hell, the number of the muses) that haunted the poet's life. The sighting of Beatrice, dressed in red, was a conversion experience, the birth of a new religion. *Incipit vita nuova*. When he saw her, a new life began.

Exactly nine years later, at the ninth hour of the day, Dante again met Beatrice, this time dressed in white. She looked at him and greeted him. Back in his room, Dante had a vision of a man holding the naked Beatrice, wrapped in a crimson cloth, and feeding her a burning object—as it happened, Dante's heart. After this ghoulish meal, the man in the vision began to weep, enfolded the lady in his arms, and the pair ascended to heaven. Dante then gives us the sonnet that his imaginings inspired, a toned-down version of his dream, a poem that conceals a hidden writing lesson on how to turn morbid fantasy into art.

And so goes the *Vita Nuova*, in forty-two sections written between 1292 and 1300 and constructed on the frame of a love affair, with its predictable milestones—Beatrice grows jealous (Love, in another vision, dictates the poem that pacifies her), Beatrice mocks the poet—events that serve as pretexts for floods of feeling, exquisite self-contemplation, more sonnets, ballads, and songs. Beatrice's father dies, she too succumbs to the plague. Begun two years after her death, *Vita Nuova* displays its author's remarkable powers of recall as Dante reports every word of an inner conversation he had with himself in Latin when he was nine—a three-way chat involving his heart, his brain, and his animal instinct. The final chapter offers a promise to honor Beatrice's memory in a new, more noble way, a vow that Dante kept in the *Paradiso*.

The *Vita Nuova* is at once a send-up of conventional contemporary poetry with its formulaic declarations and vaporous fainting fits, its swooning obeisance to the God of Love—and an authentic record of the poet's love for a woman named Bice, the daughter of Folco Portinari and later the wife of a banker. Part of our ceaseless fascination with the couple derives from the myth of the boy who saw his child-muse from afar and felt her image branded on his heart forever, as well as our intuition that Dante is speaking of something deeper and more complex than this story of childhood infatuation. In any case, the Florentine poet and his muse have maintained such a hold on subsequent generations that centuries later Dante Gabriel Rossetti would press himself and his muse, Lizzie Siddal, into the mold of Dante and Beatrice, confusing their lives and identities with those of the long-dead couple and ignoring, with tragic result, the realities (Bohemian poverty, opium addiction) that distinguished Pre-Raphaelite London from Dante's Florence.

Reviving a past century's muse was a project doomed to failure. Because what the lives of the muses demonstrate is that every historical period re-creates the muse in its own image. Each era endows the muse with the qualities, virtues, and flaws that the epoch and its artists need and deserve. In eighteenth-century London, where Samuel Johnson's fame relied on a conjunction of an eloquent prose style and dazzling social skills, Mrs. Hester Thrale—a sharp-tongued, lively, intelligent woman married to a rich brewer who gave lavish dinner parties at which his wife and Dr. Johnson could *talk*—functioned as the muse of literature and of conversation. The Victorian muses—Alice Liddell, Lizzie Siddal—come to us trailing clouds of innocence, naïveté, and repression, as well as various unsavory Victorian fantasies about children and young women. Serially involved with Nietzsche, Rilke, and Freud, Lou Andreas-Salomé was the muse most suited to bridge the nineteenth and twentieth centuries. More recently, the brilliant photographer, Lee Miller, deployed the skills she'd learned as Man Ray's muse to progress from muse to artist.

Like Gala Dalí, the twentieth-century muse could double as publicist and agent, a vital sideline to inspiration in a society just beginning to appreciate the commercial benefits of commodifying the celebrity artist. Yoko Ono was, in many ways, Gala's spiritual heir; coincidentally, the two muses and their artists lived in New York's St. Regis Hotel at the same time. For all her ingeniousness, Gala could hardly have imagined the scale and efficacy of Yoko's promotional abilities, though, to be fair, the muse of the charismatic Beatle had an easier time in the marketplace than did the muse of the greasy mustachioed Surrealist, obsessed with grasshoppers and goat shit. Yet Yoko had doubts that Gala did not, for Yoko harbored reasonable suspicions, shared with her female contemporaries, about the drawbacks of being a muse rather than an artist. Initially, she attempted a sort of job-sharing arrangement with her husband, an admirable if impossible effort that she ultimately abandoned, and struggled with him, even after death, over who was the real artist, and who was the muse.

Not that either Ono or Lennon would have used the word *muse*, for the concept of musedom has become progressively more ironized in our unromantic times. Even in the longest lists of acknowledgments, contemporary writers are reluctant to identify or thank their sources of inspiration—dreading, perhaps, the test case laying claim to a percentage of their profits. Such fears will hardly be assuaged by the title character in Albert Brooks's 1999 film, *The Muse*. As played by Sharon Stone, the Hollywood goddess of directors and blocked screenwriters is shallow, frivolous, fickle, and above all, mercenary as she trades high-concept film ideas for costly gifts from Tiffany's.

The word *muse* itself has become so paradoxically fraught and extraneous that, among modern muses, only Suzanne Farrell is widely referred to as a muse—perhaps because the ballet is still so firmly rooted in the aesthetic and the language of the past. The term does appear periodically in an essay or article. A *New York Times* review of Yoko Ono's winter 2000 retrospective art exhibition at the Japan Society identified her as a muse, a designation that could hardly have thrilled the artist. But by and large, as Arlene Croce pointed out in her provocative 1996 *New Yorker* essay "Is the Muse Dead?" the notion of the muse incarnate—"devastating to modern feminism" and at odds with the most basic tenets of Freudian psychology—has become a quaint, even suspect anachronism: "At the end of the American century, making art and thinking about art seem increasingly wistful, not to say futile, occupations. Mention the Muse and people smile. We don't know who that is any more, and we may never know."

Certainly, feminism has made us rethink musedom as a career choice. Doesn't the idea of the muse reinforce the destructive stereotype of the creative, productive, active male and of the passive female, at once worshiped and degraded, agreeably disrobing to model or offer inspirational sex? Shouldn't the muse be retired for good, abolished along with all the other retro, primitive, unevolved sexist myths? A more generous solution might be to offer more choices rather than fewer, to give men and women equal opportunity to be either artist or muse or both, though cases such as John and Yoko (and F. Scott and Zelda Fitzgerald) point up the difficulty of equitably dividing the labor of creation and inspiration.

Perhaps uniquely in the lives of the muses, the partnership of Suzanne Farrell and George Balanchine suggests that the roles of inspired and inspirer, artist and muse, *can* be divided and shared between a man and a woman, two artists collaborating to produce work that neither could accomplish alone. But this blurring of boundaries was not expressly acknowledged. Farrell was inevitably described as Balanchine's muse, and no one seems to have proposed that the reverse was also true.

To say that Farrell and Balanchine might have been each other's muse raises the complicated, thorny questions: Do women artists *have* muses, and are there male muses? For whatever reason, these are, almost inevitably, the first questions people ask when the subject of muses arises. The facile answer is that male artists get muses, while their female counterparts—Virginia Woolf, for example—are more often given (in lieu of a muse) male psychiatric nurses like Leonard Woolf.

There's probably no biological reason why a man *can't* provide the elements of inspiration: energy, passion, the spur of satisfied or unrequited love. Indeed, the lives of the muses repeatedly demon-strate that such details as gender, physiology, and what is generally considered to be "normal" or "appropriate" heterosexual desire have little bearing on the alliance of Eros and creativity. Consider such unusual couples as Charles Dodgson and Alice Liddell, or Gala and Salvador Dalí. History abounds in same-sex artists and muses—Diaghilev and Nijinsky, W. H. Auden and Chester Kallman, Natalie Barney and Romaine Brooks—men and women who worked their inspirational magic often despite the additional strains and chal-lenges of social censure and the need to keep their connection se-cret. Gertrude Stein's most appealing and accessible book was, after all, the putative "autobiography" of her loyal muse, Alice B. Toklas.

One of the likelier candidates for the role of male muse may be Denys Finch Hatton, Isak Dinesen's dashing aviator lover. Her de-scription, in *Out of Africa*, of her joy in telling him stories during his visits to her Kenya plantation is one of literature's most luminous accounts of the way in which love can arrange the conjunction of in-spiration, appreciation—and editing:

"Denys had a trait of character which to me was very precious, he liked to hear a story told. . . . Fashions have changed, and the art of listening to a narrative has been lost in Europe. The Natives of Africa, who cannot read, have still got it; if you begin to them: 'There was a man who walked out on the plain, and there he met another man,' you have them all with you, their minds running upon the un-known track of the men on the plain. But white people, even if they feel that they ought to, cannot listen to a recital. If they do not be-come fidgety, and remember things that should be done at once, they fall asleep. The same people will ask you for something to read . . . They have been accustomed to take in impressions by the eye.

"Denys, who lived much by the ear, preferred hearing a tale told, to reading it; when he came to the farm he would ask: 'Have you got a story?' I had been making up many while he had been away. In the evenings he made himself comfortable, spreading cushions like a couch in front of the fire, and with me sitting on the floor, cross-legged like Scheherazade herself, he would listen, clear-eyed, to a long tale, from when it began until it ended. He kept better account of it than I did myself, and at the dramatic appearance of one of the characters, would stop me to say: 'That man died at the beginning of the story, but never mind.' "

On the surface, the passage offers a luminous vision of the storyteller inspired and encouraged by the acutely attentive, profoundly comprehending listener—an image not unlike that of Charles Dodgson enchanting Alice with his tales on their golden afternoon. And isn't the ability to make the artist feel that he (or she) is in the presence of the perfect audience one of the essential attributes of such famous muses as Lou Andreas-Salomé, whom Freud described as "the great understander"? But certain revealing turns of phrase hint at the ways in which Karen Blixen's relation to Denys Finch Hatton was in fact quite different from that of male artists to their muses.

Comparing herself to Scheherazade, Blixen raises the possibility of the homicidal sultan as Scheherazade's harsh muse, threatening death as the ultimate penalty for artistic failure—an effective, if somewhat drastic, mode of providing inspiration. Consciously or unconsciously, Blixen was equating the fiercely independent Finch Hatton with the wild beasts—lions, birds of prey—that frequented her farm. His presence could be neither summoned nor compelled, he came only when he chose to, and she had some reasonable anxiety about keeping his attention. And so the stories functioned as a means of securing and ensuring his love, and perhaps (in the tradition of Scheherazade) of extending their life together—that is, the length of his visits.

Few male artists seem to have suffered from similar concerns, nor did many of them appear to have been much troubled by the possibility of boring or tiring their muses. Whether we like it or not, the distribution of power is simply different, depending on the gender of the artist and the muse. Of course, the muse's ability to grant or withhold inspiration is an important ability, which explains the blocked screenwriters flinging pale blue Tiffany boxes at the muse-as-Sharon-Stone. But even when the muse retains her strength and influence by remaining elusive or unobtainable, the male artist is generally less preoccupied by the challenge of staying fascinating or attractive to her than he is engaged by the evolution of his own feelings. Artists rarely create *for* the muse, to win or keep the muse's love and admiration, but rather for themselves, for the world, and for the more inchoate and unquantifiable imperatives of art itself. Their muses are merely the instruments that raise the emotional and erotic temperature high enough, churn up the weather in a way that may speed and facilitate the artist's labors.

That so many of the muses seemed to have functioned as nearly blank scrims for their artists to project on points to yet another reason for the rarity of male muses. Though one hesitates to generalize, women seem less inclined to idealize men to the point of featureless abstraction. Perhaps for reasons connected with the survival of the species, women are trained to pay close attention to the particular needs, the specific qualities of an *individual* man, while men often find it more useful for the purposes of art to worship a muse who fulfills a generic role: the Ideal Woman, or in Charles Dodgson's case, the Ideal Child Friend.

Not entirely coincidentally, the various subsidiary activities included in the muse's job description—nurturing, sustaining, supporting, encouraging—are traditionally considered to be woman's work. It's difficult to imagine Denys Finch Hatton fussing, as did so many female muses, over questions of household management and the nutritiousness of Karen Blixen's diet.

In any case, we are, these days, more likely to agree that a city, a country, or a continent can function as a muse than to cite a woman *or* a man as the source of inspiration. Like the Greeks, who thought that pilgrims might hear helpful or instructive voices at certain springs and the homes of oracles, we believe that a change of scenery can aid the creative process. When Lafcadio Hearn moved to Japan, he altered his formerly purple prose style to match the spare, elegant sensibility of his adopted country. Delacroix, Matisse, and Paul Bowles found a congenial climate for art in North Africa, Gauguin in Tahiti. A recent show at New York's Museum of Modern Art, "The Museum as Muse," explored the ways in which artists have been influenced by the places where their work has been exhibited.

We have, as a culture, reached the point at which nearly any-thing—geography, ambition, expensive tastes, an abusive childhood, poverty—seems a more probable motivation for making art than the promptings of longing or love. Gauguin, among countless others, was driven by the craving for fame and success. Hunger—the wolf at the door—has had a long and brilliant career as muse. So has subli-mation, according to Freud. And then there is always debt. A suc-cessful eighties art dealer was rumored to have kept her painters productive by introducing them to trendy restaurants, Cuban cigars, and flashy cars. A compulsive shopper, Balzac provided himself with similar reasons to keep writing. He was also a caffeine addict, which sped the process along.

For to take the muse incarnate seriously makes us acutely self-conscious, which is perhaps why the muse is now most readily in-voked in the ironic orbit of the fashion industry. It's no longer the heterosexual poet or painter seeking the erotic spark generated by a mistress and muse, but rather the gay designer observing how a styl-ish woman chooses a wardrobe and puts herself together—how a goddess channels the secrets of female beauty and narcissism. Loulou de la Falaise, we hear, was Yves St. Laurent's muse. Accord-ing to an item in the January 1, 2001, issue of *New York* magazine, "Designers Marc Jacobs and Stephen Sprouse must have been plenty inspired at the December 11 opening of the new Louis Vuitton store on Fifth Avenue. There were muses all over the place! Jacobs arrived with Zoe Cassavetes, Michelle Hicks, and Deborah Harry."

Perhaps the fashion muse marks a return to the spirit of the Renaissance, when the muse was under no obligation to *do* anything, but simply to be beautiful, or even more simply to *be*. Beatrice had only to smile or not smile at Dante, while Laura became Petrarch's ideal, and the Renaissance's second most celebrated muse, merely by leaving a church in Avignon on April 6, 1327. Though, or because, she was married to someone else and the mother of several children, though she never returned Petrarch's affections, and though they were separated for long periods, Petrarch continued to adore Laura until her death in 1348. His love is the subject of the hundreds of poems in *Canzoniere*.

Accidentally, or unconsciously, Dante and Petrarch, medieval and Renaissance poetic tradition discovered that the absent, distant, or unattainable muse was an ingenious solution to the question of what to do when the muse *did* descend from the airier realm and incarnate herself as a woman. Problems would naturally arise when an artist didn't much like women—so much more difficult, willful, and stubborn than a Greek water sprite, dancing into one's studio with her lyre or laurel wreath.

In some cases, the whole idea of muses can inspire a certain sort of man to get in touch with his inner misogynist, a special liability for the muses' biographers, who often despise their subjects with such venom that books such as Rudoph Binion's *Frau Lou: Nietzsche's Wayward Disciple* provide the horrific fascination of watching a posthumous mugging. Such responses represent a venerable tradition, dating back to Hesiod railing against the lazy, materialistic "deadly female race and tribe of wives." Just the thought of the muse can trigger a related compulsion—the urgent need to explain why a woman can never hope to graduate from muse to artist:

"She is either Muse or she is nothing," wrote Robert Graves. "This is not to say that a woman should refrain from writing poems; only, that she should write as a woman, not as an honorary man . . . It is the imitation of male poetry that causes the false ring in the work of almost all women poets. A woman who concerns herself with poetry should, I believe, either be a silent Muse and inspire the poets by her womanly presence . . . or the Muse in a complete sense . . . impartial, loving, severe, wise."

In his 1953 book, *A Choir of Muses*, the French historian and philosopher Étienne Gilson echoes Graves's pessimistic assessment of women's creative potential: "It may prove that social conditions inhibited woman's creative powers . . . Often one hears this urged; and it is plausible if it is not wholly convincing. . . . With so many women musicians, why no equal, I will not say of Bach, but of Mozart or even Chopin? The very emotions of women seem to need male musicians to express them."

And yet the life of Lee Miller suggests that the muse *can* change jobs and become as serious an artist as the one she inspired. Among the lives of the muses, her story stands out as one in which a muse went on to produce important work, after which she succumbed to the absolute worst-case scenario of domestic hell, alienation, and creative sterility.

Both Gilson and Graves confidently explain that wives cannot be muses, that certain disqualifications—excessive familiarity, for one—prevent an artist's wife from inspiring her mate. Darkly, Graves warns that the domestication of the muse can actually destroy the poet's talent. "The reason why remarkably few young poets continue nowadays to publish poetry after their early twenties is not necessarily—as I used to think—the decay of patronage and the impossibility of earning a decent living . . . the reason is that something dies in the poet. Perhaps . . . he has also lost his sense of the White Goddess: the woman he took to be a Muse, or who was a Muse, turned into a domestic woman and would have him turn similarly into a domesticated man. Loyalty prevents him from parting company with her, especially if she is the mother of his children and is proud to be reckoned a good housewife; and as the Muse fades out, so does the poet. . . . The White Goddess is anti-domestic; she is the perpetual 'other woman,' and her part is difficult indeed for a woman of sensibility to play for more than a few years, because the temptation to commit suicide in simple domesticity lurks in every maenad's and muse's heart."

Well, perhaps not *every* maenad and muse. The lives of the muses are filled with the extreme measures that muses have taken to keep from committing career suicide through domesticity, from being demoted to art wives. The willed or instinctive strategies they employed to avoid becoming the sturdy linchpins holding together the machinery of daily art production range widely. Mrs. Thrale resisted by having servants to do the work of the art wife; Lizzie Siddal rendered herself helpless with opium addiction; Lou Andreas-Salomé withheld sex; Lee Miller protected her interests with competence, restlessness, and flight, and later with drinking and depression. Alice Liddell had her youth and her ferocious mother; Gala Dalí her own nastiness. Suzanne Farrell nearly sacrificed her career to avoid becoming an art wife, while Yoko Ono attempted to persuade Lennon that he *was* one.

So the muses struggled against the dubious lure of supplementing their inspirational capacities with the humbler duties of child care and housework. In some instances, one might wonder why they bothered. The humble, reliable Rose Beuret—the mistress whom Rodin finally married after decades during which her chores included wetting down his maquettes—fared better than his more glamorous muse and fellow sculptor Camille Claudel, who went mad, destroyed most of her own work, and was dispatched to a mental asylum.

But other cases, such as Charis Weston's marriage to the photographer Edward Weston, illustrate what her sister muses were resisting: the unpleasantness that can result when the muse's duties change from posing nude in the sand dunes to cataloguing negatives and shopping for organic crackers. The understandable resentments and unconscious hostilities of the art wife may result in the demoted muse wanting credit for her contribution to the artist's work—a fatal mistake that, Gilson warns, the true muse never makes. The aggressive faux-muse "only too easily wants to be a more active collaborator than her function as Muse allows; she will not be content just to be there and let the artist do the rest. She will interfere in the work, fancy that she had some share, and claim rights of origination . . . Obviously it is not pleasant to find oneself relegated to the rank of occasional cause, and when the Muse makes claim for the recognition of her usefulness, the artist is in for trouble. Dante placed Beatrice in heaven, but he never said she had written the *Divina Commedia*. From the moment the Muse claims rights over his work, other than those recognized by the poet, irreparable misunderstandings arise, and it is time for them to part."

Understandably, Charis Weston wants credit. At eighty, Alice Liddell was still enjoying, and trading on, her position as "the moving cause" of Lewis Carroll's books. Hester Thrale counted the works she inspired Dr. Johnson to write: three political pamphlets, the new edition and revision of his Dictionary, and *The Lives of the Poets*. In her memoir and in a TV documentary, Suzanne Farrell describes *Meditation* as the first of the ballets Balanchine made for her. Muses know they are muses, though they can accept or resist it. That it might be in the muse's best interests—psychological, fiscal, or professional—for her to acknowledge her musedom was a possibility that Gilson and Graves would hardly have factored into their recipes for the muse incarnate.

Meanwhile, the artist's own preference for the fantasy muse over the real-life woman is not entirely about clinging to the ideal in order to evade the messy realities of sex, jealousy, domestic tedium, and so forth. For artists, like the rest of us, sooner or later notice that the power of longing is more durable than the thrill of possession. Perhaps what makes unsatisfied desire thrive in the jungly climate of the creative psyche is the artist's insistence on retaining access to the emotions and perceptions of childhood and adolescence, stages at which romantic fantasy is safer than, and even preferable to, erotic gratification. And unrequited desire may itself be a metaphor for the making of art, for the fact that a finished work so rarely equals the initial impulse or conception, thus compelling the artist to start over and try again.

Longing is an intense emotion, and artists cling to the belief or experience that art is born of strong sensations, preferably, as Wordsworth suggested, recollected when tranquillity makes it easier to do the work. Strong emotions are what artists crave from their love affairs with the muse, and so the lives of the muses are nothing if not intense—before, during, and after the time during which they actively inspire their artists. The force of the connection is such that the sudden withdrawal of the muse's affections—as when Lou Andreas-Salomé broke with Nietzsche and then with Rilke—can affect the artist, to put it crudely, like turning on a faucet.

Feelings this heated inevitably shade into the erotic. Bonnard's early portraits of his wife Marthe so accurately and lovingly capture the intimacy and abandon of sex that they seem almost too personal for strangers to see. The painter never lost his obsessive fascination with her body, which appears in canvas after canvas, portrayed—in the bathroom and the tub—with a ripe, unhurried sensuality belying the fact that Marthe was by many accounts a peevish, mendacious hypochondriac and recluse whose frequent baths may have been related to her chronic ill health.

Throughout, the lives of the muses greatly expands our limited notions of Eros. Lewis Carroll's photograph *Portrait of Alice Liddell as the Beggar Child* is suffused by erotic desire, though like the photographer's attachment to his model, it is not explicitly sexual. Lou Andreas-Salomé maintained a chaste relationship with two of the three geniuses she inspired. Though Suzanne Farrell may never have slept with Balanchine, it's hard to imagine a more impassioned romance.

By contrast, Charis Weston's affair with Edward, Lee Miller's with Man Ray, and (at least at first) Yoko Ono's with John Lennon were exuberantly carnal. Moreover, these three muses were gifted with such a rare degree of sexual confidence that, in defiance of Gilson's belief that true muses do not choose their poets, they courted or pursued their artists and took decisive action when the men proved hesitant or shy.

If certain artists require the goad of unsatisfied longing and if others, conversely, utilize the power of sex to generate energy, raise the spirits, and focus the mind, still others seek from their muses not pleasure but forgiveness—what Étienne Gilson calls "the nostalgic luxury of sanctuary." The dramatic scene that ratcheted up the level of intimacy between Samuel Johnson and Hester Thrale involved his anguished sense of sin and his pleas for pardon, a request echoed years later in the famous letter in which he asked his muse to confine him to his room, possibly in the padlock and fetters he entrusted to her care. The horror of the vile but nameless evil that Charles Dodgson noted in his diary and which kept him awake at night intensified his devotion to the ideal of a spotlessly innocent child. John Lennon would recall the acceptance and permission he received from his first encounter with Yoko's work. "I climbed the ladder, you look through the spyglass and in tiny little letters it says 'yes.' So it was positive. I felt relieved. It's a great relief when you get up a ladder and you look through a spyglass and it doesn't say 'no' or 'fuck you' or something, it said 'yes.'"

Every chapter in the lives of the muses adds to the infinite variety of what can transpire between a muse and an artist. Some muses, like Lou Andreas-Salomé, Alma Mahler, and Vera Stravinsky, operate serially, progressing from genius to genius, while some artists—Picasso was one example, Balanchine another—tire of their muses, discard them, and acquire new ones.

Possibly because we tend to idealize the alliance between artist and muse, we imagine that the young, idealistic, and innocent artist is most in need of the muse's intercession. We think of Lou Andreas-

Salomé jump-starting the young Rilke's poetic gift by introducing him to the pleasures and pain of love, by bolstering his sense of mission, by helping him turn experience into art, and by offering him experience suitable for transformation. Yet the artist can be any age; Samuel Johnson was fifty-seven when he moved in with Hester Thrale. Morever, the relationship between an artist and a muse can change over time. Gala's initially salutary influence on Salvador Dalí's work became destructive when his increasingly greedy goddess advised him to sign blank sheets of lithographic paper on which someone else could print, lowering the value of his art and wrecking his reputation. The songs on *The White Album, Plastic Ono Band,* and *Imagine*—inspired by Lennon's love for Yoko—are among his best compositions. But in the less palmy days of their marriage and the final years of his life, Lennon produced (with Yoko's help) shallow, facile recordings that cannibalized his early work.

Given the vast differences that divide the lives—and even the stages in one life—of one muse from another, is it possible to generalize about the muses? Certain themes emerge. Many of these muses seem to have provoked the intense dislike of their contemporaries. Nearly everyone hated Gala. The ferocity with which John's fellow Beatles and fans resented Yoko resulted from a mixture of jealousy, race and gender bias, and simple irritation. William Rossetti's hostility to his brother's muse seems mostly based on the fact that Lizzie Siddal was intelligent, dignified, and, like her husband, took too many drugs.

Rather than thanking the muses for doing their demanding, important jobs, we tend to be jealous of them, envious of some aura of glamour that we imagine surrounding them. We resent their inconsiderate insistence on standing in the way, on disrupting and triangulating the fantasy love affair between art lover and love object—*our* romance with the artist. One possible solution to our muse-envy is to put ourselves in their places, to identify with them, to project our feelings onto them, just as their artists so often did.

All of which suggests another common motif in the lives of the muses: inspiration as a social and communal activity. The muses and their artists attract the curiosity and attention of the neighbors and of the larger world. Lewis Carroll's friendship with young Alice Liddell and her siblings received enough notice that he found it wiser not to discourage rumors that he was in love with their governess. When Yoko's and John's community became global, their love affair raised a tempest of press coverage and public debate. The sexual and private lives of the muses have often provoked fantastic rumors, feverish speculations that long outlive them. Lizzie Siddal's biographers weigh in authoritatively on the subject of her sex life; when Suzanne Farrell returned to the New York City Ballet from the exile that followed the disintegration of her romance with Balanchine, the entire company turned out to watch their first rehearsal together. Predictably, such scrutiny decreases the chances of the muse and her artist having a "normal" relationship, although— given these lovers' personalities—the odds for normalcy would at best have been slim.

At the same time, the cultural and personal mythology—the sense of themselves as heroic, as larger-than-life—to which these couples subscribed was part of what sustained their love and inspired the artist. Though their trip to Russia was among the great tourist disasters, Lou Andreas-Salomé and Rilke enshrined it as a major turning point in the poet's development. At eighty, Alice Liddell was still actively dining out on whatever transpired between her and Charles Dodgson on the "golden afternoon" of July 4, 1862. Gabriel Rossetti's conviction that he and Lizzie Siddal were the reincarnations of Dante and Beatrice led to the full flowering of the Pre-Raphaelites' obsession with the Middle Ages. In the fairy tale version of John's and Yoko's love, the night they recorded *Two Virgins* was the scene in which the prince and princess ride off into the sunset, and their desire to recapture that experience resulted in years of unfortunate collaborations.

In some instances, art draws successfully on the private iconography that the couple has adopted. Balanchine's *Don Quixote* features a moving duet between a shuffling old man and a lithe, energetic young woman, a visual metaphor for the choreographer's feelings about his relationship with Suzanne Farrell. And the visual symbols Dalí employed to represent Gala—a rose, a classical bust—provide the grammar of the secret language spoken by his paintings.

Despite their quirks and eccentricities, these artists and their muses turn out to share certain qualities, experiences, and patterns of behavior with ordinary lovers. The muse is often that person with whom the artist has the animated imaginary conversations, the interior dialogues we all conduct, most commonly with someone we cannot get out of our minds. That Samuel Johnson's *A Journey to the Western Isles of Scotland* evolved from letters to Mrs. Thrale suggests that, during his travels, he was editing and selecting the impressions that he hoped would most engage and please her.

Like many lovers, artists display an endearing tendency to overestimate the beloved. Nietzsche thought that Lou's sentimental lyric, "Hymn To Life," was a poetic masterpiece. And Lennon seems to have believed that Yoko was a genius. In return, muses provide a high degree of sympathetic comprehension, which may make their artists feel as if they are being *seen* to a depth that no one else has fathomed.

Finally, muses assumed a responsibility that was, in retrospect, inevitable when the muse's nature shifted from divine to human, and installed itself in a body. Like many women, the muses concerned themselves with what their lovers ate. Lou had Rilke dining on groats and combing the forest for nuts and berries, Lee Miller put Man Ray on a bizarrely restrictive diet, Yoko introduced John to the joys of a strict macrobiotic regimen.

Nurturer and diet police, understander and mirror—these attributes of the muse are the familiar roles that women have been expected and obliged to play, just as they are aspects of essentialist male-female behavior. And yet none of these muses was a "traditional" woman—assuming that such a creature exists.

Every one of them was extraordinary, either for who she was, or what she did, or for the unique and heroic qualities with which her artist endowed her. Each was a product of her time, and each moved outside and beyond it, either through personal courage, originality, and determination, or through her mysterious role in the process that turns experience into art. The lives of the muses at once illumine and deepen the mysteries of Eros and creativity, as each muse redraws the border between the human and the divine, the mortal and the eternal.

HESTER THRALE

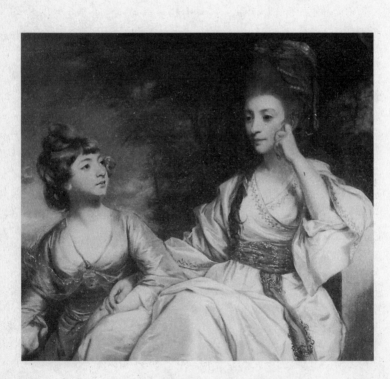

Mrs. Thrale and Her Daughter Hester (Queeney).

(Sir Joshua Reynolds)

ON A SPRING MORNING in 1766, Henry and Hester Thrale visited Dr. Samuel Johnson in his rooms at Johnson's Court.

The lively, attractive young couple had known the famous writer since 1764, when the playwright Arthur Murphy had brought Johnson to dinner at the Thrales' estate in Streatham Park, a few miles from central London. Since then, he had been a regular guest at Streatham, and at the Thrales' city place in Southwark, on the grounds of their profitable brewery. But lately, Johnson's visits had tapered off, and the Thrales had reason to suspect that he was suffering from one of the profound and terrifying fits of melancholia that had plagued him for most of his fifty-seven years. Already, they had grown close enough for Johnson to have confided his fears about "the horrible condition of his mind, which he said was nearly distracted."

Unlikely on the surface, the friendship was a tremendous coup for the socially ambitious Thrales. Johnson was famous not only for having written the *Dictionary*, the *Rambler* essays, *The Life of Savage*, and *Rasselas* but for his witty conversation. Among fashionable Londoners, watching the doctor talk had become a sort of spectator sport; at parties, guests crowded, four and five deep, around his chair to listen.

Johnson brought his own celebrity talking-and-sparring partners—David Garrick, Oliver Goldsmith, Sir Joshua Reynolds—along with him to Streatham, possibly because brisk repartee was not his host's strong suit. Well meaning and personable, properly insistent on his masculine right to overeat, hunt, and cheat publicly on his wife, Henry Thrale lacked, according to Johnson, the finer social skills. "His conversation does not show the minute hand; but he strikes the hour very correctly." He was the sort of rich, dull, solid fellow—"such dead, though excellent, mutton," to quote Virginia Woolf's wicked assessment of Rebecca West's husband—who turns up, with surprising frequency, in the lives of the muses.

Johnson liked the wealthy brewer; he admired the manly way he ran his household, and enjoyed the benefits of his expensive tastes in food and wine. Driven by an increasing horror of solitude and a craving for human companionship, the writer was drawn to the vibrant domesticity of Streatham, and especially to his hostess, a slight, dark-eyed Welsh fireball, who was disputatious, flirtatious, quick, well educated, and (unlike many of their contemporaries) unafraid of a man whom she described as having "a roughness in his manner which subdued the saucy and terrified the meek; this was, when I knew him, the prominent part of a character which few durst venture to approach so nearly."

Chroniclers of the period record the sparkling sorties that flew back and forth across the table between Samuel Johnson and Mrs. Thrale. And her own *Anecdotes of the Late Samuel Johnson, LL.D.,* published in 1785, functions as a compendium not only of the writer's witticisms, but also of their exchanges on subjects ranging from faith to incredulity, from ghostly apparitions to the value of everyday knowledge, from marital discord to convent life, from the pleasures of traveling by coach to the rewards of reading *Don Quixote*, from the correct way to raise children to the necessity of constantly measuring one's minor complaints against the greater sufferings and privations of the poor.

The Thrales were tolerant of the writer's notorious eccentricities. Eventually, they would assign a servant to stand outside his door with a fresh wig for him to wear to dinner, since he so often singed the front of his wig by reading too close to the lamp. Nearly blind, disfigured by pockmarks, Johnson suffered from scrofula and a host of somatic complaints, as well as an array of psychological symptoms that, today, would virtually ensure that he was medicated for Tourette's, obsessive-compulsive disorder, bipolar disorder, to name just the obvious syndromes. (The ongoing discussion of Johnson's "case" in medical literature has made him one of those figures, like Van Gogh and Lizzie Siddal, whose health care improved dramatically after death.) Happily, Samuel Johnson's own more permissive era was sufficiently enchanted by his intelligence, humor, and unflagging energy to overlook his rocking from foot to foot, mumbling, twitching, emitting startling verbal outbursts, obsessively counting his footsteps, touching each lamppost in the street, and performing an elaborate shuffle before he could enter a doorway.

The Thrales were used to the doctor's tics. Yet nothing could have prepared them for the scene they found on that May morning when at last they were admitted to the writer's rooms at Johnson's Court. His friend John Delap was just leaving, and it must have been instantly obvious—from how pathetically he begged Delap to include him in his prayers—that the great Samuel Johnson was veering out of control.

Left alone with the Thrales, Johnson became so overwrought, so violent in his self-accusations, so reckless in alluding to the sins for which he said he needed forgiveness that Henry and Hester were soon caught up in the general hysteria. "I felt excessively affected with grief, and well remember my husband involuntarily lifted up one hand to shut his mouth, from provocation at hearing a man so wildly proclaim what he could at last persuade no one to believe; and what, if true, would have been so very unfit to reveal."

It was an extraordinary scene: the handsome brewer clapping one hand over the mouth of London's most celebrated literary figure, while his agitated wife looked on in dread and horror. Something irreversible was happening to their friendship! The balance of power and need was being tipped forever by what Johnson was letting them see. They'd arrived as friends and hosts flattered by the doctor's affections, but uninvited, and perhaps a bit uncertain about their welcome and the future of their friendship. And now they had been drawn into this theatrical, eroticized tableau, from which they would emerge as guardians, saviors, confessors, surrogate mother and father.

Eventually, the crisis passed. Mr. Thrale left to attend to business, but not before instructing his wife to persuade Dr. Johnson to leave his house and move to Streatham, where the Thrales could look after him and help him recover his health.

That day, or soon after, Dr. Johnson did go to Streatham, where he remained, a more-or-less permanent house guest, for the next sixteen years.

INSPIRATION IS UNPREDICTABLE, it comes and goes when it pleases. The muse can appear at any time—to spur a young artist's early efforts, to pull an older one out of a stall, or to give an elderly one the will to go the distance. This last was the case with Samuel Johnson, who, by the time he met Hester Thrale, had long since perfected his brilliantly logical literary strategies, his persuasive prose style. A large part of his best work was behind him, and he had nearly finished his monumental edition of Shakespeare's plays.

But his mental instability had begun to pose an increasingly perilous threat not only to his literary productivity but to his survival. Years later, after his death, Mrs. Thrale would take credit for having functioned not just as his muse but also as the perpetually supportive psychiatric attendant who enabled Johnson to maintain the clarity—the sanity—required to continue writing. "To the assistance we gave him, the shelter our house afforded to his uneasy fancies, and to the pains we took to soothe or repress them, the world perhaps is indebted for the three political pamphlets, the new edition and correction of his Dictionary, and for the Poets' Lives, which he would scarce have lived, I think, and kept his faculties entire, to have writ-

ten, had not incessant care been exerted at the time of his first coming to be our constant guest in the country; and several times after
that, when he found himself particularly oppressed with diseases,
incident to the most vivid and fervent imaginations. I shall for ever
consider it as the greatest honour which could be conferred on any
one, to have been the confidential friend of Dr. Johnson's health;
and to have in some measure, with Mr. Thrale's assistance, saved
from distress at least, if not from worse, a mind great beyond the
comprehension of common mortals, and good beyond all hope of
imitation from perishable beings."

Hester's claims were by no means empty. Dr. Johnson himself,
and many of their contemporaries, testified to the crucial influence
she exerted on his domestic existence and on his inner life. Johnson's *A Journey to the Western Isles of Scotland*, a record of the trip he took
with Boswell in 1773 and one of the great travel books in English
literature, began as letters to Mrs. Thrale, a flurry of communiqués
mixing observation, description, reflection, and sentiments that
sound more like those of a suitor than a house guest: "I am perpetually thinking on you," he wrote. "Nothing puts my honored mistress out of my mind . . ." The ideas, and perhaps the phrases, that
comprised *The Lives of the Poets* were born and nurtured in conversation with Mrs. Thrale, and Boswell records her scolding Dr. Johnson, when he was composing *The Life of Pope*, for being too lazy to go
interview a man who had known the poet.

Their friendship was in theory platonic, though there exists one
fervid note from Samuel Johnson to Mrs. Thrale in florid French—
and in the language of bondage and restraint. And then there was
the business of "Dr. Johnson's padlock," which turned up, after her
death, among Hester's effects. Something deeper and fiercer than
simple camaraderie is suggested by the fury with which Samuel
Johnson broke off all relations with Mrs. Thrale when, after Henry
died, she married her daughters' singing instructor, the handsome
Italian Gabriel Piozzi. Though Johnson later attempted to mitigate

the violence of his first response to the news of her engagement, their relationship never recovered. The painfully contradictory portrait of the writer offered by Mrs. Thrale's *Anecdotes of the Late Samuel Johnson, LL.D.,* reflects the rage and bewilderment that persisted years after her friend selfishly tried to deny her the happiness she found with Piozzi.

Ultimately, like all the various and unpredictable pairings of artists and muses, Samuel Johnson's relationship with Hester Thrale broadens our regard for the mysteries of love. Wherever they stood on the spectrum between best friends and dominatrix and slave, they were, inarguably, the focus of one another's romantic attentions for almost two decades. Hester's wicked high energy was a blessed distraction for the depressive writer, who, in turn, diverted and consoled her as she lost, one after another, eight of her twelve children.

At the time their alliance began, more than a decade had passed since the death of Tettie, Johnson's formidable, much older wife, whom he had initially adored, then neglected, a lapse for which he suffered dreadful remorse. Despite his popularity, he missed the comforts of family, which happened to be precisely what Hester longed to escape. For by the time she met Johnson, she'd been married to Henry Thrale for two years—long enough to discover the alarmingly narrow dimensions of the domestic prison to which, she'd begun to realize, she had been condemned for life.

HESTER LYNCH SALUSBURY THRALE had not been raised for intellectual stagnation, for the need to placate an unsympathetic, unfaithful husband, for being almost constantly pregnant, and for perpetual worry about her children's survival, fears that inspired her to dose her babies with home remedies and purgatives concocted to induce "a gentle Puke." It's unclear what sort of future Hester's mother, or her alcoholic unreliable father, or her wealthy adoring older uncle (who called her "Fiddle") *could* have been imagining when they encouraged her in her studies. "Although Education was a Word then unknown, as applied to Females; They had taught me to read, & speak, & think, & translate from the French, till I was half a Prodigy."

As a girl, she was writing Italian, translating Racine, *Don Quixote,* and a treatise on the ancient gods of Spain ("This was a strange thing for a Child to do," she observed later), as well as keeping a diary in which she practiced the skills she would deploy throughout her life. A natural writer, she started off with imitations of Alexander Pope. The year before her marriage, she began contributing poems and unsigned political satires to newspapers. Later, encouraged by Dr. Johnson, she would keep three notebooks—one in which to record Johnson's sayings, another for observations on her celebrity guests, and a third for her observations on family life. To Henry Thrale's credit, he gave her the notebooks in which she recorded her *Thraliana,* a massive compilation of autobiographical anecdotes and ruminations. Eventually, she published this, as well as her best-selling *Anecdotes of the Late Samuel Johnson, LL.D.*, and an ambitious, idiosyncratic series of books on philology and history.

But neither intelligence nor education could save the bright young woman from being married off to a man she didn't love. Her father opposed the match, swearing that he would not sell his daughter "for a barrel of porter" to a well-known womanizer who would give her the pox. (Later, when Henry Thrale came down with a venereal infection, his wife would bitterly recall her father's warning.) But when John Salusbury died suddenly—in the midst of a battle over Hester's marital prospects—her fate was sealed despite "all my assurances that nothing resembled love less than Mr. Thrale's behaviour." They were married in 1763, when Hester was twenty-two and Henry was in his mid-thirties. Her uncle gave her away in church, "leaving me to conciliate as I could a husband who was indeed much kinder than I counted on to a *plain girl,* who had not one attraction in his eyes, and on whom he never had thrown five minutes of his time away, in any interview unwitnessed by company, even till after our wedding-day was done." Soon after the wedding a thoughtful acquaintance informed her that Henry had proposed to several young women, but none of them—until Hester—would agree to live in a brewery.

Decades later, Hester described her efforts to adjust to the tedium relieved only slightly when her first child, Hester Maria, was born in 1764. "Autumn came, and a daughter came, and I became of a *little* more importance. Confidence was no word in our vocabulary; and I tormented myself to guess who possessed that of Mr. Thrale . . . We kept, meantime, a famous pack of foxhounds . . . but it was masculine for ladies to ride. We kept the finest table possible at Streatham Park but *his* wife was not to *think of the kitchen.* So I never knew what was for dinner till I saw it."

Even more affectingly, she recalled her futile attempts to snag her new husband's attention: "I was now a married Woman: young enough to be proud of being such,—& silly enough to expect that my husband's heart was to be won by the same empty Tricks that had pleased my Father & my Uncle; so I wrote Verses in *his* Praise instead of *theirs* . . . These sentimental Jeux D'Esprit I had been so long accustom'd to, that It seemed odd when I observed them repress'd as Impertinent, or rejected as superfluous; but it was Natural to try, & try again: so Instead of Dressing showily, or behaving usefully—I sate at home and wrote Verses.—my *next* Effort Doctor Johnson praised as a very pretty one: though he did not see it till Years after it had been presented—neglected, & forgotten."

Both passages express an irritated turning away from Henry Thrale, and a grateful turning toward books. "Driven thus on literature as my sole resource, no wonder if I loved my books and children." Another source of solace was her new friendship with Dr. Johnson. The great man's presence at her house must have seemed to Hester a fulfillment of what she *had* been raised to do: read and write, discuss literature, and practice her charms on an older man not unlike her wealthy uncle. Not only did the muse provide her artist with his ideal audience, but the artist fulfilled a similar function for his muse. For the first time since her marriage, Mrs. Thrale had an adult (other than her widowed mother, who lived with them) to talk to, someone who would listen to her and reassure her that all her study and effort had not been in vain.

Soon after they met, they agreed to collaborate on a translation, from the Latin, of Boethius. But their budding friendship suffered a setback when Johnson traveled to Brighton to visit the Thrales, only to discover that his hosts had already gone home. Hester was about to give birth (her daughter Frances would live only a few days), and Henry had decided to run for Parliament, to which he was elected and to which he would be returned for the next fifteen years.

Initially furious, Johnson soon forgave the misunderstanding and volunteered to help Henry with his political campaign. His visits grew even more frequent—then ceased altogether during that spell of depression that confined him to his home, and which prompted the Thrales to make the fateful visit that so radically altered the terms of their relationship.

WHEN IT BECAME CLEAR that Samuel Johnson was permanently installed at Streatham and Southwark, the Thrales set aside rooms for him; soon he was fully integrated into the life of the household. He was far more involved than Henry in the upbringing of the children. It was Johnson who first began calling Hester's eldest daughter Queeney—a nickname that proved all too apt for the smart, stubborn girl who, her mother correctly feared, had "a heart void of all Affection for any Person in the World."

Johnson went fox hunting with his host, and submitted to Henry Thrale's patriarchal authority. Thrale could prevail upon him to be reasonably civil and even to change his clothes, "almost before it became indispensably necessary to the comfort of his friends." Johnson traveled with the Thrales, first on a brief trip to Kent and later on more ambitious journeys to Wales and France. Separated

from them, he sent Hester affectionate letters. "I count the friendship of your house," he wrote, "among the felicities of life."

Unsurprisingly, James Boswell had little love for Mrs. Thrale,
whom he considered a competitor for Johnson's allegiance and possibly a rival biographer. And yet we can thank Boswell—and Hester's friend, the novelist Fanny Burney—for giving us a sense of the
lively table talk at Streatham and Southwark, the flirtatiously pug-
nacious exchanges between Johnson and Mrs. Thrale. Ultimately,
even Boswell admitted that Mrs. Thrale's conversation cheered and
energized the melancholy writer, even when the two were alone.

Doubtless, their private discussions touched on subjects unsuitable for dinner conversation. Dr. Johnson entrusted Mrs. Thrale
with his hypochondriacal fears and spiritual dilemmas, including, as
some biographers have suggested, his concerns that his mortal soul
would be eternally damned because of his sexual fantasies involving
restraint and bondage.

His anxieties—and openness—on this subject peaked around
the time of Mrs. Thrale's greatest unhappiness; her mother was
dying, her daughter Penelope had lived only ten hours, the children
were down with the measles, her husband had barely survived a
public scandal and a financial crisis. It was during this anguished period that Dr. Johnson sent Mrs. Thrale the letter, in French, that has
been widely read as evidence of his masochistic desires.

In the note, Johnson asks where he may confine himself "within
prescribed bounds . . . I beg you to spare me the obligation of con-
straining myself, by taking away from me the power of leaving the
place where you want me to be . . . You must act the Mistress completely, so that your judgment and your vigilance may come to the
aid of my weakness . . ." He complains of her having neglected to en-
force certain rules, of her having forgotten so many promises that
he has been reduced to asking her (for something) so often that the
memory horrifies him. Finally, he concludes, "I want always to be

sensible of your rule, my Patroness, and I want you to hold me in that slavery which you know so well how to render pleasant."

Even allowing for the sentimental excesses of locution that can so easily lead us to misinterpret the intentions of our forebears, it *is* a peculiar letter, especially since it was meant to be sent from one room of Streatham Park to another. And Johnson's biographers have amassed enough evidence to suggest that the vocabulary of confinement and slavery was neither metaphorical nor accidental.

In a 1777 conversation with Boswell about his concerns for his own sanity, Johnson remarked, "Madmen are all sensual in the lower stages of distemper. But when they are very ill, pleasure is too weak for them, and they seek pain." Six years before, he had jotted down a brief journal entry in Latin: "*De pedicis et manicis insana cogitatio* [Insane thoughts about leg irons and handcuffs]." Even more telling was the passage Mrs. Thrale inscribed in her diary in the spring of 1779, "Says Johnson a Woman has *such* power between the Ages of twenty five and forty five, that She may tye a Man to a post and whip him if She will." In a marginal note, she added, "this he knew of him self was *literally* and *strictly* true I am sure." That winter, Hester wrote, "How many Times has this great, this formidable Doctor Johnson kissed my hand, ay and my foot too upon his knees! Strange Connections there are in this odd World!" To which she added the comment "a dreadful and little suspected Reason for *ours*, God knows—but the Fetters and Padlocks will tell Posterity the Truth." And there *was* a padlock, which, after Hester's death, was discovered among her possessions, labeled, "Johnson's padlock, committed to my care in 1768."

One can't help wondering why the muse who so loyally kept her artist's "secret far dearer to him than his Life," who guarded the confidence he entrusted to her so closely that she refrained from revealing it even to her own diary, later felt compelled to identify an artifact that might betray the nature of his tormented fantasies. But by then, she and Dr. Johnson had long since fallen out, and though she seems not to have been vindictive, she might have wondered why the man whose own private yearnings were so perverse should have been so intolerant of her ordinary, understandable wish to re-marry. And what was the Thrales' visit to Johnson's rooms, de-scribed at the start of this chapter, if not a scenario involving high drama, loss of control, and restraint?

In any case, Hester's reply to Johnson's 1773 letter asking her to lock him up and treat him as her slave remains a model of tact, lev-elheadedness, and sympathy. "What Care can I promise my dear Mr Johnson that I have not already taken . . . You were saying but on Sunday that of all the unhappy you was the happiest, in consequence of my Attention to your Complaint . . . If it be possible shake off these uneasy Weights, heavier to the mind by far than Fetters to the body. Let not your fancy dwell thus upon Confinement and sever-ity.—I am sorry you are obliged to be so much alone; I foresaw some ill Consequences of your being here while my Mother was dying thus; yet could not resist the temptation of having you near me . . ." She suggested that Johnson might wish to put some distance be-tween himself and the people or the place that stirred such unruly emotions. "Dissipation is to you glorious Medicine, and I believe Mr Boswell will be at last your best Physician. For the rest you really are well enough now if you will keep so; and not suffer the noblest of human minds to be troubled with fantastic notions which rob it of all its Quiet.—I will detain you no longer, so farewell and be good; and do not quarrel with your Governess for not using the Rod enough."

Around the time that Johnson departed for Scotland, his muse was busy coping with the latest crises in a domestic life so horrific even by eighteenth-century standards that her ability to conduct any sort of social life was a continuing miracle of pluck and resilience. Her beloved mother had just died of breast cancer. Her four-year-old daughter Lucy was in a brief remission from a fatal mastoid in-fection. Five of her children were sick with measles, and Hester, who had already lost three children and had, the previous fall, given birth to a stillborn daughter, was anxious about their health.

Henry Thrale was unhelpful, at best. He himself had barely recovered from a depression caused by a financial setback that left him nearly bankrupt, and the Thrales' marriage had been further damaged by a series of scandalous newspaper reports about the affairs of the brewer "more famed for his amours than celebrated for his beer." Still he had somehow managed to make sure that his wife was again pregnant, as she would be for most of their married life.

In late October 1773, Mrs. Thrale's beloved uncle, Thomas Salusbury, died without leaving her the inheritance to which she felt entitled, and on which she was counting. The loss of the money that would have given her a greater degree of freedom and influence in her dealings with her husband seemed the latest catastrophe in a series of disasters. By the time Dr. Johnson returned to Streatham in November, Hester had given birth to her ninth child, Ralph, who appears to have been born with brain damage ("He is heavy stupid & drowsy . . . I see no Wit sparkle in his eyes") even as her favorite daughter Lucy was dying of the infection that had spread to her brain.

Johnson was again installed at the Thrales', where he began work on his *A Journey to the Western Isles of Scotland.* This brief (compared to Boswell's account of their journey) and extraordinarily compressed book is a model of narrative authority. The calm, dignified, concentrated prose is illuminated by Johnson's sympathy and compassion, his penetrating curiosity about the world around him. The structure of the journey gives the book momentum and serves as the frame on which its author can build his reasonable, profound reflections on nature and society, politics, history, education, travel, architecture, psychology—in short, on the human condition.

It is also a book that owes its existence to the influence of Mrs. Thrale. In his biography of Johnson, the novelist John Wain observes: "In working up his book, Johnson relied mainly on the letters to Hester Thrale, though he mentions keeping a record of his impressions; this has not survived, and probably amounted to nothing more than a few notes. Boswell was the diarist. . . . Johnson, though he kept a *journal intime*, needed the sense of a receptive listener . . . left alone, (he) would become too melancholy and withdrawn to write much. Just as, in boyhood, he talked out his thoughts to Edmund Hector as they strolled about the green spaces of Lichfield, so now, writing down his impressions of the Hebrides, he needed to feel that he was writing *to* someone. The debt to Hester Thrale is thus twofold. Not only did she provide the sympathetic and receptive ear into which he poured out the story of his travels while it was still unfolding; she made the comfortable and secure anchorage in which the experiences could be 'recollected in tranquillity.' "

THAT WINTER, Hester enjoyed a brief respite from the misery of the previous two years, and by spring, the Thrales' spirits and finances were sufficiently recovered for them to contemplate a trip to Wales, where Hester had been born and where Henry wished to inspect some property she had inherited. Leaving the younger children at home and at school, the Thrales—together with Queeney and Dr. Johnson—set out in July.

It was not an easy trip; the travelers got on each other's nerves. Johnson's journal entries are terse and unexpansive. Hester was hurt by the men's obvious boredom with her homeland. Accused by Johnson of flattering their hosts, Hester replied that his rudeness required her to be civil for two. (Later, in a conversation reported by Fanny Burney, she expanded this figure to four, to include Henry and Queeney.) In her journal, she describes her loneliness and irritation. "I hear Harry has had a black eye, and Ralph cut his teeth with pain, but I have nobody to tell how it vexes me. Mr. Thrale will not be conversed with by *me* on any subject, as a friend, or comforter, or adviser. Every day more and more do I feel the loss of my Mother. My present Companions have too much philosophy for me. One cannot disburthen one's mind to people who are watchful to cavil, or acute to contradict before the sentence is finished."

At the end of September, they returned to face another hard time. Henry was reelected to Parliament after an exhausting campaign. Ralph fell ill after being vaccinated—by a primitive, perilous method—for smallpox. In April, Hester, about to give birth again, had her worst fears about Ralph's mental capacities confirmed by an expert surgeon. "Oh how this dreadful sentence did fill me with Horror! . . . Johnson gives me what Comfort he can, and laments he can give no more." That summer, Ralph died. The loss of so many of her children—three from illnesses that began with headaches— threw Hester into a panic. "It is the horrible Apprehension of losing the others by the same cruel Disease that haunts my affrighted Imagination & makes me look on them with an anxiety scarce to be endured. If Hetty tells me that her Head aches, I am more shocked than if I heard she had broken her Leg . . . What shall I do? What can I do? has the flattery of my poor Friends made me too proud of my own Brains? & must these poor Children suffer for my crime?" The intensity of Mrs. Thrale's dependence upon Johnson is the subtext of the letter she sent him from Bath: "I think you shall never run away so again. I lost a child the last Time you were at a distance."

Partly to distract Hester from her misery, the Thrales (again with Johnson and Queeney) embarked upon another expedition, this time to Paris. Though Hester had some reservation owing to the unpleasantness of their last trip, she was eager to take another. And in fact, the journey to France went well, the travelers got along, and Hester enjoyed the chance to look at paintings.

More calamities followed her homecoming. Seven-month-old Frances Ann died of influenza. One morning, in March, when Dr. Johnson was away at Lichfield, Harry complained of stomach pains. By the next day, the Thrales' beloved son and only heir was dead, apparently of a ruptured appendix. The children's tutor described the scene at Southwark: "Mr. Thrale, both his hands in his waistcoat pockets, sat on an arm-chair in a corner of the room with his body so stiffly erect, and with such a ghastly smile in his face, as was quite horrid to behold. Count Manucci and a female servant, both as pale as ashes, and as if panting for breath, were evidently spent with keeping madam from going frantic (and well she might) every time she recovered from her fainting-fits, that followed each other in very quick succession." Henry wept openly, and Hester wrote, "So ends my Pride, my hopes, my possession of present, & expectation of future Delight."

News of the tragedy reached Johnson in Lichfield, who called it "one of the most dreadful things that has happened in my time . . . I would have gone to the extremity of the earth to have preserved this boy." He rushed back to London to comfort the Thrales, advising them (as he often did) to keep busy, to channel their grief into useful activity.

By autumn, Hester had recovered enough to take Dr. Johnson's advice, and began writing *Thraliana*, which would eventually grow to 1,600 handwritten pages. "It is many Years since Doctor Samuel Johnson advised me to get a little Book, and write in it all the little Anecdotes which might come to my Knowledge, all the Observations I might make or hear . . . Mr. Thrale has now treated me with a Repository,—and provided it with the pompous Title of Thraliana; I must endeavour to fill it with Nonsense new and old." Playing muse to his muse, Johnson offered Mrs. Thrale some tips on composition: "Do not remit the practise of writing down occurrences as they arise, of whatever kind, and be very punctual in annexing the dates. Chronology you know is the eye of history . . . Do not omit painful casualties, or unpleasing passages, they make the variegation of existence . . ."

Johnson, too, soon embarked upon a major project. In March 1777, he contracted with a group of London booksellers to write a preface to a new collection of the English poets, a work that would become *The Lives of the Poets*. Johnson worked four years on the *Lives*. During this period Hester was a constant source of encouragement and inspiration. *The Life of Congreve* was "one of the best of the little lives," Johnson wrote, "but then I had your conversation." She enjoyed helping him, and he was grateful and affectionate. Frequently, Hester served as his copyist; the extant manuscript of *The Life of Pope* is in her handwriting. At breakfast, she read aloud his proof sheets, and as Fanny Burney recalled, "the discussions to which they led were in the highest degree entertaining."

In addition to her labors as secretary and muse, and to her own literary endeavors, Mrs. Thrale was engaging in some fervid social climbing. She bought stylish clothes, attended fashionable fetes and card parties; she was presented at Court and invited to experience the pleasures of the "Blue-Stocking Circle," whose leader, Mrs. Elizabeth Montagu, asked Hester and Dr. Johnson to dinner with a pair of invitations that sparked a playful rivalry between the two friends—an exchange that suggests that Mrs. Thrale's role as muse was acknowledged by her contemporaries:

" '*Your* note,' cried Dr. Johnson, 'can bear no comparison with *mine*; I am *at the head of the Philosophers*, she says.'

" 'And I,' cried Mrs. Thrale, '*have all the Muses in my train!*' "

Among these glittering parties was a musical soiree given by Fanny Burney's father, at which Dr. Johnson sulked silently throughout the awkward evening. Dr. Burney attempted to enliven the gathering with a musical performance by his friend, the attractive Italian tenor Gabriel Piozzi. During the second aria Piozzi sang to an unresponsive audience; the tension drove Mrs. Thrale to jump up and stand behind the tenor, mimicking his dramatic expressions and gestures. Horrified, Dr. Burney sent Mrs. Thrale back to her seat.

The only one who appears to have been excluded from the general merriment was Henry Thrale, whose problems multiplied even as his wife enjoyed a respite from domestic crisis. In 1776, Henry came down with a grossly swollen testicle that was feared to be cancer but was ultimately diagnosed as "venereal at last—What need of so many lyes about it!" There were continuing troubles with money and the brewery workers; and though Hester felt pressured by her husband to produce a male heir, her eleventh and twelfth children, born in 1777 and 1778, were, disappointingly, girls.

To make matters worse (for Mrs. Thrale, if not for her husband) the brewer fell deeply in love with Hester's friend Sophia Streatfield, a flirtatious beauty who possessed the irresistible (to males) ability to shed huge tears at will. One evening, Henry asked his pregnant wife to change places at the table with Sophy, who had a sore throat and was sitting in a draft. "I had scarcely swallowed a spoonful of soup when this occurred, and was so overcast by the coarseness of the proposal, that I burst into tears, said something petulant—that perhaps ere long, the lady might be at the head of Mr. T's table, without displacing the mistress of the house &c., and so left the apartment. I retired to the drawing-room, and for an hour or two contended with my vexations, as best I could."

But soon enough, Hester had reason to hope that a harmless flirtation might brighten her husband's mood. In the spring of 1779, Henry visited his sister, whose husband had just died. Together, Henry and his brother-in-law had indulged in some high-stakes financial speculation, and when the dead man's will was read, Henry realized that he might lose everything. At dinner, he suffered a stroke and was rushed to Streatham. Though he rallied enough so that Mrs. Thrale was soon pregnant again, he endured near-continuous bouts of deep depression—"the black dog," his wife called it—and displayed an alarming tendency to gorge himself on massive quantities of food.

Despite another stroke the following year, Thrale insisted on running for reelection to Parliament; though Johnson wrote his speeches, the campaign failed when his constituents saw how ill the candidate was. And on the day after an eating binge so extreme that it struck Johnson as suicidal, Henry Thrale's oldest daughter found him lying on the floor. He died the next morning.

Friends assumed that Mrs. Thrale and Dr. Johnson would at last get married. "Scott and I agreed that it was possible Mrs. Thrale might marry Dr. Johnson, and we both wished it much," noted Boswell, disingenuously. Only eight days after Henry Thrale's death, Boswell wrote a supremely tasteless poem, "Epithalamium," celebrating the couple's upcoming marriage: "My dearest darling view your slave/ Behold him as your very scrub/ Whether to write as author grave/ Or govern well the brewing tub . . ."

There had been speculation about their relationship as far back as 1773, when the newspapers reported that "an eminent Brewer was very jealous of a certain Authour in Folio, and perceived a strong resemblance to him in his eldest son." But in the aftermath of Thrale's death, Johnson slipped into the avuncular role of adviser rather than that of suitor and interceded to save Hester and her children from ruin—a valiant effort requiring that the brewery be sold and that Johnson and Mrs. Thrale function in new roles, as business partners: "If an Angel from Heaven had told me 20 years ago, that the Man I knew by the name of *Dictionary Johnson* should one Day become Partner with me in a great Trade, & that we should jointly or separately sign Notes, Drafts, &c., for 3 or 4 Thousand Pounds of a Morning, how unlikely it would have seemed ever to happen!"

Mrs. Thrale claimed that Johnson mentioned the possibility of marriage. But he was old, increasingly infirm and querulous, and Hester, who was forty when her husband died, had decided that "till I am in Love, I will not marry, nor perhaps then."

In fact, though she had not admitted it, even to herself, Hester Thrale was already in love—with Queeney's music master, Gabriel Piozzi, the tenor she had imitated at the Burneys' party. During a stay at Brighton for her husband's health she had met the Venetian singer on the street and noted that he was "amazingly like my Father." Subsequently, she hired him to entertain her guests and give her daughters voice lessons, and filled *Thraliana* with praises of his exquisite taste, his manners, his musicianship. "His hand on the Forte Piano too is so soft, so sweet, so delicate, every Tone goes to one's heart I think; and fills the Mind with Emotions one would not be without, though inconvenient enough sometimes."

Mrs. Thrale kept her crush on Piozzi a secret as she made plans to rent out her homes in London and Streatham (where Johnson said grace for the last time in October) and to take her daughters abroad, where their money would go farther, and where Piozzi had volunteered to serve as their guide. When she finally got the courage to tell Johnson that she was leaving the country, she was irritated by his stoic resignation. "I fancied Mr Johnson could not have existed without me forsooth, as we have now lived together above eighteen years, and I have so fondled and waited on him in sickness and health—not a bit on't! He feels nothing in parting with me, nothing in the least; but thinks it is a prudent scheme, and goes to his book as usual."

By the summer of 1782, Hester's infatuation with Piozzi had reached the point at which he was predicting that someday she would give him up, and she was calculating, in her journal, the consequences of wedding the Italian. That fall, she confided in Fanny Burney and Queeney. Fanny was appalled, and the initially impassive Queeney marshaled all her forces to keep her mother from marrying her "fiddler," a Catholic and foreigner who—according to London gossip—was a gold digger and possibly even Hester's half-brother.

Queeney enlisted her younger sisters in a campaign to keep from being left "like Puppies in a Pond to swim or drown," and taught the youngest to cry, "Where are you going Mama? will you leave us, and die as our poor papa did?" Such pleas were hard to resist, and, after many emotional scenes, Hester bid "Adieu to all that's dear, to all that's lovely. I am parted from my Life, my Soul! my Piozzi."

In April, Hester's youngest daughter, Harriet, died of whooping cough and measles. Two months later, Dr. Johnson described his declining health in a letter to Hester. ("I perceived that I had suffered a paralytic stroke and that my speech was taken from me. I had no pain, and so little dejection in this dreadful state that I wondered at my own apathy, and considered that perhaps death itself when it should come, would excite less horror than seems now to attend it.") Meanwhile, Piozzi's parting prediction—that his enforced separation from Hester would kill them both—began to seem prescient. Hester sank into a worrisome state of depression, anxiety, and hypochondria until finally, after nursing her daughter Sophy through a serious illness, she collapsed. Her condition seemed so fragile ("We have no Time to lose," her doctor said. "Call the Man home, or see your Mother die.") that even the heartless Queeney was moved to write Piozzi, asking him return to England. Understandably wary, the Italian hesitated until the next spring. At last, in July, the lovers were reunited at Bath, on a day that Hester called the happiest of her life.

For the past year, Hester had been corresponding with Dr. Johnson, though—due to his illness and her own precarious health—they had met only once. Now Hester hastened to inform him of her plans to marry Piozzi. In a postscript to the formal note that she also sent the executors of her late husband's estate, she added, "Indeed, my dear Sir, it was concealed only to spare us both needless pain; I could not have borne to reject that counsel it would have killed me to take."

Johnson's response was swift, and brutal:

> *Madam*
> *If I interpret your letter right, you are ignominiously married; if it is yet undone, let us once talk together. If you have abandoned your children and your religion, God forgive your wickedness; if you have forfeited your fame, and your country, may your folly do no further mischief.*

*If the last act is yet to do, I, who have loved you, esteemed you,
reverenced you and served you, I, who long thought you the first of
human kind, entreat that before your fate is irrevocable, I may once
more see you.*

Hester wrote back, defending her second husband. "Till you
have changed your opinion of Mr Piozzi, let us converse no more.
God bless you!" Johnson replied in a more conciliatory tone and offered the couple his blessing—"Whatever I can contribute to your
happiness, I am very ready to repay for that kindness which soothed
twenty years of a life radically wretched"—an overture that Hester
chose to ignore.

On July 23, Hester Thrale and Gabriel Piozzi were married in
London, in a Catholic church, and two days later were married again,
in an Anglican church in Bath. London was aghast. The newspapers
ridiculed the "Piozzified Marriage" of the forty-three-year-old
widow, and Hester's former friend Mrs. Montagu wrote, "Mrs.
Thrale is fallen below pity. I think the Women and Girls are run
mad, Heaven be praised I have no daughters." Mrs. Thrale's daughters refused to accompany the couple to Italy and were left behind,
at school and with a series of temporary, often unreliable, caretakers.
They never forgave their mother. They avoided her for long periods
and attempted to embarrass her as she had embarrassed them by
marrying Piozzi; eventually, they realized that polite coexistence
consumed less energy than a feud, and settled into a chilly truce.

Finally, in September, the Piozzis left Bath for Europe, and for
their new life together.

THE MUSE AND HER ARTIST would never meet again. Johnson was
in his mid-seventies. His health and his productivity continued to
decline. He wrote letters to Boswell and others, composed a poetic
elegy for his friend Robert Levet. He traveled to Lichfield, complained, contemplated his mortality, considered and rejected the

idea of a journey to Italy, and returned to London for good. When Fanny Burney asked if he ever heard from Mrs. Thrale, he replied, "No. Nor write to her. I drive her quite from my mind. If I meet with one of her letters, I burn it instantly . . . I never speak of her, and I desire never to hear of her more. I drive her, as I said, wholly from my mind."

And so he could not have known that, in the final days of his life, Hester had written from Italy to her friend Samuel Lysons, "Do not neglect Dr. Johnson, you will never see any other Mortal so wise or so good—I keep his picture in my Chamber, and his Works on my Chimney."

On December 7, Samuel Johnson authored his final work—a prayer for God's mercy—and, eight days later, died. It took several weeks for the news to reach Italy. "Oh poor Dr Johnson!!!" Hester wrote.

London society was quick to blame his death on the departure of his muse and to criticize her for having abandoned him in his hour of need. "I am afraid Mrs. Thrale's imprudent marriage shortened his life," wrote Mrs. Montagu, who also spread the rumor that Hester had gone insane and been incarcerated by her new husband in a convent in Milan.

In fact, the newlyweds were thriving. Hester's letters and journal entries bubble with the effervescent joy and self-involvement of someone experiencing happiness for the first time. On January 27, she wrote in *Thraliana*, "Of Course which most delights my Heart is the unfeigned Pleasure which I see my Piozzi takes in my Company—God has heard my Prayers, and enabled me to make happy the most amiable of his Sex. . . . So passes the happiest Birthday ever yet experienced by Hester Lynch Piozzi."

Traveling through Italy, enjoying the flattering attention of local intellectuals and literati, she was also deciding if, and how, she would join the group of writers rumored to be at work on biographies of Dr. Johnson. *Thraliana* documents the process by which she talked herself into staking her territorial claim to Samuel Johnson, the steps by which she convinced herself that she alone had glimpsed Johnson's soul, and that writing his life would be an almost selfless endeavor—a muse's tribute to her artist. She almost regrets the discretion that left her with scant evidence of his darkest secrets. "Poor Johnson! I see that they will leave *nothing untold* that I laboured so long to keep secret; & I was so very delicate in trying to conceal his fancied Insanity, that I retained no Proofs of it—or hardly any—nor ever mentioned it in these Books, lest by my dying first *they* might be printed and the Secret (for such I thought it) discovered. I used to tell him in Jest that his Biographers would be at a Loss concerning some Orange-Peel he used to keep in his pocket, and many a Joke we had about the Lives that would be published: rescue me out of all their hands My dear, & do it *yourself* said he."

By the spring of 1785, she had found a publisher. Writing from London, Thomas Cadell urged her to work quickly, so that her biography might come out before the rage for Johnson had peaked. That September, she sent Cadell a neatly hand-copied manuscript of her *Anecdotes of the Late Samuel Johnson, LL.D.* The first edition sold out in a single day, three more were printed within the next few weeks—and so Hester Thrale Piozzi became the first muse to discover that a decent living could be made, a more or less respectable literary reputation earned, by mining her relationship with her artist.

Divided into 195 numbered sections, each titled ("Sorrows of Vanity," "Incommunicative Taciturnity," "Needle-work," "Mental Decay," etc.) and focused on one of Johnson's favorite conversational themes, trenchant observations or pointed aphorisms, the book is so self-contradictory, so unconscious, so conflicted in its view of its subject that it is at once fascinating and disturbing to read; its effect is chillingly different from its stated purpose. Typically, Mrs. Piozzi begins with a somewhat equivocal and murky promise to tell the unvarnished truth. "I am aware that many will say, I have not spoken highly enough of Dr. Johnson; but it will be difficult for those who say so, to speak more highly. If I have described his manners as they were, I have been careful to show his superiority to the common forms of common life."

The next sections each begin by singling out one of Johnson's virtues and then turning, within a single paragraph, into a discussion of his flaws. So "Bodily Exercises" starts off by describing Johnson as "very conversant in the art of attack and defense by boxing" and ends with his clumsy attempt to leap over a cabriolet, as Mr. Thrale had just done: "*He* suddenly jumped over it too; but in a way so strange and so unwieldly, that our terror lest he should break his bones took from us even the power of laughing." A passage on Johnson's affection for his cousin Parson Ford concludes with "another story less to the credit of his cousin's penetration, how Ford on some occasion said to him, 'You will make your way more easily in the world, I see, as you are contented to dispute no man's claim to conversation excellence; they will, therefore, more willingly allow youre pretensions as a writer.'"

All of this serves as preparation for, and as evidence in support of, the centerpiece of the book: chapter 144, "Mrs. Piozzi's Account of her Rupture with Mr. Johnson"—an effort to answer her critics and perhaps to assuage her own guilt about her failure to visit her old friend during his final illness. "I had been crossed in my intentions of going abroad, and found it convenient, for every reason of health, peace, and pecuniary circumstances, to retire to Bath, where I knew Mr. Johnson would not follow me, and where I could for that reason command some little portion of time for my own use; a thing impossible while I remained at Streatham or at London, as my hours, carriage, and servants had long been at his command, who would not rise in the morning till twelve o'clock perhaps, and oblige me to make breakfast for him till the bell rang for dinner . . . and though much of the time we passed together was spent in blaming or deriding, very justly, my neglect of economy, and waste of that money which might make many families happy."

The first words in the passage—"I had been crossed in my intentions of going abroad"—may partly explain the peevishness of Mrs. Piozzi's complaints; during the period she is recalling, she had been thwarted in her hopes of marrying Piozzi, and her resultant misery and poor health had spilled over into resentment and anger at Dr. Johnson. By the time she wrote the *Anecdotes*, her happiness with Piozzi must have made her painfully aware of how much she had missed during a long, loveless marriage, the decades of loneliness and tedium relieved only by the tepid (certainly compared to the pleasures she enjoyed with Piozzi) satisfactions of hosting their famous house guest: "Veneration for his virtue, reverence for his talents, delight in his conversation, and habitual endurance of a yoke my husband first put upon me, and of which he contentedly bore his share for sixteen or seventeen years, made me go on so long with Mr. Johnson; but the perpetual confinement I will own to have been terrifying in the first years of our friendship, and irksome in the last; nor could I pretend to support it without help, when my coadjutor was no more."

Elsewhere, Mrs. Piozzi softens, and reveals the extent of the true affection that was as much a part of their friendship as her dutiful, oxlike "endurance of a yoke." Throughout the book, eruptions of temper and irritation alternate with tender, moving passages such as this one: "Conversation was all he required to make him happy . . . On that principle it was that he preferred winter to summer, when the heat of the weather gave people an excuse to stroll about, and walk for pleasure in the shade, while he wished to sit still in a chair, and chat day after day, till somebody proposed a drive in the coach; and that was the most delicious moment of his life. 'But the carriage must stop sometime,' as he said, 'and the people would come home at last;' so his pleasure was of short duration."

AFTER A EUROPEAN TOUR that took them as far as Prague, Dresden, and Vienna, the Piozzis returned to London in 1787. Though advised to keep a low profile until the scandal occasioned by their marriage had blown over, the couple went to the theater on their first night home. Hester was greeted—without much warmth—by her daughters, and before long found a house to rent in Hanover Square. Though many former acquaintances shunned her, a hundred guests attended a party she gave in May; her daughters pointedly drove by the house on their way to another event.

Even as she worked to reestablish her position in London, Hester was busily editing a volume of her correspondence with Dr. Johnson, an activity that involved substantially revising her letters to him and deleting certain annoying passages from his, neatly excising his kind words about Boswell, with whom Hester was now openly feuding. Dissatisfied with the quantity of letters she had, irritated by Queeney's refusal to let her mother publish Johnson's letters to *her*, Hester traveled to Lichfield to track down more notes and mementos, artifacts that Boswell had, for the most part, preemptively acquired.

At the same time, she was battling Queeney for her legal right to raise her ten-year-old daughter Cecilia—a privilege that Queeney had assumed in her mother's absence and was reluctant to relinquish. Finally, in April, Cecilia was brought from school to live with her mother and stepfather in Hanover Square—an event that Hester celebrated by giving a children's party, and that Queeney responded to by refusing to speak to her mother for the next six years and persuading her sisters Sophy and Susan to do the same.

When *Letters to and from the Late Samuel Johnson, LL.D.* appeared in 1788, the furor that erupted prefigured contemporary debates about the meretriciousness of survivors who profit from the literary remains of the dead. Hester's decision to print the intimate correspondence of her deceased friend was criticized and satirized in the press; she was attacked, quite nastily, by Boswell and others.

By now, however, she had observed that notoriety was not necessarily harmful to one's social status. As a rising literary celebrity, she was asked to private theatrical performances; she wrote short plays, adapted a story of Johnson's for the stage, and, in partnership with Piozzi, gave large and glamorous concerts. By the following year, even the snobbish Blue-Stockings had readmitted her into their inner circle.

The only shadow on Hester's happiness was cast by the looming iceberg of her three older daughters (who refused to communicate with her except about money) and by the miscarriage that she suffered in January 1788. At forty-seven, Hester had still hoped to have a child with her beloved Piozzi. Meanwhile, she kept writing. The chatty, badly reviewed (critics mocked her plain style and "vulgar" turns of phrase) and popular *Observations and Reflections Made in the Course of a Journey through France, Italy, and Germany* appeared in June 1789.

The next winter, after a trip to Scotland, the Piozzis reclaimed Streatham Park, where they remained, with the intractable adolescent Cecilia, for five years. Queeney, Sophia, and Susan consented to a halfhearted reconciliation with their mother. Hester wrote *British Synonymy*, a volume intended primarily for non-native speakers on the proper use of English synonyms. Perhaps it was inspired by her husband, written to spare him linguistic gaffes like this one: "Calling upon some old lady of quality, (he) was told by a servant 'she was indifferent.' 'Is she indeed?' answered Piozzi huffishly, 'then pray tell her I can be as indifferent as she,' and walked away."

Exhausted by the pressures of London social life—and disappointed by its failure to match the high standards that Johnson's conversational muse had maintained at Streatham—the Piozzis built Brynbella, a country home in Wales. Hester read, wrote to her daughters, entertained friends, nursed Piozzi through the agonizing gout from which he had begun to suffer, and anxiously monitored Cecilia's growing attachment to the rakish, unsuitable, abusive John Mostyn, with whom she eventually eloped. Steadfastly in love with a former boyfriend, Cecilia refused to sleep with her husband, and seemed not to care when he impregnated her maid.

In the hopes of providing themselves with a male heir and at least one satisfying child, the Piozzis imported from Italy—with plans of adopting—Gabriel's five-year-old nephew, who gratifyingly, if somewhat calculatedly, had been named John Salusbury Piozzi, after Hester's father. "We will see if he will be more grateful, & rational, & comfortable than Miss Thrales have been to the Mother they have at length *driven to Desperation*." Never one to let her pen remain idle, Hester published, in 1801, the two-volume, one-thousand-plus-page *Retrospection: or A Review of the Most Striking and Important Events, Characters, Situations and Their Consequences, Which the Last Eighteen Hundred Years Have Presented to the View of Mankind*—a daunting display of some of the same qualities she'd demonstrated as a young woman: lofty intellectual ambitions without a corresponding amount of depth. Again in advance of her times, she devised a marketing and publicity strategy for the book; it was scheduled to come out on New Year's Day, 1801, to celebrate the arrival of the nineteenth century.

Over the next years, Piozzi's agonies multiplied, and he endured them nobly. "He is so kind & so patient & so much more concerned for us than for Himself, that it is Melancholy to see," wrote Hester. Bedridden, tormented by abcesses, he died in March 1809, still so dear to his wife that she described their love as having "made twenty years passed in Piozzi's enchanting society seem like a happy dream of twenty hours."

Uncharacteristically, Hester's daughters rallied round to comfort their mother, who, in the course of losing so many children, had developed her own strategies for coping with grief—principally, the resumption of an active social schedule. Now at last she was able to follow the plan (that she and Piozzi had devised before he fell too ill) of spending summers in Wales and the cooler months in London and Bath. Over her daughters' objections, she formally adopted John Salusbury, whom she sent to Oxford. Having neither the en-

ergy nor the aptitude for a university career, he dropped out and retired to Wales.

Disappointed by his academic failures but thrilled that her only
son and heir was so fond of her homeland, Hester gave Brynbella
and all her Welsh property to Salusbury, who had fallen in love and
was eager to marry. Without the income from the Welsh land,
money was suddenly in short supply, and after Hester had financed
some costly but necessary repairs at Streatham, she was compelled
to rent the place and move to a modest dwelling in Bath. Eventually,
after trying unsuccessfully to persuade her sons-in-law to buy
Streatham, the estate was auctioned off, and she found a more congenial house in Bath.

Well into her seventies, Hester formed a series of intense attachments to a succession of much younger men, one of whom,
James Fellowes, would become her literary executor after her death
in 1821. Though still in mourning for Piozzi, she refused to appear
in public or be seen by visitors without her makeup. Her desire for
male attention and her ability to sustain romantic relationships outside the traditional parameters of conventional sexuality—the same
qualities that had qualified her to function as Samuel Johnson's
muse—continued into old age. Six hundred guests celebrated her
eightieth birthday in the Lower Assembly Rooms at Bath. Dressed
in an elaborate white dress and a headdress of white plumes, Hester
danced—with "astonishing elasticity," one of her young men recalled—until five in the morning.

In her final years, one of the party pieces with which she entertained friends and admirers was a dead-accurate imitation of Dr.
Samuel Johnson at Streatham, "indulging in one of his strange
whims; stepping forward, drawing back his leg, and then another
step!"—dictated by his compulsions, the ballet of gestures and ritual
tics that he was obliged to perform before he could come down to
the dinner table and blind his muse to his flaws with the dazzling
light of his brilliant conversation.

ALICE LIDDELL

By the time Alice Liddell Hargreaves arrived in New York to claim her honorary doctorate in musedom from Columbia University, seventy years had passed since the "golden afternoon" on which she seduced and pestered Mr. Dodgson into telling the story that, they agreed, became *Alice's Adventures in Wonderland*. During that time, Alice had managed to re-create some version of her connection to Dodgson with the critic John Ruskin. Later, she had an unhappy love affair with Prince Leopold, Queen Victoria's son, married a suitable country squire with social position and money, had three children, lost two in World War I, been widowed, and weathered a financially dicey period with her spendthrift youngest son, Caryl, who accompanied her to New York, where he irritated reporters by answering their questions to his mother. A lifetime separated Alice from the child beauty who had bewitched Charles Dodgson, and yet throughout the hoopla surrounding her visit—the radio broadcast, the city tour, interviews, the suite at the Waldorf, the private and public ceremonies at Columbia—Alice Hargreaves slipped quite naturally into her role as the former Alice Liddell, the infant muse whose attention and adoration had inspired an eccentric mathematician to make her the child-heroine of a classic.

Alice deserved the highest degree, for in the lives of the muses there has rarely been a more explicit recognition of a muse's role than Lewis Carroll's oft-repeated appreciation of Alice Liddell's part in the creation of his masterpiece. Throughout his life, he reminded readers that his inspiration had come on a particular day, as a result of his desire to please a particular ten-year-old girl—a debt he acknowledged first in the poetic preface to *Alice's Adventures in Wonderland*.

> All in the golden afternoon
> Full leisurely we glide;
> For both our oars, with little skill,
> By little arms are plied,
> While little hands make vain pretense
> Our wanderings to guide.
>
> Ah, cruel Three! In such an hour,
> Beneath such dreamy weather,
> To beg a tale, of breath too weak,
> To stir the tiniest feather!
> Yet what can one poor voice avail
> Against three tongues together?
>
> Imperious Prima flashes forth
> Her edict to "begin it"—
> In gentler tones Secunda hopes
> "There will be nonsense in it"—
> While Tertia interrupts the tale
> Not more than once a minute.
>
> Anon, to sudden silence won,
> In fancy they pursue
> The dream-child moving through a land
> Of wonders wild and new,
> In friendly chat with bird and beast—
> And half believe it true.

And ever, as the story drained
The wells of fancy dry,
And faintly strove that weary one
To put the subject by,
"The rest next time"—"It is next time!"
The happy voices cry.

Thus grew the tale of Wonderland
Thus slowly, one by one,
In quaint events were hammered out—
And now the tale is done,
And home we steer, a merry crew,
Beneath the setting sun.

Alice! a childish story take,
And with a gentle hand
Lay it where Childhood's dreams are twined
In Memory's mystic band,
Like pilgrim's withered wreath of flowers
Plucked in a far-off land.

The "cruel Three" were the daughters of Henry Liddell, the author, with Robert Scott, of the celebrated *Greek-English Lexicon*, and since 1855, Dean of Christ Church College, Oxford, where Dodgson taught mathematics. Shortly after the Liddells moved to Oxford, Dodgson made their acquaintance, photographed the children, entertained them with stories and games; by the time of the "golden afternoon," they were visiting almost daily.

On the afternoon of July 4, 1862, Lorina Liddell was thirteen, Edith was eight, and Alice was ten—a year older than Beatrice when Dante first fell in love. The adults and children had gone on one of the outings that they all so enjoyed, carefully planned excursions that included Dodgson's friend Robinson Duckworth and that on this occasion involved a rowboat journey upriver to Godstow, where the party had tea in the meadow.

There had been a kind of prologue to the "golden afternoon," the storm before the calm, the June 17 outing that preceded that July 4 picnic and that was a disaster, first because of the intrusive, sobering presence of Mr. Dodgson's two unmarried sisters, and also thanks to the rainstorm that soaked the entire party and is said to have been the model for the flood of Alice's tears that inundates Wonderland. Accounts of that day convey Dodgson's and the children's frustration, and the sense of urgency that must have built steadily until that afternoon which marked Victorian literature's most celebrated intervention of the muse. Few readers can date the exact birthday of *Crime and Punishment*, or *War and Peace*, but countless *Alice in Wonderland* fans know that the idea for the book came to Charles Dodgson on that hot, dreamy and, over time, increasingly mythologized and fetishized July afternoon when he and the children took shelter from the sun in the shadow of a hayrick. Indeed, so many readers have fixated on that sunny day that a revisionist movement has arisen, citing period weather reports to prove that it rained on July 4, 1862.

In an 1887 essay, "Alice on the Stage," Dodgson described his book's inception: "Full many a year has slipped away since that 'golden afternoon' . . . but I can call it up almost as clearly as if it were yesterday—the cloudless blue above, the watery mirror below, the boat drifting idly on its way, the tinkle of the drops that fell from the oars, as they waved sleepily to and fro, and (the one bright gleam of life in all the slumberous scene) three eager faces, hungry for news of fairyland, and who would not be said nay to: from whose lips 'Tell us a story, please' had all the stern immutability of Fate!

"What wert thou, dream-Alice, in thy foster-father's eyes? How shall he picture thee? Loving, first, loving and gentle: loving as a dog . . . and gentle as a fawn: then courteous—courteous to all, high or low, grand or grotesque, King or caterpillar, even as though she were herself a king's daughter, and her clothing wrought gold: then trustful, ready to accept the wildest impossibilities with all that utter trust that only dreamers know; and lastly, curious—wildly curious, and with the eager enjoyment of Life that comes only in the happy hours of childhood, when all is new and fair, and when Sin and Sorrow are but names—empty words signifying nothing!"

Dodgson marked the day "with a white stone" in his diary. And after the afternoon became known as the birthday of a masterpiece, others felt obliged to dust off their memories of the event, which at the time may have seemed no more special than a dozen other picnics. Robinson Duckworth, who would become chaplain to the queen and canon of Westminster, offered Dodgson's first biographer this recollection, in which we can still hear static crackling back and forth between the mathematics don and the dean's middle daughter:

"I rowed *stroke* and he rowed *bow* . . . when the three Miss Liddells were our passengers, and the story was actually composed and spoken over my shoulder for the benefit of Alice Liddell, who was acting as 'cox' of our gig. I remember turning round and saying, 'Dodgson, is this an extempore romance of yours?' And he replied, 'Yes, I'm inventing as we go along.' I also well remember how, when we had conducted the three children back to the Deanery, Alice said, as she bade us goodnight, 'Oh, Mr. Dodgson, I wish you would write out Alice's adventures for me.' He said he would try, and he afterwards told me that he sat up nearly the whole night, committing to a MS. book his recollections of the drolleries with which he had enlivened the afternoon."

Finally, here is Alice's account, reported in the *New York Times* on May 1, 1928, the day after her original copy of *Alice's Adventures Underground*, written in Carroll's own hand, was auctioned off at Sotheby's. "Near all of *Alice's Adventures Underground* was told on that blazing summer afternoon with the heat haze shimmering over the meadows where the party landed to shelter for a while in the shadow cast by the haycocks near Godstow . . . I have such a distinct recollection of the expedition, and also, on the next day I started to pester him to write down the story for me, which I had never done before. It was due to my . . . importunity that, after saying he would think about it, he eventually gave the hesitating promise which started him writing it down at all."

When Alice arrived to conquer Manhattan and carry off her Columbia Ph.D., yet another piece, in *Cornhill* magazine, revisited that historic occasion. This time Alice's sentimental journey was guided by her son Caryl. By then, her recall had lost a bit of its edge without diminishing her certainty about her agency in the creation of Lewis Carroll's book:

"Next Wednesday my mother will be 80 and she now has no memory of what stories Mr. Dodgson told on that famous afternoon when they had tea under the haystack at Godstow. She is certain that they must have been better than usual, because she has such a distant recollection not only of that particular afternoon but also of pestering him after that to write them out, a thing which she had never done before. It was because she kept 'going on, going on' at him that he started to write them out at all—with results that have proved more fantastic than any of the adventures which befell Alice underground."

Five years before the golden afternoon, Charles Dodgson dropped in on Alfred, Lord Tennyson, at his home in the Lake Country. Later in life, Dodgson would decline invitations to social events, telling his disappointed hostesses that their invitation had made it impossible for him to come; he would prefer to stop by, unannounced. And that—uninvited—was how he first visited the Poet Laureate, though he had taken the precaution of sending ahead a note identifying himself as the "artist of Agnes Grace and Little Red Riding Hood."

Having heard that Tennsyon, whom he admired, was interested

in photography, Dodgson had arranged to take a portrait of Agnes Grace Weld, the homely daughter of Tennyson's sister-in-law. "(Tennyson) has addressed one sonnet to the little Agnes Grace: she hardly merits one by actual beauty," Dodgson wrote, uncharitably. For the picture, he'd costumed the scowling girl in an unflattering cloak and given her a basket of goodies for Grandma; he'd sent Tennyson a copy, which the poet was said to have liked.

Dodgson had already learned that photography, like the key for which Alice searches underground, could open doors that otherwise might have stayed locked; that was how he gained access to Dean Liddell's household, by taking portraits of the children that intrigued the intellectually curious dean and pleased their mother, Lorina Reeve Liddell.

On a day that Carroll marked with a white stone, "the artist of Agnes Grace," was, as he'd hoped, welcomed by Mrs. Tennyson. She promised he could photograph her own two sons, who took to their visitor right away. "Both the children proposed coming with me when I left—how far seemed immaterial to them." Soon after, Dodgson photographed the whole family, including the Laureate, dressed in rumpled Boho high-style: crushed hat, a beard, and tweeds.

Two summers later, in 1859, Dodgson again appeared at the Tennysons' home, this time on the Isle of Wight. Tennyson failed to recognize him—"too short-sighted," was how Dodgson chose to interpret the poet's forgetfulness. The poet's son, "beautiful little Hallam . . . remembered me more readily than his father had done." It was during this visit that Tennyson admired Dodgson's newer photographs, leavening his weighty approval with a condescending joke about his guest's inferior medium: "Tennyson told us that often on going to bed after being engaged on composition, he had dreamed long passages of poetry ('You, I suppose,' turning to me, 'dream photographs?')"

But the coolness of their interchange warmed, at least by a few

degrees, when Dodgson showed the Laureate what would later become his most famous picture, the *Portrait of Alice Liddell as the Beggar
Child*, and Tennyson declared it the most beautiful photograph that
he had ever seen.

THE CHILD IS exceptionally beautiful. The bright black coins of her
eyes, the unblemished pale flesh ever so lightly grazing the rough,
mossy stone, the perfect ankles and feet, the slightly prehensile toes
curled among the nasturtiums, the ragged costume nearly comical
in its carnal suggestiveness, the crisp regularity of her features, the

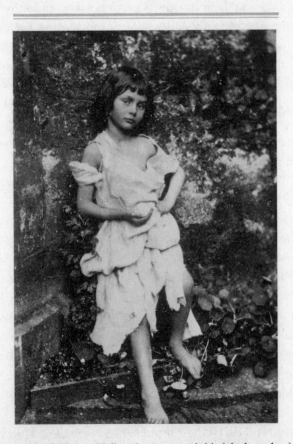

Portrait of Alice Liddell as the Beggar Child. *(Charles Dodgson)*

gleam of her hair, the naturalness of her posture, the confidence of that crooked elbow and the hand at her hip, the artistry of the composition, the graceful pose that seems so integral and ideally suited to the photograph—the cupped hand, the beggar child's supplication, not extended toward us but staying within the picture plane, more ironic, knowing, and withholding than importuning—a pose so apparently effortless that we take its elegance for granted until we compare it with another photo of Alice in the same beggar's rags, a more frontal and literal-minded shot in which the girl's hands, joined before her, resemble a baby seal's flippers.

Finally, it's the gaze that holds us and makes the photo seem so unlike any other portrait of a child—or an adult. It's the subtlety and complexity of Alice's expression, the paradoxical mixture of the sly and straightforward, the saucy and serious: the intense concentration that Alice brought to Dodgson's portrayals of her as a child, the boldness that singled her out of family groupings and then disappeared, subsumed by self-conscious melancholy, as Alice passed the age at which the child-friends ceased to interest their attentive adult companion.

The look on the beggar child's face is one we associate with intimacy: the unwavering focus an adult woman might turn on a husband or lover. No one could regard a stranger or a casual acquaintance with such sustained, undefended openness. Whom do we feel free enough to fixate on, for so long? Of course, Alice was staring at the camera and not, precisely, at the photographer. Perhaps she was envisioning some version of herself; possibly it was Dodgson's mistake to assume she was gazing at him. The result is an image that scrambles the boundaries between narcissistic introspection and erotic adoration, between helplessness and control, artistic detachment and amorous obsession.

Our awareness of the primitive photographic techniques of the period—the torturously long time, a whole minute or more, during which the little girl had to maintain that expression, that stance—makes it seem all the more extraordinary. It is not, as we have come to think of photographs, a record of one fleeting moment, but a product of many moments: the tedious processes of preparation, of posing or being posed, the frantic manipulations of plates, chemicals, and formulas necessary to develop a print. The photo does not record a gesture but rather a state of being, an emotional condition produced by an extended transaction between the photographer and his subject. The strength of that emotion—the photographer's helpless romantic longing focused on the child, and the hint, in the child's eyes, that some version of that love is returned—is part of what still has the power to move and shock us.

To look at Charles Dodgson's *Portrait of Alice Liddell as the Beggar Child* is again to be reminded that our culture has too narrowly defined the parameters of what it calls love and drastically foreshortened the continuum along which each individual passionate affair or painfully repressed romance, each homosexual or heterosexual alliance, each socially condoned or "inappropriate" attraction, is located. Instead of acknowledging that every love is different from every other love—a seemingly obvious statement underlined by the lives of the muses—we create reductive categories that fit no one and nothing. To call Charles Dodgson a pedophile is not only to misapprehend and diminish the nature of his relationship with Alice Liddell but to deny its complexity, its depth, and its essential singularity.

Their mutual fascination endured in an active form for approximately seven years—not long by standards of Victorian engagements, but very long for an unconsummated attraction that spanned almost the entire length of one lover's childhood. Moreover, there is evidence that Dodgson's infatuation survived in a vestigial form until his death, and that, long afterward, Alice's connection with "Mr. Dodgson" continued to evolve and change.

The glue that held them together was concocted from a heady recipe of yearning, affection, and play, a powerful chemistry, and one imagines, a welcome distraction from the searing attacks of guilt that Dodgson recorded in his diaries beginning in May 1862.

The source of his self-loathing has been the cause of heated debate: Was it indolence? Masturbation? Forbidden thoughts and desires? Like Samuel Johnson, the mathematics don considered himself a vile sinner in desperate need of prayer and pardon for his transgressions. And like Hester Thrale, his muse appeared to offer him distraction and forgiveness. Yet despite the torment that made Dodgson fill his journals with self-recriminations and vows to cease committing his unspecified sins, no real evidence suggests that these self-lacerations involved his child-friends, or that his relations with these girls involved anything more than kisses (lots of kisses, to be sure), hand-holding, or an invitation to sit on his lap while he told his delightful stories.

Undeniably, Dodgson's pursuit and cultivation of his child-friends had a compulsive aspect, perhaps partly due to the fact that his longings were unrequitable. Such feelings for adult women would most likely have been reciprocated eventually by one woman or another, thus obviating the need for the continuing, perpetual search. The obsessiveness of Dodgson's quest and his mathematical mind impelled him to list his child-friends, throughout much of his life. In March 1863, he recorded in his diary the names of 108 children he had photographed or hoped to photograph. In 1877, he catalogued thirty-four; two years later, he calculated twenty-two; and "sixteen new girl-friends" joined their number in 1894.

The need to acquire new friends and the fervor of these relationships must have been heightened by the awareness of their inevitable transience and brevity; as Dodgson grew older, the maximum age of his friends edged toward adolescence, but still he was heartbroken each time a girl grew past the point at which their friendship might be considered improper. He often reacted with disbelief, sorrow, and even rage when a former child-friend proved foolish enough to get married.

"Usually," he confided in Edith Blakemore, "the child becomes so entirely a different being as she grows into a woman, that our friendship has to change too, and that it usually does by sliding down, from a loving intimacy, into an acquaintance that merely consists of a smile and bow when we meet! . . . That is partly why I have written you this long letter—that you continue to honour me with an affection that is a sort of love, and that we haven't yet got to the 'smile and bow' stage!" Writing to another young woman, he combines his best wishes on her engagement with a guilt-inducing account of his own predicament: "My child-friends are all marrying off, now, terribly quick! But, for a solitary broken-hearted hopeless old bachelor, it is certainly soothing to find that some of them, even when engaged, continue to write as 'yours affectionately!' But for that, you will easily perceive that my solitude would be simply *desperate*!" And when Isa Bowman told him that she was to be married, he pulled some roses from her belt and threw them from the window, saying, "You know I can't stand flowers."

In the diaries and letters, he discusses the importance of these attachments—"The friendship of children has always been a great element in my enjoyment of life, and is very *restful* as a contrast to the society of books, or of men."—with a lack of self-consciousness suggesting that, if these relationships had been overtly sexual, Dodgson must have been extremely good, even by Victorian standards, at self-delusion and repression. The sexuality that occasionally surfaces in his imagery would seem, perhaps perversely, to argue for his innocence. A child molester could not have risked writing this madly suggestive letter to Gertrude Chataway:

"When a little girl is hoping to take a plum off a dish, and finds that she can't have that one, because it's bad or unripe, what does she do? Is she sorry or disappointed? Not a bit! She just takes another instead, and grins from one little ear to the other as she puts it to her lips . . . The little girl means *you*—the bad plum means *me* . . . and all that about the little girl putting plums to her lips means—well, it means—but you can't expect *every bit* of a fable to mean something!"

For all his otherworldliness, Dodgson was enough of a social creature to know—or suspect—that his behavior was causing gossip. He worried, in particular, about the nude photographs he took of some of the children. He reassured the mothers about his blameless—indeed, holy—responses to their daughters ("Their innocent unconsciousness is very beautiful, and gives one a feeling of reverence, as at the presence of something sacred.") and he promised Mrs. Henderson to destroy all but one print of his nude pictures of her children: "That is all I want for myself, and (though I consider them perfectly innocent in themselves) there is really *no* friend to whom I should wish to give photographs which so entirely defy conventional rules." His pained awareness of these rules was no doubt exacerbated by a letter (now lost) which he received from his sister Mary, to which he replied:

"I think all you say about my girl-guests is most kind and sisterly, and almost entirely proper for you to write to your brother . . . You and your husband have, I think, been very fortunate to know so little, by experience, in your own case or in that of your friends, of the wicked recklessness with which people repeat things to the disadvantage of others, without a thought as to whether they have grounds for asserting what they say. I have met with a good deal of utter misrepresentation of that kind. And another result of my experience is the conviction that the opinion of 'people' in general is absolutely worthless as a test of right and wrong. The only two tests I now apply to such a question as the having of some particular girl-friend as a guest are, first my own *conscience*, to settle whether I feel it to be entirely innocent and right, in the sight of God; secondly, the *parents* of my friend, to settle whether I have their *full* approval for what I do. You need not be shocked at my being spoken against. *Anybody* who is spoken about at all is *sure* to be spoken against by *somebody*: and any action, however innocent in itself, is liable, and not at all unlikely, to be blamed by *somebody*. If you limit your actions in life to things that *nobody* can possibly find fault with, you will not do much!"

His experience with the social censure that he contemptuously dismissed as the prudish influence of "Mrs. Grundy" was, on occasion, direct. A Mrs. Mayhew let him take "nudities" of her younger girl, but was so shocked at his request to photograph her eleven-year-old daughter in the nude that Dodgson was offended, and the friendship was broken off.

Yet none of the recollections of the former child-friends suggest that they found their relationship to be anything but enjoyable. In the preface to a 1954 edition of the diaries, Dodgson's niece Violet recalls the ten days she spent with her uncle at the age of thirteen: "I probably bored him. He liked children to talk and we were rather dumb. But he never let me see it and was the most thoughtful, courteous and unwearying of hosts. Moreover, he made one feel that one was of interest to him as an individual—a novel experience to a child picked out of the middle of a large family. He invited opinions and discussed them with respect and understanding. His face lighted up with appreciation of my feeble little jokes or my admiration of something he was showing or explaining. He was always a cheerful, keen and sympathetic companion, and I had never a dull moment."

The former Enid Stevens contributes this touching reminiscence: "For hours on end we used to sit curled up together—the old man and the little girl—in a big arm-chair, playing games with words, working our ciphers together, or making up strange mathematical problems . . . Over and over again he begged my mother to let him take me away with him—sometimes to the seaside, sometimes to London. The Victorian mind saw possible evil even in the association of a child of twelve with an old man of sixty-three. He must have had wonderful patience, for he tried again and again, but I was never allowed to go and shall never to the end of my days cease to regret it. Days of close intercourse with one who, however whimsical his mind, were denied me because the saint was male and I was a little girl."

In marked contrast to the harrowing, hollow-eyed photos of Victorian child prostitutes taken around the same time, the portraits of Alice and the other girls do not look as if the girls are being ill-used, harmed, or frightened, nor as if they feel in danger or at risk.

"We used to sit on the big sofa on each side of him," recalled Alice Liddell, "while he told us stories, illustrating them by pencil or ink drawings as he went along. When we were thoroughly happy and amused at his stories, he used to pose us, and expose the plates before the right mood had passed . . . Being photographed was . . . a joy to us and not a penance as it is to most children."

Just as Alice spoke of being photographed in the language of joy and penance, Dodgson described his child friendships as a spiritual experience: "Any one that has ever loved one true child will have known the awe that falls on one in the presence of a spirit fresh from God's hands, on whom no shadow of sin . . . has yet fallen." Indeed, the photo of Alice as the beggar child is a devotional picture, a retablo commemorating a Victorian miracle. In the depth and fervor of its barely concealed passion, it evokes Flemish and Italian Renaissance art, those swooning saints, Sebastian, Theresa, apparently unconscious of the eroticism of their ecstatic postures. But were they really unaware? How much does the beggar child know? Where do we draw the line between the sacred and the carnal? And whose idea, whose decision was it to slide Alice's dress off her shoulders?

DODGSON'S MUSES were children. He himself was the third of ten and the oldest son, the adored ringleader who kept his seven younger sisters busy with dramas, games, and projects he invented for their amusement. Their father was a preacher, their mother a loving Yorkshire houswife. By all accounts their childhood was happy, though Charles and all but two siblings stammered, and later, only two married. Imaginative and verbal, the little Dodgsons produced a series of in-house publications, including the *Rectory* magazine—a vehicle for hilarious doggerel like Mary Charlotte's "The Whirlwind":

> *The air was filled with shrieking mice*
> *The houses rolled along*
> *Till they reached the edge of a precipice;*
> *One crash, and they were gone.*

Composed by Charles at thirteen, the following limerick prefigures the deliriously nasty poems in the *Alice* books and displays the family talent for the sort of thing that, if written by a child now, would doubtless mandate a chat with the guidance counselor.

> *There was an old farmer of Readall*
> *Who made holes in his face with a needle*
>   *Then went far deeper in*
>   *Than to pierce through the skin*
> *And yet strange to say he was made beadle.*

So much for the treacly innocence of the preacher's Victorian darlings. In fact, Victorian culture was, like our own, schizophrenic about children, struggling to reconcile the ideal of the newborn angel-baby fresh from its prenatal layover in heaven with the grim realities of child labor and prostitution, to navigate between saccharine sentimentality and the innate distrust and jealousy of children that (as in our own time) allowed such oppressive conditions to exist. A complex view of child-nature came quite easily for Dodgson, who never forgot how it felt to be a child, and besides had an artist's ability to entertain, simultaneously, contradictory opinions and feelings. His work recognized the anarchy, sadism, and *schadenfreude* of children's personalities, as well as the unself-consciousness, honesty, and clear-sightedness that we admire in the very young.

That he saw this without judgment was partly what made his presence (and his books) so subversive, and children love subversion; they fall in love with adults who urge them to break their parents' rules. Like most children, Dodgson sometimes carried this conspiratorial fun too far—that is, to a point that makes us uneasy. Consider this letter to Tennyson's ten-year-old-son Hallam on the subject of a birthday present Dodgson had given the boy:

> *"I am glad you liked the knife, and I think it is a pity you should not be allowed to use it 'till you are older.' However, as you are older now, perhaps you have begun to use it by this time: if you were allowed to cut your finger on it, once a week, just a little, you know, till it begins to bleed, and a good deep cut every birthday, I should think that would be enough, and it would last a good long time so. Only I hope that if Lionel ever wants his fingers cut with it, you will be kind to your brother, and hurt him as much as he likes."*

But the children were not disturbed. For Mr. Dodgson paid them more attention and showed them more affection than most members of their households. His fondness for mischief, nonsense, and invention, and this fascinating anomaly—a grown-up who knew how to play—rendered him irresistible to Dean Liddell's lovely daughters.

DODGSON ARRIVED at Oxford in 1850 and remained there for forty-seven years, first as a student, then as a lecturer in mathematics, a Master of the House, and a deacon. There, he courted the Liddells through the lens of his camera. Another white stone marked the day on which Dodgson accompanied his friend Reginald Southey to photograph the cathedral from the deanery garden and wound up focusing on the dean's children, playing nearby. He had met Mrs. Liddell and her two oldest children at the boat races in February, when he'd pronounced Harry "the handsomest boy I ever saw." He'd made friends with little Lorina at a musical party given by the Liddells—so perhaps it was not pure chance that directed him and his camera to the deanery garden. All that spring and fall, Dodgson photographed the children at home and took Harry and Ina for the first of the boating excursions that would later loom so large in literary mythology.

Even through Dodgson's neutral prose, we can feel his alarm at the periodic fits of annoyance, maternal protectiveness, and (one imagines) the craving for privacy that periodically drove Mrs. Liddell to hint that he was becoming a nuisance. The first of these initially subtle and increasingly direct reprimands occurred after Dodgson asked the Liddells' governess, Miss Prickett, to arrange for her charges to be photographed with the Acland children, whose parents were friendly with the Liddells. On the appointed morning, Dodgson arrived with his camera "just in time to see the whole party (except Edith) set off with the carriage and ponies—a disappointment for me, as it is the last vacant morning I shall have in the term." Ten days later, when Dodgson went to photograph Harry and Ina, Mrs. Liddell managed to make her sentiments so obvious that not even the simultaneously hypersensitive and obtuse don could mistake them. "I found Mrs. Liddell had said they were not to be taken till all can be taken in a group. This may be meant as a hint that I have intruded on the premises too long: I am quite of the same opinion myself, and, partly for this reason, partly because I cannot afford to waste any more time on portraits at such a bad season of the year, I have resolved not to go again for the present, not at all without invitation, except just to pack up the things and bring them back."

A rapprochement was arranged, but when, in December, the ailing dean and his wife decided to spend four months in Madeira, Dodgson's offer to tutor Harry in math during their absence was frostily rejected by Mrs. Liddell, on the grounds that such lessons would claim too much of Dodgson's time. Dodgson began teaching Harry as soon as his parents left town. The following spring Dodgson again felt compelled to scale back his connection to the Liddells when local gossips theorized that the children were merely beards for the true object of his affection—their governess, Miss Prickett. "Though for my own part I should give little importance to the existence of so groundless a rumour, it would be inconsiderate to the governess to give any further occasion for remarks of the sort. For this reason I shall avoid taking any notice of the children in future, unless occasion should arise when such an interpretation is impossible."

This new resolve lasted only briefly, and Dodgson resumed his visits to the deanery. It was not long after—sometime in 1858 or in early 1859—that he took the portrait of seven-year-old Alice Liddell as the beggar child, an episode that, as we shall see, he repeatedly revisited in fantasy and memory, and that may have marked the most impassioned period of his relationship with his child muse.

The connection between photography and erotic pursuit—and frustration—was made explicit in "A Photographer's Day Out," a comic sketch Carroll published in 1860. In search of "a young lady to photograph—realizing *my* ideal of beauty," and obsessed with the name Amelia, our hero finds the object of desire in the daughter of a family he has been asked to photograph. After enduring her smug, unpleasant parents and their unruly baby, three unattractive younger sisters, and the hostility of a romantic rival, he arranges to take Amelia's portrait in a meadow—only to have his efforts stymied by two farmers who accuse him of trespassing and beat him up.

"A Photographer's Day Out" would turn out to be predictive. Three years after its composition, Dodgson, like his hero, would be forcibly prevented from taking his beloved's picture, but the mugging would occur not at the hands of "a thick-built man, vulgar in dress, repulsive in expression, (who) carried a straw in his mouth" but through the more delicate but equally thuggish agency of the bossy, snobbish Lorina Reeve Liddell—the subject of a contemporary Oxford rhyme that doubles as instruction on how to pro-

nounce the family name: "I am the Dean and this is Mrs. Liddell;
She plays the first, and I the second fiddle."

Also in 1860, Dodgson published a melancholy and eerily prescient poem, "Faces in the Fire," in a magazine, *All the Year Round*, edited by Charles Dickens. In the poem, the speaker summons up the
"magic picture" of a shy, elfin girl he knew on the farm on which he
was born:

> *Oh, time was young, and life was warm,*
> *When first I saw that fairy form,*
> *Her dark hair tossing in the storm.*
>
> *And fast and free these pulses played,*
> *When last I met that gentle maid-*
> *When last her hand in mine was laid.*
>
> *Those locks of jet are turned to grey,*
> *And she is strange and far away*
> *That might have been mine own today-*
>
> *That might have been mine own, my dear,*
> *Through many and many a happy year-*
> *That might have sat beside me here.*
>
> *Ay, changeless through the changing scene,*
> *The ghostly whisper rings between,*
> *The dark refrain of "might have been . . ."*

During the autumn that followed the "golden afternoon," Dodgson
took a photograph as striking and peculiar, if not nearly so beautiful,
as *Portrait of Alice Liddell as the Beggar Child.* This "composition picture"
(that is, a staged tableau) featured Alice Donkin, the niece of an

Oxford astronomy professor. The girl was Alice Liddell's age, eleven at the time of the photo of her in a long white dress and dark hooded cape exiting, via a hanging rope ladder, the second-story window of what was presumably her home. Revealingly, the picture is entitled *Elopement* instead of, say, *Running Away*. The fantasy of a girl stealing off to marry her future husband was clearly on Dodgson's mind.

Three years later, Dodgson's twenty-seven-year-old brother Wilfred announced that he wished to marry Alice Donkin, who by then had reached the relatively mature age of fourteen. Dodgson wrote his brother "a long letter on the subject of Alice Donkin, and suggested that he stay away from Barmby Moor, her home, for two years." Around that same period, Dodgson made two visits to his uncle Skeffington, during which they "had a good deal of conversation about Wilfred and about A.L., a very anxious subject."

What did Dodgson say about A. L., and why was the subject so anxious, and why did it come up in the context of a conversation about his brother's love for a young girl? By the time Dodgson and his uncle had these freighted dinnertime chats, more than three years had passed since his relations with the Liddell girls ceased abruptly, under circumstances thought to have been recorded on the famous "missing page"—a page torn from the diaries.

Tracing Dodgson's and Alice's progress toward that painful break has all the gloomy fascination of watching the inevitable happen to a bubble. The summer of 1862 had included more river excursions—on August 2 and on August 6, when "we tried the game of 'Ural Mountains' on the way, but it did not prove very successful, and I had to go on with my interminable fairy-tale of *Alice's Adventures*."

A month after the text was completed, Alice sent Dodgson a note asking him to escort her to the Oxford illuminations, the official celebration of the Prince of Wales's wedding to the Danish princess Alexandra. Holding hands, accompanied by Charles's brother Edwin, Charles and Alice threaded their way through the crowds to watch the fireworks and view the shapes—a miter, a

crown, the initials of the royal couple—outlined by lamps and blazing gas jets against the nighttime sky. "It was delightful," noted
Dodgson, "to see the thorough abandonment with which Alice enjoyed the whole thing. The Wedding Day of the Prince of Wales I
mark with a white stone."

Three days later, Dodgson spent two hours walking with Alice,
Edith, and Miss Prickett, and wrote, "I began a poem the other day
in which I mean to embody something about Alice (if I can at all
please myself by any description of her) which I mean to call 'Life's
Pleasance' "—a pun on Alice's middle name. The poem begins:

> Child of the pure unclouded brow
> And dreaming eyes of wonder!
> Though time be fleet, and I and thou
> Are half a life asunder,
> Thy loving smile will surely hail
> The love-gift of a fairy-tale.

And it ends as follows:

> And, though the shadow of a sigh
> May tremble through the story,
> For "happy summer days" gone by,
> And vanish'd summer glory—
> It shall not touch, with breath of bale,
> The Pleasance of our fairy-tale.

When spring returned, there were more long strolls and river
excursions, more days marked with white stones. In April, Dodgson
called on Alice, confined at home with a sprained leg. "Alice was in
an unusually disagreeable mood by no means improved by being an
invalid." He consoled and distracted the children during the fatal
illness of their baby brother Albert Edward Arthur. "I met the chil-

dren in the meadow in the morning, and their account gave no hope
of the little one. We walked round the meadow, grave and nearly
silent, a great contrast to yesterday's walk. I offered to take them on
the river, as a change from the dullness of a sick house." And in June,
Dodgson spent the day helping the Liddells at their stall in the
bazaar held in honor of the Prince and Princess of Wales's visit.

ON JUNE 25, Dodgson described yet another excursion in his
diary:

> *About 10 o'clock Alice and Edith came over to my rooms to fetch me
> over to arrange about an expedition to Nuneham. It ended in our
> going down at 3, a party of ten . . . We had tea under the trees at
> Nuneham, after which the rest drove home in the carriage (which
> met them in the park), while Ina, Alice, Edith and I (mirabile dictu!)
> walked down to Abingdon-road Station, and so home by railway; a
> pleasant expedition, with a very pleasant conclusion.*

And that was it. The end. The end of the rambling walks, the end
of the river journeys, the end of the games and storytelling sessions
in his rooms. The brief entry for June 27 includes a sentence that begins, "Wrote to Mrs. Liddell urging her either . . ." The last word has
been crossed out, and the sentence resumes, "to send the children to
be photographed." The next page—the notorious "missing page"
ripped from the diary, allegedly by one of Dodgson's relations after
his death—is almost as legendary as the "golden afternoon."

No one knows what the torn page contained. The Liddell children vanish from the diaries for the rest of that summer and fall, an
absence particularly striking given the frequency of the outings that
preceded the fateful train trip back from Nuneham. The next mention of them, in early December, is, to say the least, terse. Attending
a Christ Church theatrical, Dodgson observed that, "Mrs. Liddell
and the children were there—but I held aloof from them as I have

done all this term." Two weeks later, he was granted a partial and, as it turned out, temporary reprieve, an invitation to the deanery: "The nominal object of my going was to play croquet, but it never came to that, music, talk, etc. occupying the whole of a very pleasant evening. The Dean was away: Mrs. Liddell was with us part of the time. It is nearly six months (June 25th) since I have seen anything of them, to speak of. I mark this day with a white stone."

LIKE EVERYTHING IN Dodgson's life, his break with the Liddells has been subjected to intense scrutiny, speculation, and projection. According to Oxford gossip, the thirty-one-year-old Dodgson made the fatal error of asking for Alice's hand in marriage. Given the prevailing Victorian notions of childhood, adulthood, and marital eligibility, such a request would not have been interpreted as evidence of pedophilia, but merely of impatience. Consider Dodgson's own brother, Wilfred, who tempered his passion for another Alice—the model for Dodgson's *Elopement*—until Alice Donkin was nineteen, and they married. Had the poor mathematics don been wealthy or aristocratic, it's probable that Mrs. Liddell, whose fierce social ambitions for her daughters made her a figure of fun in the university community, might have counseled Dodgson, as he advised Wilfred, to be forbearing and bide his time.

In any case, there is nothing—and no one—to confirm or deny the story of the proposal. The only evidence concerning the end of Dodgson's friendship with the Liddells is a 1930 letter to Alice from her older sister. The eighty-one-year-old Lorina apparently feared that she might have said too much in an interview with Florence Becker Lennon, then researching her biography of Carroll, *Victoria Through the Looking Glass*: "I suppose you don't remember when Mr. Dodgson ceased coming to the Deanery? How old were you? I said his manner became too affectionate to you as you grew older and that mother spoke to him about it, and that offended him so he ceased coming to visit us again, as one had to give some reason for all intercourse ceasing . . . Mr. Dodgson used to take you on his knee. I know I did not say that! Horrible being interviewed if your words are taken down."

But what does "too affectionate" mean? Possibly, Alice's experience resembled Atty Owen's, of whom Dodgson wrote: "She does not look 14 yet, and when, having kissed her at parting, I learned . . . that she is 17, I was astonished, but I don't think either of us was much displeased at the mistake having been made!" Even after sending an apologetic letter, he found himself in the Owens's "black books." Or perhaps the break with the Liddells paralleled the end of Dodgson's friendship with Agnes Hull, whose son told Carroll's biographer, Morton Cohen, that "Agnes Hull . . . broke off the friendship with Charles when she felt that one of his kisses was sexual."

Kissing was an essential element of the child friendships. Of a visit to see a performance of *Cinderella* with seven-year-old Irene Burch, Dodgson noted, "They let me bring her in without a ticket, to sit on my *knee*: and about once in every half-hour she turned round to give me a kiss." In a letter to Mrs. Stevens, he confided, "I would very much like a kiss from another daughter of yours, besides Enid (as to whom I took it for granted that *any* child under 12 is 'kissable')." To the mother of seventeen-year-old Ethel Rowell, he wrote to inquire, "if I may regard myself as on 'kissing' terms with her, as I am with many a girl-friend a great deal older than *she* is."

Always one to acknowledge a creative debt, Dodgson traces *Alice's Adventures in Wonderland* to a kiss, or the hope of a kiss, from a child: "The why of this book cannot, and need not, be put into words. Those for whom a child's smile is a sealed book, and who see no divinity in a child's smile would read such words in vain; while for any one who has ever loved one true child, no words are needed . . . No deed of ours, I suppose, on this side of the grave, is really unselfish. Yet if one can put forth all one's powers in a task where nothing of reward is hoped for but a little child's whispered thanks and the airy touch of a child's pure lips, one seems to come somewhere near this."

Could the "*very* pleasant conclusion" of that last trip to Nuneham have involved a good-bye kiss that crossed the line between the chaste and carnal? What exactly *is* that line? And who would have known, or noticed? The only witnesses would have been little Edith, and Lorina, who—unlike Alice—had at least a vague sense of why Mr. Dodgson's visits to the deanery had so abruptly ceased. Did Ina tell her mother, or did Mrs. Liddell pick up something unassisted on what passed—in that family, in those days—for maternal radar?

If there are any clues, they may lie in yet another of Dodgson's maudlin, predictive poems. The knightly hero of "Stolen Waters"— published three months before the "golden afternoon"—makes the mistake of kissing the "lithe and tall and fair" maiden with whom he has fallen in love ("I kissed her on her false, false lips—/That burning kiss, I feel it now!") and tragedy ensues:

> In the gray light I saw her face
> And it was withered, old and gray;
> The flowers were fading in their place,
> Were fading in the fading day.
>
> Forth from her, like a hunted deer,
> Through all that ghastly night I fled,
> And still behind me seemed to hear
> Her fierce unflagging tread;
> And scarce drew breath for fear.

FLIGHT AND ESCAPE, fear and violence, and the chaos of the ghastly night are always in the background, or more accurately, just below the surface throughout *Alice's Adventures in Wonderland* and *Through the Looking Glass*. Terrifying physical transformation (growing, shrinking) is an omnipresent danger. Nearly every conversation is confusing, rude, or abrasive, and of all the unpleasant talking animals, by far the most savage and brutal are, as it happens, adult women; a maniac queen swings a flamingo and gleefully orders up beheadings, a duchess nurses and shakes her pig-baby to the lullaby of literature's most horrific child-rearing advice:

> *Speak roughly to your little boy,*
> *And beat him when he sneezes*
> *He only does it to annoy*
> *Because he knows it teases.*

Yet the plucky heroine soldiers through this hostile chaotic world. More has been said about the Freudian or pharmaceutical significance of the caterpillar than about Alice's amazing singularity as the heroine of a novel for children—or adults. She's courageous, tenacious, inquisitive, thoughtful, and precise. Every interchange crackles with her personality or with the other characters' consciousness of her presence. The story that the Dormouse tells at the Mad Tea-Party, the marvelous tale about three sisters living at the bottom of the treacle well, depends for its bounce and humor and rhythm on the sensibleness and intelligence with which Alice plays straight man. The result is perfection, a literary conjuring trick, a house of cards constructed with words, and from which it is impossible to remove a single word: a glimpse of vaudeville slapstick written by a genius.

The lively intelligence, the bravery, and the supreme self-confidence with which Alice tries to make sense of the Dormouse's absurdities are a model of youthful, or adult, conduct. Carroll's heroine was his *truly* ideal child-friend, and it seems unlikely that the flesh-and-blood Alice (or any child) could have equaled this paragon of bravery and reason. As so often happens in the lives of muses, the "real" Alice mattered only partly for herself, and partly for her ability to provide a blank screen on which Charles Dodgson could project his ideal, or his memory of himself as a child among his own first child-friends—that is, his siblings.

On November 13, 1862, Dodgson noted that he had begun "writing the fairy-tale for Alice," adding that he hoped to finish by Christmas. He missed his deadline by two months, then continued working on the illustrations. The book *was* a Christmas present for Alice—two Christmases later than planned. By the time Dodgson gave her the manuscript, it was late November 1864, seventeen months after Mrs. Liddell had ended their friendship.

In May, Dodgson had written, "During these last few days I have applied in vain for leave to take the children out on the river, i.e. Alice, Edith and Rhoda; but Mrs. Liddell will not let any come in future—rather superfluous caution."

The diaries do not mention his giving the book to Alice. She disappears from them until this entry the following spring: "Met Alice and Miss Prickett in the quadrangle: Alice seems changed a good deal, and hardly for the better—probably going through the usual awkward stage of transition."

FIVE YEARS LATER, Mrs. Liddell brought Ina and Alice to Dodgson's studio to be photographed, presumably for the Victorian equivalent of those chilling snapshots of Asian mail-order brides. The difference is that the would-be brides are beaming, eager to please, while among proper Victorian maidens, eligibility was signaled by submissive melancholia. Dodgson's portrait of Alice at eighteen might pass for that of a normally demure 1870 virgin unless we compare it with the *Portrait of Alice Liddell as the Beggar Child.* The comparison makes her downcast eyes and avoidance of the camera seem nearly as alien and extreme as the contorted grimaces or catatonic vacancy of the madwomen photographed by Hugh Diamond in British insane asylums. Alice looks unhappy to find herself once again in the rooms where she had spent so many happy hours, the Eden from which she had been expelled by her own mother.

How perverse and cruel of Mrs. Liddell, or at best, how thoughtless to ask the rejected suitor to photograph the girl he'd loved and photographed so expertly—this time, for what amounted to a Victorian personals ad. How could Alice have looked at him, how could she have confronted the camera and seen, in its eye, confirmation of everything that she and Mr. Dodgson knew had occurred?

Among the events that had happened during their separation was the composition of *Through the Looking Glass*, the less buoyant, subdued sequel to *Alice in Wonderland*. In the Looking Glass world, the misunderstandings and insults that Alice must endure are more pointed and personal than they were in Wonderland. The talking flowers are remarkably nasty in their assault on Alice's stupidity. "Her face has got *some* sense in it," says the Rose, "though it's not a clever one!" And Humpty Dumpty's parting words to Alice are a devastating critique of her ordinariness: "I shouldn't know you again if we *did* meet . . . you're so exactly like other people." In 1870, the year in which he took the last photos of Lorina and Alice, Dodgson was arranging to give Alice an elaborate presentation volume of the second Alice book, a volume in which he hoped that a mirror could somehow be embedded.

FOUR MONTHS BEFORE Mrs. Liddell brought Alice and Lorina to Dodgson's studio, John Ruskin gave his inaugural lecture as Oxford's first Slade Professor of Fine Art. Inevitably, the celebrated critic was drawn to Mrs. Liddell's equivalent of a salon, to the social and musical evenings at the deanery, where the thrum of excitement was amplified by the dean's power, by the company of the most important men at Oxford, and by the presence of the Liddells' attractive daughters. The spirit that animates Jane Austen novels was alive and well in Mrs. Liddell's efforts to marry off her girls, strategies and machinations conducted so publicly and with such disregard for the young women's privacy that her husband-hunting became the subject of a verse satire, *Cakeless*, which made the rounds of the university and got its author expelled.

By the time he arrived at Oxford, Ruskin was fifty-one. At twenty-nine, he had married Euphemia Gray, who was ten years younger, and whom he had met when she was a preadolescent. Their marriage was annulled when Effie—who later wed the painter John Millais—proved that it had never been consummated, allegedly because Ruskin was so unnerved by his first sight of female pubic hair. Since then, he had been involved in a tortured romance with Rose la Touche, whom he met when she was ten.

The story of Ruskin's passion for Rose is frequently invoked to prove that Dodgson's infatuation with young girls was not nearly so rare in his own time as it would be considered today. But it is less often pointed out that Alice Liddell was, remarkably, involved with both of the nineteenth century's most famous lovers of girl children.

Both men were friendly with successful children's book illustrators and asked them to portray their sprites and prim maidens unclothed. "I do *not* admire naked *boys* in pictures," Dodgson wrote Gertrude Thomson, whose drawings of nude female fairies accompanied a volume of his poems. "They always seem . . . to need *clothes*; whereas one hardly sees why the lovely forms of girls should *ever* be covered up." Kate Greenaway was less obliging when Ruskin requested, "Will you . . . draw her for me without a cap . . . and without her—frock and frills? And let me see exactly how tall she is—and—how—round." Ruskin criticized William Richmond's portrait of Edith, Alice, and Lorina Liddell because Ina was depicted wearing shoes, instead of barefoot. ("Perugino would never have made such a mistake!") Alice, who had some talent for drawing, became Ruskin's student, and his notes to her rapidly took on a coyness that resembled and outdid the flirtatiousness of Dodgson's letters to his child-friends.

What subliminal signals drew these men to Alice, and Alice to these men? What needs of her own inspired her to re-create, with Ruskin, something like her relationship with Dodgson—a friendship mutually understood as a subversive intrigue that thrived on discovering clever ways to outsmart the grown-ups? What seems clear is that Alice was by no means a frail flower attracting these predatory bees; she pursued and encouraged their attentions. It was *her* invitation to a concert that prompted Ruskin to reply, "I am sure I shall like to hear you telling me about the music—much better than any music (unless you would sing it without all the organs and trumpets and showmen and things). But even in that bright historical light I'm afraid I shall never come to feel Bach more than wonder of Wonderland. But I'll come of course—on any pretense—being ever your Faithfullest servant."

Alice was a full participant in the plot that led to a visit that Ruskin paid the Liddell sisters, an incident that conjures up the whole history of secret adventures that Dodgson and the children enjoyed, out of sight of the Liddell parents:

"The planet Saturn had treated me with his usual adversity in the carrying out of a plot with Alice in Wonderland. For, that evening, the Dean and Mrs. Liddell dined by command at Blenheim: but the girls were not commanded; and as I had been complaining of never getting a sight of them lately, after knowing them from the nursery, Alice said that she thought, perhaps, if I would come round after papa and mama were safe off to Blenheim, Edith and she might give us a cup of tea and a little singing, and Rhoda would show me how she was getting on with her drawing and geometry, or the like. And so it was arranged. The night was wild with snow, and no one was likely to come around to the Deanery after dark. I think Alice must have slipped me a little note, when the eastern coast of Tom Quad was clear. . . .

"Well, I think Edith must have got the tea made, and Alice was just bringing the muffins to perfection . . . when there was a sudden sense of some stars having been blown out by the wind . . . and there were the Dean and Mrs Liddell standing just in the middle of the hall, and the footmen in consternation, and a silence,—and—

" 'How sorry you must be to see us, Mr Ruskin!' began at last Mrs. Liddell.

" 'I was never more so,' I replied. 'But what's the matter?'

" 'Well,' said the Dean, 'we couldn't even get past the parks; the snow's a fathom deep in the Woodstock Road. But never mind; we'll be very good and quiet, and keep out of the way. Go back to your tea, and we'll have our dinner downstairs.'

"And so we did, but we couldn't keep papa and mama out of the drawing-room when they had done dinner, and I went back to Corpus, disconsolate."

What's stunning is Ruskin's intensity, the dreamlike fixation on Alice that beclouded his awareness of any presence but hers, the violent sense that the stars had been blown out by the wind, of having been cursed by Saturn, and that last word: *disconsolate*. What did he imagine would happen, what fantasies or hopes were dashed by the unexpected arrival of his coconspirator's parents?

Alice's hold on these men continued. On May 4, Alice's birthday, a year after that final photo session, Dodgson recorded that he'd visited a dying, consumptive carpenter, to whom he read two psalms and a favorite hymn. He'd spent the rest of the day giving a lecture, taking brief walks with colleagues, delivering the corrected proof of a paper entitled *Suggestions for the Committee Appointed to Consider Senior Studentships*, working on another lecture. It would be hard to imagine a more penitential celebration of the birthday of the girl who had brought him such delight.

ALICE'S CAREER as Mr. Dodgson's model may have ended, but her gifts—or her stamina—as a photographic subject inspired Julia Margaret Cameron to ask her to sit for the sort of portrait that Dodgson, who disliked Cameron's work, dismissed as "out of focus." The results are instructive—revelatory of the different person Alice had become, or at least of the different face she showed Cameron.

The beggar child's sly sauciness and unself-conscious humor

have been thoroughly obliterated. In the 1872 *Alethea*, Alice looks, in profile, wan, peevish, and strained. And *Pomona*, taken the same year, is shockingly unlike Cameron's typically demure, blushing maidens. Alice confronts the camera, direct and almost defiant. Her large jaw, her tight-set lips, and her wide-open unblinking eyes hint at something unattractive: the unsympathetic willfulness with which she treated the hapless servants after she married and assumed command of Cuffnells, the Hargreaves family estate.

Or perhaps what we are seeing is the determination that impelled her—with tragic miscalculation—to outdo her mother at her own game of orchestrating an upwardly mobile romance. The year that Alice's portrait was taken by Julia Margaret Cameron, Queen Victoria's youngest son, Leopold, came down to study at Oxford, where he met and fell in love with the enchanting Alice Liddell.

Frail, hemophiliac, plagued by ill health, the bookish prince thrived under the attentions of the dean and his family. He studied with Ruskin and Dodgson, and was soon spending much of his time in the company of the Liddells. When Lorina married a prosperous landowner, W. B. Skene, Leopold attended the celebration. His romance with Alice blossomed—and then ended.

For the Liddells discovered that social striving and class snobbery, the same ambitions and calculations that may have factored into Dodgson's exile from the Liddell household, were, as it were, a two-way street. Queen Victoria disapproved of her son's attachment to the daughter of an academic, even the author of the *Greek-English Lexicon*. The love affair came to nothing, though later Alice would name her second son Leopold, and Prince Leopold (who married Princess Helene Frederica Augusta of Waldeck-Pyrmont) named his daughter Alice. As a child, this royal Alice visited Charles Dodgson in his rooms at Christ Church, a day that he would mark in his diary with a white stone.

On September 15, 1880, Alice and Reginald "Regi" Gervis Hargreaves—who met Alice when he was an Oxford undergraduate—

were wed in Westminster Abbey. The brooch pinned to the front of
Alice's satin dress was a present from Prince Leopold, who chose to
skip the ceremony. At twenty-eight, Alice was almost geriatric for a
Victorian bride, so perhaps she hardly minded that the handsome,
good-natured Regi was no match for the geniuses who had frequented the deanery. A devoted athlete and cricket player but a
mediocre student, Regi had taken six years to finish university.

Regi was, however, rich. After a honeymoon in Scotland and
Spain, the newlyweds repaired to Cuffnells, the 160-acre Hampshire
estate replete with lavish gardens, an orangery, a well-stocked lake,
and a home with gargantuan public spaces and a "gold room" undis-
turbed since King George III spent the night there. In transforming
herself from an Oxford bluestocking into a lady of the manor, Alice
became, or surrendered, to that part of herself that always was a version of her mother. Conscious of class and position, she set about
making Cuffnells a center of rural high society. She was reputedly
hard on her servants, whom she paid poorly, watched vigilantly, and
penalized for minor infractions. (This conservative, hierarchical
habit of mind was apparently inherited by her third son, Caryl,
who—returning home after accompanying his mother on her trip to
receive the doctorate from Columbia—published an essay blaming
the woes of Depression-era America on its excessive democracy.)

Caryl's birth in 1887 followed that of his two brothers: Alan in
1881 and Leopold in 1883. (Alice claimed that her youngest son's
name had nothing to do with Lewis Carroll, but had been inspired
by a character in a novel.) Avid athletes and horsemen, the boys resembled their father. Alan attended Sandhurst and went off to fight
in South Africa. Leopold, known as Rex, was a businessman, while
Caryl, the family artist, became an amateur writer and pianist with
a talent for spending large quantities of family money.

All three of Alice and Regi's sons fought in the First World War.
In 1915, Alan died while leading an assault on Fromelles, not far

from Armentières. A year later, Rex was felled by "friendly fire" in the trenches of northern France. Alice's beloved sister Edith died—in agony, on the eve of her wedding—of peritonitis. Prince Leopold succumbed to a brain hemorrhage in 1884. Four years later, Charles Dodgson and Dean Liddell died within four days of each other. At Regi's death in 1926, the *Times* memorialized him as "more than a commonly good shot, fisherman and cricketer."

His widow was left with a generous but insufficient inheritance that—combined with Caryl's spotty money-management skills—nearly added Cuffnells to the long list of painful losses, until her old friend Mr. Dodgson came posthumously to her rescue. In 1928, her manuscript of *Alice's Adventures Underground* was auctioned off at Sotheby's, fetching a record sum—more than $75,000—from an American collector, Dr. A. S. W. Rosenbach; the sale shored up Alice and Caryl's finances, which had grown so wobbly that Cuthnells had displayed a sign reading: "To rent, furnished, this historic mansion."

Mr. Dodgson's continuing help was not only financial. Alice's honorary doctorate in musedom provided some brightness and consolation amid the series of diminishments that marked her final years. Addressing the dignitaries assembled in Low Library, Alice spoke of her former admirer—dead for more than forty years—in the present tense.

"Mr. Dodgson knows and rejoices with me in the honor you are doing him," she declared, as if the spirit of the awkward, stuttering, lovesick don were alive, returned to the earth one last time and permitted to gaze adoringly at the elderly beggar child through the lens of his old-fashioned camera.

AMONG THE FEW surviving letters that Dodgson wrote Alice (those she'd recieved as a child were destroyed by Mrs. Liddell) is one from 1885, requesting the loan of her copy of *Alice's Adventures Underground* so that it might be reprinted in a facsimile edition.

My Dear Mrs. Hargreaves,

    I fancy that this will come to you almost like a voice from the dead, after so many years of silence—and yet those years have made no difference that I can perceive in my clearness of memory of the days when we did correspond. I am getting to feel what an old man's failing memory is, as to recent events and new friends (for instance, I made friends, only a few weeks ago, with a very nice little maid of about 12, and a walk with her—and now I can't recall either of her names!) but my mental picture is as vivid as ever, of one who was, through so many years, my ideal child-friend. I have had scores of child-friends since your time: but they have been quite a different thing.

How much those brief paragraphs reveal, in the rapid shift of tone from the coy flirtatious blackmail of that "nice little maid of about 12" to the undefended openness of Dodgson's declaration of feeling for the "ideal child-friend," of love that has endured more than twenty years of separation: "I have had scores of child-friends since your time: but they have been quite a different thing."

"Scores" was putting it mildly. Hundreds of relationships fill the diary with arrangements for meetings with children approached on trains and at the seashore, taken to plays and shopping. And the diaries confirm what the children said: Mr. Dodgson *knew* them, and unlike other adults, recognized their intricate, playful, and imaginative selves. So Dodgson observed the character of little Emma ("Emsie") Bowman with closer scrutiny than it probably received from another human being: "At the Aquarium we had some original remarks from Emsie, who seemed to pity the bear for having no tail, and the seals for not being provided with towels—remarks worthy of a child who once wanted to hem a pocket handkerchief for a cat who had a cold in its head."

His relationship with Emma's sister Isa, the child actress who played Alice in an early theatrical production, was protracted and intense. Later, Isa wrote a somewhat steamy memoir emphasizing the passion of Mr. Dodgson's kisses. But Alice was still the *ideal* child-friend, tied forever to his masterpiece. The following summer, after a brief exchange of letters explaining that the proceeds from the sale of the book would be donated to children's hospitals and convalescent homes, he wrote:

"It is very pleasant to think that you are connected with the facsimile edition. Of the existence of the original you were the chief, if not the only cause."

Sometime later, as Dodgson attempted to reconcile his memory of Alice with the utterly confounding image of her as a wife and mother, the Alice he kept returning to—the Alice with whom he was most in love—was in fact not the ten-year-old for whom he wrote his books but rather the seven-year-old who posed for him as the beggar maid.

Here is how Dodgson reported meeting Regi Hargreaves, in *his* new incarnation as Alice's husband: "Skene brought, as his guest, Mr. Hargreaves, (the husband of 'Alice'), who was a stranger to me, though we had met, years ago, as pupil and lecturer. It was not easy to link, in one's mind the new face with the olden memory—the stranger with the once-so-intimately known and loved 'Alice,' whom I shall always remember best as an entirely fascinating little seven-year-old girl."

But that is precisely what Dodgson does, linking the two with ease, skipping instantly from the unimaginable, unendurable Regi to the entirely *fascinating* (a word of ambiguous erotic charge) girl of seven. That is the age of the heroine of the Alice books: the Alice whom Dodgson knew, and whom Regi never would.

Yet another letter, headed "Christ Church, Oxford. December 8, 1891," includes one of the most well-known textual revisions in literary biography.

My Dear Mrs Hargreaves,

I should be so glad if you could, quite conveniently to yourself,
look in for tea any day. You would probably prefer to bring a compan-
ion: but I must leave the choice to you, only remarking that if your
husband is here he would be most [most is crossed out] *very wel-*
come. (I crossed out most because it's ambiguous; most words are, I
fear.) I met him in our Common Room not long ago. It was hard to
realise that he was the husband of one I can scarcely picture to myself,
even now, as more than 7 years old!
Always sincerely yours,
Charles Dodgson.

Your adventures have had a marvelous success. I have now sold
well over a 100,000 copies.

The tempered politeness crashes and burns at the crossed-out
word, the change from *most* to *very*, wreckage followed by the seemingly apologetic clarification, in itself a secret message from a writer
of two books—two books about *her*—full of ambiguities and misunderstandings, of puns flung around like the duchess's flamingos; it
goes without saying that Carroll himself chose words with extreme
precision. And at last he is moved to tell Alice what earlier he told
the diary: that the two of them remember something that Regi can
neither touch, nor alter.

Again, it's not the ten-year-old with whom he shared the
"golden afternoon" but the child of seven to whom Dodgson flees,
the child who lives forever, whose seductive vitality still spills out of
his photograph of the beggar girl, a century and a half—two life-
times—after it was taken.

THE FINAL PARAGRAPHS of *Alice's Adventures in Wonderland* contain
some of the loveliest and most moving prose in the English language.

"But her sister sat still just as she left her, leaning her head on her hand, watching the setting sun, and thinking of little Alice and all her wonderful Adventures, till she too began dreaming after a fashion, and this was her dream . . .

"The long grass rustled at her feet as the White Rabbit hurried by—the frightened Mouse splashed his way through the neighbouring pool—she could hear the rattle of the teacups as the March Hare and his friends shared their never-ending meal, and the shrill voice of the Queen ordering off her unfortunate guests to execution—once more the pig-baby was sneezing on the Duchess's knee, while plates and dishes crashed around it—once more the shriek of the Gryphon, the squeaking of the lizard's slate-pencil, and the choking of the suppressed guinea-pigs, filled the air, mixed up with the distant sob of the miserable Mock Turtle.

"So she sat on, with closed eyes, and half-believed herself in Wonderland, though she knew she had but to open them again, and all would change to dull reality—the grass would be only rustling in the wind, and the pool rippling to the waving of the reeds—the rattling of the tea cups would change to tinkling sheep-bells, and the Queen's shrill cries to the voice of the shepherd-boy—and the sneeze of the baby, the shriek of the Gryphon, and all the other queer noises, would change (she knew) to the confused clamour of the busy farm-yard—while the lowing of the cattle in the distance would take the place of the Mock Turtle's heavy sobs.

"Lastly, she pictured to herself how this same little sister of hers would, in the after-time, be herself a grown woman; and how she would keep, through all her riper years, the simple and loving heart of her childhood; and how she would gather about her other little children, and make *their* eyes bright and eager with many a strange tale, perhaps even with the dreams of Wonderland long ago; and how she would feel with all their simple sorrows, and find a pleasure in all their simple joys, remembering her own child-life, and the happy summer days."

The beauty of these sentences resides partly in their graceful rhythm, their paradoxically unadorned lushness, the quiet resignation, the sincerity and intensity of feeling; the dreamy accuracy with which the vision of the present projects into the future, the lens wide enough to reveal many ages at once, the Alice of the moment, the Alice she will become, and the secret Alice, already disappeared, the perfect seven-year-old who has already become the pale imitation of ten. The consciousness that informs the last paragraphs already knows this. The narrator is well aware of how briefly childhood lasts and that it will never come back, no matter how desperately we try to submerge our adult selves in the games and stories and riddles, in the company of children. It knows this even as it addresses its nominal muse, the ten-year-old, who like some devouring mythical creature has, by an inexorable law of nature, already subsumed the body of the true muse, the seven-year-old beloved.

The sensual grief, the pleasurable melancholy of contemplating these facts suffuses the final passages of *Alice's Adventures in Wonderland*. On the surface, the section is written from the point of view of Alice's sister, fallen asleep on the riverbank and dreaming a reprise of Alice's dream, only far more fragile, more subject to breakage and disruption. But who is it, really, staring into the green haze on that "golden afternoon" and seeing there a vision of his dear small muse, or perhaps of his own vanished childhood, lost to time and lost again with every second that passes?

ELIZABETH SIDDAL

THE BRIEF, LAMENTABLE LIFE of Elizabeth Siddal offers a cautionary lesson in how the muse can inspire art that never progresses beyond the concerns and limitations of the tender age at which the muse and her artist first met. Elizabeth Siddal's twelve-year relationship with the Pre-Raphaelite poet and painter Dante Gabriel Rossetti was an ongoing drama, first joyous, then stormy, then estranged, then domestic, then horrific, and all of it intensified by the parallel drama of her debilitating and eventually fatal laudanum addiction.

Both Lizzie and Gabriel painted and wrote poetry, and much of their oeuvre took the form of loosely encoded dispatches and pointed messages to each other, disguised as illustrations of Arthurian legends, Renaissance masterpieces, and currently popular poems. Their anguished conversation continued after Lizzie's death and left an artistic legacy that speaks to its audience in the language of the gifted teenage contributor to the high school literary magazine. If Charles Dodgson's inner world involved a paradoxically playful and desperate retreat to childhood, Dante Gabriel Rossetti's interior landscape was mired forever in adolescence, and the two artists' choices of love objects and muses reflected the longings and ideals of those consecutive but very different stages of life.

Like their art, the Pre-Raphaelites' daily existence was mannered, self-conscious, theatrical, and stylish. Perhaps some confused art history student of the future will have trouble distinguishing the Pre-Raphaelite Brotherhood from the gang at Andy Warhol's Factory. Rossetti and his associates *lived* the Merchant-Ivory film, inhabited the Arts and Crafts Movement issue of the shelter magazine, played out the tragic opera tarted up with elements of the Broadway musical, *La Bohème* meets *My Fair Lady* meets *The Phantom of the Opera*, the pure Bohemian love dream *and* the ghoulish special effects.

IN AUGUST 1869, Dante Gabriel Rossetti wrote his friend Charles Howell, authorizing him to exhume the body of Rossetti's wife, Elizabeth Eleanor Siddal, who had died seven years earlier of an overdose of laudanum, and in whose coffin the grieving widower had placed a manuscript of his poems, nestled amid the flowing red-gold hair that had inspired so many of his paintings. Rossetti had become obsessed with the notion that retrieving the book was essential to rekindling his career as poet. The mysterious Howell—a pathological liar, con man, and forger—may have intuited that gossip about the manuscript's disgusting provenance would greatly boost the book's sales. In the exchange of letters preceding the mission for which Howell appears to have volunteered, Rossetti's squeamish circumlocutions and pleas for absolute secrecy alternate with breezier offers of gratitude and more tangible rewards—"If I recover the book, I will give you the swellest drawing conceivable . . ." The poet also devised a clever plan for obtaining official permission for the exhumation from the Home Secretary, an old acquaintance.

On the night of October 9, Howell, a Dr. Llewellyn Williams, and two men from the Blackfriars Funeral Company built a fire in Highgate cemetery, raised the coffin, and removed the manuscript, as directed. "The book in question is bound in rough grey calf and has I am almost sure red edges to the leaves. This will distinguish it from the Bible also there as I told you." Howell was quick to reassure Rossetti that Lizzie, and especially her glorious hair, was still beautiful, untouched by rot or decay—a detail of great significance to the founder of a movement with a near-pathological fetish about great masses of women's hair. But the manuscript had, alas, proved more vulnerable to corruption, and Dr. Williams was assigned the task of disinfecting the soggy, worm-eaten pages, separating and drying them.

The violation of Lizzie Siddal's grave was only the coarsest and most explicit manifestation of the necrophilia that had tainted her relationship with Rossetti from the start. One senses that Rossetti's attraction to Lizzie had less to do with passion or admiration for a flesh and blood woman of the nineteenth century than with the imaginative role he assigned her as a reincarnation of Dante's Beatrice.

Rossetti's father, Gabriele, was a Dante enthusiast and scholar who, on board a ship docked in Naples, had a life-changing vision of the Florentine poet. His fascination with Dante would become a family obsession, inspiring his oldest daughter Maria to write her own book, *A Shadow of Dante*. Not only did Gabriele name his son Gabriel Charles Dante Rossetti (a name the younger Rossetti reshuffled into its more familiar form) but wrote a book explicating the secret meanings of the *Divine Comedy*, and another claiming that Beatrice was never a historical figure but merely an idea. His son argued for the reality of Beatrice's existence but ironically seemed to prefer the idea of Dante's muse, dead for five hundred years, to the actuality of his own model, mistress, muse, and wife.

In 1861, a year after his marriage to Lizzie, Rossetti memorialized his father in a sonnet, *"Dantis Tenebrae,"* which begins with the revealing lines:

> *And didst thou know indeed, when at the font*
> *Together with thy name thou gav'st me his,*
> *That also on thy son must Beatrice*
> *Decline her eyes according to her wont,*
> *Accepting me to be of those that haunt*
> *The vale of magical dark mysteries*
> *Where to the hills her poet's foot-track lies . . .*

Much about his romance with Lizzie suggests that Rossetti had essentially, if unconsciously, shopped around for a woman to match (and with whom he could act out) his fantasies about Beatrice—the muse whom Dante met in childhood and immortalized in works that celebrate his undying adoration of the dead beloved. Conveniently, Gabriel conflated his muse with Dante's until—or so that—he was able to portray Elizabeth Siddal in the guise of Beatrice. Every Beatrice he drew was Lizzie, wrote Gabriel's brother William.

Rossetti's inability to distinguish Lizzie from a girl who died in Florence in the thirteenth century would necessarily have diminished any ethical reservations about disturbing the grave of a woman who—despite the length and closeness of their attachment—never fully existed for him. The relationship between her function as muse and her ability to excite Rossetti's romantic, adolescent, necrophiliac longings began on the day the Pre-Raphaelites extracted her from the milliner's shop where she was employed and endured long after Rossetti encouraged Howell to attend to the "matter" he could hardly mention even after the pages on which his poems could barely be discerned were drying in the doctor's office.

By the time Rossetti met Siddall (whom he later persuaded to drop the final "l" in her name) in 1850, he was already translating the Italian Renaissance poets and must have noticed that Lizzie's charms—long coppery hair, pale skin, an ethereal aura—corresponded to the Renaissance ideal of female beauty. Months before their meeting, he wrote a short story, "Hand and Soul," in which a swooningly handsome thirteenth-century painter is saved from spiritual doldrums and artistic self-doubt by the apparition of a beautiful golden-haired woman who tells him that he can save himself by painting her.

The story of Elizabeth Siddall's "discovery" by the Pre-Raphaelite painters follows the Cinderella, star-is-born arc later associated with movie stars plucked from their earthy origins (Lana Turner, Schwab's drugstore) and installed in the Hollywood firmament. Walter Deverell—the handsomest of Rossetti's friends, the one who was said to think the Pre-Raphaelite Brotherhood's initials were an acronym for Penis Rather Better—spotted the lovely red-haired milliner's assistant in a Cranbourne Alley shop and, using his mother as a go-between, enlisted her to model for Viola in his painting of *Twelfth Night*.

Two years before, Rossetti and six friends had formed the Pre-Raphaelite Brotherhood, vowing to liberate painting from the artificial strictures imposed by the Royal Academy (an institution personified by Sir Joshua Reynolds) and to restore the purity and brilliance that had been leaching out of art since the Renaissance. In retrospect, what's striking is how few of the Brotherhood's ideals—simplicity, clarity, the direct, accurate representation of nature—ever made it onto canvas or into their domestic aesthetic. One reason for this disjuncture was their reductive assumption that naturalism and accuracy could be achieved by using each other as models in romantic scenarios with the female parts played by the working-class "stunners" (their term) whom they hunted with the urgency of vampires seeking fresh blood. In his diary, William Rossetti describes meeting Millais "parading Tottenham Court Road, together with Hunt and Collins, on the search for models."

In paintings such as Edward Burne-Jones's *King Cophetua and the Beggar Maid* and William Holman Hunt's *The Awakening Conscience*, they channeled the erotic appeal of the lower classes into moral and religious tableaux and returned to the noble subject of the attractive prostitute's redemption. They also knew that these were not women to be brought home to mother; Gabriel neglected to introduce his muse to *his* mum until Lizzie had been vetted by John Ruskin's elderly parents. Behind all this were the class distinctions and social snobbery that prompted Gabriel to change the spelling of Lizzie's last name (he considered one "l" more elegant), that led Walter Deverell to note that "while her friends, of course, are quite humble, she behaves like a real lady," and that made William Rossetti feel compelled to assert that "Miss Siddal—let me say here once and for all—was a graceful lady-like person, knowing how to behave in company. She had received an ordinary education and committed no faults of speech."

Her humble origins were a source of some discomfort, or at least ambivalence, for Rossetti and the Brotherhood. In fact, the Rossettis were no richer than the Siddalls; the difference was that Mr. Siddall was a cutler or ironmonger, whereas the impecunious Professor Rossetti wrote books about Dante. Gabriel took on the job of Lizzie's gentrification, a process that began with drawing lessons; among her early efforts was a watercolor based on Wordsworth's "We Are Seven." Rossetti's brother noted the downside of their tutelary relationship ("He had his defects and she had the deficiencies of those defects.") while in his hilariously hostile 1928 biography of Rossetti, Evelyn Waugh sniped equally at Gabriel's abilities ("Rossetti's ignorance of perspective was almost invincible; its rules seemed to him unintelligible and their application patently absurd.") and at those of his pupil, whose drawings "have so little real artistic merit and so much of what one's governess called 'feeling'; so tentative, so imitative, and flickering with the live intensity of the souls that sighed about the Blessed Damozel." Touchingly oblivious to the shortcomings being passed between them like some sort of virus, Rossetti sketched himself in the act of sketching Lizzie, and also drew Lizzie drawing and stepping back to contemplate a painting.

Even as Lizzie and Gabriel were falling in love, she continued to model for Millais, Deverell, Madox Brown, and Hunt. Gradually, Gabriel stopped her from sitting for his friends, but partly to repair the dent that her brother's recent death had put in her family's income, she agreed to pose for Millais's celebrated depiction of the drowned Ophelia floating downstream. The details of the disastrous 1852 session—lying in a full bathtub, Lizzie became ill after the lamps used to heat the water went out—are well known, but what's less often remarked upon are the implications of the fact that some combination of job anxiety and passivity kept Lizzie from complaining about the chill, and of the fact that Gabriel was smitten with a woman so compliant and desperate for money that she had risked her health for the privilege of being painted as a beautiful corpse.

Among the first portraits Rossetti made of Lizzie was a watercolor, *Beatrice Meeting Dante at a Marriage Feast, Denies Him Her Salutation*. Her face appeared in *Giotto Painting the Portrait of Dante*, in *Dante Drawing an Angel*, in the morbid *Dante's Dream at the Time of the Death of Beatrice*, and yet again in the nearly orgasmic *Beata Beatrix*, which he completed after her death and which would become one of his best-loved works. Early in their relationship, he made so many sketches of his beloved that his friend and teacher Ford Madox Brown diagnosed his fixation on her as being "like a monomania with him."

Rossetti's paintings of Siddal bear only a casual resemblance to her own self-portrait, or to the likenesses of her executed by other Pre-Raphaelite artists. "Rossetti's innumerable portraits and drawings of Lizzie . . . are sometime, in fact, so 'idealized' that they fail to dispel the uncertainty about the significant details of Lizzie's appearance," writes Rossetti's biographer, Oswald Doughty, who goes on to quote Lizzie's "sensible" friend Bessie Parkes on the ecstatic *Beata Beatrix*: "I feel puzzled by the manner in which the artist took the head and features of a remarkably retiring English girl . . . and transfused them with an expression in which I could recognize nothing of the moral nature of Miss Siddal. She had the look of one who read her Bible and said her prayers every night, which she probably did."

A similar lack of focus characterizes Rossetti's letters, which exult in Lizzie's artistic achievements or report worriedly on her health but fail to give much sense of what she was actually like. Writing to his sister Christina, he refers to his beloved as a "meek unconscious dove." Frequently he drew a dove as a symbol for the woman to whom he gave an array of unattractive nicknames, including "Guggums," "Gug," and "the Sid."

Ford Madox Brown and others describe her looks ("thinner & more deathlike & more beautiful & more ragged than ever, a real artist") without bothering to comment on her personality. Despite, or because of, his barely concealed dislike, Gabriel's brother and loyal apologist William has given us the most sustained and useful account of his sister-in-law's temperament, a portrait notably unlike that of Gabriel's timid little bird:

"Her character was somewhat singular—not quite easy to understand, and not at all on the surface. Often as I have been in her company . . . I hardly think that I ever heard her say a single thing indicative of her own character, or of her serious underlying thought. All her talk was of a 'chaffy' kind—its tone sarcastic, its substance lightsome. It was like the speech of a person who wanted to turn off the conversation, and leave matters substantially where they stood before . . . She was not ill-natured in talk, still less was she scandal-mongering, or chargeable with volatility or levity personal to herself; but she seemed to say—'My mind and my feelings are my own, and no outsider is expected to pry into them.'"

William's account of Lizzie's dignified insistence on her privacy—or, alternately, her standoffishness—is corroborated by Deverell's statement that she "knew how to keep people at a respectful distance." And the reference to her "chaffish" conversation is the only suggestion of a character remotely capable of having written the note Lizzie sent Gabriel from the south of France. Reflecting a sensibility that could hardly be less dovelike or more unlike the melancholy, anemic wraith Rossetti painted, Lizzie's letter is graced by trenchant observation, irony, and humor, qualities in notably short supply among the Pre-Raphaelite Brotherhood:

"On leaving your boat, your passport is taken from you to the Police Station, and there taken charge of till you leave Nice. If a letter is sent to you containing money, the letter is detained at the Post

Office, and another written to you by the postmaster ordering you to present yourself and passport for his inspection. You have then to go to the Police Station and beg the loan of your passport for half-an-hour, and are again looked upon as a felon of the first order before passport is returned to you. Looking very much like a transport, you make your way to the Post Office, and there present yourself before a grating, which makes the man behind it look like an overdone mutton-chop sticking to a gridiron. On asking for a letter containing money, Mutton-chop sees at once that you are a murderer, and makes up its mind not to let you off alive; and . . . demands your passport. After glaring at this and your face (which has by this time become scarlet, and is taken at once as a token of guilt) a book is pushed through the bars of the gridiron, and you are expected to sign your death warrant by writing something that does not answer to the writing on your passport. Meanwhile Mutton-chop has been looking as much like doom as overdone mutton can look, and fizzing in French . . . But now comes the reward of merit. Mutton sees at once that no two people living and at large could write so badly as the writing on the passport and that in the book . . . but gives me the money, and wonders whether I shall be let off from hard labour the next time I am taken, on account of my thinness. When you enter the Police Station to return the passport, you are glared at through wooden bars with marked surprise at not returning in company of two cocked-hats, and your fainting look is put down to your having been found out in something."

How regrettable that the force of personality expressed in this letter went unremarked by the diarists and memoirists who documented the Pre-Raphaelite movement. Our vision of Lizzie Siddal is so clouded by her pitiful death and grotesque afterlife that we have lost sight of her as a brave and unconventional Victorian woman living on her own and then, during a tempestuous ten-year "engagement," with her lover. She painted, earned money from her work, exhibited in public, wrote poems, and maintained male and female friendships, all despite being a severe invalid and drug addict.

Except for Lizzie's letter from France, William's Rossetti's account, and the testimony of Swinburne, who adored and admired her "grace, loveliness, courage, endurance, wit, humour, heroism, and sweetness," only her own formulaic, sodden poetry remains to help us understand who she was. Interestingly, Christina Rossetti's 1856 poem "In an Artist's Studio" demonstrates a sharp awareness of her brother's selective myopia:

> *He feeds upon her face by day and night,*
> *And she with true kind eyes looks back on him,*
> *Fair as the moon and joyful as the light:*
> *Not wan with waiting, not with sorrow dim:*
> *Not as she is, but was when hope shone bright;*
> *Not as she is, but as she fills his dream.*

In the absence of evidence, the rather large crowd of critics and historians that has, over the years, joined Charles Howell and Dr. Williams in attendance over poor Lizzie's corpse has rushed to fill the vacuum surrounding her with unprovable speculations on topics ranging from her sexuality to the thoughts that "must" have gone through her mind as she downed the fatal dose of laudanum. In her melodramatic biography, *The Wife of Rossetti*, Violet Hunt, the former mistress of Ford Madox Ford, accuses Gabriel of having been a womanizing pig and at the same time finds Lizzie guilty of frigidity. Rossetti's infidelities, *The Wife of Rossetti* suggests, were naturally to have been expected by a woman less sexually relaxed and generous than Violet Hunt herself.

CONTEMPLATING THE START of Lizzie's affair with Gabriel is like watching a Puccini opera for the third or fourth time; from the first poignant bars of the overture, we know precisely how the lovers' unhappy fate will play out. Yet none of that diminishes the sweetness of the early duets, nor makes them any less convincing, nor prevents us from hoping that the doomed couple will somehow prevail.

When they met, Gabriel was twenty-two, Lizzie was seventeen. His letters and the diary entries of their friends are charged with the heady, solipsistic optimism that persuades lovers that everything is possible, that their passion will last forever, and that the world will be only too glad to provide for their needs. "That she was sincerely in love with him—he being most deeply and profusely in love with her—is readily to be presumed," wrote William Rossetti, getting it right for once, though he hesitates to say how long the process took. "Not long after Miss Siddal had begun to sit to Deverell, Dante Rossetti saw her, admired her enormously, and was soon in love with her—*how* soon I cannot exactly say." Madox Brown was bolder in dating the start of their romance: "Rossetti once told me that when he first saw her he felt his destiny was defined."

In letters written during the early 1850s, Rossetti continually finds excuses to mention Lizzie and to boast about her gifts and charms. His first allusion to her involves her art; his playful warning to Christina that her drawings must not compete with "the Sid's" was perhaps not the most tactful way to introduce your mistress to your sister. Like John Lennon a century later, Rossetti persuaded himself that his muse was a genius, a touching conviction in a lover, and a convenient way for Rossetti to rise above the problematic aspects of a serious relationship with a lower-class woman. "Her fecundity of invention and facility are quite wonderful," he wrote, "much greater than mine."

Gifted, charismatic, and handsome, Gabriel and Lizzie soon attracted the attention of John Ruskin, who returns for another appearance in the lives of the muses, this time evincing the fascination that the sexually confused or insecure often display for couples whom they see as models of healthy heterosexual passion. Ruskin seems to have fallen for, and flirted with, both of them at once. Much as he did in his account of his ultimately "disconsolate" evening with Alice Liddell, the theoretically proper Victorian reveals, in a passage of unguarded prose, a tangled snarl of longings, blighted hopes, and frustrations. "I wish Lizzie and you liked me enough to—say—put on a dressing-gown and run in for a minute, rather than not see me . . . But you can't *make* yourselves like me, and you would only like me less if you tried."

Like the lovers themselves, he alchemized romantic ardor into faith in their talent. He bought Rossetti's paintings and in 1855 offered to buy Lizzie's entire output for 150 pounds a year. ("The plain *hard fact*," he wrote her, "is that I think you have genius; that I don't think there is much genius in the world; and I want to keep what there is, in it . . . Utterly irrespective of Rossetti's feelings or my own, I should simply do what I do, if I could, as I should try to save a beautiful tree from being cut down, or a bit of a Gothic cathedral whose strength was failing.")

William had a less flattering opinion about the appeal of Lizzie's drawings: "Although far from blind . . . to their executive shortcomings . . . Mr. Ruskin committed one of those unnumbered acts of generosity by which he will be remembered." But only someone blinded by love could have told Gabriel, "I really do covet your drawings as much as I covet Turner's; only it is useless self-indulgence to buy Turner's, and useful self-indulgence to buy yours." As the couple's adviser and patron, Ruskin dispensed tips on painting, arranged medical care for Lizzie, engineered her trip to the south of France, and offered the financial help that, he hoped, would permit them to get married. "I should be very glad if you thought it right to take me entirely into your confidence, and tell me whether you have any plans or wishes regarding Miss S. which you are prevented from carrying out by want of a certain income, and if so what certain income would enable you to carry them out."

For some time, there had been talk of an engagement, but there *were* no plans for marriage, with or without Ruskin's assistance. According to Ford Madox Brown, the subject was a source of tension between Gabriel and his Guggums. ("Why does he not marry her?"

Brown asked, in his journals.) Not until Lizzie nearly died did Gabriel get a marriage license, confiding to William, "I still trust to God we may be enabled to use it." It's chilling to track, in his correspondence, Lizzie's metamorphosis from the "meek unconscious dove" in whom he takes such pride to the invalid, to the troublesome invalid, to the critically ill invalid, to the invisible presence whom he hardly mentions and who nearly vanishes from his letters until she reappears, at the point of death, just before their wedding.

The first of these ominous tonal shifts occurs in 1853, within a single paragraph of a note to Madox Brown: "Lizzy has made a perfect wonder of her portrait, which is nearly done, and which I think we shall send to the Winter Exhibition. She has been very ill though lately." The next year, two letters written on successive days illustrate the precarious balance that Gabriel was struggling to maintain. To William he expressed his continuing faith in Lizzie's talent: "Tell Christina that if she will come here on Thursday Lizzy will be here and she can also see that Gug's emanations." But to Madox Brown he was at once less sanguine and more forthcoming about her health: "Lizzie has been very unwell lately . . . The Howitts insisted on Lizzy's seeing a Dr. Wilkinson, a friend of theirs, and I believe an eminent man. He finds that the poor dear has contracted a curvature of the spine, and says she ought not to paint at present; but this, of course, she must."

At this stage, the frequent health bulletins ("apparently rather better," "upon the whole a little better," "very unwell," "moderately well") were still leavened by affection for Guggums. In 1855, Ruskin's offer to pay Lizzie an annual stipend inspired this burst of emotion from Gabriel: "I love him and her and everybody, and feel happier than I have felt for a long while."

But Gabriel's letters to William Allingham suggest that anxiety about Lizzie's condition was already cooling the heat of their romance: "Lizzie is a sweet companion, but the fear which the constant sight of her varying state suggests is much less pleasant to live with. . . . It seems hard to me when I look at her sometimes, working or too ill to work, and think how many without one tithe of her genius or greatness of spirit have granted them abundant health . . . while perhaps her soul is never to bloom nor her bright hair to fade, but after hardly escaping from degradation and corruption, all she might have been must sink out again unprofitably in that dark house where she was born. How truly she may say, 'No man cared for my soul.' I do not mean to make myself an exception, for how long have I known her, and not thought of this till so late—perhaps too late. But it is no use writing more about this subject; and I fear, too, my writing at all about it must prevent your easily believing it to be, as it is, by far the nearest thing to my heart."

Careful readers will note how precipitously Gabriel's attention turns from Lizzie to himself; or perhaps he had simply stopped being able to tell the difference. And yet, to Gabriel's credit, he seems never to have considered leaving Lizzie, though it would have been easy for an ambitious young artist to divest himself of a lower-class ex-model and opium addict. Instead, he took her around to doctors, in London and in Oxford, where, according to Violet Hunt, she spent a pleasant afternoon with Charles Dodgson.

Curvature of the spine was only one of the contradictory diagnoses to emerge from Lizzie's unprofitable encounters with Victorian medicine. She was thought to be consumptive, but Oxford's esteemed Dr. Acland—the eminent friend of Dodgson and Dean Liddell—examined her and concluded that "her lungs, if at all affected, are only slightly so, and that the leading cause of illness lies in mental power long pent up and lately overtaxed." Acland's prescription, that Lizzie stop painting, must have seemed to him easy to follow, given his patronizing response to her watercolor *We Are Seven*: "That a girl brought up in London, within a street or two of the Elephant and Castle, should have selected such a subject and executed it from pure imagination, is most remarkable." William Rossetti offered yet another scientific opinion: "phthisis, with the accompaniment of a great deal of acute and wearing neuralgia. It was for the neuralgia that she had been authorized or directed to take frequent doses of laudanum."

Frequent, indeed. Lizzie herself described ingesting "quarts" of laudanum, and at the inquest following her death, Gabriel testified that "he had known her to take as much as a 100 drops at a time" of opium dissolved in alcohol. Through much of the 1850s, Lizzie downed prodigious doses of the narcotic routinely prescribed to soothe the psychic and physiological complaints of nineteenth-century invalids and malingerers—especially women. Lizzie refers to her drug of choice in an alarming pun ("Laden autumn, here I stand") encrypted in one of her death-obsessed last poems. To this day, Lizzie's case continues to interest diagnosticians, some of whom have suggested that her illness was a form of anorexia. But it's generally agreed that her symptoms—restlessness, weakness, compulsive vomiting, the inability to eat—were more likely indicative of an opium habit.

IF GABRIEL'S LETTERS are all solicitous concern spiked with bursts of desperation and self-involvement, if William Rossetti's memoir suggests that his brother's home life was all mutual respect and moral probity, Madox Brown's journals offer a different account of the stormy battles and damaging rifts that divided the couple. Brown's wife, Emma, was not only Lizzie's close friend but, according to Gabriel, the troublemaker who encouraged Lizzie to criticize him. Brown describes Gabriel's tirades at Emma for keeping Lizzie away from him, and for encouraging her to express her dissatisfaction. "Miss Sid complains enough of his absurd goings on not to require that sort of thing," observes Brown, acidly.

The first mention of serious trouble occurs in August 1855: "Rossetti and Miss Siddall here behaving (Rossetti) very badly." A month later, Lizzie left for Paris, where she quickly ran out of money. When Gabriel went over to rescue her, their reunion was so affectionate that the painter Alexander Munro wrote W.B. Scott: "Rossetti is every day with his sweetheart, of whom he is more foolishly fond than I ever saw lover."

But by the time Lizzie returned from the south of France the next spring, she had plenty to complain about—specifically, the triangulated relationship among Gabriel, William Holman Hunt, and a woman named Annie Miller. "Hunt stayed," wrote Brown, "& told me . . . about Annie Millars love for him & his liking for her & perplexities, & how Gabriel like a mad man increased them taking Annie to all sorts of places of amusement . . . to dine at Bertolini's & to Cremorn, where she danced with Boyce, & William takes her out boating forgetful it seems of Miss R., as Gabriel, sad dog, is of Guggum. They all seem mad about Annie Millar & poor Hunt has had a fever about it."

Soon Lizzie was drawn into the swirl of rivalry surrounding Annie Miller: "Emma called on Miss Sid yesterday who is very ill & complaining much of Gabriel. He seems to have transferred his affections to Annie Millar & does nothing but talk of her to Miss Sid. He is mad past care." And what could Lizzie have felt when she saw that one of Gabriel's current projects, *Dante's Dream at the Time of the Death of Beatrice,* portrayed Lizzie as the dead Beatrice and Annie Miller as one of her grieving but robustly healthy handmaidens?

In fact, half the Pre-Raphaelite brethren were infatuated with Annie Miller, a gorgeous barmaid with masses of long blond hair. Annie had been introduced to the group by Hunt, who hired her to model for *The Awakening Conscience,* an allegorical portrait of a fallen woman depicted at the moment of being shocked back to her senses. A bolt of moral awareness has rocketed the attractive harlot straight out of her seducer's lap and brought her nearly to her feet; half crouching, she stares up and out of the canvas with a transfixed stupefaction intended to represent transformation. "I arranged the two figures," wrote Hunt, "to present the woman recalling the memory of her childish home, and breaking away from her gilded cage with a startled holy resolve, while her shallow companion still sings on, ignorantly intensifying her repentant purpose."

Among the most neurotic of the brethren, Hunt fell in love with his model and promptly resolved that, like the hussy in his painting, Annie should be converted into a lady. Immediately decamping for the Holy Land, he left his friend Frederic Stephens with a generous allowance and full instructions for Annie's improvement (she should be taught to read, wear underwear, clean her fingernails and so forth) and for keeping her out of the clutches of other men—an obviously flawed plan that failed, thanks to Rossetti and numerous rival suitors.

By autumn, "Gabriel has forsworn flirting with Annie Millar it seems, Guggum having rebelled against it. He & Guggum seem on the best of terms, now, she is painting at her picture." A few weeks later, Gabriel told Brown that he meant to marry Lizzie immediately and take her off to Algeria, where the climate was believed to be salutary for consumptives. But Gabriel seems to have had second thoughts, and Lizzie left for Bath, instead.

That winter, the couple had a dreadful fight over a plan that Rossetti, Hunt, Morris, and Burne-Jones were devising for a "college" in which the artists would share studio space and, along with their families, living quarters. Gabriel described the argument to Brown: "Last night a misunderstanding occurred between Lizzie and me about what passed, when you were there, concerning the scheme of a college ... I *had* spoken of the scheme to her several days ago, but she seemed to take little interest in it, and I did not say much. She now says that she understood only a range of studios, and would strongly object to the idea of living where Hunt was ... She seemed last night quite embittered and estranged from me on this account, whether for the moment or permanently I cannot yet tell, and it has made me most unhappy ever since, more so than anything else could make me."

Perhaps disingenuously, Gabriel blamed Lizzie's response on illness. Doughty, his sympathetic biographer, traces her antipathy to a practical joke Hunt played years before, when he tried to persuade a friend that Lizzie was his wife. But William Rossetti offers a judicious version of what was more likely the truth—that Lizzie objected to living with Annie Miller, whom Hunt was still planning to marry. "If my reader chooses to ask the old question, 'Who was the woman?' he will not be far wrong . . . The incident belongs to the year 1857. It behoves me to add that Mr. Hunt was wholly blameless in this matter; not so my brother, who was properly, though I will not say very deeply, censurable."

The affair with Annie Miller—which, despite Gabriel's claims, continued for several more years—was only a dress rehearsal for his far more serious involvement with Fanny Cornforth, which had already begun, and which lasted intermittently from 1856 until his death in 1882.

All the accounts of Gabriel's meeting with Fanny—whose real name was Sarah Cox—embody two essential elements of Pre-Raphaelite culture: hair fetishism and erotic slumming. In one version, Gabriel and some friends spotted Fanny at a fireworks display and, attracted by the abundance of what William Rossetti called her "harvest-yellow" hair, they contrived to bump into her so that her hair cascaded down her back. In another account, by Bell Scott, "He met her in the Strand. She was cracking nuts with her teeth, and throwing the shells about. Seeing Rossetti staring at her, she threw some at him. Delighted with this brilliant *naivete*, he forthwith accosted her, and carried her off to sit to him for her portrait."

Fanny's own description of her first modeling session—"He put my head against the wall and drew it for the head in the calf picture"—gives some sense of the "brilliant naievete [*sic*]" that Gabriel found so refreshing after the more rarefied and strained atmosphere of daily life with Lizzie. While Fanny may have committed all the "faults of speech" that Lizzie did not, she was unburdened by Lizzie's illness, her art ambitions, and her difficult, "chaffish" intelligence.

The "calf picture" was *Found*, on which Rossetti worked for decades, refusing to finish or abandon his version of Hunt's *The Awakening Conscience*. In *Found*, a young man in ersatz-Renaissance costume lifts up a blond beauty who has slumped against a low brick wall. Everything about the painting is breathtakingly literal-minded—the fact that the fallen woman has literally collapsed on the street, that her suitor is actually lifting her up, and that her position and plight are echoed by the unfortunate calf, trussed up in a wagon. (Painting the calf was part of what gave Rossetti such trouble, and Brown expressed an untypically snide opinion of his method: "He paints it all in like Albrecht Durer hair by hair & seems incapable of any breadth.") The final touch of obviousness is the use of the prostitute Fanny to play the luscious whore saved by her loyal knight, presumably for virtue's sake.

Unsurprisingly, the radiant Fanny Cornforth (the brethren's pet name for her was "the elephant") outlasted the skeletal, drug-addicted "Miss Sid." Twice married, once widowed, Fanny continued to live near Gabriel and kept house for him after Lizzie died.

BY THE LATE 1850S, Lizzie's position was a sorry one, for a muse. Repeatedly, she returned to London from various health spots to find her lover immortalizing Annie Miller and Fanny Cornforth, not one but two glorious, long-haired, demimonde sex goddesses. Georgiana Burne-Jones describes a visit to the bedridden Lizzie during which everyone seemed to know that Gabriel was in another room, painting Fanny. Yet Gabriel and Lizzie continued to play their established roles in the drama that was becoming increasingly operatic and mythological; they remained each other's obsessive poetic and pictorial subjects, and the inspiration for feelings that— often with numbing literalism—inspired yet more art.

By 1857, they had been together for seven years; a crisis was brewing. Two weeks after their argument about the communal "college," Madox Brown wrote, "Miss Siddall has been here for 3 days and is I fear dying. She seems now to hate Gabriel in toto. Gabriel had settled to marry . . . & and she says told her he was only waiting for the money of a picture to do so, when, lo the money being paid . . . never a word more about marriage.

"After that, she determined to have no more to do with him. However, he followed her to Bath & again some little while ago promised marriage immediately, when since he had again postponed all thoughts of it till about a fortnight ago, having found Miss Sid more than usually incensed against him, he came to me and talked seriously about it . . ." Rossetti borrowed money for the license from Brown, which he promptly spent, and immediately borrowed more. "Of course I am very glad to lend it to him but he has quite lost her affection through his extraordinary proceedings. He does not know his own mind for one day."

That spring, the couple's problems occupied a good deal of the Browns' time. "All day with Gabriel who is so unhappy about Miss Sid that I could not leave him. In the evening to fetch Emma from Miss Sid at Hampstead . . . Went off to tell Gabriel what Miss Sidall [*sic*] said of him. Put him in much affliction & brought him back with the intention of walking over to Hampstead and to try and induce her to give him an interview . . . This we did but on getting there she would not see him nor me . . . Gabriel in a sad state."

It was the next year that Gabriel met Fanny Cornforth. A year later, he used her likeness in his painting *Bocca Baciata*—"the mouth kissed"—a title taken from a line of Boccaccio's: "The kissed mouth that loses not its fascination, but renews itself as does the moon." Responding to the painting's vaguely pornographic sheen, Swinburne called its subject "more stunning than can decently be expressed."

IN HIS MEMOIR, William Rossetti cites his sister-in-law's "deplorable" health as "the first and foremost" reason for the length of her ten-year engagement. But plotting Lizzie's illness against the

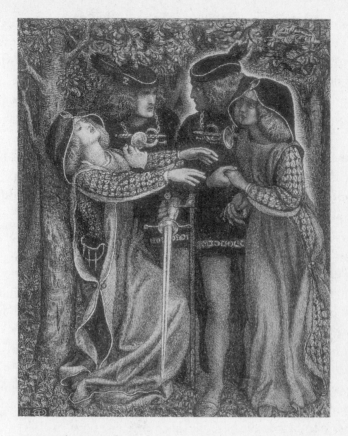

How They Met Themselves, 1851–69. (*Dante Gabriel Rossetti*)

history of her relationship with Gabriel suggests that the converse might have been true—that her anxiety about Rossetti's reluctance to marry her exacerbated her addiction. Although she had been at death's door only days before and was thought to be too ill to attend the ceremony in a drafty church, she and Gabriel were finally married in 1860. Lizzie made a miraculous recovery during their honeymoon in Paris. On the other hand, sojourns in Hastings, Bath, Paris, and Nice did little for her health, possibly because she could so easily have taken along her own laudanum, which would have seemed even more appealing as it became clear that Gabriel was spending her absences painting other women. From Matlock, in Derbyshire, where Lizzie went in November 1857 to take a "hydropathic cure," she wrote Gabriel a pitiful note requesting his help with a painting because "I am too blind and sick to see what I am about."

Ultimately, Lizzie's health grew so poor and her romance with Gabriel so estranged that drastic measures seemed called for: They decided to get married. In April 1860, a flurry of letters from Gabriel to his family and friends announced his upcoming wedding, his abject guilt, and his fear that Lizzie was dying.

"Lizzy and I are going to be married," he wrote his mother, "in as few days as possible . . . Like all the important things I ever meant to do—to fulfill duty or secure happiness—this one has been deferred almost beyond possibility. I have hardly deserved that Lizzy should still consent to it, but she has done so, and I trust I may still have time to prove my thankfulness to her. The constantly failing state of her health is a terrible anxiety indeed; but I must still hope for the best . . ."

Around the same time, Gabriel wrote his brother yet another letter that shifts rapidly from Lizzie's problems to his own: "Till yesterday she had not been able to keep anything—even a glass of soda water on her stomach for five minutes . . . She gets no nourishment, and what can be reasonably hoped when this is added to her dreadful state of health in other respects? If I were to lose her now I do not know what effect it might have on my mind, added to the responsibility of much work commissioned and already paid for, which still has to be done—and how to do it in such a case?" And he confided in Brown, "I have been, almost without respite, since I saw you, in the most agonizing anxiety about poor dear Lizzie's health. Indeed it has been that kind of pain which one can never remember at its full, as she has seemed ready to die daily and more than once a day. It has needed all my strength to nurse her through this dreadful attack. Since yesterday . . . she has been able to get up and come downstairs, and eats just now—though not much—without bringing up her food—which she has done till now, generally a few minutes after swallowing . . . It makes me feel as if I had been dug out of a vault, so many times lately has it seemed to me that she could never lift her head again." (That *dug out of a vault* gives one pause—perhaps a clue to a habit of mind that, almost a decade later, would agree to the proposed exhumation.)

Just when it had begun to seem that there would be no Lizzie to marry, Gabriel wrote Brown from Hastings, where they were wed. "All hail from Lizzie and myself just back from church. I am sorry I cannot give you any good news of her health, but we must hope for the best."

The newlyweds spent the first week of their honeymoon at the Hotel Meurice in Paris, a romantic splurge that ended when they moved to cheaper lodgings. Separated from the familiar scenes in which so much had gone wrong, far from Annie Miller and Fanny Cornforth, Lizzie thrived. "Paris seems to agree so well with her that I am fearful of returning to London . . . lest it should throw her back into the terrible state of illness she had been in for some time before." Indeed, back in London, Fanny had reacted badly to the news of the marriage: "It appears she frets constantly about R, who is with his wife in Paris . . ."

From France, Gabriel dispatched a breezy note to William Allingham, mentioning that he and Lizzie might relocate to Paris. At the Louvre, they were thrilled by the most heroic of all wedding pictures, Veronese's *The Marriage at Cana*.

Meanwhile, he was completing *How They Met Themselves*, a drawing of a meeting between two ersatz-medieval, doppelgänger couples—two identical men and women; one of the women appears to be half-dead or at least fainting.

"As he was not a little superstitious, and sensitive to ill omens, I am somewhat surprised," wrote William Rossetti of his brother's new work. "Here the lady—studied from Lizzie, and very like her—

is represented swooning away as she encounters her own wraith—not to speak of her lover or husband, who grasps his sword on seeing the wraith of himself. To meet one's wraith is ominous of death, and to figure Lizzie as meeting her wraith might well have struck her bridegroom as uncanny in a high degree. In less than two years the weird was woefully fulfilled."

William was not alone in using the lens of hindsight to magnify the predictive aspects of this grisly drawing. Several of Rossetti's biographers refer to the artist's prescience. Yet Gabriel hardly needed ESP to put Lizzie and Death in the same drawing. It's just as likely, and more in keeping with his habitually direct use of autobiographical material from his own life, that the drawing is a reference to Lizzie's recent brush with eternity. In any case, it's hardly a hopeful vision of marriage, and what makes it all the more disturbing is that we can fairly well assume that Gabriel showed it to Lizzie. How unnerving to find that your husband of less than a few months is depicting you at the moment of meeting your demise!

By then, Lizzie was accustomed to being portrayed in a state of moribund repose or actually dead, as Millais's waterlogged Ophelia and as Gabriel's departed Beatrice. Her rivals, Fanny Cornforth and Annie Miller, were painted very differently: Their bodies, their faces, and most of all their hair look terrifyingly alive. Their eyes gaze liquidly out of the canvas, enticing and inviting—so unlike Lizzie's eyes, which in Gabriel's rendering are always lidded, downcast, evasive. And what did Lizzie entitle the drawing *she* did during their wedding journey? *The Woeful Victory.*

The romantic, sadistic, or depressive message encoded in *How They Met Themselves* was the first postnuptial dispatch in a long series of communications between the couple, encoded as paintings and poems. The affected allegory of such Rossetti paintings as *Found* seems drawn from the same inspirational well as Siddal's efforts, so many of which seem like updates on the status of her relationship with Rossetti. Her *Lovers Listening to Music* depicts an affectionate idyll not unlike the sweet satisfactions of their early days together, while her version of Tennyson's *Lady Clare* evokes a legend in which a knight agrees to marry his lady even after he learns the truth of her humble birth; *Pippa Passes the Loose Women*—a portrayal of Browning's innocent Pippa skimming past the prostitutes—seems like a protective charm to ward off the sexual temptations that contributed to the couple's disintegration.

Like the images Lizzie and Gabriel drew, her poems seem generated by the adolescent idea of art as a pipeline for raw untreated emotion. This view, together with their technical limitations (Waugh was not far wrong about their draftsmanship) and their derivative subject matter, helped prevent them from transforming those feelings and experiences into something much beyond the versified love letter to one's high school sweetheart.

Lizzie's poems rarely surpass the heartfelt doggerel of "The Passing of Love":

> *O God, forgive me that I ranged*
> *My life into a dream of love!*
> *Will tears of anguish never wash*
> *The passion from my blood?*

Many of her lyrics are laments for lost love, or longings for death, or maledictions heaped upon the faithless lover:

> *And turn away thy false dark eyes*
> *Nor gaze into my face;*
> *Great love I bore thee; now great hate*
> *Sits grimly in its place.*

Only rarely does her verse transcend the cliché and the banal, except perhaps in this terse, barbed indictment of a lover's self-centered shallowness and inconstancy:

I care not for my Lady's soul
Though I worship before her smile;
I care not where be my Lady's goal
When her beauty shall lose its wile.

Low sit I down at my Lady's feet
Gazing through her wild eyes
Smiling to think how my love will fleet
When their starlit beauty dies.

According to William Rossetti, Gabriel's brief marriage coincided with a period of enormous productivity. Installed in a rented house at Hampstead with Lizzie, Gabriel completed a series of canvases and drawings on assorted grim themes: Lucrezia Borgia preparing a dose of poison, Cassandra predicting Hector's death. He also painted his most lubricious portrait of Fanny as *Fair Rosamund*, that is, as Henry II's mistress anticipating a visit from her lover, a virtual declaration of the fact that marriage had failed to temper his taste for what William called amours and entanglements: "My brother, at the age of thirty-two, was less likely to settle down into the ordinary habits of married life than many other men would have been . . . His propensity for doing whatever he liked simply because he liked it, and without any self-accommodation to what other people might like instead . . . made it improbable that he would prove a complaisant or well-matching husband."

Around the time of his marriage, Gabriel wrote a poem called "The Song of the Bower"—still more barely disguised reportage, this time about lovers menaced by an unnamed evil personified in the form of a dying woman. Swinburne believed that Gabriel was again expressing his thwarted passion for Fanny. "In fact, I may almost say I know it, from Gabriel's own admission—implied when he and I were discussing that yet unpublished poem, which in the early days of 'Bocca Baciata' may not have been so comically exaggerative as it seemed to me even when I first met the bitch."

Once more Lizzie's health suffered a decline that at once resulted from, and contributed to, her opium consumption. "She was compelled," wrote William, "no doubt under medical advice—to take laudanum or some opiate continually, and stimulants alternated with opiates." Gabriel's letters are filled with bulletins about her symptoms, and Georgiana Burne-Jones returned from visiting Lizzie with "an impression which never wore away, of romance and tragedy between her and her husband."

Exhausted by all that romance and tragedy, Lizzie fled to Brighton, from where she sent her husband a cringing, defeated letter that seems to have been written by a different woman than the one who, five years before, described the annoying habits of Monsieur Mutton-chop in Nice. It might be argued, however, that a similar level of literary skill was required to produce a text as guilt-inducing as this one:

"I am most sorry to have worried you about coming back when you have so many things to upset you. I shall therefore say no more about it. I seem to have gained flesh within the last ten days, and seem also much better in some respects, although I am in constant pain and cannot sleep at nights for fear of another illness like the last. But do not feel anxious about it as I would not fail to let you know in time . . . I should like to have my water-colours sent down if possible, as I am quite destitute of all means of keeping myself alive . . . I can do without money till next Thursday, after which time three pounds a week would be quite enough for all our wants—including rent of course."

Eventually Lizzie did return. And though some of her biographers would have us believe that Gabriel and his ethereal Beatrice never had sex, that he worshiped Lizzie's spirit and reserved his earthier attentions for his mistresses, Lizzie managed to get pregnant. They returned to Chatham Place, where for a while things went well. Lizzie kept at her art, and Gabriel sent Allingham another of his remarkably mixed messages: "I feel surer every time she works that she has real genius—none of your make-believe—in conception and color, and if she can only add a little more of the precision in carrying out which it so much needs health and strength to attain, she will I am sure paint such pictures as no woman has painted yet. But it is no use hoping for too much."

Despite his brother's and his friends' misgivings about his talent for middle-class marriage, Gabriel enjoyed a rare moment of domestic bliss. A newsy letter to Allingham bursts with practical plans for bolstering his income by opening a furniture-making shop with William Morris, and with cheerful home-decorating chat: "We have got our rooms quite jolly now. Our drawing-room is a beauty I assure you, already, and on the first country trip we make she shall have it newly papered from a design of mine which I have an opportunity of getting made by a paper-manufacturer . . . When we get the paper up we shall have the doors and wainscoting painted summer-house green." These domestic progress reports appear in the same letter as Gabriel's announcement of Lizzie's pregnancy: "Lizzie is pretty well for her, and we are in expectation (but this is quite in confidence as such things are better waited for quietly) of a little accident which has just befallen Topsy and Mrs. T who have become parients. (sic.) Ours, however, will not be (if at all) for two months."

That chilling phrase, "little accident" serves as preparation for the "if at all," which stops us cold. We know, from William, that Gabriel was superstitious, so perhaps the conditional phrase is just a propitiatory nod to Nemesis, a verbal knock on wood. It's also likely that Gabriel doubted the ability of his frail, opium-addicted, possibly consumptive wife to carry a child to term.

Gabriel's concerns proved justified. On May 2, 1861, he wrote four letters, all variations on this brutally frank note to his mother:

"My dear Mother, Lizzie has just been delivered of a dead child. She is doing pretty well, I trust. Do not encourage anyone to come just now—I mean, of course, except yourselves." He informed Ford Madox Brown that "Lizzie has just had a dead baby. I know how glad Emma and you will be to hear that she seems as yet to be doing decidedly well." That same day, Rossetti conveyed the sad news to Mrs. John Dalrymple and to his new friend, Alexander Gilchrist, the biographer of Blake; he hastened to assure Gilchrist that "Swinburne and I will be with you on Saturday."

Lizzie was slow to recover. Gabriel's letters detail the gradual return of the old, familiar symptoms—lack of appetite and so forth—as well as the appearance of disturbing new ones: a tendency toward erratic behavior, which twice caused her to suddenly disappear from a house in which she was staying and, without alerting anyone, to make her own way home. In her book, *Pre-Raphaelites in Love*, Gay Daly astutely points out that there were healthy new babies in both of the houses (first the Browns' place, then the Morrises') from which Lizzie fled. And a pharmacologist could probably calibrate the dose of laudanum required for her to have cried, "Hush, Ned, you'll waken it!" when Burne-Jones and his wife arrived at Chatham Place to find Lizzie brooding beside an empty cradle.

Yet no one seemed to find this unusually troubling. If the suicidal title and refrain of Lizzie's last poem, "Lord, May I Come?"— "Hollow hearts are ever near me/ Soulless eyes have ceased to cheer me/ Lord, may I come?"—failed to alarm her husband and friends, perhaps this fatal obliviousness may be blamed on the fact that the lyric represented a fairly typical addition to Lizzie's unrelievedly funereal oeuvre.

THE BRISKLY PACED newspaper article describing the postmortem inquest held at Bridewell Hospital accounts for most of what we know about the events of February 10, 1862—the night of Lizzie Siddal's death.

"Mr. Rossetti stated that on Monday afternoon, between six and seven o'clock, he and his wife went out in the carriage for the purpose of dining with a friend at the Sablonniere Hotel, Leicester Square. When they had got about halfway there his wife appeared to be very drowsy, and he wished her to return. She objected to their doing so, and they proceeded to the Hotel, and dined there. They returned home at eight o'clock, when she appeared somewhat excited. He left home again at nine o'clock, his wife being then about to go to bed. On his return at half-past eleven o'clock he found his wife in bed, snoring loudly and utterly unconscious. She was in the habit of taking laudanum, and he had known her take as much as 100 drops at a time, and he thought she had been taking it before they went out. He found a phial on a table at the bedside, which had contained laudanum, but it was then empty. A doctor was sent for, and promptly attended. She had expressed no wish to die, but quite the reverse. Indeed she contemplated going out of town in a day or two, and had ordered a new mantle, which she intended to wear on the occasion. He believed she took the laudanum to soothe her nerves. She could not sleep or take food unless she used it. Mr. Hutchinson, of Bridge Street, Blackfriars, said he had attended the deceased in her confinement in April with a stillborn child. He saw her on Monday night at half-past eleven o'clock, and found her in a comatose state. He tried to rouse her, but could not, and then tried the stomach-pump without avail. He injected several quarts of water in the stomach, and washed it out, when the smell of laudanum was very distinct. He and three other medical gentlemen stayed with her all night, and she died at twenty minutes past seven o'clock on Tuesday morning.—The jury returned a verdict of Accidental Death."

Those are the facts on top of which biographers, historians, and lovers of literary gossip have embroidered layers of rumor, speculation, and conjecture. Was Lizzie's death a suicide or an accidental overdose taken by a woman whose mind was already clouded by drugs and despair? Didn't the details of the planned journey and the newly tailored mantle prove she wished to live? Was she found with a note pinned to her nightshirt? Did it contain, as William Rossetti's daughter Helen disclosed in a 1949 biography, a plea that Gabriel look after her simple-minded brother Harry? Or did the note say, as Violet Hunt reported, "My life is so miserable I wish for no more of it"?

And where exactly was Gabriel during Lizzie's final hours? Was he, as William Rossetti claimed, at the Working Men's College, though Gabriel had resigned his post there several years before? Or was he with Fanny Cornforth? And did that drive Lizzie to exceed her accustomed dose? Did the couple argue that night? Did Gabriel really drag Lizzie around by her hair? And did he, as Oscar Wilde claimed, give Lizzie the bottle of laudanum and suggest she drink it all?

Who cares? Why should it matter? Aren't the facts enough? It was night, the middle of February. Chatham Place was, in the best weather, dank and cold. Lizzie was left alone after an excruciating evening.

At first, the night must have offered some promise: dinner out with Swinburne, her closest male friend and most devoted fan among the Pre-Raphaelite circle. But before they'd even reached the restaurant, Gabriel suggested that his "drowsy" wife—who had already taken a sizable amount of laudanum—turn around and go home. Back at Chatham Place, the "somewhat excited" Lizzie grew even more agitated when Gabriel told her to go to bed, since he planned to go out.

So much for Lizzie's last evening. And what joys did the future promise? What had Lizzie to look forward to besides the journey and the new cape? More Fanny Cornforths, more Annie Millers, more financial uncertainty, more illness, more little vacations to bolster her health. Her pessimism about the chances of having another child had surfaced in her recent offer to give "a certain small wardrobe" to Ned Burne-Jones and his pregnant wife. "Don't let her, please," wrote Gabriel. "It looks like such a bad omen for us."

Who wouldn't have been tempted to seek comfort in a drug that had reliably proven its gift for blunting the edges of hopelessness and despair? Who wouldn't have decided that having survived the humiliating confrontation with Gabriel and facing the chilly, solitary night ahead justified—demanded—a dose slightly stronger than normal?

Her dying took the whole of the night, from midnight until seven. The change from comatose to lifeless must have been gradual enough to partly explain why Gabriel—who never had an especially tenacious grip on reality—refused to accept it.

"On the second or third day after death," wrote William, "Lizzie looked still lovelier than before, and Dante almost refused to believe that she was really dead—it might be a mere trance consequent upon the laudanum. He insisted that Mr. Marshall should be called in to decide—with what result I need not say."

In the midst of all this grief, the Pre-Raphaelite aesthetic prevailed, persuading the bereaved husband that a woman dead for three days looked lovelier than a live one. Yet none of these distancing observations make it less painful to imagine the scene in which Gabriel insisted that doctor be summoned to verify that Lizzie wasn't merely in a trance.

How could he not have been overcome with remorse? Standing over the coffin with Lizzie's sister and William, Gabriel cried out, " 'Oh Lizzie, Lizzie come back to me!' With a woman's kindly tact the sister felt that this was an instant when emotion should be seconded, and not controlled; and she reminded him of some old touches of sportive and now pathetic affection, to give the freer flow to his tears." Swinburne witnessed Gabriel's guilt and grief: "With sobs and broken speech he protested that he had never really loved or cared for any woman but the wife he had lost; with bitter self-reproach he referred to former professions not ostensibly consistent with this assertion; he appealed to my friendship, in the name of her regard for me—such regard, he assured me, as she had felt for no other of his friends—cleave to him in this time of sorrow, to come keep house with him as soon as a residence could be found."

And finally, of course, there was the penitential gesture—the ultimate penance, for Gabriel—of putting his manuscript into the coffin as a final gift to his muse. No one saw him do it, but by the time he joined Brown and his friends, he had thought about it and framed an explanation for his impulsive act: "I have often been writing at those poems when Lizzie was ill and suffering, and I might have been attending to her, and now they shall go." Brown asked William to reason with his brother and make him reconsider, but William replied, " 'Well, the feeling does him honour, and let him do as he likes.' " And in the memoir he added, "The sacrifice was no doubt a grave one.' "

Thirty-four, increasingly plump, Gabriel would soon develop his own serious substance abuse problems; heavy self-medication with chloral and alcohol facilitated his occasional freefalls into psychosis. He abandoned Chatham Place and moved to Cheyne Walk, where he intermittently lived with, and continued to paint, Fanny Cornforth. He fell madly in love with William Morris's wife Jane, whose portraits he painted and to whom he wrote his most erotic and successful poems. He cultivated his eccentricities and collected the large private menagerie that he half-seriously represented (again, Warhol's Factory comes to mind) as an image-enhancing publicity stunt that might help to sell his work. When asked why he wished to buy a small elephant, he replied, "I mean him to clean the windows, and then, when someone passes the house, they will see the elephant cleaning the windows and will say, 'Who lives in that house?' And people will tell them, 'Oh, that's a painter called Rossetti.' And they will say, 'I think I should like to buy one of that man's pictures'—and so they will ring, and come in and buy my pictures."

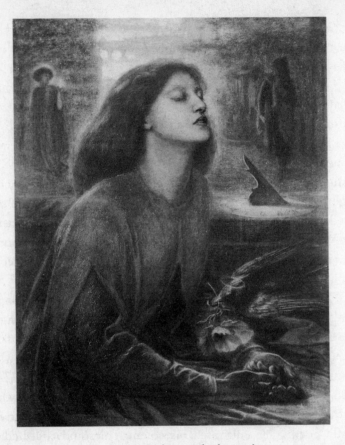

Beata Beatrix. *(Dante Gabriel Rossetti)*

And Lizzie haunted all of this, just as was always intended, all
the time that she and Rossetti played at the drama of Dante and
Beatrice: the muse who was even more beloved, more inspirational—and consequently more useful for the purposes of art—
dead than alive. Not long after that February night, Rossetti
finished *Beata Beatrix*—the ecstatic portrait of Siddal complete with
opium poppy and the dove, the work in which Miss Bessie Parkes
said she failed to recognize Lizzie's expression. "It is not at all in-

tended to represent Death," the painter wrote, "but to render it under the resemblance of a stupor, in which Beatrice seated at the balcony overlooking the City is suddenly rapt from Earth to Heaven." Thus Gabriel's insistence that his dead muse was not really dead but merely in a trance inspired him to produce a painting that supported his opinion. Not death but rapture has closed Lizzie/Beatrice's eyes, parted her lips, and tipped back her head at an angle suggesting that her swoon is erotic. The painting's gently shaded edges and the melting posture of the figure are notably unlike the crisply chaste angularities of Rossetti's earlier drawings of Lizzie. In softer focus, less sharply drawn, less blatantly pornographic than his portraits of Fanny and Jane Morris, *Beata Beatrix* is nonetheless closer to his paintings of his mistresses than to previous renderings of his wife.

Like so much of Rossetti's work, it is a direct unmediated communication, an arrangement of symbols signifying the glories and tragedies of his life. The two figures in the background, one of Dante and the other of Love, gaze shyly at each other across the canvas, and the dove, representing Lizzie, is now a garish red—the color of Beatrice's shroud, and of the dress she was wearing on the day Dante first saw her. The dove's swoop into the painting is less suggestive of the gradual descent of the Holy Spirit than a dispatch from the devil. And what this fierce bird brings Beatrice is neither the lily that the dove brought Mary, nor the olive branch it carried back to Noah, but the opium poppy that killed Elizabeth Siddal.

Beata Beatrix is Gabriel's version of what happened to Lizzie. He wants us to know it, and he wanted Lizzie to know it, just in case she was not dead, but only "rapt," so that the dialogue that had fueled their art could continue unimpeded.

Meanwhile, he was busily seeking a still more direct way for Lizzie to keep up her end of the conversation. How convenient that spiritualism was coming into fashion! Gabriel enlisted James McNeil Whistler, his mistress Jo, and anyone else who could be persuaded, to participate in a series of séances. Lizzie's ghost aided these occult explorations, rapping on the table to spell out answers to questions, and volunteering information that only she and Gabriel could have known. Her spirit was asked if she liked Gabriel's most recent picture, *The Beloved*. She did. During another session, Lizzie confessed that it was she who had been making knocking sounds in the bedroom all night, noises that frightened Fanny Cornforth, and that Gabriel seemed not to have heard. Poor Lizzie, summoned from the beyond and taken to task for scaring the woman who shared her husband's bed!

The exhumation was inevitable. The manuscript was a pretext. Gabriel's desire was much more primitive, more infantile than the need to retrieve a few poems, most of which he already had, at least in alternate drafts. It was the result of his need to make sure that Lizzie was still there, still dead, to see if her trance had ended, to test the incorruptibility of her body against the beatific memory of her saintly existence, and to stage a repulsively literal version of Dante's reunion with his dead beloved.

And so the identification of Lizzie with Beatrice continued long after she too had passed into the other world from which she continued to inspire her lover. Like his brother, William Rossetti saw Lizzie as the modern Beatrice, and he recorded the impressions that occurred to him as he stood over his sister-in-law's corpse. Gazing at her and reflecting that "the poor thing looks wonderfully calm and beautiful," he recalled a passage from Dante's *Vita Nuova* which Gabriel had translated: "And with her was such very humbleness/ That she appeared to say, I am at peace."

But how could Lizzie have been at peace if she'd understood that the outlines of her crisp clear self were being blurred and smudged into yet another fantasy of a woman from a distant century? How could she have rested if she'd known that she was being immortalized in her artist's version of another poet's verses, in a borrowed hymn of eternal love to someone else's muse?

LOU ANDREAS-SALOMÉ

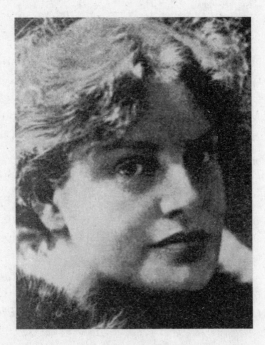

Lou Andreas-Salomé, 1897.

THE LIVES OF THE SERIAL MUSES—Alma Mahler, Lou Andreas-Salomé, Misia Sert, women said to have inspired one genius after another—suggest that the muse's work need not necessarily imply a particular chemistry between one artist and one muse, or the projection of an artist's ideal onto a particular woman or girl. Alternately or additionally, the muse's career can involve some aspect of the muse herself, some quality that draws these men toward her, and through her toward each other as the muse's romantic history becomes part of her appeal, and of her effectiveness as muse.

In the case of Lou Andreas-Salomé, this history included a stormy but platonic romance with Nietszche, nearly a half-century of chaste marriage to a professor of Persian, Friedrich Carl Andreas, and a four-year affair with Rilke, during which she rechristened the young poet, persuading him to change his name to Rainer from the less forceful René. Her friendship with Rilke lasted until his death in 1926, a quarter century after their official separation. By then she had become a disciple, correspondent, and confidante of Freud's, a practicing analyst, a sort of godmother to Anna Freud, and the author of more than twenty books: novels, short stories and essays, volumes of philosophy, psychology and literary criticism, works on subjects including Nietszche, Rilke, and Freud. And so Lou joined the subgroup of muses who, like Hester Thrale, Charis Weston, and Suzanne Farrell, wrote about their artists, though Lou was one of the *very* few muses moved to publish admiring but rigorous and even unfriendly critiques of the work she helped inspire. For much of her life, she supported herself by writing, a rare accomplishment for a woman at the turn of the century.

By 1937, Lou's reputation was such that the Gestapo waited until shortly after she died to seize her library and dump it in the basement of the Göttingen City Hall, thus thoughtfully protecting the citizenry from her contaminating association with psychoanalysis, the "Jewish science." Lou must have been a problematic figure for Aryan culture, a living bridge to the glorious past of Nietszche and Wagner, in whose orbit she had moved in Bayreuth, in 1882—*Parsifal*'s first summer there, and its composer's last. Doubtless the Nazis would rather not have seen the progression from Nietszche to Rilke to Freud as a continuum. But Lou Andreas-Salomé's memoirs might have persuaded them that the three men were not nearly so far apart as they might have assumed, or hoped; *Looking Back* reads like a work that the trio could have coauthored and channeled through Lou.

A diva with a Teutonic temperament and a proudly Russian soul, Lou viewed herself, from adolescence, as a seeker of truth, a missionary bringing happiness and wisdom to the lucky beneficiaries of her generosity and beneficence. An influential figure in literary and psychoanalytic circles, she was at the same time a sort of religious nut with all the erotic intensity and displacement so common among fanatics. She believed in the necessity of new religions, of new gods to be born out of Eros, in love that adds up to something greater and more transcendent than the sum of the lovers themselves.

The miraculous coincidence of the shared taste or idea is, of course, one of the things that confirms lovers in their sense of convergent destinies, of having been fated to be together. For Lou and her men, these common preoccupations—the overcoming of the self, the nature of God and of angels, the necessity of leading a heroic and exemplary life, the power of the unconscious—were pitched at an exceptionally high frequency. She was drawn to men such as Nietzsche and Rilke, who saw the world in the same lofty terms as she did. And in Freud, Lou found a visionary who had managed to turn his ideas into a viable system that functioned in the real world, and who offered her a chance to become a kind of intellectual consort, a disciple of a godless philosophy that fulfilled exactly her dearest fantasy of a new religion.

Reading Lou's books, Nietszche's works, Rilke's poems, their diaries and letters, one is struck by the role that God and the idea of God played in their inner lives, their everyday conversation, their writing and their art. "What attracted me most strongly to those individuals, living or dead, who dedicated themselves totally to such thoughts was always their quality as human beings. No matter how subtly they expressed it in their philosophy, you could always tell that in some deep sense *God* remained the first and foremost experience in their lives. What else in life could compare?" Lou's own philosophy conflated God, self, consciousness, and love into one joyous stream, one grab bag of animistic wonders kindly provided by nature. And the ways in which her ideas differed from those of Nietzsche and Freud involved her insistent refusal to excise the divine from her worldview.

The first fifty years of Lou Andreas-Salomé's career as muse transpired in a society balanced precariously on the edge of being changed forever by Freud. In her youth, she and her lovers acted out of unexamined compulsions and fears that, a few decades later, would have been subject to fierce investigation. When asked, in later life, if she regretted not having discovered Freud's ideas earlier, she replied that she would have hated to have missed all her youthful follies. Though Lou and her lovers behaved in not merely unconventional but often bizarre ways, she considered herself to be the picture of mental health, a model of psychic well-being. Her notions on infidelity, explicated in her *Freud Journal*, echo precisely the sorts of things she told Nietszche, Rilke, and probably others, in the process of cutting them loose: "People who are not 'faithful' do not necessarily desert one person for another, but are often simply driven *home to themselves* . . . It need not be a gesture of abandonment for them to set free the person to whom they have clung; more likely it is a gesture of reverence, returning him to the world."

Her insistence on seeing women as earthier, more elemental, more at peace with themselves and closer to the source of joy irritates feminists and may strike the modern reader as cloyingly reminiscent of New Age woman-identified tree-hugging. Her reference to the "woman who perhaps never attains the final insights of the mind but instead finds her being in the intuitive knowledge of life and mind" in the *Freud Journal* is characterisic. So, too, is her fantasy about a farewell speech she wished she'd given after the last of Freud's Wednesday evening lectures, an oration that would have ended, "For men fight. Women give thanks."

For all her flaws and blind spots, Lou Andreas-Salomé possessed prodigious powers of concentration, and the ability to sustain long, lucid (despite an excessively floral prose style) arguments on the page and in person. Thanks to an instinctive, unconscious or at least unacknowledged grasp of how sex, beauty, and intelligence could be used to manipulate others, she managed to achieve a phenomenal amount of independence and power for a woman of her era. Throughout her life, she behaved as if she had never heard anyone suggest that a woman couldn't do entirely as she pleased.

Though Lou enjoyed quoting Freud's flattering (or so she assumed) description of her as a "Sunday" in the midst of his more somber colleagues toiling at their weekday researches, the fact is that she and the men she influenced could hardly have taken themselves more seriously. All of them thought in large, abstract terms and were driven by a powerful messianic imperative. No one in the unusual group that Lou selected out of the available mass of humanity doubted for a moment that his work was a matter of life and death, and part of Lou's effectiveness as muse can be traced to her belief that they were right.

WHAT COULD THE Swiss photographer have made of the woman and the two men who arrived at his studio and, assuming those peculiar poses, asked him to take their picture? Little in M. Bonnet's experience staging formal portraits of the haute bourgeois of Lucerne could have prepared him for the moment when his customers spotted the donkey cart (in which he was accustomed to corral his clients' uncomfortable, overdressed children) and decided that the two gentlemen, yoked together with rope, should pretend to pull the wagon in which the severely pretty young woman perched, holding a riding crop decorated with lilacs.

It was the thirteenth of May, 1882. Friedrich Nietzsche, the philosopher Paul Rée and their twenty-one-year-old friend Lou von Salomé had just come from the park, where, near the famous lion statue, they'd agreed, to everyone's relief, that Nietzsche and Lou would not be getting engaged. Marriage, Lou argued, would cost her the pension to which she was entitled as the daughter of a deceased Russian army general, and, worse, would taint the purity of their visionary plan to live together, all three of them, in a cozy, chaste, and impeccably high-minded household, reading and studying.

All of this was very new, very sudden, and all-consuming. Barely two months had passed since Lou—who had left her home in St. Petersburg for university in Zurich, then gone to Rome for her health—had met Paul Rée, the author of two books on morality, and a compulsive gambler. They were introduced at the salon centered around the emigrée bluestocking, Malwida von Meysenbug. From the start, Lou and Rée scandalized even this liberal community by taking unchaperoned midnight walks through the streets of Rome, talking constantly, fervidly, discussing Life and Death, God and Man, Morality and Religion, and also the plan—Lou's plan—to form their own little monastery for two.

"In it I saw a pleasant study filled with books and flowers, flanked by two bedrooms, and us walking back and forth between them, colleagues, working together in a joyful and earnest bond."

Lou, who already had a history of growing close to men and then being shocked when they fell in love with her, much preferred her airy scheme to Rée's more pedestrian notion: that they get married. As the moonlight puddled around them on the ruins of the Roman forum, Rée was ultimately persuaded, or worn down, to Lou's way of thinking—thus making her probably the only twenty-one-year-old Russian girl in 1882 to convince a man that they live together without marriage and sex.

Through March and early April, they discussed various locations for their tiny commune: Paris, Vienna, Genoa, Munich. Eventually Rée proposed that their idyllic "Winterplan" might be broadened to include his friend Friedrich Nietzsche, an idea amenable to Lou, who must have intuited that the love triangle (with herself at the apex) was the perfect configuration for maximizing her own power.

Rée wrote to Nietszche in Genoa, a letter apparently spiced with tantalizing allusions to the "Russian woman." At thirty-eight, Nietzsche was adrift, migrating—at times accompanied by his suffocatingly devoted sister Elisabeth—from one squalid Italian boardinghouse to another. Severe ill health (he suffered from syphilis, among other complaints) had forced him to give up his teaching position at the University of Basel. His much-valued friendship with Richard Wagner had ended when the composer disapproved of Nietzsche's *Human, All Too Human* and of his eugenically ill-advised friendship with Rée, a Jew so self-loathing that Rée allegedly fainted the first time Lou heard about his ethnicity.

Nietzsche replied to Rée in a tone that would characterize the trio's subsequent exchanges: confused, overheated, charged with eroticism and a strained, near-hysterical irony: "Greet this Russian girl for me, if there is any sense in doing so: I lust after souls of this kind. I even plan to go out on the prowl for them—I need them because of what I want to do in the next ten years. Marriage is another matter. I could agree at most to a two-year marriage . . ."

Given that Rée was in love with Lou, such a letter might presumably have made him wonder if the proposed threesome shouldn't be scaled back to a couple. But throughout the "Pythagorean" (as Nietzsche called it) turbulence that would engulf the three for months and would take years to subside, logic was beside the point, as was common sense, rationality, instinct, self-preservation, and most ordinary definitions of love. So the preparations went forward for the eagerly anticipated meeting between Nietszche and Lou, a drumroll that built for weeks until the April day when Nietszche found Lou and Rée in the only setting that could possibly have sufficed: St. Peter's Cathedral. There, in the side chapel where Rée liked to study, Nietzsche greeted Lou with what must be the most dramatic pickup line in the history of the muses: "from what star have we fallen together here?"

His question was like the pistol shot at the start of a race. Throughout the next six months, as loyalties and alliances fluctuated, as the trio exchanged enraptured vows and jealous reproaches, the two men learned to measure power by their closeness to Lou, who stayed firmly in control; the Lucerne photo was no joke. Lou's previous romantic experiences in St. Petersburg had demonstrated the advantages to behaving as if sex and marriage were at once beside the point and beneath consideration—a strategy that would later serve her well in her battle for dominance with her husband, Friedrich Carl Andreas. At the same time, she was discovering the strategic benefits of a triangulated relationship—a lesson she would draw on throughout her life, even as her alliances shifted from the romantic to the cerebral and professional.

Intoxicated by visions of the heady new life they planned to share, the three began to travel, together and separately, north through Italy, with Lou chaperoned by her widowed mother, still bravely struggling to rein in Lou's unconventional impulses.

In the town of Orta, north of Milan, Lou and Nietzsche left Lou's mother and Rée, and hiked up Monte Sacro. From the base to the summit was not a long distance, but the pair was gone for hours, and Rée and Madame von Salomé watched anxiously for the couple's reappearance. Nietzsche and Lou must have been aware that their return was being awaited, and so their prolonged absence must have taken on a thrilling urgency, as if they were not merely climbing the mountain but throwing themselves from its peak. That walk was, Nietzsche told Lou, "the most enchanting dream of my life, that I owe to you." In the meteoric trajectory of their friendship, it would assume enormous significance, much like Charles Dodgson's and Alice Liddell's "golden afternoon." Later, the "Lou of Orta" would become the adored love object whom Nietzsche could not reconcile with the difficult Lou who seemed to have usurped her place. Lou

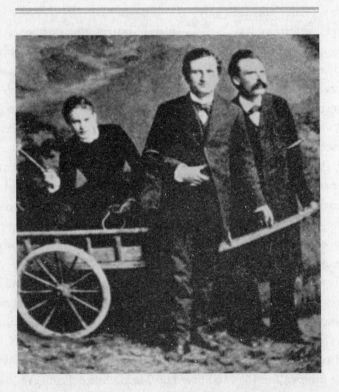

Lou von Salomé, Paul Rée, Friedrich Nietzsche, 1882.

claimed not to remember if she kissed Nietzsche on the Monte Sacro, but obviously she recalled the occasion as one which would have raised the question of whether or not a kiss was exchanged.

Nietzsche proposed marriage or didn't, depending on whom one believes. More three-way negotiations ensued, more letters avowing love and friendship, until at last—on May 13, 1882, in the Lion Park at Lucerne—they restored the balance of the "Holy Trinity," which would devote itself to work and study, and simply not bother about the fact that both men were in love with Lou.

That was the historic detente that the Lucerne photograph commemorates. In her memoir, Lou suggests that the tableau was Nietzsche's idea, but certain of her biographers—an especially disputatious and partisan crew—have argued that only the bossy Lou could have stage-managed the perverse scenario.

Farthest away from the camera, roped to one pole of the cart, Nietzsche alone seems focused on the brave future they are facing together. Mustachioed, myopic, he stares into the beyond, his entranced, otherworldly determination in ironic counterpoint to the yoke and to the riding crop his lady friend is holding. All of Rée's energy is absorbed in the effort to disappear from the picture; his palpable discomfort, preserved here for the ages, erupts in a note he wrote Lou a month or so after the photo was taken: "Picture arrived yesterday. Nietzsche superb; you and I hideous, we can argue over who should get the prize for ugliness."

Neither of them is ugly. What's striking about Lou is how she looks almost precisely the same as she does in other portraits from that period, formal pictures of her alone. Of the three, only Lou gazes into the camera with a bemusement that the tense stiffness of her shoulders belies as she simultaneously expresses and transcends her own unease in that strange tableau and her discomfort in the cart she recalled decades later as being way too small. It's us she's looking at, holding that whip. We are the ones on whom she is practicing the skill that she perfected in her career as muse: the ability to make others see the world as she does and maintain the faith that this vision is a dream that they have always shared, and are inventing, minute by minute.

THE TENSIONS, PASSIONS, and contradictions that drove Lou von Salomé inform her memoir, *Looking Back*, a book that reveals the influence of the men in her life and also bears the hallmark of her singular self-image: a female Russian mystic turned Freudian psychoanalyst.

The first thing Lou wants posterity to understand is her childhood belief in God, a close relationship with a kindly deity she conceived of as "a grandfather who spoiled me mightily, who approved of everything I did, who enjoyed giving me gifts so much it seemed his pockets were overflowing." Lou's faith in this "God-grandfather" ended after an incident involving the melting of two snowmen, a crisis which presumably seemed more serious to little Lou than it will to the adult reader.

Confronted with "the unalterable fact of a universe abandoned by God," Salomé rerouted her spiritual quest toward a "feeling of a deeply shared destiny with all things." Moving along from God to Love, she spends a chapter defining her theory of human relations: "Activated by Eros, beyond all those things which bind two beings personally or procreatively, there is another deeper relationship . . . The ecstasy which transfigures them both is not turned upon each other, but toward a third object of their mutual desire, which lifts them from the profound depths of being into their own sight, so to speak, into their own vision."

Not until the book is well under way does Lou descend to the facts of her biography: her St. Petersburg childhood in a compound facing the czar's palace, her parents, her five brothers, three of whom survived to adulthood. Her most vivid memories suggest the sort of oedipal moments one dredges up in analysis, though Lou herself was never formally analyzed; she recalls her terror that a mad dog would bite her, which would in turn make her bite her beloved papa, and her desire that her mother go swimming and drown.

Discreetly, Lou never mentions the name of Henrik Gillot, the Dutch preacher whose sermons were the rage of St. Petersburg and who was the first of the charismatic men with whom she allied herself. As always, seemingly oblivious to the limitations imposed upon her by gender, the seventeen-year-old Lou persuaded the forty-two-year-old Gillot to teach her theology, philosophy, world religions, French and German literature—subjects she pursued with an avidity her family considered unhealthy. In fact, she began to have fainting spells, one of which occurred, inconveniently, as she sat on Gillot's lap.

Gillot was the first of many men who shocked Lou by proving so dim and unevolved as to confuse the intellectual with the carnal. Gillot's plan to leave his wife and two teenage daughters and marry Lou so horrified his pupil and her mother that they fled St. Petersburg for Zurich. Lou's welcome escape from the increasingly confining city of her birth offered an early, instructive testament to the power of thwarted male desire. In Zurich, one of her professors, the esteemed theologian Alois Biedermann, wrote a description of Lou that prefigures Nietzsche's view of her and that gives the first clear indication of how she was seen by the world—the smitten male world—around her: "She has a childlike purity and integrity of character and, at the same time, a quite unchildlike, almost unfeminine, direction of her mind and independence of will."

But Zurich did nothing for Lou's health; by now she was coughing blood. And so her long-suffering mother took her to Rome and her fateful meetings with Rée and Nietszche.

DESPITE THE CREEPY NAÏVETÉ of its unintentional disclosures, the Lucerne photograph marks the most innocent, optimistic moment in the three-way misunderstanding that would prove so catastrophic not only for the lovers themselves but for a cast of subsidiary players. Within days the trio dispersed and began wrangling, by mail, about where Lou would spend the summer—with Rée's family in Stibbe, or with Nietzsche and his sister in Naumburg. Blinded by idealism and by Lou's hypnotic ability to convince them that their feelings were entirely about her *mind*, the men were unable to see—or acknowledge—the stress fractures already marring their seamless "Winterplan."

Meanwhile, there were more endearments and love notes. Rée addressed Lou as "my little snail," while Nietzsche seized every opportunity to remark on how similar he and Lou were—how readily they understood one another. ("I wonder if there has ever existed before such a *philosophical openness* as exists between us.") In the diary she kept during her visit to Nietzsche in Tautenberg, Lou wrote: "Talking with Nietzsche is very exciting, as you know. But there is a special fascination as you encounter like thoughts, like sentiments and ideas—we understand each other perfectly. Once he said to me in amazement: 'I think the only difference between us is that of age. We have lived alike and thought alike.'" Significantly, Nietzsche seems not to have thought of the other obvious difference: gender. What gives this passage additional pungency is the fact that Lou was keeping the diary for Paul Rée—evidence that Lou must have, at least on the surface, assumed that her two new life-partners were above jealousy or possessiveness, beyond taking any of this personally.

Nietszche's and Andreas-Salomé's biographers have ferociously debated the question of whether he was in love with her, a dispute that should have been resolved (regardless of what one concludes about the nature of Nietszche's sexuality) by the extreme emotionality of his letters, his unreasonable joyousness, the reports of recovered health, the expressions of hope, the anxieties on not hearing from her, the professions of admiration, the assurances that she is always on his mind: "I have thought of you much, and have shared with you in thought much that has been elevating, stirring and gay, so much so that it has been like living with my dear friends. If only you know how novel and strange that seems to an old hermit like me! How often it has made me laugh at myself!"

And what else besides love could have caused Nietzsche to so admire Lou's poem, "Hymn to Life," that he wrote a musical setting for the sentimental lyric, which ends with two lines that touched him most deeply: "If you have no more happiness to give:/ Give me your pain." Writing to his friend, the composer Peter Gast, Nietzsche seemed pleased by Gast's mistaken assumption that Nietzsche was the author of "Hymn to Life"—oddly, the same mistake that Freud would make thirty years later. "That poem was not by me. It is among the things which quite overpower me; I have never been able to read it without tears coming to my eyes; it sounds like a voice for which I have been waiting and waiting since childhood. The poem is by my friend Lou . . . She is as shrewd as an eagle and brave as a lion, and yet still a very girlish child, who perhaps will not live long."

Yet already there was trouble in this paradise of exalted ideals and delayed gratification. Lou's trip to Bayreuth with the possessive Elisabeth Nietzsche was a disaster during which, as Elisabeth reported (perhaps erroneously) to her brother, Lou flirted outrageously with the Russian artist Paul von Joukowsky, allowing him to design a dress on her body. Lou charmed Cosima Wagner and the entourage surrounding Richard Wagner, whose lost friendship was still painful for Nietzsche; worst of all, Elisabeth claimed that Lou was showing off the Lucerne photograph and boasting about the projected "Winterplan," which Nietzsche had asked her to keep secret.

During the journey from Bayreuth to Tautenberg, the tensions between Lou and Elisabeth erupted in the most celebrated catfight (no other word will quite do) in the history of philosophy. When Elisabeth criticized Lou's flirtatiousness at Bayreuth and warned her—as a sister, naturally—about the damage her reputation would suffer if she lived with Nietzsche and Rée, Lou declared (or so Elisabeth insisted) that she could spend a whole night in a room with Nietzsche without feeling the faintest temptation to sin, and that it was Nietzsche who threatened their idyll with his "dirty design of a concubinage."

The trusty Elisabeth reported this bad news to her brother, thus casting a bit of a pall on his reunion with Lou at Tautenberg. Happily, Lou and Nietzsche soon settled their differences and achieved such blissful communion that, as Lou wrote provocatively to Rée, everyone took them for a couple. But already Lou was harboring doubts about Nietzsche and about the disloyal remarks he had begun to make about his rival. ("If I ask myself what it was that began to affect my inner feelings toward Nietzsche, it was his increasing tendency to imply things with the intention of making me think less of Paul Rée.")

Once more the pair separated. Lou met Rée in Berlin, while Nietzsche went on to Leipzig, from where he wrote gloomy letters as he waited for the other two to join him. During this interval, something happened; the rivalry between Nietzsche and Rée intensified; Lou had more reservations about Nietzsche's "dark dungeons and hidden passages" and about sharing her life with the troubled philosopher.

By the time that Lou and Rée finally arrived in Leipzig, in October, the trio's enthusiasm for their "Winterplan" had ebbed. Lou and Rée returned to Berlin. Nietszche left Leipzig for Italy. In late November he sent Rée a touching note: "From time to time we shall see each other again, shall we not? Do not forget that, *from this year on*, I have suddenly become poor in love and consequently very much in need of love." As resignation—and hope—shaded into rage and disappointment, Nietzsche's correspondence grew more bitter and manipulative:

"Do not be upset by the outbreaks of my 'megalomania' or of my 'injured vanity'—and even if I should happen one day to take my life because of some passion or other, there would not be much to grieve about. What do my fantasies matter to you? (Even my truths mattered nothing to you till now.) Consider me, the two of you, as a semilunatic with a sore head who has been totally bewildered by long solitude . . . Friend Rée, ask Lou to forgive me everything—she will give me an opportunity to forgive her too. For till now I have not forgiven her."

Over the ensuing months, Nietzsche's tone turned rancorous. He called Lou a "cat, a beast of prey that pretends to be a domestic animal," a monstrosity, a brain without a soul, "this dry, dirty, nasty-smelling monkey with her false breasts." He implied that, having come from her, the poem "Hymn to Life" could only have been a gross lie, and he repudiated the lyric's totemic role in their romance. He wrote but never sent an especially vituperative letter to Rée: "So the defamation of my character stems from *you*, and Miss Salomé was only the mouthpiece, the very unclean mouthpiece for *your* thoughts about me? . . . You it was who maintained that I pursued the dirtiest of designs in regard to Miss Salomé beneath the mask of ideality?" In what may be the most revealing letter of all, the most illuminating on the subject of what Nietzsche saw in his muse and why she meant so much to him, he wrote Rée: "I would like to erase the memory of this whole painful year—not because it offends me, but because of the Lou in me."

That same December, Nietszche wrote his friend Franz Over-beck: "This last morsel of life was the hardest . . . unless I discover the alchemical trick of turning this—muck into gold, I am lost."

The need for this alchemical magic sent Nietzsche back to his work. In the six months after his final meeting with Lou and Rée in Leipzig, he had succeeded in minting gold; he'd completed the first two books of *Thus Spake Zarathustra*, and in the next few years went on to write *Beyond Good and Evil* and *The Genealogy of Morals*. Everything we imagine, or think we know, about Nietzsche militates against the suggestion that he did his most profound thinking in response to a broken heart, but that is precisely what a number of scholars and critics have suggested, most notably William Beatty Warner: "After the trauma of the Salomé episode, Nietzsche prescribes a goal for himself: to find a way to stand over and above his own experience . . . This is how Nietzsche sought to say 'yes' to the most difficult experience of his life: by reliving as Zarathustra his love affair with Lou Salomé."

Indeed, the details of Nietzsche's involvement with Lou and the language in which he described their friendship and its dissolution resonate in his work: the warnings against jealousy, the embrace of solitude, the insistence on "self-overcoming" as an analgesic, the ideal of becoming a Superman whose sights are fixed above the demeaningly human sufferings that ordinary souls must endure. The disorienting shifts in dominance and allegiance that characterized the love triangle would certainly have focused Nietzsche's attention on the "will to power." Who else but Lou is Zarathustra speaking of when he says, "Woman is not yet capable of friendship. Women are still cats and birds, or at best cows"? And how can one read Zarathustra's famous lines—"Are you visiting women? Do not forget your whip!"—without thinking of the trio in the Lucerne photographer's studio?

Unlike Lewis Carroll publicly thanking Alice for inspiring his books, unlike Rossetti compulsively painting Lizzie as Beatrice, Nietzsche never said that he wrote his great works because a twenty-one-year-old muse had put him through six months of joy and hell. It's impossible to prove that the words—power, cat, whip—so evocative of Lou made their way into Nietzsche's work because of his feelings for "the Russian woman."

So let us consider what *is* documented—and what we ourselves have observed of human behavior. Lou was not merely young and beautiful, but also convinced that the ideas she and Nietzsche discussed on the Monte Sacro and in the forest at Tautenberg were as important as life itself. And Nietszche was thirty-eight, almost blind, dependent on his sister. After *Human, All Too Human*, he had said that he would not write another book; Wagner's dislike for the work had ended their friendship and significantly reduced the social possibilities and the borrowed glamour of Nietszche's life. His letters leave no doubt that Lou made him feel energetic and hopeful, convinced that his work was worth doing. What faltering, syphilitic, solitary middle-aged man would not have been inspired by an attractive muse with such impassioned faith in his ideas—ideas that they shared?

For among Lou's qualifications as muse was the ability to recognize extraordinary men who were terrified of being *ordinary* men and to convince them of their chosenness. The courage of Nietszche's *Übermensch* would reappear in Rilke's vehement refusal to live a conventional life, and both men burned with the fire that blazes in every sentence of Lou's version of her life story.

EVEN AS NIETZSCHE was entering the period of feverish productivity that would be granted him before he collapsed in 1889 and endured eleven years of agony until his death in 1900, Lou von Salomé and Paul Rée were continuing with their plans for a studious, chaste alliance, "meant to last forever." They set up housekeeping in Berlin, amid a circle of prominent academics who referred to Lou as Her Excellency and to Rée as her Maid of Honor. Both began writing books (Lou's first novel, *Struggling for God*, was written during this interval) despite the distractions of the ongoing public scandal manufactured by the tireless Elisabeth Nietzsche, whose fury at Lou boiled on even after Lou had disappeared from her brother's life. She wrote slanderous letters about Lou to family and friends, and even suggested that the Berlin police arrest the couple for living in sin. "I warn Miss Salomé to watch out," she wrote the Overbecks. "If she should ever dare again to come near Fritz . . . and ruin poor Fritz's reputation by her compromising presence—but I will say nothing more . . ."

But the real threat to Rée and Lou's happy home was not, in the end, their former friend's shrewish sister. In 1886, Lou met a stocky,

dark-bearded, part-German, part-Armenian, part-Malaysian lin-
guistics scholar, Friedrich Carl Andreas, a meeting that she describes
as an encounter with an intractable force of nature: "Irresistible because it did not begin by manifesting itself with the force of an in-
stinctual desire, but simply appeared as an unchangeable *fact* . . . It is
almost a matter of indifference whether one compares it with colos-
sal, powerful forces, with the unrestrained actions of huge animals,
or to the effects of the most delicate, helpless creatures, like a little
bird one cannot bear to step upon."

In fact, Lou's attempt at resistance was quickly—if not easily—
overcome by Andreas's near-mad determination to marry her. On
the eve of their engagement, during a disagreement, he stabbed
himself in the chest with his pocketknife, inflicting a wound so unpleasant that the doctor called in to treat the unconscious man suspected Lou of attempted murder. How could Lou not have married
Andreas, even though her decision resulted in a final break with
Paul Rée, who was unconvinced by Lou's promise that marriage
would not affect their relationship. Perhaps Rée would have been
consoled if Lou had explained that she didn't plan to sleep with Andreas, either. But she feared that such a disclosure might compromise Andreas's reputation—a worry that apparently had ceased to
bother her by the time she wrote *Looking Back*. In the spring of 1887,
Rée concluded a night of soul-searching with Lou by leaving a note
that said, "Be merciful—Don't look for me" and heading out into
the early-morning rain.

If, as Lou later implied, she allowed Andreas to strong-arm her
into getting engaged, she was more successful in resisting his efforts
to consummate their marriage. Lou fought valiantly against her
husband's beastly nature, which she associated with his affinity for
"the world of animals." This aspect of his personality was, she believed, illustrated by a "characteristic" episode: his testing of their
new watchdog, a huge Newfoundland, by stripping naked and pretending to be a prowler. The confused pup, no doubt noticing that

the "intruder" smelled like his master, responded by growling—and jumping into Andreas's arms.

Little wonder that the philologist had a difficult time taming his baser instincts in compliance with Lou's regime, and that their struggle for dominance took the form of a battle over sex. Lou tells of waking from a nap to find Andreas trying to force himself upon her while she slept. "What seemed to first wake me was a sound; a weak sound, but one of such strange vehemence that it swept through me as if it came from an infinite distance, from some other star . . . Then my eyes opened: my arms were near a throat. My hands were encircling the throat and choking it. The sound was a rattle." This harrowing incident apparently persuaded Andreas that Lou's "physical alienation" was not merely the result of "girlish ideas, which in time would pass."

Their platonic marriage lasted for forty-three years. When Andreas was asked why he didn't divorce Lou, he replied that he couldn't imagine himself *not* married to her. Over time, they grew more estranged. ("I so seldom came to my husband with anything which concerned me deeply on a daily basis, that . . . when I did, it was like visiting a strange and distant part of the world I'd never set foot on before.") Yet later Lou would describe the pleasure she felt when, near the end of Andreas's life, he came to see her daily during the six weeks she spent in hospital; each visit was like "a reunion of two people who had returned home from a great distance."

Lou's ambivalent "sketch" of Andreas is saved for the last two chapters of *Looking Back*. Festschrift-like testimony to his gifts as a teacher alternates with acidic allusions to his shortcomings: "He could never finish anything . . . Because he could not look back upon finished and completed work, his weeks seemed to lack Sundays . . . It reached the point where I didn't share things with him which might have distracted him, even though he would have found them interesting (and what didn't interest his lively mind!)."

AFTER THEIR WEDDING, they settled in a suburb of Berlin, where their circle included artists, intellectuals, and writers such as Gerhart Hauptmann, Max Reinhardt, and August Strindberg. In the course of her travels to Paris, Vienna, and Munich, Lou befriended a host of important cultural figures, among them Knut Hamsun, Arthur Schnitzler, and Frank Wedekind, with whom she had another typical misunderstanding when he misinterpreted Lou's willingness to come to his room as a sign of sexual interest.

Whatever fragile accord Lou and Andreas reached was threatened when Lou fell in love with the journalist George Lebedour. "The first time we met I missed his name, as often happens, nor did he hear mine. The next time we were introduced I noticed that he was examining my hands very closely . . ." What Lebedour's scrutiny revealed was that Lou wore no wedding ring; he promptly intuited the truth about her marriage, and informed Lou that she was not a woman, but a girl—a line that appears to have stirred her even more deeply than Nietzsche's inquiry about which star they had fallen from together. The murderous crisis that ensued—Andreas, wrote Lou, "would rather simply stab the other person to death rather than talk things over with him"—caused the couple to renegotiate the terms of their marriage. Lou renounced Lebedour, but insisted on the freedom to go where, and do as, she pleased. In return, Andreas acquired a surrogate wife, a housekeeper whose two illegitimate children were rumored to be Andreas's and who moved with him and Lou to Göttingen when Andreas was made chair of the university's department of Asiatic Languages.

By forcing her—at long last—to acknowledge the possibility of adult sexual attraction and to reach an understanding with Andreas that would permit her to act on this somewhat tardy discovery, Lou's unhappy affair with Lebedour paved the way for her 1897 meeting with the young poet who had begun sending her his poems because he had already fallen in love with her essay, "Jesus the Jew"—and was intrigued by their shared interest in the human nature of Jesus. "Jesus the Jew" posits a Christ whose belief is severely tested and ultimately lost during his agonies on the cross, while one of Rilke's poetic "Visions of Christ" dispatches a disappointed Jesus to converse with the ghost of the mystic Rabbi Loew in the Jewish cemetery in Prague.

Fascinated by Nietzsche's work, Rilke was captivated by the idea of a woman known to have had an entanglement with the philosopher. Lou had prefaced her 1894 book on Nietszche with a letter he'd written her twelve years before, during that hopeful autumn before their friendship ended—the buoyant note in which he suggested that his musical setting of her poem "could indeed be the one small path by which we would reach the afterworld together" and importuned her, "Come to Leipzig soon! Why wait until October 2?"

Rilke, who was twenty-two, was introduced to the thirty-six-year-old Lou by a mutual friend in Munich, where Lou had gone on an extended visit and where Rilke had moved, not long before, from his native Prague. In May, Rilke—after having sent her, anonymously, a series of his poems—requested permission to call on "the famous authoress." Not long after, they spent several days together in the mountain village of Wolfrathausen, and the tone of his letters changed: "I want to see the world through you; for then I shall not be seeing the world but only you, you, you! I have never seen you without thinking that I should like to pray to you. I have never heard you without thinking that I should like to believe in you. I have never longed for you without thinking that I should like to suffer for you. I have never desired you without thinking that I should be allowed to kneel before you." Already the couple felt as if they had been predestined to find each other and chosen to stand outside (and above) the rest of the complacent, unenlightened world.

Together with Lou's friend Frieda von Bulow and intermittently with Lou's husband, Rilke and Lou began living together at Wolfrathausen. That fall, Rilke installed himself in lodgings near the Andreas home in Schmargendorf, a suburb of Berlin; not only did

Andreas tolerate this unconventional arrangement, but he appears to have welcomed the company of his wife's young friend, whom he encouraged to follow the salubrious regime he practiced with Lou: wearing loose clothing, taking nature walks, dining on whole grains and berries.

"A path through the forest led to Paulsborn, a few minutes away, past tame deer who sniffed at our pockets as we strolled along barefoot. Rainer often helped me cook in the little apartment, where the kitchen was the only place other than my husband's library that was somewhat like a living room; particularly when I was making his favorite dish, Russian-style groats, or also borsch . . . He would help me chop kindling or dry dishes in his blue Russian shirt with the red shoulders, then we would both continue quietly working in our separate studies."

The routine Lou established with Andreas and Rilke was much like the life she had imagined leading with Nietzsche and Paul Rée—another triangle, more work and study. But this time, Lou arranged things herself, having learned from sad experience to avoid the complications of including men in the planning stages. Of course, the most significant deviation from the "Winterplan" was that Lou was having a sexual relationship with one of the two men.

Like the erotic lives of so many muses, Lou Andreas-Salomé's romantic history has inspired considerable posthumous speculation— in her case, a debate about whether the sexual component of her long romance with the Viennese Dr. Friedrich Pineles preceded her involvement with Rilke. At the heart of Lou's biographers' somewhat prurient curiosity is the question of whom the virgin of thirty or so first slept with. But what set Lou apart from the muses who preceded her is her willingness to tell us about her romantic history, to offer her forthright, if poeticized and pumped-up, version of events.

In a section of her memoir apostrophizing Rilke, she writes: "If I was your wife for years, it was because you were the first *truly real* person in my life, body and man indivisibly one, unquestionably a fact of life itself. I could have confessed to you word for word what you said in declaring your love: 'You alone are real.'" The same chapter includes a story about a postcard from Rilke that makes it clear the couple was spending their afternoons in darkened, shuttered rooms:

"You wanted to remind me," Lou wrote, "of our little room on the ground floor, where you used to close the shutters to keep passersby from looking in, and only a little daylight would come in through the star-shaped hole in the shutter. When this lyrical postcard was delivered to me, filled in with black ink, bearing no message but the star-shaped space left undarkened at the top—I immediately jumped to the delighted conclusion that it was the evening star in the darkened heavens . . ." Later, when Rilke and Lou joked about their misunderstanding—the celestial spin that Lou put on Rilke's carnal reference—they concluded that "We were thinking about *our* stars, which were neither poetic nor prosaic as they rose before us, or shined down upon us, and whose reality—blessedly joyful and thrillingly serious—could never be adequately expressed."

Lou's intensity was matched and outdone by Rilke, who was even more open than Lewis Carroll in expressing his gratitude to his muse, and in celebrating her role in his work. In a poem addressed to Lou, Rilke wrote, "All that I am/stirs because of you." And in the *Florence Diary*, which Rilke kept during his 1898 voyage to Italy and which he addressed to Lou (the seemingly counterintuitive idea of a journal addressed to another person recalls the inflammatory diary of her sojourn with Nietzsche in Tautenberg that Lou passed along to Paul Rée), he wrote: "When You asked me about the future and I lay helplessly and remained awake that whole night wracked by this worry, then I knew, when in the morning I found You again, that you are the ever New, the ever Young, the eternal Goal, and for me there is one fulfillment that includes everything: to move toward YOU."

Combining febrile outpourings like these with cooler observations on Italian cities and Renaissance painters, and with reflections on the responsibility of the artist, the *Florence Diary* was intended as a love token from Rilke to Lou. The young poet was shattered when she seemed insufficiently impressed. Critics have blamed her tepid response to the *Diary* on its effusive emotionality, and on the unmistakably Nietzschean tone of many of its aphorisms, a timbre that might have had an upsetting resonance for Lou. But it's also possible that Lou, childless by design, may have been put off by Rilke's cogitations on the subject of women and maternity: "Woman's way goes always toward the child, before her motherhood and after . . . For her path is meant to lead into Life."

Shaken by the turmoil that followed in the wake of Lou's dispiriting response to the *Florence Diary*, the couple resolved that their next trip would be undertaken together. They turned their sights toward Russia, which had always played such a vital role in Lou's identity and self-presentation, and threw themselves into the study of Russian language and literature. In late April 1899, Rainer and Lou—accompanied by Andreas—set off on a pilgrimage to Lou's homeland. In Moscow, they met local writers and painters, attended an Easter mass at the Kremlin, and were granted an interview with Tolstoy. By the time they returned home, the expedition had left them thirsty for whatever they imagined they had begun to tap from the deep wellsprings of the Russian earth and the Russian soul.

A GROUP PORTRAIT, taken on a farm near the Russian village of Nisovka in the summer of 1900, is as eloquent and sly, as self-ironic and self-mythologizing as the Lucerne photograph of Lou, Nietzsche, and Paul Rée, and reveals as much about Lou's romance with Rilke as the earlier photo did about her relationship with the two philosophers, eight years before. The 1900 photograph was shot outside the home of Spiridon Drozhzhin, the so-called "peasant poet," with whom Lou and Rilke had invited themselves to stay, to the obvious consternation of the peasant poet and his family.

Lou and Rainer were on their second journey to Russia. They had come—this time without Andreas—in search of Mother Russia, and in the spirit of those Teutonic tourists one meets at Native American powwows, those busloads of Japanese jazz buffs disembarking in Harlem, soaking up local color, seeing their preconceptions confirmed, and missing the larger, truer picture. Rilke sought the Dostoyevskian sinner, the Tolstoyan peasant weeping before his waxy icons, the man of the people whose history, wrote Lou, "had been one of oppression and misery, yet whose basic nature combined submission *and* faith . . . This people called their faith by the name of 'God': no high and mighty power who lifted their burden, but someone near to them, protecting them, someone preventing any final destruction from drawing too near to this heartfelt intimacy . . ." It will be noted that the God Rilke hoped to find in Russia was nearly identical with the God-grandfather whose loss Lou reports in the beginning of *Looking Back*.

Accounts of their journey suggest a goofy, innocents-abroad comedy of errors. Their second visit to Tolstoy, at his estate at Yasnaya Polyana, was a social disaster that began with the great man's opening the door to Lou and slamming it in Rilke's face, then vanishing, leaving them to chat with his son while, from distant rooms, came the screams of a domestic fight, until at last the author reappeared, and treated them to a brisk walk around the garden and an unsolicited diatribe on the pointlessness of lyric poetry. Lou's account of the forest walk is painful and unintentionally humorous— painful, that is, for Rilke, forced to hear his hero dismiss his vocation, and humorous in that Tolstoy paid absolutely no attention to the "aged pilgrim" they encountered, the wandering holy man who was precisely the sort of character that Lou and Rainer had traveled to Russia to see.

In her memoirs, Lou chooses to recall the day as a joyous occasion: on the walk, Tolstoy lifted clusters of blue forget-me-nots to his face, as if drinking them in. And in a letter to Sofia Schill, a friend who had helped arrange the Russian tour, Rilke wrote, "We took leave of the Count with a feeling of childlike thankfulness and rich with gifts of his being."

Soon after came the visit to the "peasant poet," whose poems Rilke had translated, despite his shaky command of Russian. Drozhzhin had ignored Sofia Schill's repeated requests that he invite the couple to stay, perhaps because he had nowhere to put them—a problem solved, expensively, by building them their own hut. Well connected in Moscow and St. Petersburg literary circles, Drozhzhin was not precisely the grimy primitive Lou and Rainer had in mind, and the strains of the visit appear to have gotten to Lou, who had just come from a stay in a hut she described as having left "splinters in my fingernails and in my nerves."

The photo, taken on the steps of Drozhzhin's house, shows the hosts and guests grimly soldiering through. At the center of the group stands Lou, like a heroic statue of Victory, bearing as her weapon a garden rake, which she grasps with a corner of her paisley shawl, presumably to avoid more splinters, or dirt—a squeamishness at odds with whatever organic impulses fueled Lou and Rainer's passion for barefoot nature walks and steaming bowls of groats. Off to one side, Rilke (hands jammed in his pockets, head tilted at an awkward angle) could hardly appear more ill at ease, while Drozhzhin—with his belted smock, high boots, wild Rasputin-like hair, droopy mustache, and an open book—plays the Tolstoyan farmer-poet straight from central casting. Completing the picture are two of the poet's children, and standing at the window, a sturdy older woman—his wife?—gazes out, unsmiling as she contemplates the visitors whose presence must have occasioned so much extra work and expense.

Lou's affair with Rilke had survived periods of tension and misunderstanding, of tantrums (Rainer's) and of withdrawals (Lou's).

But by the end of the Russian expedition, Lou's nerves were so badly frayed that she began to separate from Rainer, a process she describes in *Looking Back*. After a troubling incident involving Rilke's sudden, paralyzing fear of passing a certain tree in the forest (" 'No, no! Not that one! This One!' And I could almost see the tree starting to turn eerie for you") Lou suggested that Rilke—for his own good, of course—might be better off without her: "Now it was necessary for you to enter into open spaces and freedom as quickly as possible, to develop everything within you fully."

But though the Russian trip may have exacerbated the couple's problems and driven them apart, both recalled the journey as an unqualified success and as a glorious bridge they crossed together, thrusting them into whole new lives and changing their work forever. Writing to the scholar Herman Pongs about the development of his art, Rilke thanks two muses, Lou and her native land: "Then came the influence of Russia . . . it was due to a person who was close to me and who summed it up in her own nature, and now, as you correctly realize, the way to my own individual insight was prepared." If Lou and Rainer saw in Russia only what they expected to see, what ultimately mattered was what they *thought* they saw—for example, the two peasant art critics whom Rilke observed in a museum and who would forever embody for him the pure and direct response to art, indeed, the reason for creating it:

"Standing before a large painting entitled *Grazing Cattle*, one of them remarked with annoyance: 'Cows! We know all about them! So what?' The other reproached him with an almost crafty look: 'Those cows are painted for you. So you'll love them, *that's* why they're painted. You have to love them, even though they have nothing to do with you, you see?' . . . And it was Rainer who provided the true epiphany: the way he stared at the peasant, the way the words were torn from him in his broken Russian: *'You know . . .'* "

Always eager to trace everything back to the religious impulse, Lou credits the journey with having taught Rainer to associate poetry with prayer. For Rainer, too, "prayer" and "Russian" would become a sort of shorthand for authenticity and intensity. Later, in a letter to Lou, he would summon up memories of their time in Russia and of their shared experiences, squandered because he had not turned them into lyrics, had not heeded the *necessity* of converting life into art: "Everything that is truly seen *must* become a poem." Memories of Russia would continue to resurface throughout his oeuvre, for example in the twentieth "Sonnet to Orpheus": "Thoughts of an evening long ago, it was springtime, in Russia—a horse—He came bounding from the village, alone, white, with a hobble attached to one leg, to stay alone in the fields all night, how the mane beat against his neck to the rhythm of his perfect joy . . ."

Later, Rilke would disown his earliest poems, which do in fact contain sentimental, derivative lines that might embarrass an older artist looking back on his beginnings. Yet his assessment of the *Book of Hours*, the long work he began around the time of the first trip to Russia, remained more positive. And it was during the optimistic, productive period between the two Russian journeys that Rilke wrote—in one night, he claimed—his *Lay of the Love and Death of Cornet Christopher Rilke*, which, after it was published in a revised form in 1906, would make him famous. The 1912 Insel-Verlag edition sold 8,000 copies in three weeks, and another 140,000 over the next five years.

Set in 1663, in Hungary, during the Turkish Wars, the prose poem, written in snapshot-like vignettes, narrates the story of a young Austrian cavalry soldier, exhausted by fear and homesickness, who steals a few hours of warmth, pleasure, and peace—of civilization—in the midst of a brutal campaign. Billeted in a castle, he attends a feast, falls in love with a mysterious woman with whom he spends the night, is awakened by the call to arms, and is killed the following day. Each brief section combines the silvery precision of a knifeblade with the lapidary gorgeousness of a Gothic stained-glass window, an *animated* stained-glass window. The poem is as vivid, cinematic, and noisy (thundering horses, clashing swords, the shrieks and prayers of the dying) as a battle scene in a Hollywood costume epic.

The love scene between the young cornet and the mysterious lady takes place in a dark tower room: "They grope before them like blind people and find each the other as they would a door. Almost like children that dread the night, they press close into each other. And yet they are not afraid. There is nothing that might be against them: no yesterday, no morrow; for time is shattered. And they flower from its ruins.

"He does not ask: 'Your husband?'

"She does not ask: 'Your name?'

"For indeed they have found each other, to be unto themselves a new generation.

"They will give each other a hundred new names and take them all off again, gently, as one takes an earring off."

As risky as it is to draw any sort of parallel between the life and the work, it's hard to read this passage without being struck by the fact that it was written by a man whose muse, a married woman, had, not long before, changed his name from René into Rainer.

BY THE TIME Lou and Rainer returned from their second Russian journey at the end of August 1900, it had been decided—*Lou* decided—that she would go to Schmargendorf without Rainer, who would rent a house in the artists' colony at Worpswede. Soon, however, Rilke was again staying near Lou, trying to attract her attention with poems in Russian, dreaming of yet another trip to Lou's homeland on the banks of the Volga, and writing tender letters to Clara Westhoff, a sculptor and one of the two "girls in white" who—together with her friend, the painter Paula Becker—had enchanted him in Worpswede. By the end of 1900, even Rainer had to admit that things had reached an impasse with Lou. Some time around the new year, Rainer and Clara Westhof agreed to marry.

Lou was horrified. For if she felt drained by Rainer's needs, she was still unwilling to see them fulfilled by someone else. In February, she wrote Rilke a letter she called her "last message" or "last appeal"—a much-analyzed document remarkable for the imperious, heartless self-absorption disguised (from Lou herself, one senses) as compassion and concern. What's appalling is her suggestion that her former lover would never find—nor should he bother seeking—happiness, a goal she appeared to interpret as a betrayal of their resolve to lead extraordinary lives, although, throughout her *own* life, Lou made quite a point of her natural gift for joy.

Helpfully, Lou informed Rilke that his only hope lay in his work; he was simply too mentally ill for marriage; his whiny melancholia had turned her passion for him into "tragic guilt." Having grown "into my youth" on their Russian journey, Lou had watched Rilke disappear from her sight, like a speck in the great Volga landscape. Having accepted the "great plan of my life," Lou called out to Rilke to "go the same way towards your dark God! He can do what I can no longer do with you . . . He can bless you to sunshine and ripeness." Meanwhile, Rilke should refrain from contacting her except in case of dire emergency: "If one day, far in the future, you are in despair, you have a home with us in the worst hour."

Clearly, Lou could play the punitive, sadistic mother as well as the nurturing, comforting one, and her letter reveals the aggressive, unyielding quality of her struggle for self-determination—a battle-to-the-death she fought reflexively, as if Andreas were once again pinning her to the sofa, even when her independence was not at stake. The "last appeal" is breathtaking in its sheer meanness, especially in view of what—as the future would prove—Lou still meant to Rilke.

Unhappily for Rainer, Lou's analysis of his character and his destiny was all too accurate. He and Clara were married in April. By August, he wrote his friend Emanuel von Bodman: "A good marriage is that in which each appoints the other guardian of his solitude, and shows him this confidence, the greatest in his power to bestow. A *togetherness* between two people is an impossibility . . ." Rainer's and Clara's daughter was born in December 1901, and by the following summer he had left his wife and child and gone to Paris to write a monograph on Rodin.

Two years after receiving the "last message," Rilke wrote Lou from Paris, asking if they could meet again; she replied that it would be best, for a while, if their friendship remained purely epistolary. Her grudging, partial acquiescence was all Rainer needed; it unleashed a flood of feeling and page after page of confessional prose. From Worpswede, he sent his muse an account of his time in Paris that made it seem as if he had been hoarding his memories of the city in anticipation of the day when he could hand them on to Lou. The letter is mined with references—a description of a Baudelaire poem as "awkward and beautiful as the prayer of a Russian"—evoking their shared past. Rilke held back nothing in his desperation to explain all that he had suffered: "O Lou, I was so tormented day after day. For I understood all those people, and although I went around them in a wide arc, they had no secret from me. I was torn out of myself into their lives, right through all their lives, through all their burdened lives. I often had to say aloud to myself that I was not one of them, that I would go away again from that horrible city in which they will die . . ."

Three weeks later, he sent Lou another impassioned letter in which he discussed his impressions of Rodin, and in which he formulated his ideas about the centrality of *things* in an artist's vision— a theory of poetics that marked a significant breakthrough in his own work, and which would contribute to the brilliance and originality of the lyrics in the 1907 *New Poems*. He essentially admitted that his muse was correct in advising him to sacrifice everything, to dedicate his entire existence to work: "O Lou, in one of my poems that is successful, there is much more reality than in any relationship or affection that I feel . . . I know that I too may ask and seek for no other realizations than those of my work; there my house is, there are the women I need, and the children that will grow up and live a long time."

Both Nietzsche and Rilke, it will be noted, commenced their most creative and important work in the period immediately following their separation from Lou. Perhaps it was just coincidence, and yet it seems clear that Lou (whom Freud would later refer to as "the great understander") offered both men a generous, deceptively unlimited abundance of understanding, admiration, encouragement, a sense of a common mission, a vision of the future, and the explicit or implicit promise that they would enter that future together. The abrupt and shocking retraction of that promise was (as much as Lou herself) the muse that inspired them to seek out the consolations and distractions of work, and to re-create, alone and for themselves, some version of what they had counted on sharing with Lou. When Lou ceased understanding, it was necessary for them both to make the world understand, in her place.

The countless ways in which Lou guided and instructed her adoring young pupil—from the barefoot nature walks to the Russian journey to the insistence on spiritualizing every aspect of daily experience—would reappear, transmuted, in Rilke's strongest poems, from the *New Poems* through the *Sonnets to Orpheus* and the *Duino Elegies*, transformed by Rilke's talent into something that Lou, for all her originality and Bohemian free-spiritedness, was ultimately too conventional and prosaic to fathom. In her 1928 book on Rilke, she criticized the poet as a sort of overreacher who attempted too much in his art, who had poached on the territory of religion, and in the process ruined his life. While the ideas expressed in the book are, so to speak, pure *Lou*, they fall egregiously short of offering a useful reading of Rilke, and can't help but remind readers of Lou's admission, in her memoirs, that initially she was more drawn to Rilke as a man than because of any feeling for his work.

For the rest of his life, even after Lou permitted him to see her again, even after they resumed their intense (but now platonic) friendship, traveling together, exchanging work and ideas, Rilke continued to write to her—from Italy, from Spain, from Austria— letters in which he grappled with his personal demons and reported on the satisfactions and terrors of poetic composition. In the final days of 1911, he composed the most famous of his poems to Lou.

> *Only plunged toward you*
> *does my face cease being only display, grows*
> *into you and twines on darkly,*
> *endlessly, into your sheltered heart . . .*

> *. . . all that I am*
> *stirs me because of you.*

He wrote her from Duino to describe the agony he had undergone while working on *The Notebooks of Malte Laurids Brigge*, and to thank her yet again for the all-important role she had played in his emotional life, and in his education as a poet. "God knows, your being was so truly the door by which I first came into the open: now I keep coming from time to time and place myself straight against the doorpost on which we marked my growth in those days. Allow me this dear habit and love me."

This same letter contains a paragraph suggesting that Rilke and Lou had discussed the usefulness—for Rainer—of Lou's latest intellectual passion: "I am thinking less than before of a doctor. Psychoanalysis is too basic a help for me, it helps once and for all, it clears out, and to find myself cleared out one day would perhaps be even more hopeless than this disorder."

DRAMATIC, IMPOSING, clad in furs, Lou—who had written Freud, asking his permission to attend his Wednesday Evening Lectures—descended upon Viennese psychoanalysis in the au-

tumn of 1912. A celebrated novelist and essayist, the friend of so
many artists and, as everyone knew, the former lover of two major
writers, the 51-year-old Lou dazzled Freud and at least some of
his followers with her expansive Russian soul and with her talent
for happiness. An energetic, larger-than-life woman surrounded
by more or less neurotic men, Lou was singled out by Freud for
the "Sunday" quality she brought the workaday world around her;
later he would say that she seemed to view psychoanalysis as a
"Christmas present" he had brought her. The power that happiness—that her insistent self-presentation as a happy person—
must have conferred on Lou in that somewhat gloomy crowd was
a magnified version of the power that, according to Leopardi, automatically accrues to a group of people heard laughing among
themselves at a party.

The previous fall, Lou had been introduced to the Viennese
professor at the Weimar Psychoanalytic Congress, which she attended with her friend—and much younger lover—Poul Bjerre, a
married Swedish neurologist. Freud replied to Lou's request to
audit his lectures in a friendly, jocular tone that established the
mood of the correspondence that spanned more than twenty years,
during which Freud's salutations would change from *Frau Andreas* to
Dearest Lou even as Freud would remain, to Lou, *Professor* or *Professor
Freud.* From early on, there are frequent references to Rilke, and it
seems probable that Lou's friendship with the well-known poet
(*The Lay of the Love and Death of Cornet Christopher Rilke* was a current
best-seller) added to her own appeal and increased Freud's eagerness to meet her.

After Lou mentioned a walking tour she and Rilke took together, Freud referred to his youngest son's enthusiasm for the poet.
(In this same exchange of letters, Lou asked Freud for a photograph
of himself, and Freud agreed to send one.) Thanks to Lou, Rilke
and Freud's son met, prompting Freud to write, "Please tell Herr R.
M. Rilke that I also have a nineteen-year-old daughter who knows

his poems, some of them by heart, and who envies her brother in Klagenfurt the greetings he received."

Freud was disappointed by Rilke's refusal to be analyzed; the poet "made it quite clear to us in Vienna that 'no lasting alliance can be forged with him.' Cordial as he was on his first visit, we have not been able to persuade him to pay us a second." And Lou hastened to reassure her Professor: "No, do not misinterpret Rainer's attitude. It was not due to any estrangement on his part, but only to his shattered state of mind. I know quite well what he really feels about you." But in fact, according to one of Lou's former patients, Lou had advised Rilke against psychoanalysis. "While a successful analysis might free an artist from the devils that beset him, it would also drive away the angels that help him create. A germ-free soul is a sterile soul."

The rumors surrounding Lou's involvement with Nietzsche also piqued Freud's interest. In 1932, when he heard that Lou was writing her memoirs, his thoughts tracked directly to the great mystery (and scandal) of Lou's past. "I was very pleased to hear that you are working on your memoirs. It has often annoyed me to find your relationship to Nietzsche mentioned in a way which was obviously hostile to you and which could not possibly correspond with the facts. You have put up with everything and have been far too decent. I hope that now at last you will defend yourself, even though in the most dignified way."

But in the early months of Lou's association with the Viennese psychoanalysts, her history with the philosopher and the poet seems to have mattered less to Freud than her ongoing friendship with a rival analyst. In her second letter to Freud, Lou informed him that she was considering attending Alfred Adler's Thursday Evening Discussions. "I have not yet done so, because I felt too strongly the need to assimilate quietly the impressions which I had received from you the day before. And before I do attend them I would like to tell you how these impressions predominate in everything—even in what seems to deviate from them—that occurs in my Vienna visit and how they give my visit its decisive character."

Once more, Lou's instinct for triangulation moved her to reassure Freud that he was the favorite even as she insisted on her freedom to see his rival, if she pleased. Freud submitted to this latest version of the test she had contrived to screen for male possessiveness. Indeed, Freud told Lou that she, apparently alone, was exempted from the new requirement that analysts and their patients choose between himself and Adler: "I would never dream, dear lady, of imposing such a restriction on you. Bearing this situation in mind I would only ask you—as though you were in a state of artificial split personality—that you make no reference to your contact with us when with them, and vice versa."

Lou had long since learned how to capitalize on a rivalry to consolidate her power base and intensify an alliance. Her next letter—in which she defended certain of Adler's theories and apologized for having missed Freud's lecture—elicited a reply that seems quite startling in light of the fact that only *two weeks* had passed since Lou began her studies in Vienna:

"If I understand you rightly, you would like a personal exchange of ideas. I should myself have proposed it definitely a long time ago, if the business of founding the new psychoanalytic journal had not added to my usual activities.

"I do not know whether a discussion after ten o'clock at night conforms with your daily routine, but I have no free time earlier than that. If you will do me the honor of a visit at such a late hour, I shall gladly engage to see you safely home . . . I missed you in the lecture yesterday. . . . I have adopted the bad habit of directing my lecture to a definite member of the audience, and yesterday I fixed my gaze as if spellbound at the place which had been kept for you."

However ironic and jesting its tone, Freud's confession—that he had begun to lecture to *her*, and that he had focused, "spellbound," on the place reserved for her—is a remarkable admission from a distinguished doctor (married, the father of several children and of a major scientific movement) to make to a newcomer to psychoanalysis, and a *woman*, at that. Perhaps Lou's age might have seemed to Freud (as it has, to her biographers) to defuse any suggestion that the source of the "spell" was romantic. But time had not yet eradicated her sexual appeal for the much younger men (Bjorre, Tausk, Emil von Gebsattel) with whom she conducted love affairs and passionate friendships during this same period.

The familiar patterns of Lou's relationships—the breakneck speed at which intimacy was established, the mutual intoxication of mission and communion, and the inevitable triangulation—asserted themselves once again in this, the most amicable of Lou's meetings with remarkable men. Just as Lou saw no reason for any ill will between Nietzsche and Paul Rée, she refused to choose between Freud and Adler.

In the spring of 1914, in response to a letter from Lou suggesting that she had begun to side with Freud, Adler sent Lou a vituperative reply on the subject of Freud and his followers, "their busy-busy grabbing and pilfering," their cynicism and self-delusion. Just as she had thoughtfully confronted Nietzsche and Paul Rée with evidence of the other's betrayal, Lou passed the slanderous note on to Freud, who wrote, "That you should have permitted me to see your correspondence with Adler I take as a sign of great trust on your part. The letter shows his specific venomousness, and is very characteristic of him . . . He is a loathsome individual."

But if Lou's handing over of the letter signaled a declaration of allegiance—the choosing of Freud over Adler—she had already introduced another male into the equation. Viktor Tausk was "the most unconditionally devoted" of Freud's disciples, but unlike Lou, he had the misfortune to irritate his teacher. Pondering "the whole tragedy of Tausk's relation to Freud," Lou examined her own problems with her younger colleague in a passage that explicitly recalls her misunderstandings with Gillot, Nietzsche, Andreas, and all the other luckless suitors whose intentions fell so far short of Lou's hopes and plans for them: "He is deceiving himself about me. In the long run no helpful relationship is possible; there can be none when reality is cluttered by the wraiths of unabreacted primal reminiscences. An impure tone resonates through everything, buzzing as it were with murmurings from within."

In Lou's insistence that her friendship with Freud be "free from the usual conventionalities and politenesses," one can hear echoes of what she must have told Nietszche, Rée, Rilke, and Gillot. In her letters to Freud, we can observe the style and hear the voice that must have entranced Paul Rée on those moonlit walks among the ruins of the Forum: the seductiveness, the admiration, the conspiratorial sympathy, alternating with, and underlying, the airy flights into the realm of pure ideas. And beneath everything, the sublime *understanding* that made Lou the ideal muse.

When Freud responded coolly ("It may seem boring and insincere if I reply to each of your letters with compliments.") to the news that Lou had sent "a little book" about psychoanalysis to the printer, Lou wrote him an uncharacteristically insecure letter in which she expressed her worries about the depth and accuracy of her comprehension: "I am particularly anxious to avoid any sort of misunderstanding." And Freud's reply seems, almost spookily, like something that could have been written by Nietzsche, Paul Rée, or Rilke.

"You are 'an understander' *par excellence*; and in addition your commentary is an amplification and an improvement on the original. I am always particularly impressed when I read what you have to say on one of my papers. I know that in writing I have to blind myself artificially in order to focus all the light on one dark spot, renouncing cohesion, harmony, rhetoric and everything which you call symbolic . . . Then you come along and add what is missing, build upon it, putting what has been isolated back into its proper context. I cannot always follow you, for my eyes, adapted as they are to the dark, probably couldn't stand strong light or an extensive range of vision. But I haven't become so much of a mole as to be incapable of enjoying the idea of a brighter light and more spacious horizon, or even to deny their existence."

Their correspondence would continue until Lou's death in 1937, two years before Freud's. After Lou returned to Göttingen and began to practice analysis, she frequently consulted her teacher on individual cases, and they communicated, often at great length, on those aspects of psychoanalytical theory (the nature of narcissism and of sublimation) that engaged them both. Freud appears to have been genuinely intrigued by Lou's observations on female sexuality, though on occasion—mostly in the early letters—he expresses a certain impatience with her compulsive need to synthesize, a tendency which led to excessive abstraction and to the disorderly, illogical, conflation of disparate ideas: "Every time I read one of your letters of appraisal I am amazed at your talent for going beyond what has been said, for completing it and making it converge at some distant point. Naturally I do not always agree with you. I so rarely feel the need for synthesis."

Later, in 1930, Freud would reflect more charitably on the broadly inclusive nature of Lou's mind ("You are always able to add depth and to connect things; I am happy if I succeeded in isolating something.") and on the long-term benefits of their intellectual relationship: "I am delighted to observe that nothing has altered in our respective ways of approaching a theme, whatever it may be. I strike up a—mostly very simple—melody; you supply the higher octaves for it; I separate the one from the other, and you blend what has been separated into a higher unity; I silently accept the limits imposed by our subjectivity, whereas you draw express attention to them. Generally speaking we have understood each other and are at one in our opinions. Only, I tend to exclude all opinions except one, whereas you tend to include all opinions together." In addition to a passing reference to her as his muse and to the suggestion that part of his research may have been built on ground first broken by Lou ("If I should be in a position to continue to develop my theories you may perhaps recognize with satisfaction several new things as having been anticipated or even announced by yourself."), this marks the extent of Freud's admission of a scientific or philosophical debt to Lou.

Such acknowledgments were notably low key compared to the expressions of gratitude she had come to expect from Rilke. But Lou seemed glad enough to exchange the responsibility of being a pioneer and guide for the less demanding duties of a follower and colleague. Lou seemed not to have minded (or noticed) the patronizing quality of Freud's reaction to her book *My Thanks to Freud*. After counseling her to change the "all too personal title," Freud remarked that "for the first time I have been struck by something exquisitely feminine in your intellectual approach. When in my annoyance at the eternal ambivalences I am prepared to leave everything higgledy-piggledy, you tidy everything up, put everything in order and show that it is possible to be quite comfortable in that way too." In a subsequent letter, he comes up with an alternate title ("My Thanks to Psychoanalysis") and offers a double-edged appraisal of the work: "It is the finest thing of yours I have read, an involuntary proof of your superiority over all of us—in accord with the heights from which you descended to us . . . Not everything you deal with was immediately intelligible to me, and not all of it equally worth knowing." All of this presages the somewhat equivocal tone of the tribute to Lou that Freud wrote after her death: "She was of an unusual modesty and discretion. She never spoke of her own poetic and literary productions. She obviously knew where the real values of life were to be sought."

In the autumn of 1921, Freud asked Lou to stay at his house in Vienna. Freud confessed that he had invited Lou mainly for his daughter Anna, whose female friends had all left town. His plan worked beautifully. Lou and Anna discussed beating fantasies and daydreams, and the next year, Anna paid Lou a return visit. Her ten days in Göttingen allowed them to continue their conversation, though Anna reported having some trouble in keeping up with Lou, who at sixty-one still retained the ability to think out loud that had dazzled Rée in Rome and Nietzsche on the Monte Sacro.

Though Lou was never Anna's analyst, their friendship—which deepened over the course of Anna's frequent stays at Göttingen— performed such an obviously therapeutic function that Lou and the Professor discussed "Daughter-Anna" much as they did the cases Lou saw in practice: "Anna is splendid and self-assured," wrote Freud, "and I often think how much she probably owes to you." In 1922, while Anna was staying with Lou, an incident occurred that must have brought back fond memories of Lou's past: The mathematician Paul Bernays attempted to kiss Anna, and the distraught young woman rebuffed his attentions. With maternal pride, Lou told Freud, "Altogether Anna has stirred up quite a storm of passion here, as she will tell you, but nevertheless returns home totally unseared by the flames."

Freud's gratitude for Lou's success with his daughter may have influenced his suggestion that she be accepted into the Vienna Society, a project that Anna, who had recently gained admittance, supported. Exempted from the requirement of giving a formal lecture, Lou expressed her relief: "What Daughter-Anna succeeded in reality in doing, i.e. in giving the lecture required for membership, I should never have achieved successfully."

Clearly, Freud, Lou, and Anna enacted their own perverse family romance. Happily for the sake of domestic harmony, all three were relieved when Lou advised Anna to ignore the misdirected friends who counseled her to leave home and separate from her father. Anna's determination to stay, and Freud's desire to have her stay, were reinforced in 1923 when Freud became ill and underwent the first of the many disfiguring surgeries that made his final years a torment. "You are right," Anna wrote Lou, "I would not leave him now under any circumstances." And Lou understood, though loyalty in sickness and health was not her particular talent.

As Lou and Freud grew older, age became an increasingly common theme in their correspondence. In a 1927 letter wishing Freud well on his birthday, Lou painted her current life in the joyously affirmative tones that had become her trademark:

"I am stretching my old bones in the sun today, and my husband is doing the same. This brought us to discuss the fact that old age really has its 'sunny aspects' . . . I am frankly curious about what remains unraveled for me in the wondrous skein of life . . . I admit unreservedly the almost idiotically infantile nature of this inner attitude. Nevertheless it continues to laugh mockingly at all my superior wisdom . . . bestowing on the whole ensuing day something of this blissful idiocy."

For once, Lou's good mood proved too much for Freud, whose dejected reply was barely brightened by its grudging pinch of hope: "How wonderful—there you have a husband and wife, the one ten years older and the other ten years younger than oneself, and they still enjoy the sun. But with me crabbed age has arrived—a state of total disillusionment, whose sterility is comparable to a lunar landscape, an inner ice age. But perhaps the central fire is not yet extinguished, the sterility only affects peripheral layers, and later perhaps, if there is time, another eruption may come."

Lou seems to have interpreted those *eruptions* in a somewhat more physiological and less cerebral sense than Freud apparently intended. Tellingly, she relegates such eruptions to the past and puts the cheeriest possible face on the losses of age. ("Such a series of eruptions is after all a series of splendid benefactions, and our grateful memory of them can never really die away.") And she rapidly segues from celebrating the compensatory pleasures of age into

boasting about how slow her own old age—specifically, meno-
pause—was in finally arriving:

"I had feared that old age might set in too late (because speaking physiologically it had only set in at sixty) and that in this way I
might be cheated of what old age specifically has to offer . . . For
when one leaves erotic experience in the narrower sense, one is at
the same time also leaving a cul-de-sac, however marvelous it may
be, where there is only room for two abreast; and now one enters
onto a vast expanse—the expanse of which childhood too was a part
and which for only awhile we were bound to forget."

Despite Lou's good cheer, Freud's illness worsened. On hearing
that her beloved Professor had been in pain, she described the mugging she would inflict on the person responsible for his suffering, if
such a person could be found. It never occurred to Lou to lay a shred
of blame anywhere near the all-powerful, all-knowing God she so
adored, nor did she feel the need to reconcile the idea of God with
the problem of evil. It was as if she had settled that during her
childhood spiritual crisis over the melting snowmen, and was free to
do what she claimed we all did: to create a God in her own image,
and to let that image shape her. For Lou, God was essentially like
herself: a joyous, generous being, incapable of causing the slightest
pain.

Lou's account of her last visit to Freud in 1928 is deeply moving.
Though it was hard for him to speak, they carried on a lively conversation during which Lou reminded him of how, early in their
friendship, he had made fun of her poem "Hymn to Life," the lyric
that had played such a central role in her relationship with Nietzsche, and which Freud had mistakenly believed to have been written by the philosopher himself. In response to the poem's last
lines—"If you have no more happiness to give:/Give me your
pain."—Freud had said, "For me it would be enough to have one really bad cold in the head to be cured of such wishes." Recalling those
verses as she spoke with the gravely ill professor, Lou burst into

tears and exclaimed, " 'The very thing I once wrote that enthusias-
tic drivel about—you have done it!' ".

Freud, Lou reported, didn't reply, but simply put his arm around
her.

BY THEN, Lou had already gained a certain amount of practice in
the art of saying farewell to the men she loved; only Freud outlived
her, and not by very long. In 1901, Paul Rée died in a suspicious fall
from a mountain during a hiking expedition, an apparent accident
rumored to have masked a suicide. In her memoir, Lou mourns the
fact that Rée was born too early to have reaped the benefits of psychoanalysis, which, she hints, might have saved him. But the talking
cure did little to rescue Viktor Tausk, who killed himself in 1919,
and whose death prompted a chilling exchange between Lou and
the Professor.

"Poor Tausk," wrote Freud, "who you for some time favored with
your friendship, committed suicide on 3.7 . . . I confess that I do not
really miss him; I had long realized that he could be of no further
service, indeed that he constituted a threat to the future . . . I would
have dropped him long ago if *you* hadn't raised him so in my estimation." Lou absorbs the shock of her former lover's death so well that,
after briefly mourning that "frenzied soul with a tender heart," she
goes on to join Freud in their frosty *pas de deux* on Viktor Tausk's
grave:

"What you write: 'that fundamentally you do not miss him,'
seems to me not merely understandable; for I too felt him to be a
kind of 'threat to the future' both for you and for psycho-analysis . . .
He knew my misgivings about him, and my apprehensions about his
determination to pursue an academic career in Vienna. In March he
wanted to come to Munich, but I was against it. His last letter, like
many earlier ones, I did not answer. And he was justified in writing
a year ago: 'No one wants the company of an unhappy wretch—not
even you.' No, not even I."

None of this would have come as a surprise to Poul Bjerre, who, in an interview with H. F. Peters, remembered being shocked by Lou's nonchalant response to Paul Rée's suicide. " 'Don't you have any pangs of conscience?' I asked her. But she merely laughed and said that conscience was a sign of weakness. I realize that this may have been bravado, but she did seem unconcerned about the consequences of her actions and was in this respect more like a force of nature than a human being."

Bjerre, too, had not entirely shaken off the effects of Lou's spell, and some lingering chemistry of enchantment and disillusion enabled him, decades later, to give a penetrating summary of Lou's character and of her effects on others; his layered, ambivalent portrait described her ability to function as muse for the men she inspired. "She had the gift of entering completely into the mind of the man she loved. Her enormous concentration fanned, as it were, her partner's intellectual fire . . . Her unusually strong will liked to triumph over men . . . I think Nietzsche was right when he said that Lou was a thoroughly evil woman. Evil, however, in the Goethean sense: evil that produces good. She hurt me much but she also gave me much. . . . In my talks with Lou things became clear to me that I might not have found by myself. Like a catalyst she activated my thought processes. She may have destroyed lives and marriages but her presence was exciting. One felt the spark of genius in her. One grew in her presence."

Grief and regret were incompatible with Lou's dedication to her own unwavering happiness, and when Friedrich Carl Andreas died suddenly, in 1930, at the age of eighty-four, she recorded "a feeling of purest joy, like a miracle, like grace," occasioned by the fact that her husband had not been forced to endure the agonies that her dear Professor had suffered for so long. Indeed, the kindest things Lou says about her late husband in *Looking Back* concern his ability to understand and appreciate *her* exuberance and bliss:

"No matter how busy he was, my husband always had a wonderful sense of one thing: whether and to what extent the other person was happy and at peace. One proof of this made a deep impression on me. I had started to write a story, something that was out of character for me by then, since I'd completely given up the habit of writing once I started working with psychoanalysis—and the overload of the two types of concentration had totally absorbed me. When I was finished, I laughed and said, with a somewhat guilty conscience, that I must have been hard to be around, and quite worthless, during all that time. To which my husband replied, almost in jubilation, with a shining face I'll never forget: 'You've been so happy!' "

FOR ALL THE BUBBLY joyfulness that, in theory, leavened Lou's daily existence, the fact is that she and her men took nothing lightly. It was to be expected that they would not easily let one another go, and that the ties binding Lou to Nietzsche and to Rilke remained in place, alternately tightening and slackening, until all of them were dead.

Dying of leukemia, in a Swiss sanitarium, at the end of December 1926, Rilke kept importuning his doctors to consult Lou Andreas-Salomé, who would know what was wrong with him and could make sense of his terrible death. Two weeks earlier he had written Lou: "I don't know how many hells, you know how I have placed pain, physical pain, in my orders, unless it's an exception and again a way into the Open. And now it covers me. It unloosens me. Day and night." Rilke's doctors informed Lou of the gravity of his condition and of the necessity that the patient be kept ignorant of how little time he had left. Lou acceded to this medical advice—the conventional wisdom of the day—but began to write Rainer daily.

By then, Nietzsche had been dead for a quarter century. After a long period of increasing mania and euphoria, he collapsed on the street in Turin, his arms around the neck of a horse he had watched being beaten. Eleven years of madness followed, of hospitalizations and releases, of delusion and paralysis, until he died in 1900. Confined to a clinic in Basel, where one physician's diagnosis read, "claims he is a famous man and asks for women all the time," he drew a picture of a lion that resembled the lion statue in the Lucerne park where he and Lou pledged to share a future of work and study. In Nietszche's drawing the Swiss shield and cross share the page with two lovers embracing in the shadow of the lion.

And Lou? Nietzsche—and his parting insults—must have remained on her mind. After her mastectomy, in 1935, she said that Nietzsche was right, after all. Now she did have a false breast. According to her notably unsympathetic biographer, Rudoph Binion, Lou took on the traits that she observed—and ultimately rejected— in Nietzsche. "She contracted personal habits of his, such as alternately working long weeks or months in solitude, then living socially awhile. She took up physical attitudes of his . . . such as his cautious, pensive gait and his air of 'hearkening to all things' . . . But what she took from Nietzsche was chiefly intellectual, from pet expressions (such as going out 'among men' and returning 'to myself') to historical theses . . . by way of his new psychological approach according to which the psyche is an archive, culture denotes inhibition, memory is weaker than forgetfulness, perception works to prevent seeing too much and intellection to prevent understanding too much . . . and one's sexuality informs the highest reaches of one's mind." Of course the ideas that Binion claims Lou absorbed from Nietzsche could just as easily have been borrowed from Rilke or Freud. For in her capacity as the muse and great understander—the great synthesizer—Lou managed to combine, in herself, the ideas of three apparently different men.

After an old age spent tranquilly in Göttingen, working on her memoir, enjoying the privacy interrupted only by visits from admiring young men and women, including her devoted literary executor, Ernst Pfeiffer, Lou died in 1937, at the age of seventy-five, of uremia and not of the breast cancer that she had supposed would kill her. In her final hours, she said that when she allowed her thoughts to roam, she found no one but herself.

GALA DALÍ

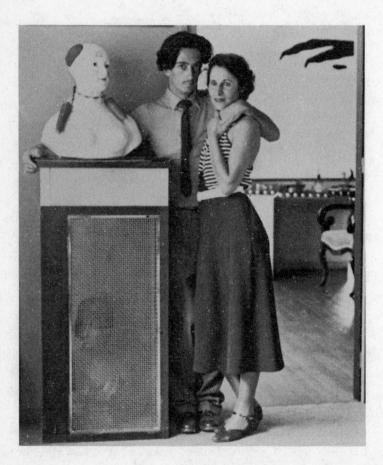

Salvador and Gala Dalí. (Brassaï)

Few artists have prepared more elaborately for a visitation from the muse than Salvador Dalí did on that August morning in 1929 as he dressed to spend a day at the beach with the exotic band of Surrealists who had descended on his family home in the fishing village of Cadaqués. The poet Paul Eluard, his wife Gala, their daughter Cecile, René and Georgette Magritte, Luis Buñuel, the art dealer Camille Goemans and his girlfriend Yvonne Bernard had traveled down from Paris for a late summer vacation, during which Buñuel and Dalí would collaborate on a scenario planned to capitalize on the recent success of their film, *The Andalusian Dog*.

In his memoir, *The Secret Life of Salvador Dalí*, the painter describes that morning's tortuous toilette: "I tried on my sister's earrings several times. I liked them on myself, but decided they would be a nuisance for the swim. Nevertheless I put on my pearl necklace . . . I took my finest shirt and cut it irregularly at the bottom, making it so short that it did not quite reach my navel . . . I began to tear it artfully: one hole, baring my left shoulder, another, the black hairs on my chest, and a large square tear on the left side exposing my nipple that was nearly black." Briefly confounded by "the difficult problem" of his sporty bathing trunks, Dalí decided to wear them inside out, so as to expose the stains on the cotton lining of the shorts.

Dalí was not merely trying to make a good impression. His couture choices were also being dictated by existential panic and hysteria. He was twenty-five. He had recently returned from Paris, where despite the popularity of *Un Chien Andalou*, he had felt like a failure.

After suggesting he purchase a suitable dinner jacket, his fellow Catalan Joan Miró took him out into French society; he advised the shy Dalí not to talk too much and to work on his physique with a personal trainer. Dalí's romantic life was confined to long, depleting sessions of masturbation in front of a mirror, and after succumbing to a violent case of tonsillitis followed by chest pains, he had, in a delusional moment, operated on himself, gorily excising a birthmark, which he mistook for a bloodsucking cockroach.

Perhaps his expectations had been too high ("Caesar or nothing!") when he arrived in Paris like a Balzac hero, expecting to be embraced by his fellow artists, stampeded by beautiful women, and to fulfill the dreams of glory he'd had as a high-strung boy whose tantrums could only be calmed when his mother let him dress up in his holiday costume for the Day of the Three Kings. Now, back in Cadaqués, he was experiencing a renewed connection to the childhood horrors and fantasies he was maniacally incorporating in his work even as he battled the paralytic terror of an adult returned (forever, he feared) to the family home.

And so, on the morning of his fateful date with Gala Eluard, Dalí attempted to calm his nerves just as he had as a child—that is, by finding an outfit that would express his fabulous self: "What else could I do on the necessarily limited 'theme' of a swimming costume? . . . I now shaved the hairs under my arms . . . I went and got some laundry bluing, mixed it with some powder, and dyed my armpits with this. The effect was very fine for a moment, but immediately my sweat caused this makeup to begin to run . . . Then I had a new idea . . . Dried and coagulated blood on this part of the body ought to make an extraordinary impression . . . I took my Gillette and began to shave again, pressing harder so as to make myself bleed. In a few seconds my armpits were all bloody . . . My transformation appeared to me more and more desirable, and each moment I fell more in love with my appearance. Adroitly I stuck a fiery-red geranium behind my ear."

ON HIS RECENT TRIP to Paris, Dalí had met the Surrealist poet Paul Eluard in the Bal Tabarin. The two men ogled pretty girls, and, after several bottles of champagne, boozily conceived the plan of August in Cadaqués. Eluard, his family, and friends would join Dalí in the picturesque village where he had spent holidays in his youth. But when, that summer, the Eluards finally checked into the Miramar Hotel, the poet's wife Gala was grumpy about the prospect of their cut-rate vacation and took an instant dislike to Dalí's eccentric dandyism, his pomaded hair, and "professional Argentine tango slickness." As the evening wore on, however, Gala—who, at thirty-five, was ten years older than Dalí—warmed to "the rigor which I displayed in the realm of ideas," while Eluard impressed Dalí as "a poet of the category of Lorca—that is to say, among the greatest and most authentic."

In Eluard's presence, Dalí was magically cured of the hysterical laughing fits that had plagued him for years and that had lately become a source of acute anxiety for Dalí's father and sister. These attacks were precipitated when Dalí imagined an owl sitting on the head of whomever he was speaking to—an owl that had, on its own head, a piece of Dalí's shit. With Eluard, Dalí was inexplicably unable to summon this dependably mirth-inducing image and had to kick his fantasy up to another level. He imagined his owl upside down, his head stuck to the sidewalk by Dalí's excrement. This made Dalí laugh so hard that he rolled on the ground before he could go on with his walk.

The Eluards were among the glamorous Surrealist couples whose marriages and love affairs fueled the erotic aura and the reputation for sexual adventurousness that surrounded the movement. Gala and Paul had met and fallen in love as teenagers, in 1912, when both were inmates of a Swiss tuberculosis sanitarium. Four years later, after their release, Gala traveled alone, from her native Russia, through the chaos of World War I in order to rejoin her lover, who had been drafted into the French army and was on furlough at his family home in Paris. They married in the winter of 1917, and by summer Gala was pregnant.

Though, decades later, she would send her daughter packages to offset the shortages and privations of post–World War II France, and though Eluard's letters kept her informed of Cecile's moods, her health, her education, and her two early marriages, Gala seems never to have displayed more than a passing interest in her child. On being called the Mother of Surrealism, Gala replied, "You can call me *merde* but don't call me *mère*," as if she was the putative mother *only* of an artistic movement, forgetting that she was the actual parent of a child who might be hurt by her mother's feisty repudiation of the maternal role. As she grew older, Gala's behavior toward Cecile turned brutal, but no more so than her relations with others, including Dalí.

At an early age, baby Cecile was remanded into the care of Paul's mother, and her parents plunged into the artistic and social whirl, the heady and (despite itself) chic world of Breton and Aragon, Tanguy, and Max Ernst. During a group holiday in the Austrian Alps, Ernst fell in love with Gala, left his wife and young son, Jimmy, and went to live with Gala and Eluard. Thus Ernst's wife, Lou, became the first of many to paint an unflattering portrait of the siren who had vamped her husband, "that slithering, glittering creature with dark falling hair, vaguely oriental and luminant black eyes and small delicate bones, who had to remind one of a panther. This almost silent, avaricious woman, who, having failed to entice her husband into an affair with me in order to get Max, finally decided to keep both men, with Eluard's loving consent." Actually, this "loving consent" may have been closer to resignation; Eluard is reported to have said, "You don't know what it is like to be married to a Russian female."

Gala, Eluard, and Ernst began to live together in a ménage à trois. In *Investigating Sex*, a series of Surrealist colloquies on the subject of sexuality, Eluard described having sex with a man and a woman more passionate than either of her male partners, which prompted Breton to remark, "She was pretending." After two years of psychodrama, separations, and reconciliations, Eluard embarked on a solo journey around the world. Left to her own devices, Gala auctioned off her husband's cherished art collection to pay for a ticket to Saigon, where she, Ernst, and Eluard were reunited. When they returned to France, the Eluards—without Ernst—were a couple once more.

News of this sort traveled fast, expedited perhaps by the nude photo of Gala that Eluard was fond of passing around. Gala's reputation (she had also, with Eluard's approval, had a brief affair with de Chirico) could only have increased the fixity of purpose with which Dalí anointed himself to meet his new friends:

"I should have liked some kind of perfume, but I had only Eau de Cologne, which made me sick to my stomach. I would therefore have to invent something else for this . . . I began to boil some water in which I dissolved some fish glue . . . While waiting for this to boil I ran out in back of the house where I knew several sacks of goat manure had been delivered . . . Back in my studio, I threw a handful of this manure, and then another, into the dissolved glue . . . I let the whole thing jell, and when it was cold I took a fragment of the paste that I had made and rubbed my whole body with it.

"Thus," Dalí decided, "I was ready." But at that moment he glanced out his window and saw Gala, whose bare back, so like an adolescent's, "served as an infinitely svelte hyphen between the willful, energetic and proud leanness of her torso and her very delicate buttocks" convinced him that he was beholding the woman of his dreams. He frantically began to scrub the stench off his body and jettison his more original fashion accessories, though he retained the pearl necklace and the red geranium.

But Dalí's new resolve to be suave was subverted when his imaginary owl alighted on Gala's head. Laughing too hysterically to speak, the painter fussed over her—fetching cushions, a glass of water—and somehow managed to make a date for the following evening.

Unbeknownst to Dalí, Gala had been delegated to settle a matter of some concern to Dalí's dealer and colleagues. That summer, Dalí had worked on a painting that Eluard entitled *The Lugubrious Game*, one of those stretchy lunar landscapes populated by overtly sexual and personally resonant figures and body parts. Its subject matter reflected an oxymoronically orthodox Surrealism; the movement, was, after all, dedicated to dredging the unconscious, shaking off the repressive censorship of the intellect and of conventional morality, and spreading the flotsam across the page or the canvas. In their efforts to lure the subconscious to the surface, they played games like Exquisite Corpse and practiced automatic writing. But what burbled up from Dalí's id was perhaps *too* automatic, and what strained even the elastic bands of Surrealist good taste was the figure in the lower-right-hand corner of *The Lugubrious Game*, a man whose pants are stained with splotches of excrement, which Dalí had compulsively painted and repainted, so as to get them just right.

A question bothered his colleagues: Was Dalí a genuine coprophage? On their first date in Cadaqués, Gala made it clear that, if this were the case, she would be too repulsed to continue their friendship. If not, if he was just *toying* with the idea of scatological obsession—if he just *happened* to prepare for their meeting by smearing himself with goat shit, just *happened* to imagine an excrement-encrusted owl perched on the heads of his pals—he risked reducing his work to "a mere psychopathological document." Dalí was tempted to lie, to confess to coprophagia in order to make himself appear more interesting. But Gala's "purity" and "honesty" so moved him that he assured her: His painting was not autobiographical, except in that he considered "scatology as a terrorizing element, just as I do blood, or my phobia for grasshoppers."

In response, Gala took Dalí's hand, provoking a fit of "catastrophic" laughter. Most women would have taken one look at this giggling, bizarrely dressed coprophiliac and run in the opposite direction. Gala, however, understood that she had found her soul mate. For the exact nature of Dalí's erotic fixations was merely a detail compared to what she must have intuited—that Dalí had located, and pressed, the sore spot on which even the Surrealists (so tough, so nervy, so open about sex!) were sensitive. His work shocked them and made them talk, and more important, would shock others, and cause *them* to talk, and eventually this gossip and outrage would translate directly into notoriety, fame, and more money than her poet husband could ever hope to make.

"My little boy!" Gala cried. "We shall never leave each other."

EVEN AS A TIMID CHILD, Salvador Dalí craved attention. At school he discovered, quite by accident, the reputation-enhancing aspects of flinging himself downstairs. "I threw myself from the top of the stairway during the second recreation period, at the moment when the animation in the yard was at its height . . . Before flinging myself down I uttered a shrill scream so everyone would look at me . . . This was a definite encouragement to continue, and from time to time I repeated my fall. Each time I was about to go down the stairs there was great expectation. Will he throw himself off, or will he not? What was the pleasure of going down quietly and normally when I realized a hundred pairs of eyes were eagerly devouring me?"

Perhaps more (or more consciously) than any artist before him, Dalí wanted to become famous. And his muse, his Gala, ever attuned to celebrity and image, combined the muse's traditional functions (inspirer, facilitator, lover, mother, accountant, nurse) with the newly required skills of a spin doctor and an impresario who gave Dalí the confidence to successfully market himself as a personality.

Gala and Dalí were born for each other. Beneath their superficial differences, they belonged to the same species. Both were paradoxically evasive and exhibitionistic, troubled by childhood secrets, ambitious, acquisitive, self-mythologizing, and gifted with a talent for intuiting the spirit of the age and for calculating the precise chemistry of outrageousness and titillation that would grab and hold the popular imagination. Gala and Dalí were geniuses at public relations and promotion, adepts who complemented each other's skills, and who formed, as a couple, the perfect artist and muse for an era about to discover the magical—indeed, phenomenal—ways in which the lofty aims of art could serve, and be served by, the baser interests of commerce. Splashed across *Life* magazine, enlivening the gossip columns, awaiting a summons from Disney in a Pebble Beach hotel, hobnobbing with Ultra Violet and Andy Warhol, Gala-Dalí—for that is how the artist began signing his canvases—was their most successful creation, an icon as recognizable as the pointed mustache, the melted clocks and birds.

Always gratuitously, deliriously extreme, Dalí raised the bar for the artist who chose to make a public declaration of gratitude to his muse. If Lewis Carroll repeatedly thanked Alice for having inspired two books, if Rilke fervently acknowledged his debt to Lou, Dalí credited Gala—over and over, on every possible, appropriate or inappropriate, occasion—not merely for having influenced his work and his philosophy, but for having taught and enabled him to survive—"how to dress, how to go down a stairway without falling thirty-six times, how not to be continually losing the money we had, how to eat without tossing the chicken bone at the ceiling, how to recognize our enemies . . . Gala, with the petrifying saliva of her fanatical devotion, succeeded in building for me a shell to protect the tender nakedness of the Bernard the Hermit that I was, so that while in relation to the outside world I assumed more and more the appearance of a fortress, within myself I continued to grow old in the soft, and in the supersoft. And the day I decided to paint watches, I painted them soft."

With their outlandish costumes and high-concept personalities,

Dalí and Gala inaugurated a new way of thinking about the artist—or a new way of the *media* thinking about the artist. Dalí's portrait (by Man Ray) on the cover of a 1936 *Time* magazine predated by more than a dozen years Jackson Pollock's appearance on the cover of *Life*. It initiated the current trend toward the commodification of the celebrity artist, a trend that reached its apogee in the eighties, then subsided as interest in contemporary art ebbed. By 2000, it took (at the Brooklyn Museum's controversial *Sensation* show) the unlikely congruence of elephant dung and the Virgin Mary—a combination that would have thrilled Dalí—to get media attention. Just as Gala was considered the Surrealist muse (when an artist was working especially well, he was said to be in love with Gala) she was also the muse of a new vision of the artist.

IT WAS THE EARLY 1930S that Dalí first signed his canvases with both his and Gala's names. " 'It is mostly with *your* blood, Gala, that I paint my pictures,' I said to her one day, and since then I have always used her name with mine in signing my work." By then, their identities had merged so seamlessly that it is hard to know how much of their accounts of their hideous childhoods represent a collaborative effort.

Dalí's upbringing seems calculated to have produced a Surrealist plagued by morbid fantasies. He was named after a brother who died before he was born and whose photograph, enshrined over his parents' bed, portrayed a pretty child his mother called a genius and whose legacy drove Dalí "to prove that I am not the dead brother, but the living one." It has been suggested that Dalí was molested by an eccentric schoolmaster, that he had an affair with his younger sister, Ana Maria, and that, as an older boy, he continued to sleep naked with his mother, possibly to console her for being neglected by her husband, who was allegedly sleeping with his wife's younger sister, whom he married after Dalí's mother died at an early age.

Rising from this domestic wreckage, the young Salvador took his name literally. "I was destined, as my name indicates, for nothing less than to rescue painting from the void of modern art." His faith in his own specialness—and his talent as a draftsman—took him from his birthplace in the Catalan backwater city of Figueres to Madrid, where he enrolled in art school, from which he was expelled twice, once for refusing to take an exam because, he said, his professors weren't qualified to test him. He lived at the Residencia de Estudiantes, where his dormmates included Federico Garcia Lorca and Luis Buñuel, who became his close friends. Lorca was in love with Dalí; at least briefly, the two were lovers. Though biographers have suggested that Dalí's horror of being touched precluded consummation, Dalí remarked, "I felt that he was a great poet and that I did owe him a tiny bit of the divine Dalí's asshole."

Elsewhere, Dalí implied that he was virgin until he met his muse, and informed Brassai, who photographed the couple in their Paris atelier, that he "had been impotent until the age of twenty and had finally been able to experience sex only with the Beatrice of his life." On the subject of his delayed sexual development, he wrote: "I would sometimes see two of my friends go off after exchanging a look that haunted me for several days. They would disappear to some solitary spot, and when they came back they seemed transfigured—they were more handsome! I meditated for days on what 'it' might well be and would lose my way in the labyrinth of false and empty childish theories, all of which constituted a gross anomaly in view of my already advanced adolescence." These fantastic theories made little Salvador an interesting boy. His refusal, as an adult, to cease his childlike interrogations of reality—Why, he would ask, is champagne always served chilled while disgusting, sticky telephones are handed to us warm?—became the most engaging trait of the exasperating grown-up.

As a boy, Dalí claimed, he pushed a playmate off a bridge just for fun and bit into a dead bat crawling with ants. But the fact is that by the time *The Secret Life of Salvador Dalí* was written, the adult Salvador

had an investment in portraying his younger self as a twisted creature already bearing the earmarks of the madcap adult. In an essay
on Dalí, George Orwell suggested that the painter's memoir was
not a record of events, but of fantasies and desires.

Gala also seems to have tinkered with her history—the only
conceivable explanation, besides a horrible memory, for her incon-
sistent accounts of her childhood. Anyone can forget the year of her
birth, but whether or not her mother was married to her first or
second husband, and which one was her father, and who exactly had
molested her would surely stick in the mind. Helena Deluvina Diakonovna was born in Kazan, sometime around 1895. Her father
(or stepfather) was a lawyer, probably Jewish. The theme of
prospecting for gold—a pursuit in which her mother's first husband
was allegedly killed in Siberia, though in reality he may simply have
deserted his family—recurs frequently in her depiction of her past.
In some versions, he took Gala with him on his gold-mining expeditions. Either Gala *was* the daughter of a gold digger—compelling
evidence of the power of heredity—or else the importance of gold-
digging in her personal mythology proves that even the most calculating minds are subject to reflexive, Tourette-like contributions
from the unconscious.

More likely, it was the lawyer-father (as opposed to the prospector-
father) who financed the ailing Helena's sojourn at the Swiss clinic,
from which she returned cured, renamed Gala by Eluard, and determined to leave Kazan for Paris. No one knows how the young
woman accomplished this perilous wartime journey. The story of
her adventures might have gained Gala a certain cachet among the
Surrealists, but it would hardly have made her unique. Paris was full
of beautiful muses (Kiki of Montparnasse, Nusch, Alice Apfel) who
had somehow made their way alone to the city, where they scratched
out a living or were supported by artist-lovers.

Because there was a limited number of marginally solvent
artists, the muses of Montparnasse were, by necessity, competitive

self-marketers, capitalizing on their image. Gala was the dark Russian: smoky, sexy, mystical, superstitious, famous for her accurate tarot card readings and for her laserlike gaze; her eyes could pierce through solid walls, said Eluard. She also became notorious for her erotic restlessness and her *"qualités putainesques."*

Understandably, Gala preferred the role of Surrealist gypsy sex goddess to that of the impecunious Russian girl whom Eluard rescued from the Swiss sanitarium. A Russian aristocrat to whom she was later introduced would imply that Gala's Russian was decidedly lower class; and Gala saw no profit in trading on her dubious background or on anything that contradicted her image as Montparnasse free spirit. In his letters to Gala, Paul Eluard deplores her lack of interest in the past. "I don't like, I can't get used to the idea of what you told me during those last days in Arosa: that you have no memories, that you don't like to have any."

Among the facts that Gala seems to have remembered only hazily was her domestic situation at the time she fell in love with Dalí. Later she would claim that she threw over Max Ernst for Dalí as soon as she realized that Dalí was going to make more money. Actually, Ernst had already remarried and was living with his new wife.

Time would prove that Eluard, too, was confused about his marriage. When he left Gala and Cecile with Dalí in Cadaqués and went back to Paris, he believed that he was returning to prepare his family's new flat on the rue Becquerel. He was also under the impression that he and Gala would continue having affairs whenever they pleased without loosening their powerful grip on one another. And he thought, or hoped, that Gala would, by any means necessary, persuade Dalí to let her take *The Lugubrious Game* back to Paris, where Eluard partly supported them by dealing art.

Evidently, Gala and Eluard saw this outrageous painting as a potential moneymaker, and it is likely that Eluard had some hand in its sale to the Vicomte de Noailles. (Occasionally, in Eluard's letters, the stolid French bourgeois can be seen peeking out from beneath the anarchistic Surrealist exterior, expressing sensible concerns about inheritance and the market value of art; one letter includes Eluard's manifesto calling for the abolition of private property *and* his wish that his mother would sell her house and take over the mortgage payments on his apartment.) It was Eluard who eventually advised Gala to marry Dalí, so as to prevent Dalí's father from seizing his son's valuable work in the event of the painter's death.

As Dalí and Gala performed their demented-peacock mating dance on the cliffs of Cadaqués, Eluard continued to send her the sort of feverishly pornographic letters that he would write her for at least another five years—after he found another girlfriend, the beautiful Nusch; after Gala was married to Dalí and she and Eluard saw each other infrequently, but continued to sleep together at those rare reunions. His *Letters to Gala* is a remarkable document, as dirty as the most over-the-top of Joyce's letters to Nora. But because Paul and Gala were separated for so much of their marriage, the letters (unlike Joyce's) continued, their passion undiminished as Gala and Eluard reminded each other (certainly Eluard reminded Gala) that their relationship was *about* sex.

The leitmotifs running through his correspondence are Surrealist gossip; health, travel, money; Eluard's loneliness, his desire to have sex with Gala, and the pale consolation of masturbating while fantasizing about having sex with Gala. "This morning I jerked off magnificently while thinking of you. And my imagination isn't weary. I see you everywhere, in everything, above everything. I love you to death. Your sex swallows mine, covers my face, it covers me with your beauty . . . your genius. Everything about you is beautiful: your eyes, your mouth, your hair, your breasts, your pubes, your ass, your sex, your legs, your sex, your hands that can't let go of what they're jerking off, that space between your thighs, near your sex, your shoulders."

This is not Lou von Salomé and Nietzsche walking through the woods and talking about God and the soul! Absence kept Eluard's

longing intense and raw, and what makes his letters painful to read
is their detailed, nuanced charting of his gradual realization—and
his stubborn refusal to believe—that he was losing Gala.

Eluard's correspondence provides the raunchy yet lushly romantic background music piping beneath the early years of Gala's affair
with Dalí. If anything can be extracted from accounts of the Dalís'
fifty-three-year marriage, it is that the creature they spawned together, their cash cow, the Gala-Dalí, did not feed principally, if at
all, on erotic passion. Sex had little to do with the longevity and endurance of their productive and ultimately tortured partnership.
The question of Dalí's disliking to be touched remained at issue, as
did his homosexuality. When Lorca heard that Dalí had fallen in
love with Gala, he is said to have exclaimed, "It's impossible! He can
only get an erection when someone sticks a finger up his anus!"
Masturbation and voyeurism seem to have remained Dalí's favorite
modes of gratification, and at the orgies he staged in his heyday as a
sixties superstar, he directed the revels—and watched.

Long before Dalí reached this level of accommodation and comfort with his erotic disposition, Gala had sexual confidence to spare.
And she must have drawn on it heavily during those first days in
Cadaqués, as the muse enthralled her skittish artist with seductive
hints about what she wanted him to do to her—intimations, Dalí
believed, of submission to his most depraved fantasies. But when
Dalí finally found the nerve to ask her *what* exactly she wanted, she
replied that she really wanted him to kill her.

Or that's what Dalí decided she said. The verb she used, *"faire
crever,"* means to kill and to make burst. It is used when someone
expires from heat, and when a lobster is boiled in a pot. Was Gala
making a pun that spanned murder and sex? Dalí chose not to think
so. He believed that she wanted him to throw her into the sea. He
realized that she was entrusting him with her deepest, darkest secret—a secret, he says, that she gave him permission to tell, but
which he decided to keep *for* her. Finally, he persuaded himself (this

took a while longer) that he was not going to kill her, although he had, on their walks along the cliffs, been tempted to give her a push.

"Gala's fantasy of seeking death at an unplanned and happy moment of her life was not simply a childish and romantic urge . . . Gala's idea constituted indeed the very basis of her psychic life, and in the lovely expression of her face at the moment she made her avowal I saw all the fibres of her flayed sensibility converge into a pyramid . . ."

Later, Dalí claimed that whatever passions were stirred by their curious death-tango on the rocks of Cadaqués would not be consummated for three months, during which he channeled his preconjugal jitters into *The Great Masturbator* and *Accommodations of Desire*. With their peekaboo erotic symbolism, their coy invitation to the viewer to practice the most obvious sort of amateur-Freudian interpretation, these paintings offer two of art history's most blatant representations of sexual anxiety.

While Dalí was turning his terrors into art, Gala returned to Eluard and Paris, where Dalí joined her later that fall. His account of their reunion is a tender parable about finance, sacrifice, and surrender: Buying red roses to bring her, he misunderstood the price and spent his last centime on flowers for his beloved. In fact, Gala had earned it, for during his absence she had edited "the mass of disorganized and unintelligible scribblings that I had made throughout the whole summer" into a presentable manuscript, *The Visible Woman*—which would appear with her portrait on the cover—and prepared the way so that "my work could be taken half-way seriously even if only by the group of friends most prepared to admire me."

Back in Paris, Dalí soon discovered he had been granted, as if by magic, the gift of speech—the ability to communicate with the same artists who had once dismissed him as a "cretin." Although Dalí credits alcohol for this new facility, he also acknowledged Gala's role in his socialization: "The alcohol I had drunk in Madrid rose in the tomb of my palate like the mummy of Lazarus. 'Walk!' I commanded. And it walked . . . Its resurrection made me eloquent again. Thereupon I said to this mummy, 'Speak!' And it spoke. It was a discovery to discover that besides painting what I was painting I was not an utter cretin. I also knew how to talk, and Gala with her devoted and pressing fanaticism furthermore undertook to convince the Surrealist group that besides talking I was capable of 'writing,' and of writing documents whose philosophic scope went beyond all the group's previsions." Though Dalí, on occasion, portrays himself as a Spanish bumpkin who played Galatea to Gala's savvy Pygmalion, the fact is that he too had an instinct for self-advancement through flattery and charm, as evidenced by his pre-Gala 1929 visit to Picasso's atelier, where he told his fellow Spaniard that, on arriving in Paris, he'd headed there directly, instead of bothering with the Louvre.

Though Gala continued to live with Eluard, she and Dalí were rapidly closing ranks to form the samurai army of two with which they prepared to vanquish their fellow Surrealists and go on to conquer the world. "One maxim became axiomatic for my spirit: If you decide to wage a war for the total triumph of your individuality, you must begin by inexorably destroying those who have the greatest affinity with you. All alliance depersonalizes; everything that tends to the collective is your death; use the collective, therefore, as an experiment, after which strike hard, and remain alone!"

ONLY THE CLEAR SIGHT of retrospect could make Dalí and Gala's love seem not only comprehensible, but preordained. Lorca was puzzled, obviously; Buñuel was so furious at Gala for having diverted Dalí's attention from their film collaboration that, on an outing in Cadaqués, he pretended to strangle her—a playful bit of theater that terrified poor Cecile. The most surprised and distressed of all was Dalí's father, an autocratic, opinionated notary whose idea of early childhood sex education was to leave open, on the piano, a textbook with pictures of genitals hideously corroded by venereal disease.

Señor Dalí's rage increased after Dalí exhibited, in his successful 1929 show at Camille Goemans's Paris gallery, a drawing incorporating the words, "Sometimes I spit for pleasure on the portrait of my mother." (For all the Freudian working-over that Dalí has received, no one seems to have noted the coincidence and the implications of the fact that the act of spitting on a dead parent's portrait occurs in Proust, during a homosexual love scene.) Señor Dalí disinherited his son, who—on hearing of his "irrevocable banishment from the bosom of my family"—again sought consolation in a fashion make-over. He shaved his head, buried his hair clippings on the beach near Cadaqués, and had Buñuel take an unsmiling mug shot of him with a sea urchin on his head, a painful little crown of thorns that would become an important element in the Dalí-Gala iconography. (In another famous photo, the couple contemplates a meal of sea urchins, lined up in an orderly grid on a white tablecloth.) Standing at attention before the shadow that his bald head and sea-urchin topknot cast on the wall, Dalí first glimpsed the image that would become shorthand, in his work, for his relationship with his father: the legend of William Tell. In the photo, Salvador plays William Tell's son, waiting bravely for the arrow that will pierce the sea-urchin apple on his head or turn him into St. Sebastian, whose legend had played a critical role in his friendship with Lorca.

Like many parents who meddle in their children's love lives, Señor Dalí only succeeded in cementing the relationship between his son and the despised paramour—the married, adulterous Russian art hussy. And so the father's fury played into Gala's hands. With one scalpel-like incision, Señor Dalí severed the artist from his sole-surviving parent and from Ana Maria, the adoring sister who to her dying day refused to believe that Lorca was homosexual, who wrote a book about Dalí, and about whom Dalí wrote a poetic tribute:

The image of my sister
her anus red
with bloody shit
my prick
semi-erect
leaning elegantly
against
an immense
lyre . . .

Dalí's biographers have speculated about whether the poem represents confession or fantasy, without much noting that merely to write and publish such a poem about a Catholic woman in a provincial Spanish city was an act of rebellion, rage, and hostility roughly akin to spitting on a dead parent's portrait.

Disinheritance suited Gala, even when Dalí's father sent the Civil Guard to throw the lovebirds out of Cadaqués. Dalí's family money was not what she had been counting on. Now Salvador was hers alone, and after his banishment, Gala did everything to bind him to her. Somehow it seems unlikely that it was Dalí's idea for them to hole up in a series of hotels and vacation spots, improbable that "the most ambitious of all contemporary painters decided to leave with Gala on a voyage of love two days before the opening of my first painting exhibit in Paris, the artistic capital of the world."

Later that winter, "while waiting for society people to begin to want me," Dalí and Gala left Paris for a small inn Gala knew, at Carry-le-Rouet, on the coast near Marseilles. "Gala understood that we had to flee the world so as to temper ourselves as a couple in the crucible of life alone together." There, claimed Dalí, they spent two months without going outdoors, "two months of voluntary confinement, during which I knew and consummated love with the same speculative fanaticism that I put into my work." This idyll, which he celebrated with a drawing of lovers embracing on the floor in front of a fireplace surrounded by stacked firewood, would become an essential part of their mythology as muse and artist, the equivalent of Alice Liddell and Charles Dodgson's "golden afternoon," Nietzsche and Lou von Salomé's hike up the Monte Sacro, the night John and Yoko recorded *Two Virgins*: "This period has remained engraved in Gala's and my memory as one of the most active, exciting and frenzied periods of our lives. And several times, during those long reveries which come over one on train-trips, just at the moment when each of us seemed to be wandering in the most distant of his memories, it has happened that both of us would exclaim at once, 'You remember the time at Carry-le-Rouet?' "

As dedicated exhibitionists, Dalí and Gala expected and allowed their erotic lives to come under intense scrutiny. Perhaps more than any other modern painter, Dalí has had his sexual preferences discussed and debated: Did he masturbate exclusively? Was he homosexual? Asexual? A voyeur? What of his fascination with excrement, his terror of being touched?

Whatever happened in that hotel room at Carry-le-Rouet, Gala and Dalí saw their stay there as their true honeymoon, one of those enchanted respites from time when the desires and pleasures of the body occupy the lovers' attention and the extraneous, boring world vanishes beyond the edge of their peripheral vision. Among the things that seem not to have mattered were Eluard's progressively dirtier and more desperate letters.

Meanwhile, Dalí was hard at work, painting *The Invisible Man,* a canvas to which he ascribed occult powers—a protective fetish designed to safeguard Gala and himself. Gala whiled away the hours in their darkened, shuttered rooms, compulsively reading her tarot cards and receiving reassuring messages from the deck. As with John and Yoko, the private mythology of this artist and his muse included elements of magic—of Gala's prescience, and of the preternatural gifts with which she would free them both from ordinary cares and render them invulnerable, an idea to which Dalí subscribed with the blind faith of peasant armies who believe their leaders impervious to bullets. ("Gala . . . is a true medium in the scientific sense of the word. Gala is never, never, never wrong. She reads cards with a paralyzing sureness. She predicted to my father the exact course of my life up to the present moment.") Gala's clairvoyance was confirmed when she predicted that good news about money would come from a dark man; soon afterward, Dalí received a check for twenty-five thousand francs from the Vicomte de Noailles (who was also bankrolling Buñuel's and Dalí's *L'Age d'Or*), more than enough to tide the artist over when the Goemans Gallery closed.

In March 1931, in Barcelona, Dalí delivered a controversial lecture on Surrealism, in praise of paranoia and "the pleasure principle." How it must have thrilled Gala to see her true love use even this modest venue (a respected city club) to generate the maximum notoriety and scandal. "It is the duty," Dalí proclaimed, "of our intelligence to embark upon a rabid defense of all that which—despite the abominably mechanical nature of practical life, despite ignoble humanitarian sentiments, despite the pretty phrases (love of work, etc. etc.) which we Surrealists all heap with shit—can lead to masturbation, exhibitionism, crime, love." In the same speech, Dalí connected the death wish with a wife's blighted love for, and hatred of, her husband—a veiled reference to his own mother's death that, he knew, would be reported back to his father.

Señor Dalí was angry enough to persuade the local hotel owners to refuse his son lodging when he and Gala returned to Cadaqués. Undeterred, the couple retreated to the fisherman's shack they had bought on the waterfront at Port Lligat, a dwelling they would expand until they had erected a stylish seaside mansion and monument to themselves. But the hut proved uninhabitable. The couple fled to Paris and then to Torremolinos, where Gala necked in public with Dalí, strolled bare-breasted through the village, and exchanged lurid letters with Eluard.

It was around this time that Dalí began to incorporate images of

Gala in his paintings. Evolving over their five decades together, his vision of his muse mapped the trajectory of their relationship, and the arc of her centrality in his domestic and creative life. At first, Gala played a marginal role in the hallucinatory tableaux that animated his desolate, extraterrestrial landscapes. In the earliest of these works (*Imperial Monument to the Child-Woman, Gala; Memory of the Child-Woman*) Gala assumed her place among the obsessional symbols—lions, fish, eggs, genitalia, birds, grasshoppers, Napoleon, the *Mona Lisa*—that her lover's "paranoiac critical method," the "spontaneous methods of irrational knowledge based on the interpretive-critical association of delirious phenomena" salvaged from his unconscious and combined in theatrical scenes of anguish, perversion, dismemberment, castration, etc. He also conscripted her to play victim and bystander in a series of horrific oedipal scenarios (*William Tell and Gradiva; The Old Age of William Tell*) featuring images of the Swiss hero, the symbolic stand-in for Señor Dalí, depicted in a range of threatening stances toward his son's beloved: menace, attempted seduction, repudiation, assault.

During the early and mid-1930s, Gala (often portrayed wearing a colorfully striped jacket) dispelled the frenetic terrors of the suggestive moonscapes and took possession of the canvases with a sphynxlike calm that nonetheless managed to suggest tension, an implacable melancholy, and even the capacity for violence. Frequently (in paintings such as *The Angelus of Gala* and *Gala and "The Angelus" of Millet before the Imminent Arrival of the Conical Anamorphoses*) her figure appears in conjunction with the couple from Millet's *The Angelus*, that sentimental portrayal of two peasants pausing to pray, in which Dalí claimed to see a predatory praying-mantis woman, a man hiding an erection with his hat, and, between them, the buried coffin of the child they are mourning.

Later still, in Dalí's religious-historical paintings of the 1950s and '60s, and in his scientific extravaganzas of the following decade, his images of Gala become comically grandiose. In *The Discovery of*

America by Christopher Columbus, Gala—enraptured, haloed, her hands clasped in beatific ecstasy—has become St. Helena, the discoverer of the true cross, her figure emblazoned on a banner, her white robes trailing down to gird the loins of the pretty-boy Columbus, about to set foot on the newly discovered land. Gala reappears as St. Helena, floating among the clouds in *The Ecumenical Council*, and in *The Madonna of Port Lligat*, she assumes the prayerful majesty of a virgin in a Renaissance altarpiece. In the 1965 *Apotheosis of the Dollars*, a hymn to the happy marriage of big money and oversize art, Gala takes her place in a pantheon of the great—Velázquez, Goethe, Duchamp—and in *Corpus Hypercubus*, the regal, heavily robed Gala has been chosen from all humankind to witness the miracle of Jesus and His cubical crucifix, levitating in mid-air.

IN DALÍ'S 1930 PAINTING *The Bleeding Roses*, a naked woman with roses on her belly—a bouquet from which red blood dribbles down her thighs—wraps herself around a column in an attitude of languid suffering and ecstatic exaltation reminiscent of St. Sebastian. Perhaps Dalí's extravagant, impoverishing expenditure on the bouquet of roses for Gala was still fresh in his mind. Already a part of his personal iconography, the rose womb had made earlier cameo appearances in *The Old Age of William Tell*, and in *The Invisible Man*, on which Dalí worked during the idyll at Carry-le-Rouet. During this time, Gala suffered from gynecological symptoms so severe that Eluard's letters are filled with reference to her "flows"; mostly he is advising her to time her visits home so that menstruation won't interfere with their sex life. In addition, she experienced lung trouble that turned into pleurisy and resisted the therapeutic benefits she and Dalí sought in healthful climates.

In 1931, Gala was found to have fibrous tumors in her uterus and her lung, for which she was operated on (Eluard gallantly agreed to pay half the expenses) in a Paris clinic. In the first chapter of his memoir, Dalí describes this traumatic experience:

"In 1936 in Paris in our apartment at number 7 rue Becquerel . . . Gala was to undergo an operation the following morning and had to spend the night at the hospital for preparatory treatments. The operation was considered very serious. Nevertheless, Gala, with her unfailing courage and vitality, seemed not at all worried, and we spent the whole afternoon constructing two surrealist objects. She was happy as a child: and with graceful arched movements, reminiscent of Carpaccio's figures, she was assembling an astounding collection of items . . . Later I realized that this object was full of unconscious allusions to her impending operation. Its eminently biological character was obvious: membranes ready to be torn by the rhythmic movement of metal antennae, delicate as surgical instruments, a bowl full of flour serving as a shock absorber for a pair of women's breasts so placed as to bump against it . . .

"I, meanwhile, was putting together a 'thing' which I called the 'hypnagogic clock.' . . . At nightfall Gala had completely finished her object, and we decided to take it to André Breton to show him before going to the hospital . . . We hurriedly carried Gala's object into a taxi." A sudden stop made the objects topple, and, to the driver's consternation, covered the couple (and presumably, the taxi) with flour.

"All these incidents made us forget the hospital, where we arrived very late," and where the arrival of the high-spirited, flour-drenched couple shocked the nurses on duty. Still dusting off the flour, "I left Gala at the hospital and hurried back home . . . I dined on a few oysters and a roast pigeon, which I ate with excellent appetite. After three coffees I went back to work on the object I had begun in the afternoon . . . This complete indifference toward the being whom I believed I adored presented to my intelligence a very interesting philosophical and moral problem to which, however, I found it impossible to give my attention immediately.

"Indeed I felt myself inspired, inspired like a musician: new ideas sparkled in the depth of my imagination. Still engrossed in the

importance of the object I had just constructed, I finally went to
bed at about two in the morning. With the innocence of an angel I
fell immediately into a deep, peaceful slumber . . . At five I awoke
like a demon. The greatest anguish I had ever felt held me riveted to
my bed . . .

"Gala, Galuchka, Galuchkineta! Burning tears welled up one by
one into my eyes, awkwardly at first, with spasms and the pangs of
childbirth . . . Each time the flow of my tears began to subside there
would immediately arise before me an instantaneous vision of
Gala . . .

"Like one possessed I ran to the hospital, and I clutched at the
surgeon's uniform with such a display of animal fear that he treated
me with exceptional circumspection, as though I had been myself a
patient. For a week I was in an almost constant state of tears and
wept in every circumstance in which I found myself . . . A Sunday
came when Gala was definitely out of danger . . . Galuchka was smiling, and at last I held her hand pressed against my cheek. And with
tenderness I thought: 'After all this, I could kill you!' "

All sorts of truths, attitudes, personality traits, and unintentional revelations surface in this section, so much like Dalí's painting in its mixing of the accidental and the calculated, the heartfelt,
the chilly, the impassioned and outrageous. To begin with, he has his
dates wrong, by a factor of about five years, but why should the divine Dalí bother about that? He is so caught up in a dream of the
self that he imagines the nurses, years later, still scratching their
heads about the identity of that fascinating, flour-covered couple.

The three-page scene speaks volumes about the artist and his
muse. Regardless of her true feelings on the eve of a surgery that
must have seemed terrifying, especially in 1931, she could not afford to be afraid. Only recently had she assumed the role of Dalí's
courage, of the muse who emboldened a genius so phobic that he
suffered a fit of paralytic terror when Yves Tanguy left him alone
on the Paris Métro, and who, later in life, would demand—in

Gala's absence—to be walked home after dinner a few houses away.

Here, however, Dalí revels in his independence. He describes the meal he enjoyed in Gala's absence, and after puzzling over his coolness to her plight, segues into a description of the way that art can take us out of ourselves. But what's most striking about the passage is its portrayal of the couple's early life together. Not only is Gala, as well as Dalí, engaged in the construction of Surrealist sculpture, but the touching playfulness of their efforts to get through a difficult day, to distract themselves (in Dalí's case perhaps too successfully) from their anxieties is utterly at odds with the grimy patina that time has layered onto our image of Gala-Dalí— the ambitious publicity-seekers and social-climbers grasping at fame and fortune.

Only gradually did the seriousness of Gala's operation sink in; later she would complain bitterly that the doctors had "emptied her completely." Eluard brightened her recovery with letters intended to demonstrate that Gala's hysterectomy had not diminished her sexual appeal. Everyone seems to have known about her surgery, and, in Surrealist circles, Gala's reputation changed from that of the erotically insatiable Russian witch to the "violent and sterile woman" described in Eluard and Breton's 1938 *Abridged Dictionary of Surrealism*. (That Gala was already the mother of a daughter appears not to have figured into this equation.) And by the time she returned to Paris after her convalescence at Vernet-les-Bains, something *had* grown more violent—her determination to parlay Dalí's eccentric genius into the kind of security that would forever safeguard them from the perils of poverty and illness.

IN THE PHOTOGRAPH of Gala-Dalí that Brassai took in what he pointedly calls *their* studio, the couple stands, pressed together. Dalí drapes his arm over Gala's bare shoulder; she covers his hand with hers. Lurking in the shadow of a pedestal supporting the plaster bust of a nude woman sporting a necklace of corn cobs, Dalí, in a shirt and tie—alarmingly thin, wildly handsome, dark-eyed, dark-haired, not yet thirty and still charged with skittish adolescent intensity—fixes his Svengali-like gaze on the camera. Fleshier, softer, more solid, Gala (in a full dark skirt and a skimpy, revealing striped blouse) tilts her pelvis toward Dalí's hip and gives the impression of simultaneously supporting and leaning against him as she trains a half-seductive, half-mournful hint of a smile on Brassai, whose image can be seen in a mirror—like Velázquez's in *Las Meninas.*

The setting is very different from the dark streets and louche whorehouses that provide the background for Brassai's better known work. Though none of the furnishings seem expensive, the studio looks elegant and stylish. Still, the couple projects something like the rapt carnality that Brassai discovered in his photos of gangsters and their molls, of lovers in Paris cafés. Gala-Dalí's sexuality is more androgynous, enigmatic—and, therefore, even more intriguing—than that of the obviously heterosexual and homosexual couples whose images Brassai captured. Huddled together, gazing out at the world, Dalí and Gala seem fully prepared to do whatever is needed—to use their beauty, their allure and their air of secrecy and mystery as a ladder to scale the heights of Paris society.

One of their secrets concerned their dire financial situation. Preferring to have people think they were dying of indigestion rather than of hunger, the couple concealed their poverty. Still, Gala often set out with Dalí's constructions and canvases under her arm, hoping to sell them for quick cash, and it was Gala who begged the Prince Faucigny-Lucinge for support, lest Dalí be obliged to commercialize his genius.

Their ambition was what Brassai remembered when, in 1982, he included the double portrait in *The Artists of My Life,* and wrote with an obvious pleasure (and a hint of the rancor that the artist who has maintained his integrity can't help feeling for the colleague who has sold out and gotten rich) in naming names, "With an avid, frenzied snobbery, Dalí and Gala set forth to conquer 'society.' They met

Coco Chanel, Elsa Schiaperelli, Misia Sert; they were invited to Prince Mdvani's and the Maharajah of Kapurthala's; to the homes of Princesse Marie-Blanche de Polignac, the daughter of the couturier Lanvin; the Prince de Faucigny-Lucinge; millionaire Señor Ancherena; and the wealthy Chilean Arturo Lopez-Willshaw . . . For four years Gala and Dalí paid constant court to such people, even though the Dalís considered them blasé, boring and stupid." Brassai was forthcoming about Gala's role as muse: "At once Dalí's inspiration and mentor, Gala disciplined him, soothed him, protected him; she managed to relieve his anxieties and fears. She took control of the 'Dalí phenomenon,' and its enormous success is due in great part to her. A remarkable businesswoman, she was the one who negotiated and signed his contracts."

Among these contracts was the one that established the Zodiac Club, a plan that Gala implemented to guarantee a steady income while Dalí was changing dealers and establishing his reputation. Twelve wealthy art collectors were invited to join a sort of subscription service; each patron would choose, by lot, a particular month, and during that month would buy a work from Dalí, at a price guaranteed in advance. The ingeniousness of this marketing plan resided in what the Zodiac offered—an ennobling opportunity to support, and hobnob with, Paris's hottest artist couple, combined with the cachet of belonging to an extremely exclusive club.

Its membership was not only international but, eventually, transatlantic. In 1933, Dalí had his first one-man show at Julien Levy's gallery in New York. The artist and his muse did not attend, partly because of Dalí's phobia of travel, especially across water. Gala plays a curiously minor role in Caresse Crosby's account of how in 1934, on the occasion of Dalí's second show, Caresse (the notorious heiress, the putative inventor of the brassiere, and the widow of Harry Crosby, publisher of the famous literary magazine *Black Sun*) facilitated their traumatic passage to America on board the SS *Champlain*.

According to Crosby, Dalí spent the voyage huddled in his cabin, so paranoid that he tied his canvases to his clothing with strings. Gala and Dalí made only one public appearance, dressed in raffish Boho finery that upset the first-class dining room where the Dalís, who were traveling third class, came as Caresse's guests. When the ship landed in New York, Crosby thoughtfully diverted the reporters who had come to see her flash some leg by telling them that the *real* story was the arrival of a great modern painter. Dalí failed to rise to the occasion until Crosby hissed, in French, "This is the press, they can take you or leave you." The artist finally got with the program and informed the reporters that his favorite of his own paintings was a portrait of his wife with lamb chops on her shoulders, a response that got the flashbulbs popping. *Painter Here with 'Chop' on Shoulder,* read one headline.

Dalí caught on quickly. Not only was the show a hit—paintings sold to the Museum of Modern Art and the Hartford Atheneum—but, thanks to dozens of articles, interviews, and reviews, the soi-disant John the Baptist of Surrealism in the United States made hordes of American converts. Free from the social constraints of Europe and the disapproving eye of their fellow Surrealists, Gala-Dalí demonstrated their brilliant flair for generating publicity. At the conclusion of their triumphant stay, Caresse Crosby decided to give the Dalís a farewell party, a gala costume Dream Ball to which the guests were invited to come dressed as their favorite recurrent nightmare.

Society women with green snakes emerging from their heads arrived with their masked, half-naked escorts at the Coq Rouge, the Dalís' favorite restaurant. There, they wandered through the Dalínian wonderland (bartenders sporting neckties made from human hair, a cow carcass containing a gramophone playing French songs, a hundred-pound block of ice tied with a red satin ribbon, a bathtub full of water about to slide downstairs) to meet their host, whose head was bandaged with gauze and who was attired in a shirt with its front cut out to reveal a tiny pair of women's breasts. Their hostess, her face covered with dead vegetation and fake ants, wore a headdress studded with baby dolls, an outfit that some interpreted as a reference to the recently kidnapped and murdered Lindbergh baby.

The populace was so outraged by this sacrilege that Dalí felt compelled to deny that Gala had intentionally alluded to the crime, and the couple returned home to face the Surrealists' ire at their cowardice in disowning this sublimely provocative gesture. A few years later, Breton, whose enmity toward Dalí—the only Surrealist who succeeded in making a fortune from his art—had grown steadily, would coin the famous anagram on Dalí's name: Avid A Dollars.

Gala-Dalí rapidly became expert at calculating the limits to which they could push public opinion in order to generate maximum attention. Twice, in Gala's absence, Dalí took things too far. In London, he nearly suffocated while giving a lecture dressed in an old-fashioned diving suit, complete with helmet; in 1939, he smashed the window at Bonwit Teller to protest the department store's modification of the outré window display he and Gala had designed. Thus he exposed himself to dangers that must have confirmed his belief that Gala's presence was essential to his survival. And once more, Dalí's wayward impulses had a beneficial effect. His arrest—on charges of malicious mischief, reduced to disorderly conduct—made front-page headlines that drew even larger crowds to his show at Julien Levy's gallery.

The Dalís were taken up by the wealthy, eccentric, bisexual British poet Edward James, who later claimed to have been Dalí's lover, and to have bought Gala off with jewelry after she discovered that Dalí had deceived her in order to spend the night with James. He also reported that Dalí encouraged his wife to take lovers, because the prospect excited him. So perhaps something other than (or in addition to) greed motivated Gala to cheat on the terms of the contract stipulating that James would pay Dalí a monthly stipend and have the option of purchasing all the work Dalí produced for three years, from 1936 through 1939. This was, of course, the period of the Spanish Civil War, during which Dalí's aristocratic, right-wing, opportunistically pro-Franco sympathies alienated him from his fellow Surrealists, and from colleagues such as Picasso and Miró. He and Gala waited out the war—and World War II—in rural France, Italy, and America, though Gala did make one perilous trip to Paris around the time of the German invasion, braving bombs and chaos to salvage money and as many of her husband's paintings as she was able to transport or have shipped.

Edward James's patronage liberated Gala from the need to find customers for Dalí's work and freed her to attend to other essential details—locating the best paints and brushes, and the expensive antique frames Dalí insisted on. In addition, Dalí's muse began to perfect the look befitting her new position as a society figure, cultivating Coco Chanel and Elsa Schiaparelli, who gave Gala her latest, most daring designs. And when, in 1940, the Dalís installed themselves in Hampton Manor, Caresse Crosby's Virginia mansion—along with a colorful group of houseguests that included Henry Miller and Anaïs Nin—Gala made sure the others knew their place. Thanks to the "organizational powers of Mrs. Dalí," wrote Nin, "we were not allowed to enter the library because he was going to work there . . . Would I mind translating an article for him? Would Caresse invite *Life* magazine to come and visit? So we each fulfilled our appointed tasks. Mrs. Dalí never raised her voice, never seduced or charmed. Quietly she assumed we were all there to serve Dalí, the great, indisputable genius."

Having exhausted Caresse's hospitality, the Dalís left for California, where Dalí enchanted Harpo Marx, for whom he designed a harp with barbed-wire strings; the artist recoiled from Greta Garbo's proffered kiss, created the dream sequence for Alfred Hitchcock's *Spellbound*, and planned a project with Disney that was never carried out. Eventually, the couple retreated to the Monterey

Peninsula, where Dalí spent his days working while the restless Gala drove her Cadillac, often at high speeds, along the coastal highway and chauffeured her husband, on Route 66, back and forth across their vast adopted country.

IN THE 1944 TO 1945 *Portrait of Galerina*—inspired, Dalí claimed, by Raphael's painting of *La Fornarina*—Gala occupies the center of the canvas. There are no tricks, no trompe l'oeil, no double images, no hacked-up body parts, just Gala, her arms crossed before her, wearing a filmy white blouse unbuttoned to reveal her left breast and the jeweled bracelet, in the form of a snake, that she received from Edward James after the contretemps over Dalí's infidelity. Though Gala's face, in studies for the painting, is severe and confrontational, it is harder to read the expression in the finished work: elusive, attentive, ever so slightly simpering. The bared breast (which, Dalí claimed, signified bread) and the calm of the sitter seem meant to suggest the sort of tranquillity and fecundity one finds in Renaissance paintings of the Madonna, an irony considering that—at the time the painting was being executed—Gala had not communicated with her daughter, Cecile, for almost five years, and would not do so until the war ended in 1945.

Soon after finishing *Galerina*, Dalí painted *Three Apparitions of the Visage of Gala,* a depiction of three rocks bearing progressively sharper images of Gala with the tilted head and the beatific gaze of a quattrocento angel. This too was ironic in view of the fact that by the late 1940s, the relationship between artist and muse had deteriorated, partly as a consequence of their increasingly frantic infidelities, of Gala's growing impatience with her supporting role in the drama of the divine Dalí, and of the erosion of her character, a process which manifested itself in violent tantrums and reckless promiscuity.

Gala was cruel and vindictive to former friends and acquaintances. She refused to lend the penniless Buñuel fifty dollars, and

when Prince de Faucigny-Lucinge—whom Gala had once importuned to save Dalí from commercializing his talent—arrived in
New York and told Gala how happy he was to see her after so many
years, she replied, "You may be. But me, not at all." In fairness, neither of these unfriendly gestures seems entirely gratuitous; Buñuel
had opposed Gala's entrance into Dalí's life, and the prince, despite
his early support, seems not to have much liked her. It may be that
Gala finally felt she had the power to avenge past slights and
wrongs, but the hapless waiters, hotel employees, deliverymen, and
art dealers whom Gala kicked, hit, elbowed, and spat at could hardly
have deserved such punishment for neglecting to treat the Dalís in
the regal style to which they had grown accustomed.

When she discovered that Cecile had been forced to sell several
of Dalí's paintings from the Paris flat in order to survive the war,
Gala flew into a rage at the daughter whom she called "mean and
petit bourgeois like her French grandmother." Still reeling from the
shock of Nusch's sudden death, Eluard wrote Gala, begging her to
take pity on their "morally and materially unhappy" child. "She's got
the idea that you don't love her anymore and that she won't see you
again. Although she is fairly hardened, she cries every time she
speaks of you. Once again, my little Gala forever, don't torment
yourself over it. You can smooth it out by writing her nicely once in
a while and by sending her packages that prove you're thinking of
her." After Eluard died, Gala informed Cecile—to whom she had
not spoken in four years—that she did not wish to communicate
with her ever again.

Dalí responded, or compensated, by canonizing Gala in his art,
by portraying her as ever more saintly and even divine—a process
that culminated in *The Madonna of Port Lligat*, the painting that Dalí
(who, touchingly, still seemed to believe that Gala's image had talis-
manic and protective powers) brought to his 1955 audience with the
pope. Eluard's death, in 1952—Gala did not attend the funeral—had
enabled Dalí and Gala to be married in the Church, and Dalí wanted

Pius XII to grant his official permission. Franco had decreed that only marriages performed in Spain and during his regime were legal, and the ever-practical Gala must have realized if Dalí died before her, his family would inherit his estate. Whatever the pope thought of Gala as the Holy Virgin, permission was granted, and three years later the Dalís were married, in a quiet ceremony, in Girona.

IN THE OFFICIAL wedding portrait, the conservatively dressed couple, distinguished by the sole detail of the unmistakable Dalínian moustache, could be any middle-aged newlyweds, pleased and slightly stunned to find themselves getting married so late in life. Actually it's Dalí (in a jacket, vest, and tie, his arm crooked around a cane) who looks stunned, staring dazedly into the camera, while Gala (in a printed blouse, her arms filled with flowers, her hair rolled back from her forehead in a pompadour) appears delighted to have found, at the age of sixty-three, so suave and prosperous a husband.

No one could tell from this picture that the elderly bride had long since embarked upon a series of obsessional affairs with a succession of progressively younger and more inappropriate men. Beginning in the 1940s, friends, collectors, and casual acquaintances began to complain (or boast) about having been the object of Gala's omnivorous sexual appetites. At a dinner party, she told Paul Bowles that she longed to be his parrot and have him feed her tiny morsels of food through the bars of her cage. In 1942, she offered Robert Morse—a loyal buyer of Dalí's work—a chance to enjoy a private viewing of her husband's erotic drawings. Three years earlier, this "predatory feline," this "unchaste Diana of the Hunt after the kill" attempted to seduce Jimmy Ernst, the nineteen-year-old son of her former lover, whose marriage she had broken up. After a chance encounter in New York, she invited Jimmy to go shopping with her and Dalí—a date for which Dalí failed to appear, and which devolved into an intimate lunch at the Russian Tea Room, during which Gala rubbed her companion's leg under the table and asked him up to her hotel room. "While the opportunities for female companionship were remote in my present state," Ernst concludes, "I was certainly not desperate enough for this kind of involvement."

Given his family history, Ernst's reserve is understandable. Yet nearly every account of this period in Gala's romantic career is suffused with horror, contempt, and aspersions of psychiatric pathology. Gala's advancing age and decreasing attractiveness made her the object of pity and scorn so unlike the respect awarded Picasso for the sexual vitality he displayed well into his eighties. As Gala's biographer, Tim McGirk, writes charitably, "Those who defend Gala—few in number—describe her as a nymphomaniac." If Gala's rapacious ambition, casual cruelties, troubling prejudices, and political sympathies (she and Dalí were not only pro-Franco, but anti-Semitic) made her a problematic character in her prime, time and age transformed her into a tragic and appalling old woman. Her choice of lovers and her willingness to court them with extravagant gifts appears to have less to do with sexual insatiability (of which she is often accused) than with the impossible desire to re-create the experience of her youth—to transform the procession of slim talents and irreparable wrecks into reincarnations of the divine Dalí.

Typically, she found one of her lovers in a tenement doorway in Brooklyn: a handsome young junkie named William Rotlein, who bore a striking resemblance to the young Salvador Dalí, and whom she nursed partway back to health just as she had once shored up the unstable painter. Gala persuaded herself that he was destined for a brilliant acting career. On tour in Italy, where the couple did nothing to discourage rumors that Gala planned to divorce Dalí and marry Rotlein, Gala arranged for him to have a screen test with Fellini, who said, "The boy has the face of a bandit, and Italy is filled with men who look like bandits."

But Gala's infatuation with Rotlein was merely a dress rehearsal for the most theatrical affair of her later life. In the early 1970s,

Gala, approaching eighty, developed a consuming passion for an ethereal Midwesterner named Jeff Fenholt, who was playing the title part in the Broadway production of *Jesus Christ Superstar*, and who displayed a tendency to conflate himself with his stage role. "I am the source of God, and I have the talent of the masters," he said, with a Dalínian bravado that suggests the workings of Gala's ego-building powers. Again convinced that she had discovered a major talent, Gala brought Fenholt to Dalí's afternoon soirées at the St. Regis, where the artist introduced them as Gala and Jesus Christ.

For seven years, Gala and Fenholt spent summers at the castle at Pubol, which Dalí had bought Gala in 1969. Restored and ornately decorated, the mansion became Gala's retreat, near enough but not too near Port Lligat. Dalí was forbidden to visit without an invitation. At Pubol, Gala provided the expensive Fenholt with a grand piano and costly electronic equipment. She also gave him a small fortune in Dalí paintings and a million-dollar home on Long Island, favors Fenholt repaid by flirting with young women in her presence and going on to become a penitent televangelist who would hotly deny that his relationship with Gala had ever had a sexual component.

Gala's generosity toward her young lovers and her addiction to gambling (unwisely, in view of her weakness for roulette, the Dalís had established legal residence in Monaco to avoid paying taxes) placed a heavy burden on the household budget. Their financial problems were exacerbated by the fact that Dalí's creative output had precipitously declined. Distracted by her young men, Gala had abandoned her habit of locking her husband in a room until he completed a painting. Freed from his muse's strict regimen, the artist often found himself otherwise engaged—cultivating super-models and superstars ranging from Andy Warhol to Francis Crick and James Watson, the discoverers of DNA; presiding, in New York and Paris, over an ever-changing court of attractive sycophants and exotic exhibitionists; populating palaces with circus freaks and beauties for his spectacularly choreographed orgies and erotic

Masses; exploiting his own image in ads for sportswear and choco-
lates; and giving free reign to his fashion fantasies—the toques and
leopard-fur robes, the walking cane topped by a jeweled death's
head, the pet ocelots and cheetahs that he paraded on leashes
through the streets of Manhattan.

Most disturbingly to Gala, Dalí's court included a new friend
whom the press began to refer to as the painter's muse, a tall, beautiful transsexual named Amanda Lear (formerly Alain Tap), whom
Dalí had met performing in a Paris drag club under the stage name
Peki d'Oslo. Lear became Dalí's constant companion, and, by her
own account, was united with him in a "spiritual marriage" presided
over by a mysterious, bearded hermit on a deserted mountain top
near Girona. When Dalí's Theater-Museum in Figueres was inaugurated in 1974, Dalí escorted Amanda Lear to the opening, while
Gala searched for Jeff Fenholt, who had managed to get lost in the
crowd.

Though Dalí claimed that he spent nothing on Amanda Lear
compared to the sums Gala squandered on her boys, the fact was
that the expenses of their separate lives, combined with Dalí's de-
creased productivity, exerted considerable pressure on the couple's
finances. Beginning in the mid-sixties, Dalí—allegedly encouraged
by Gala and aided by his business manager, Enrico Sabater, who par-
layed his job into a multimillion-dollar income—began signing
blank sheets of lithographic paper, which Dalí would be paid for, and
which someone else would print. Often, Dalí would sign tens of
thousands at a time; in 1974, at the Andorra border, French customs
officials seized a vehicle carrying forty thousand autographed blank
sheets.

Dalí's reputation suffered. And Gala, the Surrealist muse who
had become the muse of media celebrity transformed herself yet
again—this time into the degraded muse of art fraud and of money.

IN 1981, DR. PIERRE ROUMEGUÉRE, a French psychiatrist who had known the Dalís for almost thirty years, told *Elle* magazine: "The truth is that Dalí has lost his will to live. What we're seeing is a suicide. She's eighty-six, she's only got two or three hours of lucidity left each day, and she uses them to think about Jeff . . . whom she also calls Salvador . . . She brutalizes, bullies and injures Dalí as much as she can. So his whole world is falling apart. You have certainly heard of babies who, brutally cut off from their mother, by war or illness, let themselves die of despair. For Dalí it's the same thing."

The doctor's diagnosis proved accurate. Dalí's physical and psychological symptoms (tremors, depression, emaciation) were exacerbated by the helpful ministrations of Gala, who was liberally dosing him with tranquilizers and amphetamines and insisting that "Dalí is an indestructible rock!" Her violence was now increasingly directed at her husband; once she assaulted him with a shoe, another time with a ring. In the winter of 1981, an argument at their suite at the Hotel Meurice in Paris left Dalí with a black eye and Gala with bruises and two broken ribs. The Dalís retreated to Port Lligat, where one psychiatrist who was called in, Juan Obiols, died of a heart attack in the midst of a house call, and his successor, Ramon Vidal Teixidor, broke his leg during his first consultation with the artist.

The following year, Gala was operated on to remove her gall bladder. Recovering, she broke her leg when she slipped in the bathtub. Senile, refusing to eat, she emerged from her fog only to complain about her unhappiness—and to call Amanda Lear and ask her to care for Dalí after she was dead. Informed of her mother's condition, Cecile Eluard rushed down from Paris. But Gala refused to see her daughter, who later sued to obtain some portion of the rightful legacy of which Gala had attempted to disinherit her.

On June 10, 1982, Gala died in Port Lligat—thus violating the terms of her own will, which stipulated that she wished to pass her last moments on earth in Pubol, where she wanted to be buried in her red Dior dress. To avoid an official inquest, it was arranged to move Gala's body to Pubol, and to certify that she died there. Propped up in the back of her Cadillac, as if she were still alive, Gala's corpse was transported to her castle, thus making the muse's final journey a piece of Surrealist theater, a scenario suggestive of the sort of absurd and terrible tableau that—in his younger, healthier, happier days—her artist might have created.

LEE MILLER

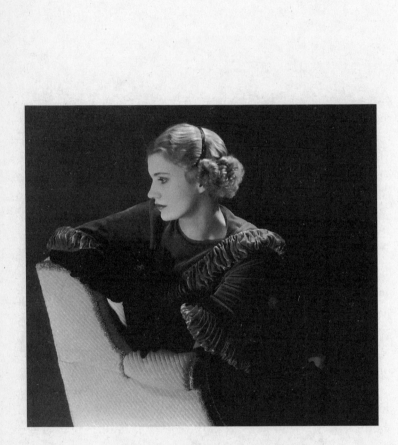

Self-Portrait, New York, 1932. *(Lee Miller)*

As far as we know, the Greek muses never matured, changed their looks, their minds, reinvented themselves and embraced new vocations. Clio never switched from history to science, nor did Melpomene abandon tragedy for something more upbeat. The whole idea of divinity—as something beyond the mutable and mortal—ensured that the major and minor deities were by definition incapable of altering their characters, their domains, or their particular preoccupations.

But as the notion of the muse was displaced from the divine to the human, and as, over centuries, women incrementally broadened their range, the lives of the muses were also transformed, until it began to seem possible that a muse could outgrow her sacred obligation to further the work of her artist and go on to lead a more independent life. She could even, potentially, *become* an artist, no longer merely inspiring, but inspired.

No one made this transition so dazzlingly as Lee Miller, the classic American beauty who served as model and muse for a series of photographers, beginning with her father and culminating with Man Ray, with whom she had a three-year affair, during which she posed for many of his most celebrated photographs and after which she continued to inspire some of his best work. By the time Man Ray was laboring over *Observatory Time*, compulsively painting and repainting her lips, like some giant, alluring, humorous, and threatening dirigible dominating the Paris skyline, Lee Miller had left him and left Paris to start her own portrait studio in New

York—just one of a series of willed self-transformations through which she became perhaps the most heroic, inventive, and determined of the muses.

Unlike the majority of the muses' life stories, hers is not primarily a duet for muse and artist but rather a solo performance with remarkable variations as she became one of the few muses—that is, former muses—to produce a body of first-rate work. Lee Miller not only succeeded as an art photographer and studio portraitist, but used her trained Surrealist's eye in her work as a courageous World War II photojournalist, reporting on the Normandy invasion, the brutal Alsace campaign, and the liberation of Buchenwald. To track Lee Miller's coverage of the war is to watch a muse discover *her* muse in the violence and horror of genocide and battle—and take an astonishing number of brilliant and lamentably undervalued photographs, underrated in part because her beauty and her legend competed with, and detracted from, the seriousness of her accomplishment.

What appears to have kept Lee Miller from settling for a career as a serial muse was a fortunate combination of personality and talent. Her most notable qualities—curiosity, the near-pathological allergy to boredom that made her restless and resourceful, the lively sense of humor that enlivened her photography—are not traits we automatically associate with musedom. What distinguished her from her sister muses was the avidity (and the success) with which she learned from the men around her, the ease with which she picked up technical and professional skills, the aesthetic acuity that she employed when she graduated from being seen to seeing, the sheer physical bravery buoyed by a fairly steady infusion of alcohol—and, above all, the high quality of the work she produced after negotiating the tricky career change from artist's muse to artist.

Of course, other muses have enjoyed the free art-education benefits of musedom, but few have used it to such advantage. Ultimately, poor Lizzie Siddal failed to benefit much from Rossetti's spirited but sporadic tutelage. While Lou Salomé's studies with Freud qualified her to become a practicing psychoanalyst, she never made a major contribution to the field, and her sense of herself as the teacher of Nietszche and Rilke prevented her from receiving some needed instruction in the art of writing. Similarly, Yoko Ono's inability to learn from John Lennon stemmed in part from her conviction that she was already an equally accomplished musician.

More than any other muse, Lee Miller was able to combine her own innate capabilities with what she acquired from the men around her. Her character, her ambition, her vocation, and her fear of boredom made her push herself to the edge, from which she would eventually draw back—with a fatal lack of nerve that nearly cost her everything she had earned.

In the best known of his dual portraits of Lee Miller and her father, Man Ray's beautiful muse shuts her luminous eyes and inclines her swan neck (two of many features that Man Ray's images of her would immortalize), curls up in Theodore Miller's lap, and pretends to snooze against his shoulder. Dressed in a girlish print dress, the nervy, gifted young woman—who, at twenty-four, had already had a career as a *Vogue* model and was in the process of taking over much of Man Ray's lucrative celebrity and society portrait business—submissively regresses into a Balthus nymphet, slumbering on the precipice of some dreamy or nightmarish awakening.

The scale of the two figures seems jarringly out of proportion. Theodore takes up all the space, while his daughter looks so diminutive that the contrast almost suggests a trick photograph, one of those sight jokes that the Surrealists so liked cooking up in the darkroom. In fact, the image has not been manipulated, though, as always, Man Ray's lighting speaks its own eloquent language, enhancing both surface and subtext. Nestled against her father, Lee appears to have shrunk into a radiant homunculus, an impression heightened by the shock of seeing a full-grown woman snuggled,

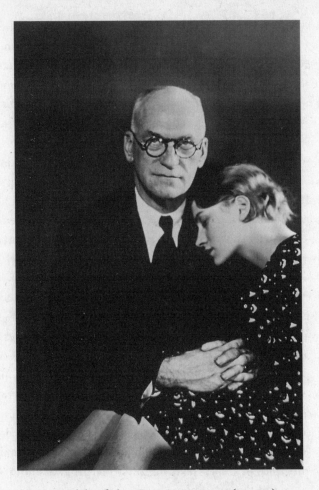

Lee with her father, Paris, January 1931. (*Man Ray*)

like a Renaissance baby Jesus, in the lap of a self-possessed middle-aged man, who looks exactly as he might alone, in a formal portrait on his office wall.

When the photo was taken, around New Year's, 1931, Miller—an engineer and executive from Poughkeepsie, New York—was traveling on business for the La Val Cream Separator Company. On his way to and from Stockholm, he stopped in Paris to visit his daughter.

Two years before, Lee Miller had shown up on Man Ray's doorstep, unannounced, uninvited, and determined to apprentice herself to the premier Surrealist photographer. And eight years prior to that, Man Ray—born Emmanuel Radnitsky, in Philadelphia—had followed his friend Marcel Duchamp from New York to Paris, where he was quickly taken up by the Surrealists and became one of the first artists to explore what the camera could do to advance the movement's principles and obsessions.

The story of Lee Miller's meeting with Man Ray (arriving from Italy to learn that he'd just left town, she caught up with him at his favorite café, Le Bateau Ivre, and announced that she was his new student and was leaving town *with* him) had already become legendary among the impecunious artists and rich socialites of Paris, who were eager to have their portraits taken by the attractive couple. Lee's leggy, blond, all-American radiance provided a titillating contrast to Man Ray's dark, stocky, saturnine good looks, and in 1930 the charismatic pair was hired to orchestrate the special effects for the legendary White Ball, given by Monsieur and Madame Pecci-Blunt. From a high window, Man Ray projected a vintage hand-tinted Méliès Brothers film onto the party guests, who were masked and dressed entirely in white, and who were transformed, by the letters in the captions on the silent film, into an animated alphabet, dancing to the music.

This dreamlike scene must have outdone even the most romantic vision of a high-Bohemian life in Paris that Lee had imagined when she'd visited the city for the first time, at eighteen. Her initial escape from Poughkeepsie had occurred when her parents jumped at the chance to send their rebellious, lovely time bomb of a daughter on an educational, chaperoned trip to France. Surely they could have predicted how quickly Lee would shake her escorts—her former high school French teacher, a certain Madame Kockashinski, and Madame's female friend—and run off to immerse herself in the art scenes of Montmartre and Montparnasse, where Lee's beauty admitted her to circles that would likely have remained closed to the average eighteen-year-old from Poughkeepsie.

It was a challenge for the Millers to get Lee home, even after Theodore came to Paris to retrieve her. The compromise was New York, where Lee's career began with a fortuitous meeting. Dressed in a chic French outfit, Lee was almost struck by a car while crossing Fifth Avenue, but was rescued at the last moment by a quick-thinking gentleman who, as luck would have it, turned out to be Condé Nast.

Lee's potential was instantly obvious to the magazine publisher, and she was soon employed at *Vogue*, modeling for Edward Steichen and Arnold Genthe, who in different ways emphasized the aspects of her beauty that made her the icon of the moment, the perfect New Woman, evolved from the *louche* kewpie-doll appeal of Louise Brooks or Clara Bow (or Kiki of Montparnasse) into a flapper raciness, a rangy, long-legged tensile strength, softened by a fresh American innocence—a sleekly handsome greyhound, starved down to go the distance. She was so obviously the New Woman that Steichen took the bold step of using her photo in an advertisement for Kotex—the first such ad to employ the image of an actual human being. Steichen and his employers turned out to have over-estimated the permissiveness of the times, and the ad caused a scandal, embarrassing even the liberated Lee.

Europe had imprinted itself on Lee, and in 1931 she snagged an assignment that enabled her to return. An American designer hired her to copy fashion details from Italian Renaissance paintings. In Florence, she discovered that it was easier to photograph than to draw the Old Master buttons and bows.

For much of Lee's working life, fashion was her day job, sup-porting her vocation as artist and even as a combat photographer covering the war for *Vogue*, then a biweekly magazine of great sophistication and intelligence. (Despite the seriousness of the *Vogue* of that period, Lee still had to alternate pieces on the Nazi death camps with pictures such as *Model Preparing for a Millinery Salon after the Liberation of Paris, 1944*.) Even after she had, like a heat-seeking missile, found Man Ray and the center of the Paris art scene, she continued to leave the neighborhood for brief excursions to the French *Vogue* office, where she earned a living (a better one, no doubt, than most of her friends) posing for George Hoyningen-Huene's theatrical glam shots, and for his student Horst P. Horst's elegant hymns to a classic ideal of female beauty.

Lee's transactions with these men were entirely professional, guided by a collegial camaraderie. But Man Ray's interest in her was of a different order, bordering on an obsession with his model and muse that had never been equaled in Lee's life—except by her father.

A bricklayer's son who had worked his way up via correspondence school from Utica to Poughkeepsie's La Val Cream Separator Company, Theodore Miller encouraged his two sons and daughter to experiment with chemistry sets and build a backyard railway. His own passion was photography, which he approached from a scientist's perspective.

Early on, he decided that his daughter was the perfect model, and he photographed her often, from babyhood. At some point, he began—and continued for years—taking stereoscopic pictures of Lee, nude. Apparently, the only time Lee objected was when Theodore proposed that the female friends she brought home to visit might want to join their experiments in nude portraiture. Just a few days before Man Ray photographed him with Lee in his lap, Theodore took a picture of his twenty-four-year-old daughter in a bathtub in Stockholm's Grand Hotel.

Whatever unease these facts and the double portrait arouse is heightened by the chilling progression of thought in this passage from *The Lives of Lee Miller*, the informative and generally sympathetic (if understandably subjective) biography—the best so far on Lee

Miller—by her only son, Antony Penrose: "The images of Lee, rest-
ing her head on (Theodore's) shoulder, affirm for us that, of all the
men in her life, he was undoubtedly the one she loved the most. The
totally abandoned way she nestles her head into his shoulder like a
drowsy puppy tells us that here is where she felt safest, tenderest,
and happiest. Throughout her life there remained a fundamental
inability to form stable relationships with her lovers. There were
many times when she wanted these relationships to endure, but
there was always some unexplainable inhibition that prevented
them from becoming completely satisfactory."

Given what we know of Lee's honesty, it seems unlikely that Man
Ray could have been unaware of her role as her father's model. And
yet this fact seems not to have shadowed the friendship that, during
that New Year's in Paris, sprang up between Man Ray and Theodore
Miller—warm feelings generated partly by a shared enthusiasm for
photographic gadgetry. And so the document endures: Man Ray's vision of a successful American businessman and his daughter, a picture that also functions as a sort of double image, since it is also a
picture of an amateur artist and his muse, a muse who doubles as the
muse of the professional artist who took the picture.

PERHAPS THE MOST remarkable aspect of Theodore Miller's nude
photos of Lee is how absent she seems, how she has managed to separate her mind—her vivid intelligence—from her body and to turn
herself into a beautiful art object. The way her arms are crossed
tightly behind her back almost suggests the broken limbs of a classical sculpture—the sort of statue that Lee would later play in
Cocteau's *Blood of a Poet*. Unless our view is tinted by outside information about the relationship of photographer and model, nothing
about the picture identifies it as a father's study of his naked adult
daughter. What does emerge is a vision of a woman mastering the
skills required for the fashion photography of the era: the ability to
represent physical beauty while disengaging from the camera and

ultimately from her own flesh. Forever after, posing clothed for strangers must have seemed, to Lee, relatively easy.

Meanwhile, Lee was learning—not only about sitting for photos, but about taking them. A committed proselytizer for the religion of science, Theodore was only too glad to instruct her in the technical aspects of their studio sessions. Lee charmed Steichen (who, she claimed, first gave her the idea of doing photography) and Genthe into disclosing the tricks of the trade—a practice she continued with Hoyningen-Huene and Horst, with whom she perfected the ability to simultaneously model and become a professional competitor. According to Antony Penrose, her "modeling sessions with Hoyningen-Huene were rather like a privileged tutorial, allowing Lee to experience the work on both sides of the camera at the same time."

By the time she apprenticed herself to Man Ray, Lee already knew so much and proved such a quick study that she was soon promoted from student to colleague. The couple collaborated on an elegant brochure for the Paris electric company and on stylish society portraits, and advanced Man Ray's efforts to shift photography from the realm of reportage to that of art. Like many modern muses, Lee took control of her artist's diet, prescribing a strict regime advised by a Dr. Hay, which prohibited the consumption of potatoes or starch on the same day on which one ate fruit, or fruit on the same day on which one ate meat.

During their three years together, Lee Miller and Man Ray worked side by side in the studio and the darkroom, and took extraordinary portraits of each other. In Lee Miller's 1929 *Man Ray Shaving*, the miracle of soap turns her lover's profile into pure Surrealism, a mystery and a joke. His hair, his eyes, and forehead are dark, while the lower half of his face is slathered in mime-white shaving cream, transforming him into a high-contrast study in black and white, rather like a cookie iced with chocolate and vanilla.

Man Ray's photos of Lee range from renderings of her classic profile to zebra-striped nudes that play with shadows cast by venetian blinds to fierce shots of her, costumed and made up as a sort of evil geisha. He incorporated her features in paintings and in constructions such as *Boule de Neige*, a glass paperweight in which a photo of Lee's eye was suspended in water swirling with "snowflakes." Unusually susceptible to the influence of his muses, Man Ray had already created *Le Violin d'Ingres* and other iconic images of his previous mistress, the fleshy, sensual, legendary art-tomato, Kiki of Montparnasse. But now he found his ideal muse in the leaner, racier Lee, whose preternatural ability to attract and reflect light (so that in his photos she often seems lit from within) made her the ideal subject for an artist determined to investigate the possibilities of illumination.

His unquenchable aesthetic interest in his lover's body, the sheer number and variety of his photos of Lee, and the renown they rapidly achieved led *Time* magazine to say that Lee Miller "was widely celebrated for having the most beautiful navel in Paris." Perhaps intuiting that *navel* was something of a euphemism for other parts of his daughter's anatomy—in one famous Man Ray photograph, a bubble lightly brushes her nipple, and a champagne glass based on the shape of her breast had already been designed—Lee's father wrote an angry letter to, and extracted an apology from, the editors of *Time*.

In a 1975 interview with art historian and critic Mario Amaya, Lee is characteristically flippant and revealing in her account of what first attracted her to photography—a seemingly casual choice that in fact reflected the restless, distractible impatience that was at once her greatest strength and her most self-sabotaging weakness: "I had given up art . . . after a long trip through Italy. All the paintings had been painted as far as I was concerned and I became a photographer. Painting is a very lonesome business whereas photography is a more friendly affair. What's more, you have something in hand when you're finished—every 15 seconds you've made something."

Throughout the interview, Lee's conversation switches fluidly between the personal and the technical. Forty-three years after their breakup, she recalls her lover in a way which swiftly conveys the force of their erotic connection: "He had an economy of motion. He never made extra gestures . . . Whether he lit his Dunhill lighter or put the key in the door, there was no lost motion. . . . His hands were not dry, but they were noticeably hot. If he took your hand or touched you, you felt almost a magnetic heat. It was quite abnormal, but not feverish." But the next moment, and for much of the article, Lee is breezily discoursing on the details of developing and printing, airbrushing and retouching. "Man put, let's say, a 60-volt lamp onto a 110 circuit so that it would burn very brightly. The lamps ordinarily burn out very fast, but he would let them light up and heat up very gradually on a rheostat so that they didn't get any shock and they didn't break right away. And you had a brilliant, clear light which is the same principal as the photoflood."

During the same conversation, Lee tells her version of how the solarization process was discovered: "Something crawled across my foot in the darkroom and I let out a yell and turned on the light. I never did find out what it was, a mouse or what. Then I quickly realized that the film was totally exposed: there in the development tank, ready to be taken out, were a dozen practically fully-developed negatives of a nude against a black background . . . Man Ray grabbed them, put them in the hypo, and looked at them later . . . The background and the image couldn't heal together, so there was a line left which he called a 'solarization.'"

During those years, Lee Miller took some first-rate photos that were nothing at all like Man Ray's or anyone else's, images that often involve visual surprises brightened by the spark of a highly individual sense of humor. In the 1929 *Sculpture in Window*, a blaze of light draws our attention to the idealized head and chest of an Attic sculpture of a young male. Only later do we notice that the statue is surrounded by knockoffs—a horse, a figure of Mercury—in a com-

mercial setting that revises our first impression of the irrepro-
ducible, ancient work of art. In the 1930 *Rat Tails*, the hilarity of four
rats' behinds with their tails hanging nearly plumb engages us for a
long time before we wonder what the rats (Are they alive or
stuffed?) are doing on their perch.

As Lee's confidence grew, she began to urge Man Ray to leave
the portrait business to her. He could stop wasting time on celebrity
photographs and concentrate on his first love, painting. Lee's account of her apparently selfless offer conveys the practicality of a
twenty-four-year-old muse trying to support herself without depending on the generosity of her artist. "I had already been there a
year and was doing his work. I was getting along very well and he
had given me jobs that he either didn't want or which didn't pay
enough. I had already had some considerable professional experience fulfilling contracts and things . . . He had taught me to do fashion pictures, he'd taught me to do portraits, he taught me the whole
technique of what he did."

Lee must have welcomed any sort of fallback plan; doubtless it
seemed improbable that she and Man Ray were destined to grow
old together. Jealously possessive, he consistently failed to rise to
the lofty high-mindedness of Lee's insistence on maintaining complete sexual freedom, a failure that prompted her to move to her
own apartment. Man Ray's recollection of the White Ball—written
decades afterward—hints at some of the reasons why their romance
ran aground:

"I was dressed in white as a tennis player, bringing as an assistant
a pupil who studied photography with me at the time—Lee Miller.
She too was dressed as a tennis player in a very smart shorts and
blouse especially designed by one of the well-known couturiers. A
slim figure with blond hair and lovely legs, she was continually being
taken away to dance, leaving me to concentrate alone on my photography. I was pleased with her success, but annoyed at the same
time, not because of the added work, but out of jealousy; I was in

love with her . . . Lee turned up now and then between dances to tell me what a wonderful time she was having; all the men were so sweet to her. It was her introduction to French society."

By contrast, Lee remembers wearing a white Madame Vionnet dress and is more technically minded than her former lover: "We must have used 35mm because I don't think there were 16 mm's around in those days. And we used bits of commercial film that Man had borrowed or picked up off some cutting-room floor without rhyme or reason." But she ends her reminiscence with an off-hand afterthought that corroborates Man Ray's version: "I met lots of handsome young men who kept me dancing so I didn't do much of the work."

Evidently, plenty of young men were eager to keep Lee dancing. She was resolutely unfaithful—by nature and on principle—and Man Ray responded to her affairs with letters like this one written during her romance with Zizzi Svirsky, a Russian emigré interior decorator: "I have loved you terrifically, jealously: it has reduced every other passion in me, and to compensate, I have tried to justify this love by giving you every chance in my power to bring out everything interesting in you. The more you seemed capable the more my love was justified, and the less I regretted any lost effort on my part . . . You met me halfway on every occasion—until this new element appeared, which has given you the illusion that you are freeing yourself from me . . ."

What's striking is Man Ray's description of the talented and resourceful Lee as merely "capable." While the pain of a lover suffering the agonies of jealousy naturally arouses one's sympathy, Man Ray manages to make every phrase seem like a tiny pump leaching oxygen from the atmosphere. Eventually, his jealousy spilled over from the erotic arena to the professional. He was enraged when his muse played a muse in Jean Cocteau's *Blood of a Poet*. Her role, as an armless classical statue, required her to have her arms strapped to her sides, to don an uncomfortable papier-mâché wig, to cover herself with a suffocatingly thick coating of white paint, and to endure a nasty confrontation with an ox rescued from an abattoir to play a bull.

The tempests generated by Man Ray's possessiveness became the normal weather of their relationship. But the climate worsened drastically in 1931, when Lee fell in love with an older, rich Egyptian named Aziz Eloui Bey. Aziz's wife Nimet was a celebrated beauty who had modeled for Man Ray, Horst, Hoyningen-Huene—and for Lee. Not long after the start of Lee's affair with Aziz, Nimet committed suicide. Man Ray threatened to do the same and took a picture of himself holding a pistol, with a rope around his neck. Finally, at the end of 1932, Lee—seeing no other way to unravel this snarled erotic embroglio—left Paris for New York, where she established her own portrait-photography business with her brother Erik.

As IT DAWNED on Man Ray that the unthinkable was occurring— that Lee was leaving him for good—he was inspired to produce some of his best pieces. And so Lee Miller's work as muse outlived the demise of their affair, thus making her one of the many muses whose departure and absence motivated their artists as much as, if not more than, their love and their physical presence.

During their last months together, Man Ray filled his journals with expressions of torment over Lee's betrayal. He drew her face in his notebook and scribbled her name over the drawing in a manic, alarming cursive. On the back of the page, which he sent Lee, he scrawled, "Accounts never balance one never pays enough etc.etc. love Man." More upsettingly, he cut out and enclosed a photo of Lee's eye, on the back of which he inscribed a poem:

> With an eye always in reserve
> Material indestructible . . .
> Forever being put away
> Taken for a ride . . .

Put on the spot . . .
The racket must go on—
I am always in reserve.

In this undiluted outpouring of passion, pride, self-pity, and self-abasement, one can see the raw material that was, even then, in the process of being turned into art. Around that time, Man Ray happened on the idea of attaching a photo of Lee's eye to the metronome arm in *Object to Be Destroyed*, a work that went through many editions, copies, and permutations when its viewers and the artist himself took its directive title seriously. Man Ray claims to have wrecked the first (1922) version himself: "A painter needs an audience, so I also clipped the photo of an eye to the metronome's swinging arm to create the illusion of being watched as I painted. One day I did not accept the metronome's verdict . . . and since I had called it, with a certain premonition, *Object of Destruction*, I smashed it to pieces." And in the 1950s, a group of anarchist students destroyed a later edition in a Paris gallery.

Like *Alice's Adventures in Wonderland*, Balanchine's *Meditation*, and Dalí's portraits of Gala, this sculpture, as well as *Observatory Time*, made reference to the artist's feelings for a particular muse. All these works may have, in some embryonic form, preexisted the muse's intervention—and been given a final push into life with her midwifely assistance. But only in the case of Man Ray was there tangible evidence that the conception *did* predate the muse and yet required her help to turn some corner—to bridge the gap that so often lies between art and experimentation.

The image of the metronome with an eye attached had first occurred to Man Ray almost a decade before. "I had a metronome in my place which I set going when I painted . . . its ticking noise regulated the frequency and number of my brushstrokes. The faster it went, the faster I painted; and if the metronome stopped then I knew I had painted too long, I was repeating myself, my painting was no good, and I would destroy it."

Around the time of his separation from Lee, Man Ray replaced the eye with Lee's, which he clipped from a photo and attached to the metronome arm with a paper clip. According to Lee, "We had quarreled rather definitively and the *Objet à Détruire* has my eye attached to the metronome; calling it 'object to be destroyed' was kind of making it a wax statue to poke needles into, I think. Because you saw this eye ticking away and you picked up a hammer and smashed it. In fact in Paris in 1958, some students actually did destroy it."

Wisely, Man Ray ensured the survival of the piece by publishing a drawing of the metronome, complete with Lee's eye, in the September 1932 issue of Edward Titus's Surrealist magazine *This Quarter*. A caption explained how the work was created, and how it was meant to be treated: "Cut out the eye from a portrait of one who has been loved but is seen no more. Attach the eye to the pendulum of a metronome and regulate the weight to suit the tempo desired. Keep going to the limit of endurance. With a hammer well aimed, try to destroy the whole at a single blow."

After the anarchist students took him at his word, Man Ray made several copies, one of which he presented to Lee. Thus he became a pioneer in the field of multiples and reproductions, territory that later would be mined by artists including Dalí and Warhol. But what matters more is that the loss of Lee Miller inspired the object that we cannot imagine without the exquisite, perfect eye at the end of the metronome arm.

He'd also begun *Observatory Time* before his separation from Lee—in fact, at the inspiration of another muse. The lipstick print that Kiki's rosebud mouth had left on his shirt collar provided the primary impulse for his painting of enormous lips undulating in the sky above the city. But only after Lee left did he realize that the shape of the floating red object needed to follow the longer, thinner, more elegant line of *her* lips—more ethereal than Kiki's and, at the same time, more biomorphic, so that each lip resembled a body pressed against its mate, squirming in the "mackerel sky" above the observatory in the Luxembourg Gardens.

Man Ray reworked the canvas until 1934—to get the lips right. In the lives of the muses, little equals the heartbreaking, operatic excess of a depressed, suicidal artist spending two years of his life painting, rubbing out, and repainting the mouth of the muse who had abandoned him.

IN NEW YORK, Lee was discovering that the Depression was not the most propitious time to start an upmarket portrait business. Even so, her studio did extraordinarily well for a Depression-era enterprise run by a woman in her twenties.

In order to open Lee Miller Studios on East Forty-eighth Street, she persuaded two businessmen (one an heir to the Western Union fortune, the other to the Fleischman's Yeast company) to back her, and with her brother's help she designed an environment that would protect her privileged, skittish subjects from having to see the nasty developing and enlarging equipment. A fanatic in the darkroom and behind the lens, Lee used the dramatic, unconventional lighting she had perfected with Man Ray to create flattering portraits of stage and movie stars (Gertrude Lawrence and Lilian Harvey), artists such as Virgil Thomson, and celebrities such as "Prince" Mike Romanoff. For her portrait of Joseph Cornell, Lee outdid herself, giving the eccentric artist the dreamy, haunted good looks of a semi-lunatic poet posed beside one of his works, an object that appears to be a hairy (or flaming) toy sailboat.

Eventually, Lee and Erik branched into the more lucrative field of advertising with a striking shot of scent bottles lined up in a glittering row. But making perfume look desirable in a Manhattan studio must have seemed a step down from projecting silent films onto the glamorous artists and socialites at the White Ball. When Aziz Bey arrived in New York to purchase equipment for the Egyptian national railway, he invited Lee to trade her demanding career for a more leisurely existence in a mansion on the Island of Giza. Surprising everyone, especially Erik, who had moved his wife to Long Island City and whose livelihood depended on the photography business, Lee married Aziz and, after a Niagara Falls honeymoon, left for Egypt.

But life in Cairo turned out to be utterly unlike whatever Arabian Nights fantasy had propelled Lee on her precipitous magic carpet ride from New York. Reading poor Aziz's letter to Lee's parents, his account of their "soft and easy" routine comprising bridge games, sea baths, and desultory Alexandria nightclub-hopping, anyone who knew his bride (except Aziz, apparently) could have predicted how soon she would grow restless: "Lee is happy. Naturally it is not easy to settle down smoothly considering her much troubled soul. Certain reactions are bound to happen. Only small things like being bored suddenly. You see she does not work any more and her brain must work to occupy Lee's time."

Visits from Paris friends, trips to St. Moritz, excursions into the desert, the arrival of Erik and his wife Mafy, and a series of casual, adulterous romances did little to alleviate the tedium, though Lee continued to take beautiful photos, finding Surrealist images in the ancient landscape. In one especially arresting shot, puffs of newly harvested cotton, emerging like some unstoppable alien life force from a stack of burlap sacks, dominate a dramatic sky filled with high, cottony clouds. Several photos—including one of a pyramid's triangular shadow falling over a dusty town—resemble Magritte paintings, and indeed Magritte claimed to have based *Le Baiser* on a Lee Miller image of a tattered tent, its ragged netting torn to frame our view of the desolate, sandy horizon. This picture displays an early manifestation of Lee's concern with composition—a formalism that would later shape her shots of nurses and doctors working in makeshift field hospitals to save the wounded victims of the Normandy invasion.

By 1937, Lee had tired of Cairo, and she fled to Paris to resume some version of the life she had left five years before. After all those bridge games in the tennis clubs of Alexandria, what a glorious homecoming it must have been, on the evening of her arrival, to attend a Surrealist ball given by the Rochas Sisters and featuring the stars of the Paris art world.

On the night of the White Ball, she had been twenty-three. Now she was thirty, Man Ray's friend rather than his lover, and officially the wife of a rich, indulgent husband back in Cairo. This time, Lee dressed more sedately, in a long blue robe. Still, feelings ran high (at some point during the festivities Man Ray gave Paul Eluard a black eye) and, even in her modest gown, Lee managed to do what she always did at the Surrealist balls—that is, attract young men. It was an activity she rarely took seriously, though maybe she should have that night, since the young man she attracted would turn out to be her future, and the full stop to which her future came.

ROLAND PENROSE would paint Lee Miller in a variety of moods and guises, in many different styles—in fact, in the styles of many different painters. Lee is the central figure in the Magritte-like *Night and Day* and *Good Shooting*, and pregnant, in the Picasso-esque *First View*. But the fact that she is never described as Roland Penrose's muse (though they were together for forty years) reminds us that the muses of failed or derivative artists are rarely celebrated for their labors. It is mostly the great work—or, as in the case of Rossetti, the showy work and the dramatic life—that moves us to look for the muse who inspired it.

In Penrose's illustrated memoir, *Scrapbook, 1900–1981*, the British painter, curator, and collector recalls the Rochas sisters' ball, to which he was invited by Max Ernst. The two friends put on old clothes, and Penrose dyed his right hand and his left foot blue, a conception with a certain obviousness and carelessness of execution, the same flaws observable in his art. Then, writes Penrose, we "appeared among an elegant crowd of dancers, whose imaginations had produced sumptuous extravagances . . . The girls had skillfully used their ingenuity to increase their natural provocation, one being clothed in little more than strands of ivy. But in spite of such obvious guile, I, to my surprise, found myself compelled to turn my attentions to a girl dressed conventionally in a long dark robe. Blond, blue-eyed and responsive, she seemed to enjoy the abysmal contrast between her elegance and my own slumlike horror." Penrose provides a capsule biography of the "fabulous beauty" and "luminous presence"—without mentioning her work except to note that she had been the studio assistant of Man Ray, "whose splendid portraits of her were widely admired," and that she had "directed her own photographic studio until she married a rich and very lovable Egyptian."

Within days after the ball, Penrose and Lee were an item; soon she joined the Surrealists (the Eluards, Max Ernst, and Leonora Carrington, among others) who arrived to stay with Penrose at his brother's house in Cornwall. Lee and Penrose traveled along with a sort of progressive house party, which moved to the south of France, where Picasso (Penrose's lifelong friend and, later, biographical subject) painted Lee's portrait.

Stirred either by conscience or by some intimation that domesticity with Roland Penrose would eventually prove more narrowly circumscribed than life with Aziz, Lee returned to Egypt, where she lasted for another year before she and Penrose embarked on a tour of the Balkans, a voyage described in his illustrated book, *The Road is Wider Than Long*. Their long-distance romance continued, sustained by periodic reunions, including a trip to Egypt during which Penrose courted Lee with two revealing love tokens: "For years I had the habit of looking for amusing pieces of sentimental jewellery . . . . These I had offered to girl-friends, feeling that their acceptance was for me in some way the symbolic equivalent of an orgasm. On one occasion a jeweller produced an exact copy of a pair of handcuffs in gold, complete with keys and signed 'Cartier.' Armed with these and the illustrated manuscript of *The Road is Wider Than Long*, bound in thick shoe leather and dedicated to Lee, I set off on my quest."

In 1939, the couple was in Antibes when they heard that Hitler had invaded Poland. Together they navigated the back roads of France to the relative safety of Penrose's house in Downshire Hill, Hampstead. There they resumed the ongoing house party, now populated by British artists, writers, journalists, and politicians. Meanwhile Lee badgered *Vogue* into putting her on staff, a job that mostly involved taking celebrity and fashion photographs; the magazine was still reluctant to disturb its readers by acknowledging the war, even after the magazine's London office was leveled by a German bomb.

From Downshire Hill, outside central London, Lee and Roland could watch the horrifying light show: the search beacons, the anti-aircraft rockets, the flames rising from neighborhoods bombed in the Nazi air raids. Penrose, himself quite anxious, noted that Lee not only remained unafraid despite the proximity of death and destruction, but seemed energized and excited by her nearness to danger.

Lee began taking the photos that would be collected in *Grim Glory: Pictures of Britain Under Fire*. These shots of bombed-out London made the war seem to have been orchestrated by a demonic intelligence with an ironic Surrealist humor and a taste for macabre, ghastly tableaux. The smashed, melted typewriter in *Remington Silent* evokes those sculptures (Man Ray's clothes iron studded with nails, Meret Oppenheim's fur tea cup) that transform a practical household object into something fantastically useless, while the bricks and rubble filling the doorway in *Nonconformist Chapel* seem like a sly awful joke—a sight gag underlined by the photo's title—on the whole idea of a doorway. Lee's abiding interest in the frame was abetted by the explosion that knocked out the center of a Knightsbridge building, leaving both sides and a connecting stretch of mansard roof to form a ragged arch that does indeed resemble *The Bridge of Sighs*, after which the photo is named.

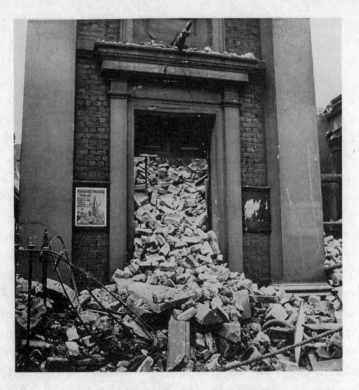

Noncomformist Chapel, Camden Town.
From *Grim Glory,* 1940. *(Lee Miller)*

Her pictures from this period are notable for their compositional and aesthetic elegance. They reflect what she learned from Man Ray, yet are entirely her own. Once we have seen them, we can immediately identify them as Lee Miller's work, not simply because of their subject matter but because of their vision, their clarity, their unique mix of compassion, formalism, and edgy, upsetting wit.

In a letter to her parents, she described her state of mind: "Feeling like a soft-shelled crab—before we had any barrage working, there was the exaltation of winning the big daytime air battles . . . we were all into the strain of what became three months of solid hell at night —and harrowing by day to get to work by some crazy route— to count noses to see if everyone had really lived through it . . ." Lee's empathy for the suffering around her, throughout the war, was heartfelt and profound; she never romanticized or understated its horrors. Her magazine articles and correspondence have a refreshing directness, a baseline layer of steely emotion (outrage at the Germans, fury and grief at the human cost of battle) unmediated by the hard-boiled matter-of-factness we associate with combat journalism. At the same time, a giddy exhilaration rises from her prose style, with its punchy elliptical images divided by dashes.

Lee was discovering the thrill of getting closer to the flame as she began to work with Dave Scherman, a twenty-five-year-old American photojournalist for *Life*, whose personal and professional attraction to Lee can still be felt in his introduction to *Lee Miller's War*, a collection of photos and essays edited by Antony Penrose. Lee and Roland befriended Scherman, and then Lee and Dave took off on their own, first to Scotland to photograph Wrens in training on the North Sea and then back to North London, to do a piece on the women who operated the giant beacon that scanned the sky for enemy planes. (Presumably, the woman-warrior angle helped Lee get permission to do the pieces for *Vogue*.) Lee's photo shows the women lined up in identical hooded parkas, their arms around each others' shoulders, like some jolly military chorus line. In this shot taken before the alarm sounded and the area was strafed by low-flying German planes, the searchlight shining in the background produces a diagonal of light as dramatic as Man Ray's trickiest effects.

Rapidly realizing what she wanted to do, Lee asked *Vogue* for tougher assignments. Meanwhile she was still taking the fashion and glam shots (Margot Fonteyn, James Mason, Bob Hope) that made her indispensable to her editors, who amid the wartime chaos must have been glad to have a reliable source for the pictures that were still the magazine's heart and soul.

Even as Lee was trying to get nearer to the front, Penrose had found a safer way of contributing to the war effort, trading on his skills as an artist and connoisseur to become an instructor in camouflage to the Home Guard. "Applying the principles of cubism to the optical disruption of form obtained by covering a surface with patterns, it was possible, given the right background, to make an object disappear as a moth does on the bark of a tree." In his experiments with the camouflage possibilities of a green ointment newly manufactured by a cosmetics company, Roland persuaded Lee, his "willing guinea pig," to strip naked except for dark shorts and cover herself with makeup. ("My theory was that if it could hide such eye-catching attractions as hers from the invading Hun, smaller and less seductive areas of skin would stand an even better chance of becoming invisible.") Dave Scherman's peculiar photo of the event depicts a wacky *déjeuner sur l'herbe*, involving two proper British couples with a picnic and tea, a thoroughly unremarkable outing except for the fact that Lee is mostly naked and entirely green.

Roland's interest in the military uses of cubism took him to Italy, where he studied the Italian army's expert use of camouflage and watched, from a distance, the assault on Monte Cassino. "Apart from this brief taste of action at the front I remained a home-bound instructor throughout the war, which gave me a sense of inferiority when I compared my own efforts to the daring exploits of Lee. On her own initiative she had become war correspondent for that elegant ladies' magazine 'Vogue.' She had landed in France shortly after D-Day and continued to follow closely the allied advance through the horrors of battle and concentration camps."

Even on the front lines, Lee photographed like a painter, conscious of geometry, of verticals and diagonals, and of the way that light could transform an image into something haunting, even supernatural. She distilled what she'd learned from Man Ray, Steichen, Genthe, Hoyningen-Huene, and Horst into a visual aesthetic that allowed her to combine (as few artists or photographers have done, and which no one has done quite so well) photojournalism and art—although in a dispatch from postwar Munich, she insisted that she was involved in nothing more glorious than pure documentation: "I'm extremely irritable quite often and especially when I don't understand people. I'm also inclined to scream at them when they try to tell me that the bombed out Hofbrau Haus won't make an interesting picture because it is all destroyed . . . The first ten times I explain that I'm busy making documents and not art, and the eleventh I start screaming, 'For Christ's sake shut up and mind your own business—all you're supposed to do is tell me what goes on in these various addresses.' "

THE GRAINY, SLIGHTLY BLURRED focus emphasizes the alien otherworldliness of the wrapped-up mummy whose white pillow and bandages cut diagonally across the image. His hands are swathed so thickly they look like boxing mitts, and some vaguely, disturbingly human expression (is it a smile, or is he just staring?) greets us from the dark strips of eyes and nose and mouth divided by strips of pale gauze. It is the lead photograph in Lee's piece, "U.S.A. Tent Hospital . . . in France," in the September 1944 *Vogue*, and the caption underneath the shot explains: "A bad burn case asked me to take his picture, as he wanted to see how funny he looked. It was pretty grim, and I didn't focus well."

The first of the major pieces that Lee dispatched from the front took readers inside the tents of the 44th Evacuation Hospital, set up in a cow pasture in Normandy a few weeks after D-Day. There, forty doctors and forty nurses took on the Herculean task of doing an average of "one hundred operations every twenty-four hours on six operating tables, as well as caring for four hundred transient patients." It's a long way from the plucky women operating the beacons outside London; the photos and text chart the vertiginous speed with which Lee was being drawn into the chaos, the excitement, the inferno that, she wrote, reminded her of a painting by Hieronymus Bosch.

In these early *Vogue* photo essays, one can watch the war seducing Lee with the ultimate remedy for boredom—the combined attractions of danger, a constant supply of arresting images, and a sense of purpose: a mission to inform the world about what she was seeing and to communicate this information in a form that aspired to art. Another caption beneath a photo from the 44th Evac Hospital hints at the effect Lee was after: "Operating room of the evacuation hospital, seen through a mosquito netting . . . a contrast of white towels, concentrated light, and khaki shadows." What comes through her texts—and especially the photographs—is the satisfaction of an artist discovering the work she was born to do, and which she undertook with a focus and dedication that obliterated her former preoccupations with how she looked and what she ate. She exchanged her chic outfits for the combat uniform she wore throughout the war, and the finicky hypochondriac who had persuaded Man Ray to adopt the restrictive Hay diet now willingly shared the rations—and the alcohol—consumed by the soldiers in the field. Dave Scherman mentions "the ingestion of gargantuan amounts of Rouyer's cognac" and describes Lee swigging straight from a jerrycan full of framboise and a lethal cocktail of whatever wines and liqueurs they "liberated" in their journey through France.

From the hospitals of Normandy, Lee traveled to the port city of St. Malo to document the fierce battle that preceded the German surrender. In another ingeniously composed photo, she used the window and the ironwork railing of her room across from the fort to create a rectangle in which a powerful napalm bomb destroys the fortress. Put under house arrest by the U.S. Army for having entered the combat zone in violation of the conditions of her accreditation, she spent her brief incarceration writing an article that ran in the October 1944 *Vogue*. From St. Malo, Lee sent Penrose a note that captures the fervor (a heat mostly absent from Penrose's account) of their attachment: "Dearest—I'm going down to an OP inside the bomblines—to watch and take pictures,—naturally, I'm a bit nervous as it'll be 200 pounders from the air—ours—I know nothing will happen to me as I know our life is going on together—for ever—I'm not being mystic, I just know— and love you. Lee."

At the end of August, Lee wrote Audrey Withers, her editor at *Vogue*, a letter vibrant with the exultation of what Lee describes as her new "taste for gunpowder": "I won't be the first woman journalist in Paris—by any means—but I'll be the first damn photographer, I think, unless someone parachutes in . . . Anyway I guess I'm the only dame who's really covered a battle."

In Paris for the Liberation, Lee was reunited with old friends—Picasso, Cocteau, the Eluards—and filed an illustrated report that combined a portrait of an important historical moment with the details (about perfume and lacy blouses, makeup and hair) that *Vogue* readers wanted. She described the extraordinary effort required to operate the one functioning beauty salon in Paris, where the hair dryers were heated by a wood furnace, and "the air is blown by fans turned by relay teams of boys riding a stationary tandem bicycle in the basement. They cover 320 kilometers a day and dry half as many heads." She illustrated her account with a photo of the bicyclists powering the dryers and another of a model leaving the hairdresser with her hair wrapped in a fetching turban. Observing the lingering effects of the Occupation and hearing the appalling reports from Germany and Poland, Lee was irritated by the *Vogue* photo editor's complaints that her shots of fashion models and chic Frenchwomen were insufficiently glossy and alluring.

Drawing on what he recalls as a mix of devil-may-care nerviness and sheer bluff, Roland Penrose managed to skip out on his war duties and get to Paris, where he found Lee at the Hotel Scribe. "Somehow it was intended that the miracle would continue." After a joyous two-day reunion, Penrose returned to England. Eluard had entrusted him with materials concerning the activities of the French Resistance, and, back home, Penrose arranged to have them published as a book, *In the Service of the People*. His memoir hardly mentions what Lee did after he left the continent, though the next months marked the most harrowing period—and the pinnacle—of her career as a wartime photojournalist.

THE SIXTEEN-PAGE celebration of the Allied victory in Europe that dominates the June 1945 issue of *Vogue* seems calculated to prepare us for, or cushion us from, the shock and brutality of its final images. The section begins with a heartening essay entitled "Half-Way to Victory," and with two photos taken on the streets of New York. In one, a flag waves amid the airborne debris of a victory celebration; in the other, a hangdog band of new conscripts marches through the parade detritus—on their way to finish the job, in the Pacific. Next comes a photomontage of thankful churchgoers and ecstatic merrymakers in Great Britain, France, and New York, then a two-page spread given over to a Lee Miller photograph of Russian and American soldiers exchanging triumphant smiles on the battlefield at Torgau.

Then suddenly, the tone darkens, all that celebratory goodwill dispelled by the first words of Lee Miller's "Germans Are Like This": "Germany is a beautiful landscape, dotted with jewel-like villages, blotched with ruined cities, inhabited by schizophrenics." Animated by the same rage that fueled the previous month's "Out of the German Prison," an essay of Lee's that included photos of the Alsace campaign and her passionate railing against the country where "the adrenalin, stimulated by hate, boils in the blood," this sequel describes her "disgusting and horrifying encounters" with Germans, none of whom will admit to having been a Nazi. Facing the text are four photographs, arranged in two sets. A shot of healthy German children walking hand in hand down the street of a pretty town has been placed beside one of the "burned bones of starved prisoners," in which a mound of charred white fragments cuts diagonally across the image. In the background are three prisoners standing over the bones; all we see of the men are their striped pants and the bottoms of their jackets. Beneath these pictures is an even more disturbing pairing: a shot of an "orderly" town rising up a hillside, beside one of a neat row of three brick ovens, "orderly furnaces to burn bodies."

But not even this prepares us for what comes next: a heap of skeletal corpses, some with their eyes still open, some naked, some wearing striped camp uniforms, a vision of horror intensified (if that is possible) by Lee's gift for lighting and composition. The headline reads: " 'BELIEVE IT' Lee Miller cables from Germany." (In fact, the unedited cable said, "I implore you to believe it.") A photo of a pile of starved bodies and another of a beaten German guard hanging from a hook are accompanied by the following text: " 'This is Buchenwald Concentration Camp at Weimar . . . Lee Miller has been with American armies since about D-Day last June . . . She cabled: 'No question that German civilians knew what went on. Railway siding into Dachau camp runs past villas, with trains of dead and semi-dead deportees. I usually don't take pictures of horrors. But don't think that every town and every area isn't rich with them. I hope *Vogue* will feel that it can publish these pictures . . .' "

By now, such images have become so much a part of our consciousness that we can no longer imagine how they affected the readers of *Vogue*. (In the same issue as Lee's photos of Buchenwald are fashion spreads with titles like "Peplums Forward," "Barebacks in Town—How and When" and "The Nightdress Idea.") On the next two pages are eight harrowing images of suffering and desolation that were among the milder photos Lee was sending back. One depicts a beautiful blond woman (who looks a bit like Lee) stretched almost voluptuously against the arm of a leather couch; her body is arched, her head back, her lips are open in what could be passion, except that she is dead: the suicided daughter of the Nazi Burgomaster of Leipzig.

CONSIDER TWO PHOTOS of Lee in the bath, taken fourteen years apart. In the first, shot in the Grand Hotel in Stockholm in 1931, Theodore Miller portrays his daughter as the shy, graceful, dewy post-nymphet who (as in his other photos of her) occupies the center of the image: a steamy, soft-focus dream without the distractions of reality, setting, and background. In the second, Dave Scherman gives his subject a considerably harder edge and pulls back from Lee (we see only her head and a discrete curve of arm and bare shoulder) to document the bathroom—Hitler's bathroom in the Führer's Munich headquarters—where Lee and Dave, en route from Buchenwald and Dachau, had arranged to stay. "I was living in Hitler's apartment," Lee wrote Audrey Withers, "when his death was announced . . . Well, alright, he was dead. He'd never really been alive for me until today. He'd been an evil machine-monster all these years, until I visited the places he made famous, talked to people who knew him, dug into backstairs gossip and ate and slept in his house. He became less fabulous and therefore more terrible, along with a little evidence of his having some almost human habits; like an ape who embarrasses and humbles you with his gestures, mirroring yourself in caricature."

Lee shed her combat boots and settled into Hitler's tub for her "first long soak in a while." Little about the bathroom suggests its original inhabitant's identity, except for the framed photo of the Führer on the rim of the tub (one suspects that Lee or Dave indulged in some set decoration) and the kitschy nude (Hitler's taste, we assume) kneeling on the edge of the counter and providing a marked contrast to the ravaged, haunted Lee. Her skin and hair have coarsened so drastically she's almost unrecognizable as the golden girl Man Ray photographed. The look in her eyes, cast slightly to one side, seems entirely appropriate for a woman who has just witnessed the liberation of the death camps, and who now finds herself bathing in Hitler's tub. In addition to all the ways in which the photo represents triumph, it also scores a private victory over the passivity and the idealized prettiness of Theodore Miller's bath-tub photo.

Later, as Lee would record in the "Hitleriana" piece that ran in *Vogue*, she and Dave went a few blocks farther, to Eva Braun's house. Lee explored Eva's "supernormal" bathroom, which contained enough drugs "for a ward of hypochondriacs," and took a nap on her bed. "It was comfortable, but it was macabre . . . to doze on the pillow of a girl and a man who were now dead, and to be glad they were dead, if it was true." Soon after, Lee and Dave followed a tip that led them to Berchtesgaden, where Lee photographed Hitler's house in flames, glowing in the dark like a monstrous jack-o'-lantern.

THE WAR WAS hard to recover from, especially for someone whose taste for gunpowder had become an addiction. The transition to peacetime was difficult for Roland Penrose, too. "The war had disrupted the way in which I had hoped to develop, and even before the war it had occurred to me that I would never attain the stature in the arts of my brilliant surrealist friends of whom I could name a score." *Scrapbook* is notably silent on the period that preceded his and Lee's reentry into each other's lives.

Lee traveled through Denmark, dutifully photographing the "gay little country that snubbed and swindled the Nazis" for *Vogue*. Back in London, she was honored for her wartime contribution with a luncheon at which *Vogue*'s managing editor praised, apparently without irony, the schizophrenia of Lee's career. "Who else can get in at the death of St. Malo and at the re-birth of the fashion salons?"

After an argument with Penrose, Lee returned to Paris, where she slipped into a depression fueled by heavy self-medication with alcohol and Benzedrine. In an unsent letter to Penrose, she complained about "a new and disillusioning world. Peace with a world of crooks who have no honour, no integrity and no shame is not what anyone fought for." Desperate to keep working and to maintain the wartime high, Lee headed east to Austria, where—with the usual bipolar focus required by her employer—she shot plump opera stars, and emaciated dying babies in a Vienna children's hospital. From there she left for Hungary, to document the ruins of Budapest and the relics of its aristocratic café society.

In a village, Lee was arrested by Russian soldiers and spent her detention (in a good hotel) teaching her captors a bar trick involving burning cigarette holes in a paper napkin until a penny balanced on the napkin drops into the glass. Freed, with the aid of a faked official pass, Lee went on to photograph the execution of the fascist ex–Prime Minister Laszlo Bardossy, facing a four-man firing squad, standing at full attention against a stack of stuffed burlap sacks heaped up between him and a curved brick wall, presumably to give the dead man something to break his fall. As always, in Lee Miller's photos, the eye is drawn to what catches the light: the burlap sacks, the cassock of the priest standing with his arms crossed, like a sentry posted between the execution and the spectators watching from the shadows.

Lee traveled with several different men; one long-range plan was to persuade Dave Scherman to return to the United States with her and work there as a team. Scherman gently discouraged her, in theory because he was reluctant to break up her relationship with Roland. Another possible reason is suggested by the testimony of the Hungarian photographer, Bela Halmi, who served as her guide: "I was not attracted to her . . . She wore those baggy army slacks most of the time and she drank too much . . . We got to be good friends and I took her home every night when she got loaded." However unpleasant, this has the ring of accuracy, and Dave Scherman must have realized that he would be taking on a handful if he cast his lot in with Lee. When he heard that Roland was being "drawn towards a permanent relationship with another woman," Dave sent Lee a cable advising her to "Go home."

The Lee who returned to England and Penrose was a mental and physical wreck. Antony's description of her confirms—and exceeds—her Hungarian friend's account: "People who knew or had heard of the fabulous beauty of Lee Miller were staggered by the red-eyed haggard apparition that confronted them." She had not only lost her looks, but she had also lost *her* muse—the war. Over the next years, and for the rest of her life, Lee would respond to the drying up of her well of inspiration with considerably less resilience and resolve than Man Ray had shown after her departure.

NONE OF THIS APPEARS in *Scrapbook*, which resumes the love story of Roland and Lee with the couple traveling to the United States. "The sense of freedom that came with the end of the war and the return of Lee from the battlefields brought back the possibility of change and travel. Lee was invited to pay a triumphal visit to the States as the heroine of Condé Nast Publications and to find her family again." The happy pair (the drinking and drugs had, evidently ceased to be a problem) journeyed from the Hudson Valley to Arizona, where Lee photographed the newly married Dorothea Tanning and Max Ernst. Among these pictures is a disturbing bit of darkroom sleight-of-hand in which a gigantic Ernst holds a teensy Dorothea beneath his fist, while the miniature woman rails up at him like some angry munchkin. In California, Lee and Roland found Man Ray married to Juliet Man Ray and living in an apartment near Hollywood and Vine, which Man Ray compared to the creative center of Paris. Lee was introduced to a number of Hollywood celebrities, whom she photographed for *Vogue*, pictures that were never published.

Perhaps this minor failure spooked her about a possible future in the United States; she may also have recalled the difficulty of running a business in Manhattan. Conveniently, another *Vogue* assignment sent her to St. Moritz, to shoot the rich at play in the snow. There, Lee discovered that she was pregnant with Penrose's child, and wrote him a letter that candidly expressed her conflicted feelings: "Physically it's heavy and lethargic-making . . . but emotionally I'm very pleased. So far no resentment or anguish or mind-changing or panic—only a mild astonishment that I'm so happy about it . . . There is only one thing—MY WORK ROOM IS NOT GOING TO BE A NURSERY. How about your studio? HA HA."

Lee spent the unusually harsh winter in Roland's unheated house, endured a miserable pregnancy, and appears to have lost her nerve in a way she hadn't during the bombing of St. Malo. Succumbing to some internal or external pressure, she resolved to put her life in order. Aziz was summoned for a Muslim divorce ("I divorce thee," repeated three times) and to spend a brief interlude in a peculiar ménage that included Roland, his former wife, Valentine, and Lee, confined to bed by pregnancy. That spring Lee and Roland were married, and the following September she gave birth to Antony Penrose.

In a photo of Lee Miller cradling her infant son, the new mother could (except for the chic outfit and the stylish hairband) pass for a madonna in a sentimental Victorian portrait by Julia Margaret Cameron. In fact, Lee looks great; having lost its ravaged wartime bloat, her face suggests an older, wiser, maternal version of Man Ray's golden muse. Lee and Roland moved to Farley Farm, a Georgian farmhouse in Sussex with enough land for Roland to try his hand at dairy farming.

Social life at Farley Farm was another ongoing party. Lee directed a large household, with a changing cast of characters that included Picasso, Henry Moore, Michel Leiris, Jean Dubuffet, and Saul Steinberg. Like Man Ray persuading himself that Hollywood and Vine was the Boulevard St. Germain, Lee clung to the belief that Farley Farm was a re-creation of the artist's life in Montparnasse, but with a better garden, better produce, and better food.

Everything was better, except for Lee's work, which took a sharp turn for the worse. In retrospect, her letter announcing her pregnancy to Roland—her preemptive defense of the workroom against the encroachment of the nursery—is chilling. She continued to get assignments, including a fashion shoot with a Sicilian background, but began to have trouble meeting deadlines. Writing, never easy for Lee, became impossible; her "verbal impotence" progressed to paralysis, and the rattling eloquence of her wartime pieces was silenced. A shrill falseness, the strained brittle tones of an English country dame pervades the last piece she wrote for *Vogue*, an essay entitled "Working Guests," outlining her technique for getting celebrity guests to help with the housework.

Farley Farm underwent successive renovations, and Roland (whose desire to make art had mostly been subsumed by the impulse to collect and show it, and to have an art career) adopted a dual identity: country squire and founder of London's Institute of Contemporary Art. Lee was unable to share in her husband's satisfaction and success. In photos taken around this time, she is clearly a ruin, and—writing about himself in the third person—Antony corroborates the distressing visual evidence with a recollection of his mother's psychological state. "By 1955 Lee was in the grip of a vicious downward spiral that nearly killed her. Following the birth of Tony, she had suddenly found herself unable to get any pleasure from sex. She was also rapidly losing her looks . . . To make matters worse, the woman who had once been described as a 'snappy dresser' was fast becoming a slob . . . It is hardly surprising that Lee became difficult and quarrelsome and that those closest to her in the firing line became the target for venomous vituperation. A vicious feud began between her and Tony. Neither missed an opportunity to snipe at the other with the knowledge that they both knew exactly where to hit to inflict the most damage."

Antony is forthcoming about the degree to which Lee's "downward spiral" was accelerated by Roland's long affair with Diane Deriaz, a beautiful trapeze artist. On the subject of his circus love, Roland is matter-of-fact to the point of sadism: "The sudden entry of Diane into my life was the beginning of years of exhilaration and tangles that only time could unravel. With her natural generosity Lee not only enjoyed the excitement caused by Diane's arrival but later eagerly offered her hospitality, creating a situation that began to alarm Lee when she realised that Diane's presence could become a danger to her. As time went by Lee refused to believe that Diane had refused steadfastly to disrupt a marriage for which she had great respect and this led eventually to the welcome guest becoming unwittingly the hated enemy."

Isolated from her husband and son, Lee confided in her friend, the painter and cookbook writer Ninette Lyon. "Even at the grandest party, Lee's tension was very near the surface. The slightest provocation would cause her to throw a scene and embarrass everyone . . . Ninette once discovered the letters NA written boldly on the mirror of Lee's dressing table. Inquiring what the letters stood for she was told: 'It means Never Answer—and it is to remind me that I am expected to carry on without protest' . . . In the nadir of her depression, she confessed to Ninette that the only reason preventing her from drowning herself in the Seine was that she knew Roland and Tony would be so happy without her."

One consequence of Lee's inability to write is that we have two versions of her later years—her husband's and her son's—but not, alas, her own. Or perhaps it's better to be spared the voice of a soul in hell, cut off from the work and the life she loved. The unsympathetic reply of the doctor to whom she complained about her depression contains both a lie, and a truth. "There is nothing wrong with you, and we cannot keep the world permanently at war just to provide you with excitement." While it's tempting to blame Roland Penrose for Lee's despair—certainly, Lee was angry enough at him— it also seems likely that drink, drugs, manic depression, and creative frustration could hardly have made her more agreeable. Antony claims that she was "repelled and frightened by the merest suggestion that she might be suffering from psychological problems."

Realizing that the art world was "dominated by Roland," who in

1960 was appointed a trustee of the Tate Gallery, where he mounted a landmark Picasso exhibition, Lee shifted her attention to the world of cuisine. She took up gourmet cooking with the zeal of a convert, collecting thousands of cookbooks, attending food fairs, spending days finding the recipe for a Confederate Soup, a dish with some putative connection to the American Civil War. "Lee's cuisine was not the art of a woman harnessed to a casserole. Preparations for supper often started early in the morning and did not preclude the elaborate preparations for lunch." At the very least, the activity and focus—together with classical music, which became another obsession—gave Lee Miller a reason to get out of bed.

Roland describes her switch from photography to cooking in a section so dismaying that it deserves to be quoted at length: "Photography had been a passion for Lee, inherited from her father and encouraged by Man Ray when, a beautiful young model, she arrived in Paris. Before marrying Aziz she had set up a studio with the help of her brother Erik in New York, and later exceeded all expectations by becoming a war correspondent . . . But after the war photography became less important in Lee's life and instead she became absorbed in another art, cooking, which gave great pleasure not only to her gourmet friends but also to the flow of weekend visitors . . . Devoted to parlour games, she found a fascinating pastime in kitchen games, competitions which she often pursued with success, winning countless gadgets for the kitchen and at one time a triumphant tour of Norway . . . as a reward for a most startling and succulent open sandwich . . ."

During this time, Lee managed to take a few pictures—the photos of Picasso that illustrate Roland Penrose's book and that tell us little about Picasso (compared to her shots of him taken before and during the war) but reveal plenty about Roland Penrose, who appears with his subject in an unflattering double portrait. As Antony remarks, "Those who knew her circumstances intimately could pick out the neat touches of barbed irony."

In fact, Lee hadn't lost her talent. The natural Surrealist survived inside the alcoholic ex-beauty and obsessive cook married to the respected art-world figure. There are a few great Lee Miller photos from this period: an eerie image of Lee taking a picture, reflected in a window through which Jean Dubuffet and Georges Limbour are looking out; and a brilliant portrait of Joan Miró as an elderly, smartly dressed Catalan gentleman feeding a magnificent toucan at the London zoo. But she hardly took any pictures, not even family snapshots, and rarely talked about her work, which she claimed had mostly been lost or destroyed in the war. The former darkroom perfectionist stored her original prints and negatives in cardboard boxes.

The consolation was a "rapprochement," with Roland and then with Tony, though Lee's reconciliation with her son occurred regrettably close to her death from cancer in 1977.

IT'S HARD TO RESIST the temptation to compare Lee Miller's career with Man Ray's. But why should we be tempted? What did they have in common except that they were lovers for three years, and that their photographic style merged so closely that they occasionally took credit for one another's work—so closely that the attribution of certain photos is still in doubt?

Even as Lee was cooking up a storm in the kitchens of Farley Farms, Man Ray was benefiting from the elegant, popular, and costly reproductions of his pieces. Critical articles and books were written about him, including the 1975 Mario Amaya interview with Lee in *Art in America*. His painting, photos, and constructions were admired by young artists. His reputation grew in Europe and in the United States, assisted by the publication of his celebrated 1963 memoir, *Self-Portrait*. His work was the subject of major retrospectives, starting with an acclaimed 1966 show at the Los Angeles County Museum of Art.

HERE IS HOW Antony Penrose and his wife discovered Lee Miller's war photos: "After her death in 1977 we began sorting through the trunks stored in the attic at Farley Farm . . . Masses of manuscripts, negatives and contact sheets were revealed, but the full scope of Lee's work did not emerge until a few years later when my wife Susanna, determined to find some pictures of me as a baby to show our children, began hunting through the dusty packages. She showed me one of her findings, the manuscript for the Siege of St. Malo . . ."

What if Lee Miller had not had a son, or a daughter-in-law eager for baby pictures of Daddy to show the kids? Is it just by lucky chance that we are familiar with the images that, once you've seen them, stay with you forever, branded so clearly and indelibly on your memory that you can summon them up merely by closing your eyes: the execution of the Hungarian fascist prime minister, the suicide of the Leipzig mayor's lovely daughter, the puffs of cotton reaching toward the Egyptian sky. And why should these images be less widely known than Dave Scherman's photo of Lee Miller in Hitler's bath, or the beautiful eye eternally swinging back and forth on the arm of a metronome?

CHARIS WESTON

How brave and resourceful the muse must be to balance, year after year, on the vertiginous high wire that her calling requires—to navigate the tightrope between imminence and absence, to be at once accessible and unobtainable, perpetually present in the mind of the artist and at the same time distant enough to create a chasm into which the muse's devoted subject is moved to fling propitiatory, ritual objects: that is, works of art. How much simpler the challenge becomes when the muse (like Beatrice and Laura) has the grace or misfortune to die young, or if she is blessed with the determination of a Lou Salomé, or if she happens to be possessed by the demons that tormented Lee Miller and Lizzie Siddal, or is simply prevented by circumstance (excessive youth, marriage to someone else) from becoming so dependable and familiar that she can no longer perform the necessary witchcraft, the magic of inspiration. What happens to the unfortunate muse who lacks inventiveness and foresight and who foolishly allows herself to wish for domestic comfort and job security?

Except in extremely rare cases—Gala Dalí's, for example—tenure is not an option in the careers of the muses. The muse who steps down from her airy perch and seeks a more solid position is (whether she knows it or not) asking to be relieved of her duties, to be replaced or at least demoted. What makes this decline so treacherous and bewildering for the unwary muse is that her artist is so often (and so understandably) complicitous, so ready to assist and accelerate her downward slide from an exalted goddess to the more human, unenviable, and inglorious role of helpmate and art wife.

History has given us as many art wives as muses, and though on occasion the line is blurred (was Mrs. William Blake a muse or an art wife?) we instinctively know the difference. Asked to identify Rodin's muse, we would more likely name Camille Claudel than the sculptor's loyal mistress and (finally) legal spouse, Rose Beuret, whose jobs included wetting down the clay maquettes to keep them pliable. And we would prefer to *be* Camille Claudel—but only until we recall her sad history: the madness that caused her to destroy her own work, and her years in a mental asylum.

If the muse—hovering above the artist and sprinkling him with the fairy dust of inspiration—throws off a glossy flash of the airborne and the divine, the art wife is plainly more matte, earthbound in ways to which we may have complex responses, reactions that rarely include the envy we feel for the muse. If we project ourselves onto the muse and resent her privileged, glamorous relationship with the artist, we can all feel a little sorry for (and superior to) the overworked, underappreciated art wife—burdened with the combined tasks of mother, companion, cook, housekeeper, business manager, agent, bodyguard, and gofer responsible for the minute chores specific to an artist's field: cataloging negatives, stretching canvases, etc.

Quite often, there is an overlap between art wife and muse. Some women have played both parts sequentially, have gravitated or been shifted from one role to the other—a process that, in the case of Charis Weston, first the muse and later the art wife of Edward Weston, is so exemplary and distressing that it makes us doubly aware of how few muses in this group of nine succumbed to the temptation or pressure to exchange the lyre and the flute for the diaper and the dishrag.

What makes Charis Weston's story all the more harrowing is that she has chosen to tell it herself and in the process has joined a new subcategory of muses: the muse as memoirist—willing, eager, and entitled to offer her own view of the mysterious transaction between herself and her artist. Of course, Mrs. Thrale recorded her anecdotal memories of dinner with Dr. Johnson, Lou Andreas-Salomé left us a Wagnerian vision of the heroes she helped boost to new heights. But only now, in the age of the tell-all memoir and the talk-show confessional, has the muse been inspired to provide her readers with an intimate account of what it means and how it feels to inspire a genius.

Charis Weston's 1998 memoir, *Through Another Lens*, represents itself as an attempt to set the record straight—in theory, to defend the photographer from such books as Ben Maddow's 1973 biography, which portrays Weston as "something of a fanatic—humorless and egotistic." In fact, humorlessness and fanaticism are the least of the faults that Charis (apparently unconsciously) ascribes to Weston in her account of the eleven years they spent together, years during which she seems to have done everything for him except take his pictures. The question of what Charis did and the insufficient thanks she received provides the subtext for her cautionary tale of how a muse gradually merges her inspirational responsibilities (like Lee Miller, Charis offered the energizing effects of a love affair *and* her services as a model) with the less attractive duties of the traditional art wife.

The memoir illuminates—through negative example—the inner strength that the muse must possess to be effective at her job and to weather the destructive tempests that typically form the climate of her relationship with her artist. Charis led the life that Lizzie Siddal might have had after divorce became a popular and viable alternative to an overdose of laudanum and the muse need no longer confine her complaints to morbidly sentimental verse but could tell the world about her artist's bathroom habits, his repulsive dietary tastes, his parsimony, his ingratitude, his sexual betrayals.

AT INTERMISSION, during a concert in Carmel, California, in the spring of 1934, Charis Wilson saw Edward Weston across the

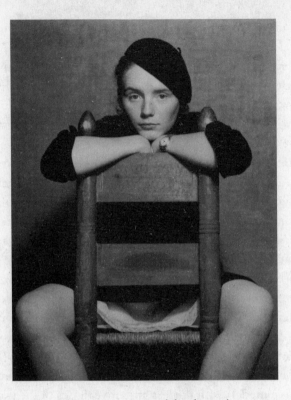

Charis Weston, 1935. (*Edward Weston*)

proverbial crowded room. "My eyes keep returning to the short man in brown clothes who is talking with friends across the room ... We have been keenly aware of each other for several minutes before he surprises me by making his way through the crooked lane of chairs and asking my brother to introduce us. Only then do I learn that he is the photographer Edward Weston ..."

Born in Illinois, in 1886, Weston, whose father was a doctor and whose mother died when he was five, began his career as a surveyor and portrait photographer. His earliest art photos—voguishly romantic, soft-focus, pictorialist studies of women in dreamy landscapes, with titles like *Summer Sunshine* and *There Are Fairies in the Grotto of My Garden*—earned him a modest critical reputation, but (influenced by the modernism of Stieglitz, Sheeler, and Strand) he became increasingly engaged by abstraction and by the hard-edged geometries of light and shadow. In 1909, he married Flora May Chandler, a wealthy, warm, and voluble woman who bore him four sons and whom he treated in the paradoxically devoted and cavalier way he behaved toward most of the women who had the dubious good fortune to stir his romantic passions.

Flora could hardly have been pleased by his eight-year affair with fellow photographer Margarethe Mather, whom he later called "the first important person in my life" or when, in 1923, he left his family to travel to Mexico with Tina Modotti. In Mexico, Modotti served as his translator, social secretary, studio assistant, and business agent, even as she was becoming an important photographer in her own right—a mistake that Charis (who intuited that Weston had a horror of female competition) was careful to avoid. Assuming that any woman who truly loved him would overcome her petty self-interest and be thrilled to learn that a new lover was facilitating his work, Weston wrote Flora about Modotti, "She is invaluable, I could do nothing alone." An entry in his *Daybooks* documents his efforts to sympathize with his long-suffering wife: "poor Flora, she has had a dirty deal from life. I must try to be tender to her, it is not easy to thrust aside such a great love as she offers me,—that is, when it comes from a distance!"

During two long visits to Mexico, over the course of three years, Weston stayed mostly in the capital, where his friends included radical American expatriates and the leading Mexican artists of the day, among them Diego Rivera. Inspired by the "direct proximity of a primitive race," the extreme contrasts of the landscape, a revelatory encounter with the art in the National Museum, and his own growing ability to "see important forms importantly," Weston formulated the spare, glossy, and rigorously formal aesthetic that would shape his future work. In 1926, Weston left Mexico and Modotti for

California, where he began taking the pictures (of shells, vegetables, the striations of cypress bark and cabbage leaves) that would make his reputation and which attracted the attention of wealthy collectors and influential curators. He began to exhibit in prestigious venues and to be included in group shows with Atget, Stieglitz, and Walker Evans. Three years after his return to California, he moved to the Bohemian enclave of Carmel.

And so by the time he met Charis, he was indeed "the photographer Edward Weston," a fact which piqued her desire to make his acquaintance: "Close up I find him even more attractive, and take him to be in his late thirties . . . He looks at me with admiration, and the openness and intensity of that look would be embarrassing if he didn't, at the same time, make it seem playful—as though we were sharing a private joke. As the three of us stand chatting, I can feel his attention focused on me . . . I say I would very much like to see his work, and before the lights blink to end the intermission we arrange for me to visit his studio the following Sunday to look at prints."

Edward Weston was forty-eight, Charis was nineteen—a rangy, beautiful, sexually confident, sophisticated, California free spirit. Soon, she began modeling for Weston, nude photographic sessions arranged during an interview (which Edward set up) with his assistant and lover of five years, the photographer Sonya Noskowiak.

Edward invited Charis to stop by his studio when he was out of town so that Sonya could show her his work, and Charis promptly took him up on the invitation. After sizing up the competition— "She was a small, shy woman with short brown hair and rather elfin features. I was a notoriously poor judge of age in those days and guessed her to be five or six years my senior when actually she was fourteen years older"—Charis underwent the conversion experience of seeing Weston's pictures. "I felt as though I had turned a corner into a sharper, cleaner, more exciting world."

When Charis asked to see Sonya's photos, her hostess demurred, "instead" (the conjunction is telling) proposing that Charis look at a selection of Edward's nudes. In fact, added Sonya, Charis should consider posing . . . "When I agreed with alacrity, she said she knew Edward would be pleased because he was always on the lookout for new models."

On the lookout for new models! Surely Sonya knew that, given Edward's history of erotic restlessness, she was vetting her own replacement—a particularly unpleasant art wife chore that Charis would later assume in 1945, when a young female student came to study with Edward for the weekend, and Charis went camping, "knowing perfectly well that Edward's student would have him in bed by nightfall." Charis *did* know perfectly well since, eleven years before, during that remarkably twisted afternoon with Sonya, she had felt Edward's talent working its magic on *her*: "As I drove slowly home, I realized I was hooked—on the photographs and on the man who had made them."

Had Charis been less impressionable, more mature, emotionally stable, or aesthetically astute, she might have formed a very different and more mixed impression of the man whose work she saw, somewhat improbably, as a sexual turn-on. In fact, it can be argued that Weston's arctic formalism delivers a sort of *anti*erotic charge, generated by the sense that nature has not been captured so much as embalmed, rendered with a sterility that Stieglitz (whose opinion mattered deeply to Weston) noted early on, and that caused the older photographer to temper his (at best, tepid) support for the younger man's work with harsh criticism. Weston's photos, he said, "lacked fire, life, were more or less dead things not part of today," and later he would tell Ansel Adams, "You know I dislike virtuosity of all kinds and I feel that above all it is the virtuosity of Weston that makes him appear more than he really is." In these offhand remarks, Stieglitz diagnosed what some feel to be the problem with Weston's art: the dazzling technique that, on close inspection, serves as a stand-in for vision.

Did Sonya show Charis Edward's 1924 portrait of Tina Modotti, a picture meant to capture the torments of their affair and which he described taking in an entry in the *Daybooks*? "The Mexican sun, I thought, will reveal everything. Some of the tragedy of our present life may be captured, nothing can be hidden under this cloudless cruel sky. . . . She leaned against a whitewashed wall. I drew close . . . and kissed her. A tear rolled down her cheek—and then I captured forever the moment . . ."

And would Charis have been capable of learning from the faintly distasteful similarities between Weston's 1925 portrait of his toilet bowl and the female nudes he took at around the same time? Weston had approached the artistic challenge posed by his commode with a missionary zeal for rendering its sensuous biomorphism: "I have been photographing our toilet, that glossy enameled receptacle of extraordinary beauty. It might be suspicioned that I am in a cynical mood to approach such subject matter when I might be doing beautiful women or 'God's out-of-doors',—or even considered that my mind holds lecherous images arising from restraint of appetite. But no! My excitement was absolute aesthetic response to form. For long I have considered photographing this useful and elegant accessory to modern hygienic life, but not until I contemplated its image on my ground glass did I realize the possibilities before me. I was thrilled!—here was every sensuous curve of the 'human form divine' but minus imperfections." Perhaps his awareness of these "imperfections" had caused him to take a more cerebral view of his nude portraits of Anita Brenner, images in which a woman's back suggests the wonders of modern plumbing: "Under cool reconsideration, they retain their importance as my finest set of nudes, that is, in their approach to aesthetically stimulating form. Most of the series are entirely impersonal, lacking in any human interest which might call attention to a living, palpitating body."

But everything about Charis's character (her youth, enthusiasm, and vulnerability) and her upbringing (her understandable desire for a sympathetic lover/father figure) would have precluded such dispassionate judgments and instead predisposed her to be "hooked" by Weston's photographs. In which case, what could a would-be muse do *but* volunteer to assist in their creation, beginning with a series of sessions during which the photographer directed his nude model in a variety of poses?

As they defused the sexual tension with breathless conversation, both model and artist were excited to discover how often "our tastes, attitudes, and even our experiences coincided." But neither dared initiate the most casual physical contact. "I half-expected a friendly pat. I certainly wouldn't have objected, but I was even more impressed when it didn't come, especially since the electric charge that had been set off between us that first night at the concert was quite evidently still present."

By the second session, Edward's shyness forced Charis to take action. "I realized that his reputation as a Lothario was wildly exaggerated. I would have to take the first step. I did so, and even though it was only a very compelling look, it soon brought photography to a halt. What followed was as great a revelation as Edward's photographs. I thought of myself as a sophisticated woman of the world, but now I learned how limited all my previous experience had been, as what had always seemed to me to be a branch of playacting became unmistakably real."

Somehow Edward had intuited that patience and restraint would be required for the great sexual "revelation." Charis had a lot to unlearn, negative lessons accrued during a rocky adolescence, years spent "in the kind of social activity that—had I been born male—would have been called sowing wild oats. I acquired a number of boyfriends, and patronized the last of the functioning speakeasies. It didn't occur to me that I was desperately unhappy, but I was secretly grateful when my mother rescued me at the end of eight months because I had an inflamed appendix. I suspect she guessed I was also pregnant, though nothing was said except by our family doctor in Carmel. After an operation in which he took care of both conditions, he said if it weren't for the regard he had for my mother he would have removed my appendix, sewed me back up, and let me suffer the consequences."

In her rebellions, as in other ways, Charis sounds remarkably modern—decades ahead of her time. What seems to have exempted her from the social norms of her era was character, upbringing, and the subculture she was born into and helped sustain: the California art scene. The dislocations, miseries, and abandonments of her childhood seem calculated to have produced just the sort of young woman most likely to be enchanted by a man like Edward Weston, most inclined to perceive her loss of self and virtual indenturement as rescue and liberation.

Charis's mother—the beautiful Helen Cooke—had sown her own wild oats in Sinclair Lewis's utopian writers' commune in New Jersey. There, Helen had commenced *her* career as muse, attracting a range of artistic suitors that included Lewis, William Rose Benet, and Arnold Genthe, who also photographed Lee Miller. At sixteen, Helen, in a rash move for which she would later make her two children pay dearly, gave up her freedom to marry the forty-three-year-old Harry Leon Wilson, a comic writer who had coauthored a successful Broadway play, and who was known (and later forgotten) for such works as *Ruggles of Red Gap*.

One difference between the ordinary muse and memoirist-muse is how much more information we have about the memoirist-muse's childhood. Gala Dalí's origins remain shrouded in the mists of prewar Russia. Lou's account of her St. Petersburg years is a fairly formal set piece—until she falls in love with her tutor. But the early chapters of Charis Wilson's book give us all the highlights, or low points, of a troubled, peripatetic childhood orchestrated by two spoiled, damaged adults. *Through Another Lens* tells us all we need to know about the rejections Charis suffered from her competitive, self-involved mother and her erratic, hard-drinking father, who blamed his lack of affection for Charis on his doubts about her paternity.

Charis's problematic family life deteriorated further in 1927, when her parents divorced; she spent the rest of her youth in a series of boarding schools and temporary homes. For the most part, *Through Another Lens* spares its readers the moralizing psychobabble and amateur Freudian analysis that so often taints contemporary memoirs. Still, Charis rather fashionably blames her youthful follies on "a kind of angry despair and what we would now call 'low-self-esteem,'" a condition that—she seems to believe, though some might disagree—disappeared the minute she met Weston. "Meeting Edward changed everything. With the first nude session, I had to revise my views on men—they weren't all alike in the matter of sex ... In a very short time we achieved a degree of intimacy I had never before experienced."

From the start, their affair burned at a high heat, fueled by a sexual chemistry that Charis recalls warmly more than sixty years later. "The pleasure he took in giving pleasure was evidence, for me, of all I had missed in the meaningless conjunctions that made up most of my sexual past." Their passion was intensified by having to conceal it from Sonya and from their nominally liberated and in fact censorious community of artists. Despite Edward's assurances that he and Sonya "were free to lead their private lives as they chose," he and Charis avoided each other in public and communicated through letters and a signal code using cards placed in his studio window.

Again, the muse-memoirist is able to tell us lots more than we've heard before—in this case, about her sex life with her artist, a subject about which the muses have been reticent, until lately. Mrs. Thrale was less than completely forthcoming about how exactly Dr. Johnson's padlock was meant to be used, and we will probably never know the provisions of the erotic truce that Gala and Dalí negotiated. Charis, however, intuits that our understanding of her relationship with Weston—and of its influence on his work—would be incomplete without some account of their intense sexual connection. The early chapters of her memoir describe the ways in which erotic heat can make the lovers see their lives as a holy mission for which they have been divinely hand-picked and brought together, a destiny foreordained by their similar "tastes, attitudes and even experiences."

Eventually, their common purpose, Edward's photography ("Edward's view was that his work was his life; everything else fit into place around the central core") brought them to Santa Monica Canyon. There, they set up house while Edward worked for the Federal Art Project, a program administered by the Works Progress Administration. "That he and I could spend whole nights together was a dizzying delight that was amplified by leisurely days."

Joined by Edward's sons, Brett, Cole, and Neil, the happy couple lived simply, thanks to a series of efficient domestic routines. Edward proved to be a bit of a health nut. "When I knew him he fasted when ill and gave himself enemas to remove 'poisons' from his system. He was a vegetarian by preference, though he would eat meat when it was served to him, and he refused to be vaccinated—no injecting of dead horse pus into his healthy tissue . . . He always squatted to defecate. It saved sitting on suspect toilet seats, and got the business over faster because it was nature's way and therefore worked better. He also was fixed in the view that a post-breakfast bowel movement was essential to good health and he'd discovered a system for provoking one when his colon didn't cooperate. Taking down dry negatives from overhead lines . . . was a job he never finished without a dash to the toilet."

Is *this* what the nine goddesses on Mount Helicon said about their artists? Or what Beatrice "shared" about Dante? And how does this information square with the enthusiasm that Weston brought to his 1925 studies of indoor plumbing? Charis tells us much more than we have ever known about most artists—*so* much that we can't help speculating on the motives of a muse who wants posterity to have this information. (In this, Charis was the opposite of Gala, warning Dalí to keep his excremental fixations private.)

Unsurprisingly, Charis has since been outdone. Another muse memoir, *Inside the Volcano*, Jan Gabrial's book about her marriage to Malcolm Lowry, makes sure we understand that her artist had an exceptionally tiny penis.

The Westons, whose pursuit of the pleasures of the senses stopped at the refrigerator door, followed a frugal, organic, unappetizing diet. Lunch meant "standing in the kitchen nibbling on whatever was handy—Rytak and cheese or avocado, dried figs, cold pea soup. This last was especially appreciated by Edward and Brett when it had been around long enough to become solid." Or even, on occasion, longer. "In the cooler I found a pot of pea soup that smelled suspicious and put it on the stove to be 'repasteurized,' that is, boiled for four minutes."

Like Lou introducing Rainer to the joy of whole grains and berries, like Lee Miller getting Man Ray hooked on a Spartan health regime, Charis took to the role of the muse as diet police, controlling and monitoring what her artist ate. Such vigilance borders dangerously on art wife territory, and Charis's attention to the culinary may have accelerated her slide.

Still, for at least a half dozen years, Edward and Charis were in love. And during this time, Charis inspired "a new series of nudes made in our upstairs bedroom, where the light—which streamed in through the glass doors from the sundeck—bounced off the white walls and reflected from the linoleum floor." Other pictures were taken on the sundeck, where not even the compliant Charis could endure more than fifteen minutes of frying on its reflective, silver-painted floor.

At first, Charis appears to have adapted to Weston's aesthetic rather than encouraging him to modify it, even slightly. In his first studies of her body, we feel Weston, as always, watching for nature to fold itself into attractive, motionless creases. Charis's breasts could just as well be seashells or cabbage leaves or the bark of a Joshua tree, and the photos of her resemble the studies of vegetables in their controlled, stage-managed beauty and in the rather pretty, designer sensibility that finally communicates little.

Weston firmly maintained that his intentions were always purely formal, and not in the least erotic. As he said of a nude he took in 1928, "How sad when my only thought was the exquisite form. But most persons will see only an ass!" *Do* most people see an ass? Looking at early photos of Charis's buttocks, most people probably see an ass, but for all the erotic charge it delivers, they might be looking at a chambered nautilus or at any of his perfectly composed and executed hymns to the beauties of nature.

But as their relationship deepened—they enjoyed companionable field trips, Edward's work was going well, Charis was learning to write captions and text—her beauty and physical vitality briefly turned up the simmer beneath the formalism that rises, like a gust of dry ice, from so much of Weston's art. A 1935 study of Charis wearing a beret and a black sweater, straddling a chair with her legs spread to reveal a fringe of lacy white slip is far sexier than any of his nudes and is perhaps the most frankly suggestive of all his photos. A sense of the couple's playfulness—or perhaps more accurately, of Charis's playfulness—informs her account of the shooting of the now-iconic image of Charis sprawled, in a state of apparently rapturous ecstasy, on the sand dunes at Oceano. ". . . The fine, soft sand, was pleasantly warm, I thought it was time for a sunbath. I called to Edward, who was working on a higher ridge and across a small valley from me . . . After Edward had made a few back views I decided to try diving down a deeper part of the sand bank. It was a giddy experience, like going slow-motion over a waterfall, and after a trial run or two to get the hang of it, I could fling myself down with abandon." One particularly striking shot of Charis on her back, with one arm behind her head and her knees parted, is given added heat and animation by grooves dug in the sand—implying that the model's pose has been achieved after a good deal of shifting and squirming.

To judge from the theatrical 1937 photo of Charis naked but for a black cloak, her hips arched against a rock at an angle that thrusts her pelvis toward the camera, her powers as muse were, by then, in high gear. The minute Weston focused on anything other than Charis's body, his vision reverted to a more typically frigid abstraction; his landscapes of the sand dunes at Oceano have a majestic grandeur and sweep, yet seem distant and inert without her vivid presence.

Meanwhile, his attempts at humor and Surrealist irony were producing some notably unfortunate results. Though his technique remained flawless, his images of bizarre roadside stands (*Mammy's Cupboard, Natchez*), outsider art (*Winter Zero Swartzel's Bottle Farm*), and bits of advertising detritus scattered across the American landscape (*"Hot Coffee," Mojave Desert*) suggest a cross between virtuoso tourist snapshots and joke postcards of jackalopes and gargantuan vegetables.

Much of their travel through the West, the South, and the Northeast was funded by the Guggenheim Foundation. Weston was the first photographer to receive a Guggenheim grant—thanks, in part, to Charis, who was quite possibly the first muse to help her artist fill out his fellowship application. "We sat together to draft an expanded proposal, listing the points from Edward's original version that he had discarded as superfluous, and adding such others as seemed to underscore the validity of photography as a means of artistic expression. . . . Edward was impressed with the product and candidly admitted that he couldn't have done it so well on his own."

Initially, Weston took his sons along on the Guggenheim expeditions, but after Charis, "in my youthful eccentricity," campaigned to "oust" the boys, the couple traveled alone. In the last year of Weston's fellowship, Weston's divorce from Flora became final, and he and Charis were married—not because they wanted to, claims Charis, but because of certain legal details connected with their joint ownership of their home, Wildcat Hill. "It seemed the practical thing." And so the muse was officially transformed into an art wife.

IN 1936, WESTON'S FRIEND, the gallery owner, curator, teacher, and later documentary filmmaker Willard van Dyke, traveled with Edward and Charis along the northern California coast. The threesome, Charis discovered, was not entirely congenial. "Ever since the first party at the Brockhurst Gallery, I had felt some hostility from him, and on the north coast trip he was direct about it. After watching me fetch a camera case for Edward when I saw that he was about to make a picture, Willard said, 'Can't you stop being so indispensable?' "

Indispensable, indeed. If Van Dyke had one word for it, Weston had another. "Edward hadn't heard Willard's 'indispensable' remark—but if he had, he would have laughed, and told Willard not to spoil his setup." It was indeed a setup for Weston, and Charis's memoir chronicles the ways in which she made herself . . . indispensable.

In addition to posing and writing proposals and texts, she oversaw their organic household. ("With a picnic tomorrow, we decided, I'd better make a run for Rytak and Jack cheese. We put our bowls down for the cats to polish; then I made the bed and ran a mop over the floor, which completed the day's housekeeping.") She kept meticulous records, listing, dating, and noting down pertinent facts about every negative. Like a wholesome Gala Dalí, Charis devised the equivalent of the lucrative Zodiac Club; twenty subscribers to the Edward Weston Print of the Month Club were offered a print every month, at the discount price of ten dollars each, twelve prints for a hundred. At the Yosemite photographic forums, where Edward and Ansel Adams taught, Charis chauffeured instructors and students around to scenic locations. When Edward photographed in winter, she and Neil Weston trudged through the deep snow and tramped it down in a circle wherever he decided to set up his camera.

Charis also labored to understand her husband's art. "My eyes would need a long re-education before I began to see Edward's photographs as he saw them . . . I avoided the flat-footed kind of question so many viewers produced: 'Why did you make *that*?' I knew if Edward could give the answer in words the picture would serve no purpose. If I didn't 'get' it, I should keep looking. . . . I wanted to understand what it was that Edward could see—sometimes, it seemed, instantly—that gave him the knowledge, as certain as a fisherman's feel for a tug on the line, that this was a live one."

Perhaps Charis was looking for more than what was there. In any event, she did learn what to *say* about Edward's work—that is, what Edward would have said. For a muse, for *anyone* who lived in such intimate daily association with the creative process, Charis's aesthetic views on photography in general and on Weston's in particular seem oddly unfocused, and most often take the form of direct quotations from Edward.

But what did we expect? An objective critical critique of the high gloss that can make the eye glide over his least successful shots? A muse who doubted her artist's work wouldn't stay a muse for very long, except in cases like Lou Andreas-Salomé's, in which doubt and correction were part of the pedagogical and inspirational process. Charis has nothing but praise for her former husband's photographs, though she does permit herself the pleasure of telling the world about his character flaws, his dictatorial nature, jealousy, bad temper, and so forth.

Did Charis ever think of Sonya welcoming her to Edward's studio, redirecting Charis's attention from her own work to his nudes? Reading the *Daybooks*, Edward's diaries, offered Charis a clear warning that, she hoped, might help her avoid the destinies of her predecessors: "Even if I had been strongly tempted to study photography—I never was—I think I would have been warned off by the fates of Margarethe Mather, Tina Modotti, and Sonya, who shared a similar progression from apprentice, to assistant, to partner, to termination." Wisely or not, Charis remained selective about the lessons she chose to learn, and the conclusions she chose to draw from the evidence of the *Daybooks*: "Particularly disconcerting were the diatribes on women . . . I could not imagine him talking or behaving that way in person. The voice in the *Daybooks* was dogmatic, didactic and judgmental, whereas Edward himself was open-minded, unpresumptuous, even diffident."

Eventually, Charis turned her savvy refusal to compete with Edward into a theory about herself: "My refusal of Edward's offers to teach me had been instinctive at first, but I had observed him with sufficient care by this point to have a more reasoned response. The discipline that enabled him to focus his whole attention and make decisions in a fraction of a second was as foreign to my psychology as the messing with chemicals in the darkroom was to my physiology . . . Instantaneous perception was beyond me."

Sounding more like Edward than Edward himself became a sort of game, with obvious benefits for their partnership. "My goal was to make the articles sound exactly like Edward, but without the broad categorical statements found in his writing . . . By then I had heard him express his ideas enough to know them by heart, but if I wasn't sure about a subject he would talk about it . . . Or I'd write a draft using my knowledge of his views and see how he liked it. It wasn't long before I could write the articles pretty much on my own . . . In some recent books and biographies, the articles I wrote for Edward are listed with both of us as authors, but for years they carried only Edward's name. This didn't bother me at all. I'd always wanted to get Edward's ideas down in writing. I liked doing it, and it was far easier for me to do than it was for him. Over the years I have enjoyed hearing often-quoted 'Weston' lines that were actually mine."

But Charis was less accepting about other, extra-literary confusions, especially when the strain of second-guessing Weston led to a progressively severe erosion of her already fragile ego. Years later, in the 1980s, an old friend of Charis's remarked that her husband had noticed how Charis's identity was overwhelmed by Edward's: " 'He thought you did too much talking for Edward and were always putting his ideas in your words,' she said . . . After some time I realized that this charge was probably true. I was not aware of it at the time, but I can see how easily it might have happened, particularly once I was in the habit of selecting and fine-tuning his words for the articles. It was only a small step to doing the same in conversation . . . It was the kind of overstepping of boundaries that is easy to spot in other people's relationships but hard to spot in one's own."

Would Erato or Clio or Calliope have known what their boundaries were? Do deities *have* boundaries, and isn't it the nature of the divine to transcend corporal and psychic borders? It's yet another sign of how far our culture has come from the notion of heavenly inspiration: The muse is human, as we now know, with sensitivities that can be impinged on, feelings that can be hurt by the artist's tendency to forget that she exists.

Tiny cries of distress echo through Charis's memoir, the faint bleats of a self as it founders, goes under, and drowns. She recounts how it demoralized her to give up writing poetry, an activity she loved but which meant little to Weston, who was, she emphasizes, not a *reader*—a surprising observation, since the *Daybooks* are (lightly) peppered with his responses to writers ranging from Melville to T. S. Eliot. Near the end of the marriage, she fell in love with someone else, an affair that seems to have amounted to little more than a serious crush; she confesses that what attracted her to this man was his knowledge of T. S. Eliot's poetry.

But though Charis had plenty to complain about, a certain amount of her unhappiness and resentment appears to have derived from a psychological state that only the modern memoirist-muse could have fully diagnosed and revealed: the muse's insecurity. Poor Lizzie Siddal must have felt a bit shaky when Dante Gabriel was off painting the luscious Fanny Cornforth, and she left behind a series of bitterly gloomy poems. But a Victorian ballad in rhymed couplets tells a less detailed story than the contemporary memoir in which the self-doubting muse struggles to convince us of how much, despite appearances, she *mattered* to her artist.

After brief prefaces by Charis and her coauthor, Wendy Madar, *Through Another Lens* formally begins with a page-long excerpt from Weston's *Daybooks*. The passage—which Charis identifies as "the last regular entry in the diaries"—describes his first meeting with Charis. Eight months after the fact, he recalls his initial sight of the "tall, beautiful girl, with finely proportioned body, intelligent face well-freckled, blue eyes, golden brown hair to shoulders" and his conviction that he had to meet her, though he never usually asked for introductions. What follows is Weston's own account of Charis's meeting with Sonya, a version which admits more than either woman was willing to acknowledge. "I left for the south before our paths crossed again. While there a letter from S. said she had a new model for me, one with a beautiful body. It was C.—Poor S.— How ironical. But what happened was inevitable."

The remainder of the quote from Weston is, presumably, meant for the reader to keep in mind while reading *Through Another Lens*. "The first nudes of C. were easily amongst the finest I had done, perhaps the finest. I was definitely interested now, and knew that she knew I was. I felt a response . . . I knew now what was coming; eyes don't lie and she wore no mask. Even so I opened a bottle of wine to help build up my ego. You see I really wanted C. hence my hesitation . . . until at last she lay there below me waiting, holding my eyes with hers. And I was lost and have been ever since . . . After eight months we are closer together than ever. Perhaps C. will be remembered as the great love of my life. Already I have achieved certain heights reached with no other love."

Well, it's hard to argue with that! Though in some sense, Charis's book is a touching account of her inability to *be* convinced and to fend off the anxieties that surfaced after the initial erotic high subsided. As late as 1994, Charis was shocked to see copies of the letters that Edward exchanged, in his first Guggenheim year, with the foundation's director, Henry Allen Moe—and to discover that Edward had neglected to mention her existence until 1938. "I felt like one of those Russian non-persons airbrushed out of photographs taken with Stalin . . . Maybe the explanation is simple: maybe Edward didn't see the need to clutter up quasi-official correspondence with references to someone he would have to explain, especially as we were not then married." She wonders if the reason why he rarely photographed her during the Guggenheim years was because she'd cut her hair. ("Edward didn't want me looking like a boy with sawed-off locks.") Though she claims that "the success of *California and the West* settled any lingering doubts I had about my value as a partner," she nonetheless recalls a painful incident during a 1941 trip through Texas, a disagreement that began when Charis suggested they leave the main road to see—and perhaps photograph—the Evangeline oak that appeared in Longfellow's *Evangeline.*

"I was about to remind Edward of the times I'd convinced him to go see something and my hunches had panned out, when the look on his face stopped me dead. His eyes blazed with an anger I had witnessed before but never felt turned against me. All he said was 'It's *my* grant,' but the effect was devastating . . . He stood there glaring at me with hostile eyes in which I could read myself as a drag, a stumbling block, and—worst of all—a stranger."

As fissures, then chasms, divided them, Weston's muse grew increasingly peeved by his refusal to recognize her contribution. What appears to have driven her over the edge was his taking credit for the garden she planted and tended, and of which she was especially proud. "Edward often mentioned the victory garden in letters, and one day when he was showing off the garden to one of our many guests, I overheard him taking credit for the work. I was shocked, because he had always made a point of telling people the garden was my creation . . . I suppose I expected Edward to credit my work because he was furiously protective of the fruits of his own creative labors."

Even when an artist is eager to thank his muse, the process of inspiration is so complex and ineffable that it's difficult to determine how much the muse *can* assume responsibility. But the question of who weeded the radishes is easier to decide, and one can hardly fault Charis for being annoyed when Weston added the tomatoes to his résumé of solitary triumphs.

Desperate to assert her independence, Charis took a job delivering mail in the Carmel Valley; she became politically active, involved in voter registration. On a visit to her dying mother in Washington, D.C., she spent the Christmas holidays in New York and experienced a brief, heady taste of freedom.

And so, inevitably, there came a time when yet another muse and her artist agreed to part. Informed of her engagement, Dr. Johnson told Mrs. Thrale never to contact him again, which is what, in similar circumstances, Lou Andreas-Salomé told Rilke. Such separations were clearly traumatic and rife with complication. But only now, in the era of memoir, do we get a play-by-play account of the breakup—a situation that, as we know, can result in contradictory versions of the truth. And who can blame the muse for wanting to tell her side, especially when her artist has already included his own grumpy account in his *Daybooks*—a passage that Charis tellingly omits from her memoir?

The besotted account of their meeting quoted in *Through Another Lens* is not, strictly speaking, the final entry in the *Daybooks*, despite what Charis claims. Dated April 22, 1944, the last section in the published edition of the *Daybooks*, edited by Nancy Newhall, begins with some apparently jocular griping that barely mask the first ominous groans and creaks of a marriage coming unglued. After a ten-year lapse, and on the tenth anniversary of his meeting with Charis, Weston confides in his diary: "Ten years ago today on a Sunday afternoon was the beginning; now Charis and I are married, have been for five years. This is the first entry in my once-well-kept daybook since 1934. I laughingly blame Ch. for cramping my style as a writer—and there may be some truth in this charge—but the fact is that I have not had much time, nor necessary aloneness for keeping an intimate journal."

So "there may be some truth in the charge" that Charis cramped his style as a writer? What kind of thing is *that* for an artist to say, however "laughingly" about his muse? The muse may be cramping the artist's prose style, but the fact is, she's doing his *writing*, which is what she thinks he wants, what *they* want, and furthermore she is priding herself on being able to write in her artist's voice. And that's the way he sees it? She is *cramping his style*?

And so the severance of the artist-muse connection begins to resemble an ordinary, messy divorce. Charis's account of their dissolution combines self-recrimination and the guilty or egoistic claim that she was solely to blame for their 1945 separation. The end of her marriage, she recalls, was "as overwhelming as it had been at the beginning, only now, in place of idolatry and carnal obsession, there was almost unbearable pain, compounded on my part by guilt and shame. I had betrayed Edward in impulse if not in fact. There were no scenes—no battles, vituperation, accusations, tears, or periods of short-lived truce. Rather, a portcullis had dropped between us and I could find no way through. In some ways this was worse than if we had fought, because everything was left to the imagination, and mine assigned me all of the blame. I became ever more fixed on the idea that my behavior, and finally just my presence, accounted for the disintegration of our shared lives."

After reaching an amicable property settlement, Charis moved to Los Angeles, where she "became active in the progressive movement." On a trip to Eureka, California, to observe a lumber company strike, she met a union organizer named Neil Harris, whom she married after her divorce from Weston became final in 1946. She and Harris had two daughters and were separated in 1967. During the 1950s, Charis continued to correspond with Weston, who had begun to suffer from the debilitating effects of Parkinson's disease. Though he could no longer work, his reputation grew, advanced by numerous books and articles, and by a series of retrospective exhibitions in New York, London, and Paris.

In 1955, three years before Weston died, Charis paid him a final visit. "His eloquent eyes peered out through eye holes in the mask that Parkinson's had made of his face and seemed to say, 'Isn't this a mess—but we can't do anything about it.' " But death, as Charis tells us, failed to sever her ties to Weston. "My awareness of the world was conditioned by him forever after. Even today a pang of loss assails me when I come upon a scene or object or quality of light that would have prompted him to set up his camera."

IN THE EARLY 1940S, around the time that his marriage to Charis began to deteriorate, Weston took a series of satiric photos, beginning with *Civilian Defense*—a disturbing nude of Charis reclining on a couch, alongside a palm frond that stretches almost the entire length of her body. She is staring at the camera, but her face is concealed by a gas mask that makes her look like a monstrous praying mantis, or an unfriendly space alien. Clearly, Weston's view of his muse has come a long way—straight down—from his vision of the gorgeous, radiantly sensuous angel sprawled on the dunes at Oceano.

Equally unflattering and even more chilling is *My Little Gray Home in the West*, one of Weston's last photos of Charis; she stands in the doorway of the Bodie Room, the little shack behind the main house, a refuge created as a writing studio for her but gradually requisitioned for broader family functions and as "my refuge from Edward's displeasure." Looking at once ironic, distracted, and depressed, the naked Charis assumes a slightly awkward, curved posture, like a Cranach Eve, "about to be banished from Eden, with the incriminating half-eaten apple in one hand and in the other a sign saying EDWARD WESTON (CARMEL, CAL.), held as a fig leaf to cover my shame." Her brother Leon leans out a window of the shack. Fully clothed, he wears glasses and tootles on a recorder.

My Little Gray Home in the West is a cartoonish art gag: part Farmer Gray, part Li'l Abner, part Erskine Caldwell, part Manet's *Déjeuner sur l'Herbe*, part camera pictorialist—a cartoon with the sign over

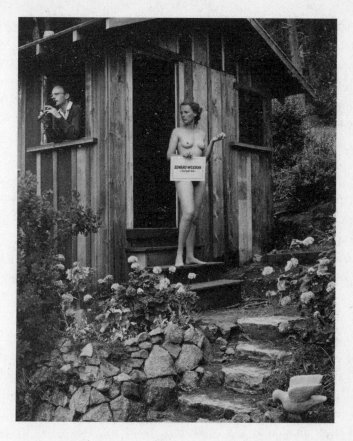

My Little Gray Home in the West, 1943. *(Edward Weston)*

Charis's groin as its smarmy caption. Actually, it is one of the nastiest photos taken by a respected American photographer, though few viewers seem to have noticed. Charis herself admits that "the mockery in some of the new and more complicated titles was evident, particularly *My Little Gray Home in the West.* Mocking or not, it was Edward's Christmas present to their friend, Bea Prendergast, who, together with her husband Don, had taken the Westons around Louisiana and stayed with them in Carmel.

Half a century later, Charis loyally defends her artist against the objections of Nancy Newhall, the *Daybooks* editor, who was dismayed by the photo, as any sensible person would be. "She was not amused by the titles or the pictures, and in response to her letter of protest Edward dispatched this remarkably unpleasant reply: 'Sorry to have upset you . . . with my 'backyard set-ups and their titles.' You guess that the war has upset me. I don't think so, not more than the average dislocation . . . No darling, don't try to pin pathology on me. Your reaction follows a pattern which I should be used to by now. Every time that I change subject matter, or viewpoint, a howl goes up from some Weston fans. So I am not exactly surprised to have you condemn . . . work which will go down in history . . . great photographs on which I will stake my reputation. I could go on, but you might think me defensive. I could explain my titles . . . but surely explanation would insult you.' "

As relieved as we are to hear that the war was only an average dislocation for Weston, and though we may be grateful for the lesson on artistic freedom, Weston's note hardly affects our sense of *My Little Gray Home in the West.* It's compelling but vile, and it makes you long for the stagy, predictable beauty of the chambered nautilus, the cabbage leaves, and those early, idealized abstractions of Charis's golden limbs. *My Little Gray Home in the West* marks the terminal stage of an eleven-year journey from the intoxicated admiration, the celebratory sexiness of the thirties nudes, to the contempt and bitterness of an artist about to be separated from his loved and despised art wife. It *is* a joke, and the joke is on the artist and his muse.

How fitting and ironic that this photo should appear along with the earlier photographs in Charis's memoir. Once more Charis and Edward have worked in "serious collaboration," her words and his pictures conspiring to tell the sad tale of how the muse can enter through one door of an artist's house and leave, as an art wife, through another.

SUZANNE FARRELL

Recall, if you will, the literary evening at which the poet announces that the lyric he will read next was inspired by, is dedicated to, and is about . . . his wife. A restive shiver runs through the crowd, not unlike the chill of unease that shakes the wedding guests as the bride and groom recite the excessively intimate vows they have written to affirm their commitment. The poet's audience sits, rigid with the effort not to glance at the hapless wife who has been singled out for glory and is beaming, or blushing, or (as is more often the case) trying to disappear. Meanwhile, cynics may find themselves wondering what new transgression caused the guilty writer to pen this sentimental ode to his faithful spouse.

Such moments make us realize how very far we have come from an era when the culture agreed that a single sighting of Laura or Beatrice could inspire a lifetime of sonnets. Perhaps we, as a species, have grown too old, too knowing and cynical to believe in the existence of an unrequited passion with the staying power to engender genius. Perhaps psychology has convinced us that the human psyche is too complex to derive something so tough and enduring as art from something so fragile and transitory as love; surely the roots of creativity are more likely to reach down into the shadowy history of the self, back to some unresolved question of sexuality, or an abusive childhood. And feminism has made us suspect the very idea of the muse as yet another passive, second-rate role to be foisted on women, an unsatisfactory substitute for the more primary satisfactions of making art of their own. Thus, to thank one's muse, let alone to claim that one *is* a muse, has become the equivalent of admitting that one is an oppressor, or, alternately, a slave who loves her chains.

"We know the arguments," wrote Arlene Croce. "Muses are passive, therefore passé. Muses are a fantasy rooted in wrongheaded notions of biological 'essentialism' (i.e. femininity). Most degradingly, Muses do not choose to be Muses; they are chosen. Since the nineteen-seventies, modern feminism has based its appeal to women on the premise that all barriers to the dream of self-realization are political. Whatever can't be acquired for oneself, invoking one's civil rights, isn't worth having, and who wants to be a symbol, anyway? The Muse is only a man speaking through a woman, not the woman herself. What male artists call Woman is a construct designed to keep women in their place."

Almost no one refers without irony to a living muse except in the world of ballet, with its language, its costumes, its heightened atmosphere so much closer to, and evocative of, an earlier, more romantic era. Rare among her contemporaries, Suzanne Farrell allows herself to be called a muse and begins her memoir, *Holding On to the Air* (cowritten with Toni Bentley) with a description of the ballet *Meditation*, which George Balanchine choreographed to express his love for her. "I was called his muse, a category not listed in the program, and when *Don Quixote* premiered the whole world had an image of his muse in action."

In the documentary film *Suzanne Farrell: Elusive Muse*, directed by Anne Belle and Deborah Dickson, the word *muse* is used (by fellow dancers Arthur Mitchell and Jacques d'Amboise, among others) with such naturalness and ease that it might as well be a category listed in the program. "He saw her as his muse," recalls d'Amboise, ". . . someone who will inspire him and for whom he will choreograph. . . . Suzanne in the later part of his life was his muse and was the great inspiration for him. He had other people after that he was inspired by . . . but no one ever in the later part of his life like

Suzanne. That was the last great muse for Balanchine." Similarly, Mitchell refers to her as "the new muse" whose romance with Balanchine severely tested his loyalty to Tanaquil Le Clercq, his wife. Yet another documentary, *Dancing for Mr. B.,* features interviews with six of Balanchine's stars, among them Allegra Kent, Darci Kistler, Melissa Hayden, and Maria Tallchief. The word *muse* is only mentioned once—to describe Suzanne Farrell, and it's used by Tallchief, Balanchine's wife before LeClercq.

Yet what makes Farrell's case so singular is not merely her widely acknowledged assumption of the muse's role, but the manner in which she performed it. For while Balanchine's feelings for Farrell and his need to translate their love affair into dance were, undeniably, the source of such masterpieces as *Don Quixote*, Farrell—again, unlike her sister muses—enabled Balanchine to realize his vision in concrete (if such a word can be used about an art form so ethereal) ways that transcended the most exalted ministrations of the average muse. Her contribution to his work, *their* work, went beyond inspiration, posing, exhorting, and encouraging, beyond providing subject matter, erotic gratification, and the fertile emotional climate (of satisfaction or longing) conducive to the production of art.

Farrell's talent, her technical skill, her sheer physical capabilities permitted the choreographer to do things that he had not been able to do until her particular gifts allowed him to imagine that such things could be done. Unique, irreplaceable, and (as Charis Wilson so wished to be) genuinely indispensable, Farrell was the rare muse who made the art physically feasible, the muse who could do something the artist could not, something that he needed and which could not be achieved by anyone else. Of the ballerinas with whom Balanchine worked, Farrell was the most acrobatic and musical, the lightest, the fastest, the least affected by gravity, seemingly the most defiant of every law of nature and biophysics; her courage, her spectacular mix of abandon and control, and her freedom set him free. In the film, she recalls him saying that, having never been on pointe, he didn't know if certain things were possible, to which she replied that they *weren't* possible, not yet . . . but perhaps they would be . . . tomorrow.

Consequently, the paradox of Suzanne Farrell's career as a muse involves both her rare willingness to be termed a muse and an equally uncommon situation in which the artist and his muse were genuine partners, true collaborators. In fact, both were artists of extraordinary stature, geniuses in their own right, and their partnership produced works of genius that, in all probability, neither could have created alone.

Yet interestingly, if unsurprisingly, no one (including Arlene Croce) ever refers to George Balanchine as Suzanne Farrell's muse; the very idea seems somehow subversive, irreverent, sacrilegious, and irreconcilable with the most basic conventions of the ballet, which derive from a prefeminist era and depend, for their power and survival, on traditional notions of masculine and feminine. One can hardly imagine Balanchine and Farrell indulging in the sort of competition—the struggle to redistribute and reclaim the roles of artist and muse—that so damaged John Lennon and Yoko Ono.

Still, watching Farrell dance Balanchine's ballets does make these roles seem simultaneously up for grabs and beside the point. It was (and is, on videotape) possible to observe his spirit inspiring her, animating her, moving through her. Near the end of *Elusive Muse*, she recalls having the fantasy that she was again dancing with him during her final stage appearance, in *Vienna Waltzes*—five years after his death. In the film, she refers to him as a god and speaks of him in much the way artists speak of their muses—repeatedly emphasizing that her work, her ability and her desire to dance were intimately, inextricably connected to her love and respect for him, to the fact of his existence.

Jacques d'Amboise describes her solo in *Don Quixote* as "one of the great performances ever *ever* by anybody. And there is an example of complete abandonment and a demon. I always say, every once in a while you see dancers, they transcend a person, they become a conduit for a force like . . . the muse of dance, the goddess of dance, using a person as a window to express or communicate something. And that person becomes transformed into something bigger than just a beautiful dancer . . . Several times in my mind and memory there's Suzanne dancing like a demon—but a goddess."

Could there be a more accurate description of an artist inhabited by, and responding to, a muse? Yet though *Don Quixote* was, and was recognized as, the most direct expression of Balanchine and Farrell's romance—at its peak, its happiest, most sustaining, most *inspirational* moment—no one seems to have proposed that the dancer's passion for the choreographer was the muse possessing *her*, driving her through that astonishing solo. So which of them *was* the artist and which the muse, and how do these terms apply in the case of a partnership, an artistic collaboration, a marriage of the psyche and the soul nearly unique in the lives of the muses?

BORN IN 1945, in Mt. Healthy, Ohio, a small town that has since been absorbed by the suburbs of Cincinnati, Roberta Sue Ficker was the youngest of three sisters and the product of a matriarchy from which men (including her father, Robert, a deliveryman for a local meat-packing company) had been weeded out by divorce. Like a striking number of the ballerinas interviewed in *Dancing for Mr. B.*, Farrell enjoyed the blessing and curse of an intensely ambitious mother.

In *Elusive Muse,* Suzanne's mom—a chipper, elderly Midwestern lady, stroking a white toy poodle that mirrors the color of her hair, her appearance, and disposition—issues alternately comical and bloodcurdling reflections on themes ranging from the historical importance of her hometown ("Cincinnati was the cradle of the stars. A lot of famous people came from Cincinnati, including Doris Day, Rosemary Clooney, Vera Ellen. So we were very conscious of the arts.") to the advice she gave her daughter on the subject of marriage. ("I told her if she couldn't marry Balanchine . . . don't get married at all. Stay single.")

Young Suzi started lessons with Marian La Cour at the Cincinnati Conservatory of Music. Through La Cour, Suzi got small parts with visiting ballet troupes, as Clara in *The Nutcracker* and as a wagon-pulling mouse in *Sleeping Beauty*. During one rehearsal, she peeled a splinter of wood from the stage of the Cincinnati Music Hall to mark her solemn decision that ballet would be her career. "I just knew at that time that I needed to be a dancer."

Such statements make one contemplate the mysteries of talent and ambition, and the rare confluence of the two. What was the relation between the girl's singular gift and the compulsion to shine and be noticed that made her ham her way through even these tiny roles? "I wanted the company to hire me. I thought that if I was the best mouse they ever saw they would be forced to take me along with them on tour, so I proceeded to do some very intricate improvised choreography enhanced by some verbal mouse behavior." What engendered the perfectionism that later compelled Farrell to grade her own daily performance in class?

In *Elusive Muse*, she reads aloud from her diary, a section dated September 6, 1960. "Dear Diary. This morning I had my first class at the School of American Ballet. I have decided to use A— excellent, B—very good, C—good, D—poor in grading my classes, okay? Being the best is my goal." And what sense of mission, of having been chosen by talent or destiny, inspired the almost maniacal singlemindedness that d'Amboise saw, early on, in Farrell? "I remember waiting to come on as the Prince in *Swan Lake*, in the back. And there is the corps de ballet, dancing. And the last girl on the edge in the dark is Suzanne Farrell dancing with all the energy and life and passion in her face . . . Extreme. I mean, *everything*. There was nothing held back. And I thought, 'My God, that girl is great. She's *never* going to fail. Because even when no one is looking in the dark she's dancing as if she's alone and it's the only performance, and the last performance of her life. It was *everything.*"

So it's hardly surprising that Suzi and her talented sisters became minor local celebrities, "big fish in the Cincinnati pond," participating in recitals and fund-raisers—playing "a domino, a Christmas card, a gazelle, a beatnik . . . an Irish lass, and a snowman who partnered ten snowflakes." After visiting one of La Cour's classes, New York City Ballet dancer Diana Adams suggested that Suzi come to New York and contact the School of American Ballet—a guarded recommendation that encouraged Suzanne's mother to move her family to the Upper West Side, and into a studio apartment in the Ansonia Hotel, which she chose because she'd heard that it had been the home of many artists who became successful. "I just didn't have one single doubt in my mind. I just decided we were gonna come, we were gonna make it, and we were gonna stay."

Clearly, a great deal was riding on Suzi's audition for the School of American Ballet, which occurred soon after her arrival, and which she remembers as a disaster. Having expected that she would be told what to do, she had neglected to prepare a routine. When Balanchine asked to see one, she offered, in a panic, to perform a dance from her June recital and accompanied herself by humming Glazunov's *The Seasons.* Balanchine watched without comment, without any apparent response, then thanked and dismissed her. Suzanne and her mother were . . . "confused. Nothing in Cincinnati had prepared us for this moment. . . . We just looked at each other and felt lost."

Perhaps Suzi might have taken some comfort from the fact that, when Balanchine himself auditioned for the Imperial Ballet school in St. Petersburg, in 1911, the nine-year-old applicant—a strikingly pretty child from Georgia—was not expected to dance at all, but merely to parade back and forth before a panel of judges trained to scrutinize prospective students "in terms of health, physique, car-

riage, general air and appearance, and such other subtle considera-
tions as the examining board had evolved through the years." After
graduating in 1921, he joined the corps at the Maryinsky Ballet, and
three years later left Russia with a group of dancers to perform in
Europe. In Paris, they auditioned for Diaghilev, and Balanchine
began choreographing for the Ballet Russe. In 1933, he accepted
Lincoln Kirstein's invitation to come to New York to establish the
School of American Ballet. After working on Broadway and in Hollywood, Balanchine—again with Kirstein's help—founded the New
York City Ballet, and by the summer of 1960, the company and the
school were doing well enough to be able to offer scholarships to
promising new students like Suzi Ficker.

A YEAR AFTER she began at the school, Suzi was invited to join the
corps de ballet, and took it as an opportunity to shed the last ves-
tiges of Mt. Healthy. "I don't know what gave me the reason to
think that I would need to have a stage name, but I thought that I
really wanted to be someone else." When Balanchine's assistant
asked her how she wanted her contract made out, the serious
eleventh-grader replied, " 'I've decided, after looking in the phone
book, that I would like to be Suzanne Farrell.' And she put paren-
theses around Ficker and typed in Farrell and said, 'Here you are,
Miss Farrell. Your contract.' "

Farrell's gradual rise through the ranks of the corps accelerated
when she agreed to learn Diana Adams's part in Balanchine's ballet
set to Stravinsky's *Movements for Piano and Orchestra*. When Adams
(who, along with d'Amboise, had become Farrell's mentor) announced that she was pregnant, Balanchine felt that his favorite
dancer had betrayed him. Having created the ballet for Adams, he
was unable to imagine anyone else in the role, and was dubious
about Farrell's ability to learn the part. His doubts were understandable; the 18-year-old dancer had only a short time in which to
master the complex steps, which Adams (confined to her couch by

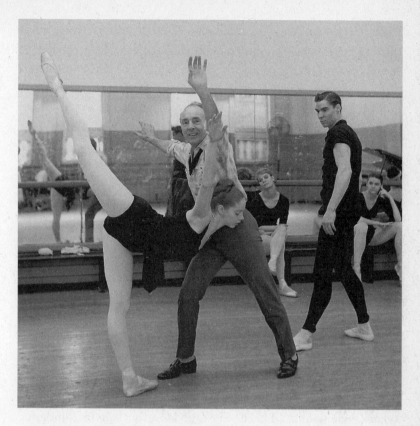

Movements for Piano and Orchestra, Jacques d'Amboise watches as Balanchine, working with Suzanne Farrell, shows him how his part should go. *(Martha Swope)*

a difficult pregnancy) demonstrated, using only her hands, while Farrell and d'Amboise practiced in Adams's living room. But when Balanchine saw Farrell dance the ballet, "Mr. B.'s eyebrows rose and his demeanor changed."

During a rocky rehearsal for *Movements,* Farrell suggested she might not be ready—not good enough—to dance the part. "Then a wonderful thing happened. He clasped his hands as if in prayer, made a small bowing gesture, and said simply, 'Oh, dear, you let me be the judge.' And so I did, forever more. This brief exchange was a turning point in a silent understanding, and our trust was sealed . . . We were both taking pretty big chances, but if he thought I could do something, I would believe him, often against my own reasoning. I trusted him not to let me be a fool, but rather a tool, an instrument in his hands. In short, I trusted him with my life."

In the memoir and the documentary, Farrell tells two slightly different versions of an exchange between Balanchine and Stravinsky on the subject of her appearance in the ballet. In the book, she reports that Stravinsky attended a rehearsal of *Movements* and asked Balanchine who she was. In the film, she described the composer visiting backstage after the first triumphant performance, a revision that gives a sharper dramatic edge to the punchline, which both accounts share. In both versions, Stravinsky asked about the new dancer, and Balanchine replied: "Igor, this is Suzanne Farrell. Just been born."

It seems clear that Farrell (who had already put in years of grueling work, practice, planning, risking everything, enduring severe physical pain) was hardly the newborn star hatched full grown from the head of the god, the mind of the artist. But of course Balanchine knew that. The neonate goddess he had in mind was Suzanne Farrell the dancer, the genius they would create together as they explored and discovered the limits (or the limitlessness) of what only the two of them, working together, could first dream and then create.

ASKED ABOUT THE FACTS of his biography, Balanchine said, "It's all in the programs." The same could be said about the course of his love affair with Farrell, which can be traced, a clear trajectory linking some of his most remarkable ballets, including *Meditation, Don Quixote, Tzigane,* and *Mozartiana,* each of which marked a new phase in their relationship. However much one hesitates to attribute a complex work of art to a particular event in the artist's life, both Farrell

and Balanchine invited such associations, suggesting—and stating—
that each ballet represented a corner turned, or nearly turned, in
their feelings for one another. If *Meditation* was a declaration of love,
Don Quixote was its fulfillment, *Tzigane* a spurned suitor's reflection
on his beloved's witchy powers of enchantment, and *Mozartiana* a
transcendent acceptance of the inevitable: mortality, transience, the
loss of love.

What Farrell wants her audience to know is that the love was
intricately, inextricably connected to the work. *Elusive Muse* begins
with her recollection of a conversation that expresses what she
and the film's directors consider the essence of her relationship
with Balanchine. "I remember very well, George and I talking . . .
And he said, 'You know, Suzanne, if I weren't a choreographer
you wouldn't look at me twice. And I looked at him, and I said,
'You know, George, if I weren't a ballerina, you wouldn't look at
me twice.'"

It is, like *Meditation*, a declaration; the lovers have reached the
point of admitting that they have looked at each other twice. But
Farrell is saying something else: not just that her artist loved her, but
that what they *did* (not just who they were, or what they felt) was
what held them together. "I think how you dance is who you are, and
that's what he fell in love with. The person sort of came along with
the dancer. And the person came along with the choreographer."

The intensely emotional, confessional, and eerily prescient *Meditation* was the first work that Balanchine choreographed for Farrell.
The title of her memoir refers to Balanchine's advice on how to
make her entrance in the ballet. "You just hold on to the air when
you're up there," he said. "You're riding on the air." And its plot provides the opening passage of the memoir: "The stage is dark, but in
one corner, in the shadows, kneels the curved, still body of a man.
His silhouette shows his face buried in his palms, as if in anguish, as
if remembering . . . or as if dreaming. Out of the darkness behind
him, in a single shaft of light, steps the figure of a young girl . . . She

reaches toward the man, but he cannot see her until she stands over him and peels his hands from his face. The stage brightens as the man rises, and it is revealed that his hair is graying at the temples and his movement is not as elastic as it once might have been."

Though the documentary was filmed more than thirty years after the first performance of *Meditation*, Farrell seems not to have entirely recovered from her surprise at learning that she had inspired the emotions that give the ballet its intensity. At the time, she found it nearly incredible that love for *her* could have moved the famously cool, austere choreographer to use the romantic music of Tchaikovsky instead of the more cerebral Stravinsky. At eighteen, Farrell (whose long hours in the practice studio had not left her much time for dating) was so innocent—she had only been kissed twice—that she was apparently the last person in the company to notice that Balanchine, who had already married four of his young ballerinas, had feelings for her that exceeded the strictly professional. In fact, her relationship with Balanchine was already (and would continue to be) the subject of much speculation and gossip among her fellow dancers, thus making Farrell one of the many muses whose sex life has excited overheated curiosity and conjecture, both in her immediate circle and among the general public.

But of course she might have been slow to recognize the signs of sexual interest in an idol, a hero who was not only an object of near-religious devotion, but who was forty years older than she was, and famously loyal to his present wife, Tanny—Tanaquil Le Clercq, who had been his star ballerina until she was paralyzed by polio. What also makes Farrell seem less naïve is that Maria Tallchief, Balanchine's third wife, reports a similar amazement on learning that the choreographer's romantic attentions were focused on *her*. "She was astonished when he proposed, for he had not previously shown any lover's ardor, and when he had turned his eyes on her, in the rehearsal hall, she had not been aware that these might be melting glances he was bestowing, but was rather painfully conscious of all the flaws he must be noting."

Even after the first rehearsals for *Meditation*, Farrell failed to note what was transpiring, nor did the truth occur to her when Balanchine (who hated to write) sent her a love letter from Hamburg, where he had gone to direct the dances for Gluck's opera, *Orpheus and Eurydice*. In *Elusive Muse*, Farrell reaches into a dresser drawer and tenderly extracts the letter, which begins with Balanchine's claim that he is writing her to describe how the male dancer in *Meditation* is supposed to feel about his partner. Next comes three stanzas of rhymed verse: "Through languor, through despair and sorrow/ Through clamor and through restless space/ I heard your voice from night till morrow/ And dreamt and dreamt of darling face." Farrell took Mr. B. at his word—that all of this was just stage directions—and fixated on his postscript ("I hope by now you are thin and beautiful and light to lift.") which she interpreted as a criticism of her weight.

Only later did she reinterpret *Meditation*, and the letter from Hamburg: "Over time it became clear that the man in the *pas de deux* was Balanchine . . . Never, though, did he say it, never would he have said it, but never was anything more apparent. I didn't have an understudy for *Meditation*, then or ever. No one else has ever danced it . . . Balanchine had not only choreographed a ballet; he had choreographed our lives."

It's no wonder that Farrell was initially unable to recognize that her idol was a human being, with human needs and desires; in the memoir and film, she refers to him as a deity. "There's something really daunting and wild about having your first love be this god . . ." Her language reflects both the Greek polytheism of classical ballet and the Catholicism that would send her to church to pray for guidance as her romance with the married Mr. B. grew more intense and bewildering.

By the premier of *Don Quixote* in 1965, four years after she joined

Balanchine's corps de ballet and two years after he choreographed *Meditation* for her, Farrell had come to share Balanchine's emotions. *Don Quixote* functioned as a public affirmation of the love that the couple had not yet acknowledged to one another, or even to themselves, an expression given added urgency and intensity by the fact that they were performing before a large and important benefit audience. Balanchine, who had not appeared on stage in seven years, announced that he would play the title role of the lovestruck, delusional knight, and Suzanne, who was dancing Dulcinea, would later understand his decision as a message, a code as readily discernible as the cards in Edward Weston's studio window.

The pairing of the aging choreographer and his young protégée was—regardless or because of its personal resonance—brilliant, visionary theater. As Farrell spins airy circles around the shuffling, disoriented old man, supporting him and leading him (Balanchine was in fact having trouble with the steps and the staging) we witness almost more testimony than we can bear to witness, more information that we can stand to process, on the themes of youth and age, tenderness and aspiration, the ideal, the beloved, and the unattainable.

"We danced entirely for each other," remembers Farrell, "and in a curious way all the emotion was a relief, a release of everything that had been building up between us without any direct expression. The ballet became a kind of public courtship, a declaration, where dance, mime, and ceremony mingled with our real lives and emotions so deeply that our on-stage and offstage selves became interwoven." Farrell's solo in *Don Quixote* was a feat of such technical daring and profound originality that "we broke one rule after the other and climbed through the walls of balletic convention to discover a whole new place to inhabit. It was not the conventional space defined by dancers of up and down, left and right; it was a tilted, revolving circle. The air there was delightfully unpolluted, and best of all, there were no laws until we made them."

Like *demon*—and, for that matter, *muse*—the word *possessed* resonates throughout the memoir and the film, and as one watches Farrell dance, holding on to the air, her body does seem to have been taken over by some supernatural force. To say that she looks *driven* is not so much a metaphor as a literal description; every movement she makes is suffused with an electricity, a transparent shimmer that readjusts our notions of how a body moves through space, of what it means to float, though there is nothing floaty about her dancing, which is always highly charged, conscious, and exacting in ways that seem, again, paradoxically masterful, controlled, and effortless.

In the film, Suzanne Farrell walks along the edge of the Seine, remembering the romantic strolls that she and Balanchine took along its banks. Energized by the New York triumph of *Don Quixote*, they had come to dance in Paris. It was the first time Farrell had been there; it was also the height of her career and of her romance with Mr. B., with whom she walked late at night, after their performances, often in silence, too deeply moved for words. "It was as if our lives had become possessed." The wispy schoolgirlish waif, the little ballerina once more possesses the body of the older woman, throws open a window on her younger self, and in doing so makes it easier for us to understand how long it took her to imagine that, during those rapturous moments of wordless communication, she and Mr. B. may have had different things in mind.

THE MOST INTENSE part of their relationship lasted for three years and followed the arc (the slow enraptured discovery of the other, the pleasure of being in one another's presence, then the drama, the jealousies and hurt feelings, the recriminations and heartbreak) of a conventional love affair. On the second page of the memoir, Farrell tells us there were kisses; halfway through the documentary, she makes it clear that there was no sex. Still, it was love, passionate enough for Suzanne to feel guilty when Mr. B. went home to his wife.

Though both the memoir and the film are discreet, what emerges is that Balanchine wanted a sexual relationship and Farrell did not. "I'm sure he wanted that . . . I don't know. Maybe it was my little Catholic upbringing, maybe it was the way I perceived love and everything. I just wasn't ready for that." Often, Farrell still appears to be having, or re-creating, the conversations and arguments she must have had with herself at the time, convincing herself, for example, that dancing not only took the place of sex but was ultimately *better* than sex. "When he was dancing with me, choreographing a ballet, it was extremely physical and extremely gratifying in that kind of way. I mean, it certainly was not the orthodox way of having . . . a relationship. But it was more passionate and more loving and more . . . *more* than most relationships. We had . . . it was terrific. We had a great time."

Her decision to remain unattainable—her refusal to be either a mistress or, ultimately, an art wife—may have reflected her religious scruples, her own reservations about adult sexuality, and certainly had a great deal to do with the guilt she and Balanchine suffered over their betrayal of Tanny, the tragic presence looming in the background, the beautiful, paralyzed, still-young wife. But it was also a matter of pride, a sense of mission that fueled her refusal to join the succession of dancers whom Mr. B. had loved, married, and replaced. "He was in the habit of falling in love and marrying his ballerinas . . . I was determined not to be another one in a long line of ballerinas. I decided I would be different—hopefully, by virtue of my dancing."

When the *Chicago Sun-Times* reported that Balanchine had announced, at a party, that he and Suzanne were going to be married, she was especially upset by the newspaper's mention of his former wives. "There was that list again with me at the end of it. It was as if I were simply the next fateful incident in the cosmic pattern of George Balanchine's many lives." Her resolve was a reasonable response to her sense of Balanchine's need for the unattainable muse, for that spur of unsatisfied longing, and to her own fear that sex and marriage would change—and damage—their working relationship. "I think having a sexual relationship with him would really have altered things."

That's certainly how Jacques d'Amboise understood Balanchine's psychology: "Many of his works have to do with a muse, a woman, an ideal that a man attempts to own, touches and passes with for a moment in his life . . . and is doomed to lose it, and it's necessary to lose it. Otherwise there's no striving for anything better any more if you achieved what you had dreamed of. You must not achieve it, you must not possess it." And Balanchine's statement of his personal philosophy, expressed in a *Life* magazine interview, supports d'Amboise's view: "Woman is the goddess, the poetess, the muse. That is why I have a company of beautiful girl dancers. I believe that the same is true of life, that everything a man does he does for his ideal woman. You live only one life and you believe in something and I believe in a little thing like that."

Likewise, Bernard Taper's biography of the choreographer suggests that a dancer who wished to remain his muse would have been wise not to become his lover, and definitely not his wife: "Each new epoch of Balanchine's creative life seems to have been associated with a new wife or love—always a dancer under his aegis, always young and not fully formed, either as person or dancer . . . They served the choreographer as both reality and potentiality—with the poignant addition that they were also the raw material out of which the finished work of art would be formed. . . . That one young woman would be supplanted in this role by another in the course of time had begun to seem by then, as with Picasso's succession of wife-mistress-models, an outward manifestation of the constantly renewed youthfulness of the artist's creative powers. 'Grow old along with me, the best is yet to be' was not a likely model for Balanchine. He lived only in and for the present. Caring intensely as he did about physical beauty . . . Balanchine always suffered to see this masterful beauty fade . . . Sometimes he would avoid meeting with beautiful dancers whom he had known in a bygone era because he cherished a precise and acute image of their beauty in his memory, which he could not bear to have spoiled for him by their present appearance."

One can imagine how Yoko Ono would have responded to this notion of a woman's proper role, but Farrell chose to see it in the most positive light. "That Balanchine spent his life building pedestals for his ballerinas to stand on is no secret, and although some might protest the position as one of inequality, no one who has been there has ever complained. It is the most humbling and beautiful place I have ever been. Balanchine was a feminist long before it was the fashion; he devoted his life to celebrating female independence . . . Paradoxically, this independence could incorporate and transcend the support and strength of a man; a partner enabled movements not possible alone, and this is why, to Balanchine, a male dancer's nobility was not to be found in bravura pyrotechnics but in the self-effacement of supporting a woman on pointe."

IN 1967, AFTER the *Chicago Sun-Times* announced Farrell and Balanchine's "engagement" with Farrell's name at the end of the list of Balanchine's wives, Farrell decided "to try to put a little distance between George and myself. Things between us were becoming more convoluted and more difficult, with no resolution in sight."

She told Balanchine it might be better if they stopped having dinner together. He promptly lost so much weight that the whole company began to worry and blamed Suzanne. "This was made most apparent to me one day when one of the company's more prominent male dancers suggested a solution to the current tension. 'Why don't you just sleep with him? It doesn't have to mean anything. Is it such a big deal?' I was deeply shocked. I had never thought of sex in that way; my life would certainly have been simpler if I could have."

Suzanne Farrell was twenty-two. Her generation (or at least the media) was celebrating the so-called sexual revolution. But Farrell's psyche existed out of time, in the pure balletic romance of the *pas de deux*. "I loved Balanchine, and I wanted him to love me in the same way—at least not to *not* love me. I was flattered by his attentions, personal and professional, yet I wasn't prepared to face the consequences of where those actions might lead." She didn't want to marry Balanchine, but she didn't want him going home to Tanny. She wanted every moment to be like those midnight walks along the Seine, like the premiere of *Don Quixote*.

"Because I couldn't give George everything he wanted, I became committed to making it up to him in some other way. I think this commitment lodged itself in my subconscious and made me a better dancer. . . . And we never talked about any of it. Maybe we both knew there was no rational, painless solution to the dilemma . . . that any talk might upset the delicate balance which allowed the ideal of our collaboration on stage to continue."

Both the memoir and the film are haunted by the question of what she would have lost by sleeping with him, by marrying him. How would it have affected the dance, which fed on unsatisfied longing? "The physical side of love is of paramount importance to many people but to us it wasn't. Our interaction was physical, but its expression was dance. We both had histories suggesting that marriage might not be the answer—George had had numerous marriages, and my family had barely survived the one that produced me. I didn't want to go home with George and be married. Even if it had been bliss, I think we would have lost something on another level. The thought frightened me."

Her mother urged her to marry Balanchine. "The age difference didn't bother me. All the marriages didn't bother me. I thought that was okay. Because he wasn't just any old man. Mr. Balanchine was a genius. He was a living working genius. And that made a big difference."

Suzanne resumed her dinners with Mr. B., who gained weight and recovered enough to help Suzanne and her mother decorate their Christmas tree. Together they created several more dances, including *Slaughter on Tenth Avenue*, in which—according to Arthur Mitchell—Farrell had some trouble projecting the sexual oomph of the Striptease Girl. Dancing in high heels and fishnet stockings, with her hair loose, she suggests, at best, a shy, reluctant teenage whore, trying hard, on her first night out.

THE FOLLOWING AUTUMN, Suzanne began a tentative, covert romance with a fellow dancer, Paul Mejia. Born in Peru, Mejia had been friends with Farrell for several years, ever since he'd joined the company. But not until Mejia made a sudden declaration of love did Farrell consider him a suitor.

"Curious as it may sound, at twenty-two I was trying, without much success, to eliminate romance from my life, and Paul didn't confuse me the way George did. Ironically, our infrequent dates took on a romantic atmosphere not so much because of any passionate feelings between us but because I felt I was always being watched, so going out with someone besides George, especially a young man, was immediately an occasion for secrecy, a real cloak-and-dagger situation." Meanwhile, there was evidence that they *were* being watched. Twice, after they arranged to meet in the morning, they ran into Mr. B., who seemed displeased to see them together so early.

Suzanne's mother was appalled by her deepening friendship with Mejia, and Mr. Balachine did what must have seemed logical, under the circumstances: He asked Suzanne to marry him so that they could have a child. When Farrell refused, Balanchine stopped speaking to her, and Farrell began to feel that Paul was her only friend, the only person who cared about her. Increasingly isolated and embattled, she and Paul decided to get married. They wed in February, when Balanchine was out of the country. Suzanne's mother sobbed openly throughout the ceremony, which Farrell recalls as a tense and confusing occasion, after which the newlyweds spent their wedding night at a hotel at Kennedy Airport.

In the film interviews, Mejia seems sweet, bewildered, fey, and more fragile than Suzanne—remarkably gracious and forbearing even when he is recalling the events that essentially ruined his career. After the wedding, Mejia (who, it appears, may never have been a favorite of Balanchine's) was fired, then rehired. Suzanne's schedule was unaffected, but she was so tormented by Balanchine's chilliness (he would turn his back on her when they met in the corridor) that she and Paul offered to leave the company. Mr. B. assured her she needn't leave, but proposed that maybe Paul should. Paul got fewer and fewer roles, and after several slights and omissions, his situation became untenable. Finally, when his name was omitted from the cast of a ballet in which he customarily danced, Suzanne sent a message to Mr. B. informing him that she and Paul would both resign from the company if Paul didn't appear in the third movement of *Symphony in C* that evening.

Before the show, Suzanne—who was scheduled to dance the second movement—sat in her dressing room, putting on her makeup "way too early" and "waiting for something to happen." At last there came a knock on the door. The wardrobe mistress took Suzanne's costume, saying, "Suzanne, I'm sorry, you're not dancing tonight." When Farrell tells this story in the documentary, her voice trembles and her eyes spill over with tears.

On the night they were fired, Farrell and Mejia sat in the audience and watched the entire performance. Then Suzanne packed a traveling case with her lucky medals and sentimental souvenirs. The next morning, every newspaper in New York reported the details of her personal drama. Barred even from using the theater rehearsal studios, the couple found themselves not only ostracized and unemployed but unemployable. No other companies would risk hiring them and possibly losing the right to perform Balanchine's ballets. They traveled, and somehow managed to earn a living; they danced on Long Island and appeared on the *Dick Cavett Show*; Suzanne modeled Vidal Sassoon hairstyles for *After Dark* magazine.

Briefly, Farrell guest-starred with the National Ballet of Canada, and, as a conciliatory gesture, invited her mother (who hadn't spoken to her since the wedding) to a performance of *Swan Lake*, during which Suzanne tore the cartilage in her knee. She and Paul returned to New York, then fled upstate, where they bought—and retreated to—their own private island. Then, just when their prospects must have seemed most bleak, Suzanne received a telegram from Maurice Béjart, a choreographer she had met in Brussels; he invited her and Paul to move to Belgium and join his Ballet du XXeme Siècle.

Interviewed in his suite at the Hotel Metropole in Brussels, Béjart recalls Suzanne as one of the few important people in his life, as a gift that he always knew was only lent to him and not given, as something he had never had before and would never have again. The footage of their collaboration provides an object lesson in how little the most generous and energetic muse can do to inspire a merely competent artist. In the *pas de deux* from Béjart's *Romeo and Juliet*, something resembling the old radiance shimmers through her, but in the service of stagy movements, of unsubtle and almost kitschy gestures.

Farrell's gratitude and affection for Béjart come through, in the book and the film. She emphasizes how happy she was; she and Paul were dancing, getting to know each other. But, she notes, there *were* the alarming, unexplained staph infections, skin eruptions that kept breaking out all over her body and that, on one occasion, sent her to the hospital . . .

In the summer of 1974, after watching *Symphony in C* and *La Valse* in Saratoga Springs, Farrell, who felt she had "nothing to lose," sent Balanchine a note. "Dear George, As wonderful as it is to see your ballets, it is even more wonderful to dance them. Is this impossible?

Love, Suzi." Intimate, slightly kittenish, intuitive, it is anything but a formal business letter, a dancer's polite request to be rehired by a former employer. A meeting was arranged. Farrell went to Balanchine's house. He uncorked a bottle of wine. As Farrell recalls, she didn't ask to come back, he didn't say she *could* come back, they just said, When do we start working? It was as if nothing had ever happened, which was how they proceeded, as if nothing had happened. The entire company turned out for Suzanne's first class with Balanchine; she simply walked over and gave him a hug. "He was sweet," she says. "He loosened his tie, rolled up his sleeves." And he ordered the class into first position.

What's most obvious is the painfully civilized repression of feeling. But what takes a moment longer to see is the lovers' commitment to protecting each other's dignity from the embarrassment of scenes and tears, confessions or accusations; and dignity is an important element in even the most free and least formal Balanchine ballet. Perhaps this also helps explain Farrell's reluctance to sleep with Mr. B., since sex is an activity in which it is ultimately counterproductive to maintain one's reserve and composure.

Among the things restored to Balanchine and Suzanne was the chance to play out their private drama on stage, to use their personal lives as material. Suzanne's return performance was a huge success. As a symbolic gesture, she danced the adagio from *Symphony in C* that she was scheduled to perform on the night she was dismissed. Making her entrance, Suzanne felt that "there was no place I would rather have been. The spotlight was my light at the end of my tunnel. I was twenty-nine and felt ageless."

None of this was lost on the audience. Farrell's fans demanded a solo bow, which she took, though company policy dictated that all four ballerinas who had appeared were supposed to bow together.

Reunited with Balanchine, Farrell resumed the repertoire of major roles, but according to Jacques d'Amboise, Suzanne and Mr. B. were now warier, more cautious, reluctant to get hurt again. In

Balanchine's first new ballet, the 1975 *Tzigane*, the prodigal muse and her artist were clearly still working things out. After having dressed the virginal Suzanne in white for years, Balanchine decided to put the new-model, married Suzanne in scarlet, a red-laced bodice and a red ribbon skirt; he gave her a long solo as the personification of female sexual sorcery waving her arms seductively to the wailings of a solitary violin. The sentimental European folksiness of *Tzigane* can at moments evoke the boiler-plate gypsy camp scenes in movies like *The Werewolf*. But, watching Farrell's performance, you can see her shaking loose the clichés she picked up during her time with Béjart.

The important thing was that Farrell and Balanchine were working together again, and *Holding On to the Air* provides a lovely account of how their collaboration resumed—and functioned. "Finally, he suggested an actual ballet step: 'Now, maybe you can do a big arabesque,' and, always wanting to give him as much as possible, I did a huge, diving arabesque penché. 'We know you can do that,' he countered, 'what else can you do?' and I flipped out of the penché into a deep backbend, head facing upward. His eyebrows rose as I looked to him for comment, and I knew then the fun had begun—we were experimenting again."

In the next years, more works emerged, surpassing *Tzigane*: the austere *Chaconne*; *Union Jack*, in which Farrell was allowed to deploy the showoffy sense of humor so evident in her mother's home movies of little Roberta Sue; and the dreamy *Vienna Waltzes*, one of the company's popular successes. For Farrell's solo, she is dressed in a regal white ballgown; she swirls and dips through a romantic *pas de deux* with an invisible partner. "At each performance I felt a gentle push from behind as my music began. It was as if George and I went on-stage together, and I could feel him following me, not literally but with his eyes. . . . Later, I decided that my partner was relegated to a phantom existence not because of the lack of men in the company but because I was dancing, once more, with George."

What is this, if not an artist talking about a muse? Who *was* whose muse, after all? And what could Paul Mejia do in the face of a love that burned as intensely as ever now that the lovers had settled their little problem about sex. In a touching interview, Mejia begins to weep when he recalls the beauty of Suzanne's return to the stage, and how proud he was of her. The unspoken subtext is the memory of his own disappointment and grief as he watched from the wings and contemplated his dismal professional future. Over the next months, his wife would be partnered frequently with the powerful Peter Martins, whose muscular Nordic blondness could not have been more unlike Mejia's olive skin and slight physique.

In 1978, Paul accepted a job in Guatemala, and later one in Chicago, where Balanchine had encouraged him to go. Maria Tallchief was there; the miles between New York and the Midwest must have seemed, to Mr. B., a healthy distance at which to keep spouses and former spouses. Persuasively, Farrell claims that, despite the long separations, the fact that Paul was working enabled their marriage to survive.

That same year, Balanchine suffered a minor heart attack. "I knew the surest way to pray for him was by dancing, so I got out onstage every night and danced for him." Illness made him reflective, and one night, over dinner, he began talking about the past. He told Suzanne that he had been wrong when he'd pressured her to sleep with him, to marry him; he'd been too old for her, he'd been wrong to think about her in that way. In the film, Farrell recalls that this was what she had always wanted to hear—and what she had never wanted to hear, for she'd never thought of him as an old man. In any event, it was a moment which the lovers drew on for a new series of ballets.

"Our conversation that night heightened our sensitivity to and awareness of each other, and some of those feelings are evident in the ballets he made during the next two years, most notably in Robert Schumann's *Davidsbündlertänze,* and *Mozartiana.* What had not happened between us had enhanced our understanding on another level, not only a dance level, but a spiritual one. If he had thought at one time that he wanted something I couldn't give him, I hoped that now he knew that in truth he did get everything . . . everything I had to give, the best of me." What comes through, of course, is Farrell's sense that—despite the sacrifices she was obliged to make, despite the damage inflicted on her personal and professional life— her decision to remain Balanchine's unobtainable muse was the correct one and paid off in the only way that mattered—that is, in their art.

The adagio in the *Davidsbündlertänze* was the last dance Jacques d'Amboise performed on stage. "Injuries were stopping me all the time . . ." Farrell's injuries worsened, as well. Her doctors prescribed knee surgery. And Balanchine was already exhibiting symptoms of a progressive—and eventually fatal—neurological illness.

When Balanchine announced his plans to choreograph *Mozartiana*, a project he'd first attempted fifty years before, Farrell (who intuited that this might be his last ballet) obtained the music so that she could prepare in advance. Before rehearsals began she had a dream in which she found herself surrounded by tall spires, startled by the "shattering, prophetic" sound of an organ: "I was walking on the vibrating spires upward from one pinnacle to another. It wasn't precarious. My footing was very stable; I was holding on to the air." The light got brighter, and suddenly Farrell was walking on the sand with Mr. B., telling puzzled onlookers, " 'Oh, yes . . . that's *Mozartiana*.' It was the answer to all questions."

This vision augured the profound effects of dancing *Mozartiana*: "He had not just made a ballet with *Mozartiana*, he had altered and extended the spectrum of my life. Having danced it, I felt that I had just begun to dance, just been borne into life itself. In *Mozartiana* George and I were at peace with each other, and the pervasive calm and corresponding strength I felt while performing it were truly transcendent.

"Balanchine at the age of seventy-seven had given us a vision of heaven . . . and it was a very beautiful place indeed, a place past desire, where dancers perform for the glory of God. My dream of climbing spires was answered—*Mozartiana* was the light. It was because this ballet existed that I could survive the death of the man who made it."

AT 4 A.M., ON April 30, 1983, Farrell received a phone call informing her that George Balanchine was dead. She wandered around her apartment, then drifted to the theater. In both the memoir and the film, she describes how alone she felt, like an orphan who would "never again be understood the way Mr. B. had understood me, I would never be used the way he had used me, I would never be loved the way he had loved me." That night, she danced the *Symphony in* C adagio "for George." Afterward, she slipped into a depression that lasted through the church service (in his open coffin, Balanchine reminded her of *Don Quixote*) and the burial, to which she was not invited, and at which she arrived after the official mourners had left.

After the funeral, Farrell returned alone to her dark apartment. She stood at the kitchen window. "I was looking out, wondering what was going to happen to me now, when suddenly my peripheral vision was lifted for the first time since George died and I felt a surge of blinding white light energizing me. It was like my dream of *Mozartiana*. Then I knew. I said to myself, 'I'm going to be all right. I'm going to survive.'" In the film, she recalls the vision as having provided a more specific direction: "After it passed I felt charged. I said, No, I really have to go on and dance."

FARRELL DANCED FOR five more years before her damaged hip ended her stage career. The dance she chose for her final performance, in November 1989, was *Vienna Waltzes*, her *pas de deux* with the invisible partner. "The trumpets were blaring, heralding my entrance. And it was as if George was standing there in the first wing again, and I felt a little push and I started walking on my ever-faithful diagonal . . . alone. And curtsying to this imaginary partner, it occurred to me, Oh, how nice, Mr. B. and I are dancing together again."

After the performance, fans showered Farrell with hundreds of white roses, while she staved off panic about retirement. "My whole existence was how I danced and who I was on stage." Waking the next morning, she was relieved to discover that she was still the same person—except that she found herself completely unable to listen to beautiful music "for the longest time" until she started to stage ballets and felt "alive and active again, physically."

Farrell still stages Balanchine's work and teaches, just as Balanchine said she would, just as he said all the young ballerinas would, though he'd said it when they were so young that none of them believed him. And in September 2000, Farrell's own troupe, the Suzanne Farrell Ballet, inaugurated its touring season with an appearance at the Kennedy Center in Washington, D.C. Farrell is, by reputation, a dedicated and demanding teacher, and some of the most engrossing footage in *Elusive Muse* is set in classrooms and rehearsal studios.

During one such scene—a rehearsal of *Chaconne*—dancer Marie-Christine Mouis, whom Farrell has been coaching, says, "I always feel like she is a direct line to Balanchine. She's so in tune with him. She's almost like a channel. Through her the choreography lives again."

The music to which they are practicing is "The Dance of the Happy Shades" from Gluck's *Orpheus and Eurydice*, which Balanchine was choreographing when he sent Farrell her first love letter, from Hamburg. Gluck's opera is, of course, based on the myth in which the poet travels to Hades, to the kingdom of the dead, to plead for the return of his lost muse, the myth that tells us that the bonds of love are as strong (or *almost* as strong) as the power of death.

YOKO ONO

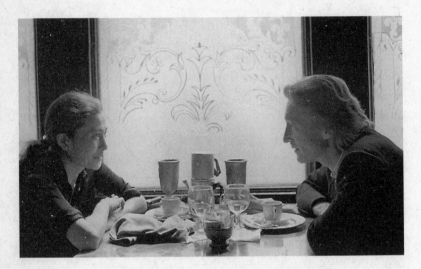

Yoko Ono and John Lennon. *(Lilo Raymond)*

Everyone knows how the story begins. Still, let's pause briefly to savor the delectable, goofy contradictions, the irresistible ironies of the love that was born when the artist met his muse at the gallery where the muse was installing her conceptual art show. If every era gets the muse it deserves, our lifetime gets John and Yoko, an artist and muse for whom, like Dante and Beatrice, Petrarch and Laura, no last names are needed.

No one could have invented a muse-and-artist myth that so seamlessly interwove the themes and conflicts of the 1960s and '70s: rock music, modern art, power and career, sex, drugs, feminism, radical activism, Vietnam, the meteoric ascendancy of the media and of celebrity worship. John's and Yoko's awkward, often excruciating efforts to question traditional gender roles cut right through our pieties on the subject and compelled us, male and female alike, to confront our true feelings about pushy, take-charge women and men publicly reminding us of feminist principles. "Only when a woman's there with you, pointing out the prejudice, did I notice it . . . It was going on all the time: pure prejudice! Continuous prejudice, night and day, I don't know how they survive."

Such statements (inarguable, but delivered in a way that sounded dutiful and robotic) only fueled the widespread resentment, the popular sense that John had been possessed by a succubus: a Japanese-woman-artist alien life-form. In fact, it's startling to find such a thoroughly modern muse evoking so many whispery accusations of witchcraft, rumors that the Lennons, in later years, did little to dispel by dabbling in Santeria, patronizing local botanicas and sketchy Colombian *brujas*. The perception that John had come to sound like Yoko—the spacey politics, the dreamy babbling about women, clouds, love, peace, and art—evoked responses that probed beneath our ideas about feminism and the avant garde to touch a major nerve and elicit the swampy oedipal feelings of confusion and abandonment that we experience when someone close to us falls in love and becomes a different person.

Everything about John and Yoko's romance seemed simultaneously of the moment and eternal. Its exterior trappings—popping flashbulbs, rock stardom, drugs, absurd amounts of money, and semiconstant litigation—were tailor-made for their era. And yet its basic structure made it seem like the "timeless" love story every age appears to require: Héloise and Abelard, Romeo and Juliet, Tristan and Isolde; erotic atttraction, obstacles overcome, life-changing passion, betrayal, separation, grief, reconciliation, the promise of a sadder but wiser future cut short by tragic violent death, long before the lovers' unsexy aging might have made us question why we'd ever invested them with so much of our own emotion.

The ballad of John and Yoko is our conceptual rock and roll grand opera, made even more timely and theatrical by the fact that, from the day John and Yoko met until now, decades later and beyond the grave, the fundamental question—who was the artist, and who the muse?—is still being settled between them.

IF MOST ARTISTS and even more muses have functioned as blank screens onto which society can project its prejudices and illusions, John and Yoko have provoked the most extreme and partisan responses in the history of the muses. There has never been a muse so widely reviled and despised for disrupting the public's imaginary liaison with the artist. In fact, no other muse has ever generated so much film, so many pages documenting so much debate.

Even the apparently straightforward account of how John and

Yoko met has come down to us in partial and variant versions. Lennon's is the prettiest: He'd stopped by the hip Indica gallery, where, he'd heard, there was going to be an art happening, a more attractive invitation in 1966 than it would be today. (Later he recalled his wistful hope that the art event might be an orgy.) As he wandered through the show, he instantly got the humor of the piece that proposed charging the viewer two hundred pounds to watch an apple decompose. Flatteringly, he fell in love with Yoko's work before he'd even met her. "But there was another piece which really decided me for-or-against the artist: a ladder which led to a painting which was hung on the ceiling. It looked like black canvas with a chain with a spyglass hanging on the end of it . . . I climbed the ladder, you look through the spyglass and in tiny little letters it says 'yes.' So it was positive. I felt relieved. It's a great relief when you get up a ladder and you look through a spyglass and it doesn't say 'no' or 'fuck you' or something, it said 'yes.' "

The gallery owner, John Dunbar, introduced the world-famous rock star to the artist with a modest reputation as a member of Fluxus, a lively group of New York artists, influenced by Dada and Duchamp, dedicated to scrutinizing and reinventing the relation of art to life, and to discovering more dynamic, less static forms of expression. Lennon claimed that he and Yoko had never heard of each other, that she didn't know who he was. "She'd only heard of Ringo, I think, it means apple in Japanese."

It's possible that Yoko Ono really didn't know who John was. In any case, her innocence or naïveté conveniently put her and Lennon on equal footing as two artists unfamiliar with one another's work rather than in the more hierarchical ranking of, say, Beatle and Beatles fan. Her claim does seem more plausible alongside the recollections of fellow performance artist, Carolee Schneeman: "Yoko was a very important Fluxus artist. And frankly, we all wondered if this . . . this . . . rock and roll guy was going to be *smart* enough for her."

Still, even if she'd never heard of Lennon, Yoko knew one thing about him. "John Dunbar had been sort of hustling her saying, 'That's a good patron, you must go and talk to him or do something' ... John Dunbar insisted she say hello to the millionaire."

By any standards, let alone those by which we presume to measure Japanese women, Yoko Ono was remarkably determined. Defying all the pressures and predictable effects of conditioning and background, she had established an art career, she was having a solo show in London, as unusual an achievement for a woman in 1966 as was Lou Andreas-Salomé's writing career, almost a century earlier. Even as Yoko made a fetish of her shyness, she possessed the social skills and the shamelessness required for self-promotion. More unpredictably still, she had found a husband, Tony Cox, willing to invest time and energy in her success.

In a 1965 letter to art dealer Ivan Karp, requesting a gallery show, Yoko proposed a guest list for the opening: "Why not have a strictly-for-the-artists preview opening 'to draw a circle'? We will invite only very selected artists—this is vulgar, but vulgarity can be very interesting. We will invite Bob Rauschenberg, Jasper Johns, etc. Some old artists such as Max Ernst, Marcel Duchamp, Isamu Noguchi are worth inviting." To which Karp replied curtly, "Max Ernst is very tired and doesn't want to travel. Most of the other famous characters despise each other and will not contribute to your panel." As hard as Yoko tried, she was only moderately good at self-marketing. Until she met John her fortunes had been, it is safe to say, downwardly mobile.

Born in 1933, into a distinguished, wealthy Japanese banking family, she was educated in Tokyo, and (after her parents moved to Scarsdale) at Sarah Lawrence, which she left to marry Ichiyanagi Toshi, an avant-garde composer. Through her husband, Yoko met John Cage, Merce Cunningham, and a circle of musicians who participated in Fluxus performance pieces. In 1955, Yoko composed a "score" that involved lighting matches onstage and watching them go out. Seven years later, she returned to Japan with Toshi, and there suffered a nervous breakdown precipitated partly by her sense that her art career had stalled. "The whole avant-garde world seemed bourgeois to me. Who was I beyond Toshi's wife and John Cage's friend?"

She was rescued from a Tokyo sanitarium by Cox, a New York filmmaker and artist who had great faith in her art, and who spent the next four years promoting her work in Tokyo, New York, and London. It was Cox who helped her film both versions of "No. 4 Bottoms"; the first featured the naked buttocks of dozens of artists, the second of 365 volunteers. The film is hilarious, instructive, and surprisingly engaging in its deadpan documentation of the variety of the human anatomy. But though it received considerable publicity when it was banned in London, a movie about bare hairy asses did not translate into money. By the time she met Lennon, Yoko was living in squalid, roach-infested poverty—a state from which she had no dependable prospects of ever extricating herself, Tony, and their daughter Kyoko, born in 1963.

Whether practical or romantic, Yoko's instincts regarding John Lennon were impeccable. Introduced to the hippie millionaire art collector whom she may or may not have recognized as a Beatle, she swung into action. Yoko gave him one of the clever cards—like business cards, but *art* cards—that echoed her "instructional paintings," works that commanded the viewer to "Let a vine grow. Water every day" and "Light canvas or any finished painting with a cigarette at any time . . ."

Breathe, said the card she gave John. "So I just went (*pant*). This was our meeting."

Getting *any* clear instruction, however precious, gnomic, or coercive, would have been a great "relief" to John, who had spent the previous months self-medicating at high dosages in an effort to obliterate what he called (with that slip into Liverpuddlian he employed for irony) "me ego." Clearly, his ego had been fried to the point at which he cared (more deeply than most of us might) whether the conceptual artist's painting said *yes* or *no* or *fuck you*, or whatever. "That 'YES' made me stay."

How soothing to the damaged ego and to the disgruntled ego-maniac to receive some version of the first command we get when we are born; soon after, Lennon would invest considerable energy and money in primal therapy's return journey to the womb and the implicit promise of a chance to start over. John read Yoko's art-instruction—and breathed. A spark traveled back and forth, a flicker of erotic possibility ignited when they strolled over to another piece.

Yoko recalls, "When 'Hammer a Nail' painting was exhibited at Indica Gallery, a person came and asked if it was alright to hammer a nail in the painting. I said it was alright if he pays 5 shillings. In-stead of paying the 5 shillings, he asked if it was alright for him to hammer an imaginary nail in. That was John Lennon. I thought, so I met a guy who plays the same game I played." John's memory is more charged: "That's when we really met. That's when we locked eyes and she got it and I got it and, as they say in all the interviews we do, the rest is history."

But now, in this modern fairy tale, the princess was obliged to make the first move when the shy prince falters. Amid the nonstop *Satyricon* (as John termed it) that constituted a Beatles road tour, John had had little trouble making first and subsequent moves, as he and his pals became the human altars on which countless groupies impaled themselves. But during the fateful meeting at the Indica Gallery, power had been traded along with the ladder, the card, the hammer, the imaginary nail. Yoko was not some . . . Beat-les fan. She was a Japanese woman artist. Something made John hesitate; besides, he was married and had a son.

John portrayed his meeting Yoko as kismet, an immutable fate—the cosmic auto wreck. "Imagine two cars of the same make heading towards each other and they're gonna crash, head-on . . . they're doing a hundred miles an hour, they both slam their brakes on and there's smoke everywhere on the floor and they stop just in the nick of time with the bumpers almost touching but not quite. That's what it was like from the first time I got to know her."

Alternate accounts suggest that (to extend the metaphor) Yoko's car was hurtling toward the collision rather more rapidly and determinedly than John's. Indeed, her behavior is often portrayed as bordering on that of a stalker, though it is equally possible to see it as the perseverance of an ambitious, poor, obscure thirty-four-year-old woman artist with a crush on a famous, attractive guy who could solve all her problems. She besieged John with cards featuring more commands. "Dance." "Watch the lights until dawn." She sent him a copy of *Grapefruit*, her diminutive book of instructions: "Hide until everybody goes home . . . hide until everybody dies."

She often waited outside his house, and after a public lecture on transcendental meditation, startled John and Cynthia Lennon by jumping into their chauffeur-driven Rolls-Royce. John was alternately alarmed, irritated, flattered, and intrigued enough so that he later recalled wishing that he could take Yoko, along with Cynthia, on the Beatles 1968 trip to India—where Yoko continued to send him letters containing further instructions ("I'm a cloud. Watch for me in the sky.") to be performed while he was in Rishikesh, studying with the Maharishi.

For almost two years, John and Yoko circled one another—a protracted mating dance that involved John's funding of Yoko's "Half a Wind" show at the Lisson Gallery, an installation composed of objects such as half a bed, a room, a basket, etc., bisected and painted white. "And I said to her, 'Why don't you sell the other half in bottles?' having caught on by then what the game was and she did that—this is still before we'd had any nuptials—and we still have the bottles from the show; it's my first."

ONE MAY NIGHT in 1968, when Cynthia Lennon was out of town, John phoned and invited Yoko over.

John and Yoko stayed awake all that night. If, as Ford Madox

Ford said, we get married to continue a conversation, nothing short of marriage could have seemed capacious enough to accommodate the dialogue that began that evening. Yoko's small talk, which ranged from Marcel Duchamp to Asian parables, was a far cry from a domestic chat with Cynthia, the pretty, pliable Liverpool sweater-girl who in art school had majored in lettering. John and Yoko listened to tapes he made when he was just fooling around, just playing, not being serious or commercial, not being a Beatle. Which meant, as Yoko was showing him, when he was Making Art.

Together—starting at midnight—they made their own art, their tape, "Unfinished Music #1: Two Virgins." At dawn, they made love. And by the time John got out of bed the next day, any doubts about his new conceptual artist had been replaced by pure faith: he'd found his soul mate, his double, his lover, his female half, "me in drag."

Rarely in the history of the muses has there been such a straight-forward recipe for—such an explicit definition—of art: the foreplay (not the prelude to a seduction, but the actual dusk-till-dawn fore-play) between the artist and the muse.

THE CURRENT CD of *Two Virgins* is a remarkable example of truth in packaging or at least of unintentional revelation in packaging. The original nude photos of John and Yoko—which caused such a furor, and attracted more attention than the album's contents when it was released in November 1968—now appear inside the plastic case, hidden by a paper jacket—designed to look like a plain brown wrapper, with trompe l'oeil peepholes permitting us to see two de-mure head shots of the couple. Presumably, cooler temperaments (and the sobering fact that many chain stores refuse to sell work displaying nudity on the cover) have prevailed over the idealistic principles that formerly caused the lovers to insist on the contro-versial packaging. And given how times have changed, it's hard to imagine nude pictures of any adults (except perhaps for iconic reli-gious leaders) sparking so much heat. Inside the paper wrapper are two identical photos of Yoko—anyone who didn't know better might conclude that *both* virgins were Yoko Ono—overprinted with "The Yoko Ono Catalog on Rykodisc." Nowhere is there a catalog of the recordings made by the other virgin, the dead one.

The recording features whistling, caterwauling, groaning, wailing, moaning, shrieking, samplings of old records, the sound of guitars being tuned and strummed, background noise, scraps of conversation. The result is so dull that only incipient passion and the promise of sex (that is, some approximate reenactment of the circumstances under which it was made) could persuade someone to listen until the end, for the chance to hear Yoko cooing, in a reedy schoolgirl's voice, a simple ditty about remembering love. One would have to be in the grip of a very high sexual fever to be charmed by this, or to imagine that it was art, or that it should have been distributed and sold. It's no wonder that Beatles fans (already alarmed by press reports suggesting that Yoko was fomenting discord among the Fab Four) felt gloomy about the prospects of further Ono-Lennon collaboration.

The clarity of hindsight enables us to see not only what came after an event but what was occurring concurrently. During the weeks and months that followed John and Yoko's first night together, the Beatles were writing and recording *The White Album*, and many of its best songs, like nearly everything John would write for the rest of his life, were both positively and negatively influenced by his relationship with Yoko.

Time has made it partly possible to separate our responses to Lennon's work from our reactions to Yoko's public persona, to her reputed or real role in the dissolution of the Beatles, her pushy intercession in Lennon's recorded and live performances, her perceived arrogance, careerism, and egomania, the insistence on being noticed that makes so much of her art seem more coy than profound. The weakest work that John did during his time with Yoko is the most collaborative and bears the hallmarks (the arty humorlessness, the refusal to acknowledge the complexity of adult life) of her worldview. And yet it's also true that much of his best music was shaped by her presence or her absence, by the offering and withdrawal of her love, and by whatever she (or his idea of her) was able to nurture and help release in him: his innate talent for concocting an utterly unique recipe of rage, honesty, passion, musical jokes, and verbal invention.

AFTER THE DEFLOWERING that *Two Virgins* immortalized, their affair progressed rapidly. A month or so after that May night, John and Yoko traveled to Coventry for their first dual performance piece: they planted two acorns near the cathedral, one facing east, the other west, to symbolize the marriage of two cultures and the couple's hopes for world peace. In July, John had his first solo art exhibition, "You Are Here," at London's Robert Fraser Gallery. Dedicated to Yoko, the show took its title from the phrase used to help London subway riders locate themselves on maps of the underground system, and featured an assortment of charity collection boxes: boxes for the blind, for spastics, for donkeys, birds, and lepers. A mechanical dog would bark, wag its tail, and lift its leg when a coin was deposited.

The art-school dropout, Teddy-boy rock-and-roller, Chuck Berry fan, and pop star had become an artist—an identity that must have fit neatly into the void left when Lennon carpet-bombed his ego with opiates, speed, and psychedelics. How patiently Yoko showed him his face in the mirror, revealed what had been there all along: a natural-born Surrealist, Liverpool's own Duchamp. And it's to Lennon's credit that he agreed to take instruction from a woman—not exactly a common predilection for a rock star in 1968.

Overnight, the rebellious student became an eager learner. "I admire Fluxus. I really think what they do is beautiful and important. (Yoko has) educated me into things that I didn't know about before . . . So I'm getting to know some other *great* work that's been going on in the past and now . . . All I ever learned in art school was about fuckin' Van Gogh and stuff! They didn't teach me anything about anybody that was alive *now*! They never taught me about Marcel Duchamp, which I *despise* them for, and Yoko has taught me about Duchamp and what he did . . . He got a fuckin' bike wheel and said, 'This is art, you cunts!' "

John had also discovered a whole new way to suffer and ennoble his sufferings, to locate his pain within a tradition. His troubles were no longer the low-rent violence and relationship problems of a kid from a troubled family, not the substance addictions of an unhappily married young musician with too much money and time, but the Kafkaesque struggles of the artist-saint and martyr. "It's no fun being an artist. You know what it's like writing, it isn't fun, it's *torture*. I read about Van Gogh or Beethoven, any of the fuckers . . . I resent performing for fuckin' idiots who won't know—who don't know—anything. Cause they can't feel—I'm the one that's feeling . . . They live vicariously through me and other artists."

So fate, as it so often does when tempted, deployed some actual suffering as a test. Cynthia filed for divorce, and a vituperative legal battle ensued. Yoko got pregnant, then miscarried shortly after the police raided their apartment and arrested her and John for cannabis possession. The Beatles' discord and financial troubles increased; John and Paul lost the rights to their own songs, the film *Let It Be* revealed the band's alienation and collective depression. By now, John and Yoko had together embraced heroin's ability to soothe even the agony of an artist. Lennon claimed they'd turned to drugs because of the pain caused by their conflict with the Beatles. Yoko took a more offhand view: "Drugs make life less boring."

Still, John and Yoko kept working, turning obstacles (the constant media scrutiny, their increasing isolation) into photo ops and sound bites, all in the service of peace, love, and art. Having divorced their spouses, the couple wed. They made more recordings, shared the stage at concerts, shot films, and released a *Wedding Album,* which provided a copy of their marriage certificate, a booklet, a poster, and photos, including one of a slice of wedding cake. Beginning with the celebrated Bed-Ins for Peace (in Amsterdam, Vienna, and Montreal) the couple began to tease fans with their sexuality; wearing chaste white nightclothes as a message to the reporters who came to the bed-ins to observe a sexual act, and then publishing John's erotic lithographs, graphically portraying what they'd kept private from the reporters.

The Beatles separated amid allegations that Yoko was to blame and counteraccusations about the rudeness with which the other band members treated her. (In fact, Yoko's presence merely seems to have given John the courage to take a step that was, by then, inevitable.) John released his first solo album, *Plastic Ono Band,* which included a number of powerful and haunting songs, as well as others in which one can hear the influence of Yoko's fondness for screeching along to music and of John's attempt to use the blues as a bridge between screaming and rock and roll. While the new record displayed far more unmediated intensity than any of the Beatles' previous work, the playful humor and irony of *The White Album* was (except for a few songs, such as "Well Well Well") missing. The deadpan jokiness of "Happiness Is a Warm Gun" and "Glass Onion" are gone. Instead we get the obsessional rawness of "God" and "Mother," two songs that cut directly to the chase; in place of parody, there is a serious homage to Dylan, "Working Class Hero."

With Yoko's encouragement, Lennon endeavored to get beyond and beneath whimsy, metaphor, and self-protection to communicate on a truer, deeper level: "I started from the 'Mother' album onward trying to shave off all imagery, pretensions of poetry, illusions of grandeur ... Just say what it is, simple English, make it rhyme and put a backbeat on it and express yourself as simply (and) straightforwardly as possible."

An artist had taken a turn in his work, an aesthetic shift that incited passionate private and public arguments for and against the "new" Yoko-fied John Lennon. But what changed more dramatically than Lennon's music (as with any artist, certain threads and obsessions run through from beginning to end) was the scale of his ambition. Years had passed since he'd publicly remarked that the Beatles were more popular than Jesus, but now, pumped by his new muse, he'd come to think that perhaps he *was* Jesus, or perhaps he and Yoko were Jesus, and could, by sheer effort of will, bring about something like the Second Coming. "We're all responsible for war. We all must do something, no matter what—by growing our hair long, standing on one leg, talking to the press, having bed-ins—to change the attitudes. The people must be made aware that it's up to them. Bed-ins are something that everybody can do and they're so simple. We're willing to be the world's clowns to make people realize it."

All this seems less ridiculous and delusional when we recall that John was representative of an era in which the prevailing youth culture—from flower-power hippies cavorting at love-ins to grim cadres of Maoists leaving college to organize the workers—was fueled by faith that social transformation was possible, that the world was ready, that radical change could be effected by love or revolution. Love or revolution? Violence or nonviolence? It's hard from this distance to imagine the intensity with which ordinary people discussed and debated such questions.

Yoko and John did support liberal and radical causes; they campaigned for Attica prisoners, Native Americans, the withdrawal of American troops from Vietnam, the release of imprisoned political figures including Michael X. and John Sinclair. The misguided sweetness and idealism, the fundamentally well-meaning innocence of John's political pronouncements during this period secured him a place on the continuum ranging from, say, Ken Kesey to Eldridge Cleaver. Asked to sum up his philosophy, the musician replied: "Peace, just no violence, and everybody grooving, if you don't mind

the word. Of course, we all have violence in us, but it must be channeled or something. If I have long hair, I don't see why everybody
else should have long hair. And if I want peace, I'll suggest peace to
everyone. But I won't hustle them up for peace. If people want to be
violent, let them not interfere with people who don't want violence.
Let them kill each other if there has to be that."

Yoko's politics seem, if possible, even more naïve; spacier, airier,
not merely evasive but suggestive of a defiant refusal to even halfway
think things through. How is any sentient being supposed to respond to her theory about using love and sex to combat the evils of
fascism? "If I was a Jewish girl in Hitler's day, I would approach him
and would become his girlfriend. After ten days in bed, he would
come to my way of thinking." On what planet is it true that "Working people in this age have at least two weeks' holiday, even office
girls." And what favorable construct can possibly be put on her jaw-
dropping analysis of poverty? "There must be a line where it becomes masochism. I'm sure there is a way of getting out of poverty,
and there's a point where you decide to either get out or not. . . . It's
like saying, 'I'm starving, but I've never been a whore,' so that means
she prefers to starve rather than being a whore. There are certain
kinds of rules they have that make them stay in that position."

HOW BIZARRE AND POIGNANT it is, the nimble artistry with
which memory retouches and overpaints the eternally unfinished
canvas of the past! By 1998—three decades after she first fell in
love with John—Yoko had persuaded herself that her association
with a Beatle represented a downward career move. "Before meeting John, I was doing two concerts and lectures a month. I was in
demand. I was able to express myself all the time. Suddenly, by becoming the wife of a Beatle, what was required of me was to shut
up. Or if at all possible, to overdose and die. I took it as a challenge,
like how can I create new works in jail? It was like a prison. A
strange, rare, invisible prison."

From this invisible prison, Yoko and John held a press conference (doubtless the first occasioned by the publication of a book by a Fluxus artist) to annnounce the reissue of *Grapefruit*. John seized the opportunity to scold British critics for their crass insensitivity: "In England I'm regarded as the lucky guy who won the pools. She's regarded as the lucky Jap who married the guy who won the pools. In America we are both treated as artists. . . . In New York there's these fantastic twenty or thirty artists who all understand what I'm doing and have the same kind of mind as me. It's just like heaven after being here."

The Lennons soon left for America, where until then, the highlight of their dual career had been a concert with Frank Zappa at the Fillmore East. "I did rhythm and booze, and Yoko sang on stage with what she calls voice modulation, which to the layman is screaming!" New York was also a more logical place from which to stage Yoko's ongoing custody battle with Tony Cox over Kyoko, a struggle that would consume vast amounts of time and money, and result in minimal satisfaction: Kyoko spent much of her childhood with Cox and his second wife.

Not long after their arrival in Manhattan, Yoko was invited to mount her first major career exhibition at the Everson Museum in Syracuse, New York. Invitations to the opening were written in disappearing ink that mentioned John Lennon, then vanished except for a phone number, an RSVP request—and Yoko's name. According to David Ross, then a curator at Everson, "When the exhibition opened on October 9, 1971, over 5,000 people were camped out in the cold Syracuse rain to ensure their place among the first to experience the show. On the eve of Lennon's thirtieth birthday, the exhibition was a gift from Yoko to John (whose active participation led to his listing as "Guest Artist") and an extension of their love for each other. As sentimental as this may sound, it was far from a corny show-business gesture. It was, and remains to this day, a primary example of how Yoko managed to use the simple concept of love as a universal social construction as the content for her own aesthetic and philosophical stance."

In any case, it was the first and quite possibly the last time that five thousand fans camped out overnight to attend the opening of a Fluxus show. Yoko seems unaware of the probable reason for this cultural anomaly—which, she seems to think, simply meant that her art was finally getting the attention it deserved. John, who had a somewhat clearer view of the forces at work, railed about the unjust obscurity from which he had saved her. "I don't think the poor bastard will get recognition til she's dead . . . I could count the people on one hand that can have any *conception* of what she is or what her mind's like or what her *work* means to this *fuckin'* idiotic fuckin' generation . . . But in general she can't be accepted, because she's so far out, man, it's hard to take! Her pain is such that she expresses herself in a way that *hurts* you! That you cannot take it! That's why they couldn't take Van Gogh and all that shit, it's too *real*! It *hurts*! That's why they *kill* you!"

With heroic resourcefulness and determination Yoko had persevered until she found a millionaire-artist-rock-star not only willing to say such things but to accept second billing as guest artist. And with rare grace, John agreed to play "Ike Turner to her Tina, only her Tina was a different, avant-garde Tina"—a willingness that fueled the widespread sense of him as a class and gender traitor, a red-blooded white male who had fallen under the spell of a Japanese witch, a working-class boy unmanned by a spoiled Asian princess.

Yoko's alliance with John was, for her, a social and professional coup. Still, almost everyone (except for the most hostile biographers) agreed that Yoko Ono and John Lennon were genuinely in love. In fact, the couple provide a straight-up clinical textbook case of love as the French diagnosed it—*une folie à deux*, shared madness. All the classical symptoms were present, magnified by the fact that the lovers were so much larger than life.

Love, John and Yoko reminded us, was the paradoxically accurate and distorting mirror that shows us our real selves. It confers an eagerness to learn whatever the beloved knows ("I learned everything from her"), the exaltation of having found one's other half ("He was definitely my other half, my mirror image, strangely, in the body of a man."), and the reluctance to be separated, even for a moment: "There is no reason on earth why I should be without her. There is nothing more important than our relationship, nothing. And we dig being together all the time."

John and Yoko were walking advertisements for love's power to transform us into new and superior beings. Lennon—who at various points in his life had had trouble controlling his violent temper—had been reborn, thanks to Yoko, as the Prince of Peace. And at the same time they offered cautionary reminders of the transfixed solipcism that can cause lovers to lose sight of everything beyond themselves. ("Whatever happened to us was partly our creation. And it was probably to do with complete self-involvement and not really taking care of business on an outside level and looking where we were going, you know, instead of looking . . . down the road, we were always looking into each others' eyes.") Endearingly, both displayed the lover's predilection for idealizing the other's beauty, gifts, and charms; Yoko compared John's drawings to those of da Vinci and Goya. John seemed also to have believed that Yoko was a genius fully capable of producing his records: "She has a musical ear and she can produce rock & roll. She can produce me . . . You don't have to be born and bred in rock. She knows when a bass sounds right and when the guy's playing out of rhythm . . ."

In the footage of their concerts and recording sessions, Lennon never once betrays his beloved by smirking at his bandmates or by winking at the camera so as to distance himself from the intrusive warbling and shrieking captured in such films as the Rolling Stones' documentary *Rock and Roll Circus*. Yet, sadly, there is evidence to sug-

gest that John Lennon may have overestimated the benefits of his
muse's input.

THREE QUARTERS OF THE WAY through *Gimme Some Truth*, a documentary about the 1971 recording of John Lennon's *Imagine*, Lennon
and his band are rehearsing "How Do You Sleep?"—"the nasty one,"
as John says, the accusatory, contemptuous one, the song about Paul
McCartney. It's a fraught situation, incestuous and claustrophobic,
complicated by the presence of another former Beatle, George
Harrison, sitting in on guitar, and of Yoko Ono, to whom McCartney was unfriendly, and who (along with Phil Spector) is supervis-
ing the record production in a sound studio in Tittenhurst Park,
John and Yoko's Ascot mansion.

It takes a while to get in the groove. John describes a rhythm
change, a reggae hiccup he wants in the bridge, and gradually the
musicians forget themselves, the implications, the history, the old
scores being settled, forget everything but the music until at last
they're jamming along with the bluesy snake charmer's vocal, the
piano and guitar supplying sly New Orleans–style fills—and the
music takes off, less like one rock star savaging another than like
some swinging, beautiful voodoo malediction.

It's by far the most exciting moment in the film. And then, suddenly, it ends. The music trails off, and Yoko appears on screen,
whispering in John's ear.

John says, "What do you mean, *it's too free?*"

Yoko says, "It's too free. They're improvising too much."

A beat passes. Another beat.

John tells the band, "Stop improvising and just keep it solid.
Really tight. You've just got to think it's nasty. It's a nasty song. I
don't want it to swing too much."

And after that, it doesn't. Everyone's a professional, the band
gets it back together in a version that isn't bad, and is certainly better than the one (backed by a lush Phil Spector wall of strings and

hardly any piano) that eventually wound up on the record. But still it's a long way from the trancelike virtuosic beauty that Yoko interrupted.

Yoko, who produced the 1999 film, seems not to have noticed. Like so much of the information that has come to us about John Lennon since his death, *Gimme Some Truth* seems like propaganda closely supervised by Yoko, the minister of information operating with a cultural minister's blinkered self-assurance.

Throughout, the not-so-hidden subtext of *Gimme Some Truth* is the central role that Yoko Ono played in the creation of *Imagine*. During the recording of the lilting, tender "Oh, Yoko," its muse is shown yelling at the recording engineer who can't find the take John wants. She discusses the instrumentation for "Oh, My Love"; and scenes of John performing the song are interspliced with an interview in which John and Yoko offer their opinions about love and sex. (Love is about "relaxation," asserts Yoko—not exactly the first word that comes to mind in regard to the Lennons.) Shots of John singing "Jealous Guy" are superimposed on an image of Yoko's tear-streaked face, a visual aid to help us recall whom, exactly, John's jealousy hurt.

There are also snippets (the white room, the chess game) from their extended-rock-video film of *Imagine*, dramatic scenarios of John and Yoko running through the verdant English landscape, calling each other's names, John dressed in a gaucho hat and opera cape, Yoko in leather hot pants, boots, a beret, and a bandolier across her chest. Scenes of their lives together feature cameo appearances by such fully credentialed hip celebrities as Andy Warhol and Miles Davis. All of which makes *Gimme Some Truth* the first documentary produced by a muse that shows—in real life, real time, and in detail—the muse at work, the actual process by which the muse inspires or ruins the artist.

ARTISTS KNOW there is no clear path on which to trace one's steps back to the wellspring of a work. To attempt to analyze or quantify inspiration is as futile as trying to describe a mystical state, which is what inspiration is.

But artists get worn down. It's easier, when repeatedly asked, to falsify a little: Ah yes, I remember exactly what I was thinking about, what got me started. If Shakespeare had been interviewed as frequently as John Lennon, we'd know who the dark lady was, the occasion for each sonnet, and what friend or enemy was the model for King Lear. In *Gimme Some Truth*, there's a scene in which a young stoner fan comes to John's door, apparently to test out his theory that John's songs are about *him*. "How can they be about you?" John says logically. "I don't even know you. They're about me, or at best Yoko, if it's a love song. I'm saying I had a good shit today, and this is what I'm thinking about, and I love you, Yoko."

Repeatedly, John described his songs on *Abbey Road* as encrypted messages of secret love for Yoko. " 'She's So Heavy' was about Yoko . . . I just sang, 'I want you, I want you so bad, she's so heavy, I want you,' like that. I started simplifying my lyrics then, on the double album." Years later, he traced a song on *Double Fantasy* to a similar source: " 'Woman' came about because, one sunny afternoon in Bermuda, it suddenly hit me. I saw what women do for us. Not just what Yoko does for me, although I was thinking in those personal terms. Any truth is universal." And he was equally forthcoming about the extent to which certain songs came out of the miseries of his eighteen-month separation from Yoko in 1973.

Though it's not uncommon for artists to credit their muses, Lennon is one of the few to apologize for not having given his muse *enough* credit. Discussing "Imagine," Lennon admits, "actually that should be credited as a Lennon/Ono song, a lot of it—the lyric and the concept—came from Yoko, but those days I was a bit more self-ish, a bit more macho, and I sort of omitted to mention her contri-bution, but it was right out of *Grapefruit*, her book, there's a whole pile of pieces about imagine this and imagine that and I have given her credit now long overdue."

It's hard to imagine Man Ray lacerating himself for having undervalued Lee Miller's contribution to his oeuvre; and if Dante Gabriel Rossetti felt remorse over his mistreatment of Lizzie Siddal, his attempt at making amends—by tossing his manuscript into her coffin—was a long way from acknowledging her influence on his poetry and his painting. But what distinguished John and Yoko from other artists and their muses was their *insistence* on the fact that they were peers and equals, a notion which made their romance vulnerable to special strains and stresses. When her professional and personal ambitions threatened to conflict with Man Ray's, Lee Miller fled his atelier—and Paris—to establish her own business across the Atlantic. Likewise, Suzanne Farrell's desire for autonomy in her private and artistic life drove her to take the one step guaranteed to sever her connection with Balanchine.

But once again in perfect accord with her times, Yoko Ono chose to remain and fight for her right to be the artist. And as the fading of their early infatuation dispelled the illusion of being one person, John and Yoko became increasingly combative and competitive.

It's easy to sympathize with Yoko's fear of losing the identity she had struggled so hard to establish. "When he was alive, I used to always try to keep my independence, because he was such a strong, powerful energy. With the whole world behind him as well, by the way. So if I didn't keep my independence, I would have been swallowed up. Whenever somebody called me 'Mrs. Lennon,' I used to say, 'Mrs. Lennon? I'm Yoko Ono, thank you.'" But empathizing is not the same as wanting to watch these conflicts enacted.

In a 1971 interview, John and Yoko gave us a harrowing portrait of how romantic slippage can manifest as artistic competition: "Yoko and I have clashed artistically. Our egos have smashed once or twice. But if I know what I'm doing as an artist, then I can see if

I'm being hypocritical in my reactions. I sometimes am overawed by her talent. I think, fuck, I better watch out, she is taking over . . . When she wants the A side, that's when we start fighting. The reasons the covers of our albums are similar is that I wanted us to be separate and be together, too . . . because they're dying for us to fall apart, for God knows what reason. It's just that everybody doesn't want anybody else to be happy, because nobody's happy."

At this, Yoko interjects, somewhat plaintively, "I think it's a miracle that we're doing all right. But we're doing all right, don't you think, John?"

John's reply is neither as romantic or reassuring as Yoko might have hoped: "It's just handy to fuck your best friend. That's what it is. And once I resolved the fact that it was a woman as well, it's all right. We go through the trauma of life and death every day, so it's not as much of a worry about what sex we are anymore. I'm living with an artist who's inspiring me to work. And, you know, Yoko is the most famous unknown artist. Everybody knows her name, but no one knows what she does."

A revealing scene in *Gimme Some Truth* indicates how these skirmishes played out in everyday life. The musicians making *Imagine* are eating at a long table. George Harrison asks Yoko for some tea, possibly because she's standing directly over the teapot. John bridles, arches his back, drums his finger on the table, and announces, "This is a Beatles wife fixing the tea for one of the Fab Four . . . uh . . . Fab Three."

Indicating John, Yoko says, "This is *my* wife."

And John says, "I'm Beatles Wife Number Three."

It's all very quick and ironic. And you're glad you're not actually there, just as you're glad you're not one of the studio musicians who cannot even be permitted the luxury of an expression change when Lennon's muse appears, and tells them how to play.

On its own such creative competition, this jockeying to be recognized as the *real* artist, can make intimacy a mine field for the artist couple—for example, Scott and Zelda Fitzgerald. To which John and Yoko added the extra demands of numerous full-time jobs: buying and taking drugs, managing a fortune, withstanding business pressures, and dealing with multiple law suits, including the continuing struggle with Tony Cox for custody of Kyoko. Eventually, their marriage imploded, sending John into the arms of Yoko's pretty assistant, May Pang, and into a downward spiral that involved heroin and other mind-altering substances—perhaps most incredibly, the massive consumption of Brandy Alexanders. John sought solace and distraction at a nonstop Los Angeles party attended by an ever-changing cast of debauched rock and rollers, and by reporters eager to tell the world about the fallen Prince of Peace wearing a Kotex on his head and heckling the Smothers Brothers.

Despite the continent between them, the Lennons' marriage remained a potent force. Yoko was the steamroller, John the rampaging herd of elephants, and to get in their way was to risk being flattened and trampled. That was what happened to the unfortunate May Pang, the young working-class Chinese-American secretary who, understandably if unwisely, failed to see the end of her affair with John foreshadowed by its beginning, determined from the moment that Yoko fixed her up with John. So profound was May Pang's shock, according to one of Lennon's biographers, that when John returned to Yoko, she wondered if Yoko might have used occult means to summon her zombie husband home. This high estimation of Yoko's gifts was shared by others, including Lennon himself. "John looked to her as a sorceress, as a high priestess, a magician," said a friend, Elliot Mintz. "I'm a fairly pragmatic guy and consider myself to be a realist. But I am now a believer in her abilities. She is telepathic . . . I do know she reads minds."

Obviously the muse-witch still retained her powers. With John's collusion, Yoko found the perfect way to repair the damage sustained by the myth of life-changing love. It was a drama in two parts. First, the artist (or in any case, the one whom the public *considered* to be the artist) had to acknowledge that he could not survive, that he was literally killing himself without his muse: "I'm the one who's supposed to know everything, but she's my teacher. She's taught me everything I know. The lessons are hard and I can't take it sometimes and *that's* why I freaked out. When we were separate, it was *me* making an asshole of myself in the clubs and in the newspapers. It wasn't her. She missed me as a human being and she loved me but *her* life was ordered. *I* went back to *her* life. It wasn't the other way round."

Second, the event that precipitated the reconciliation had to be as romantic and sexy (or nearly so) as the making of *Two Virgins*. On Thanksgiving 1974, John Lennon made a guest appearance at Elton John's Madison Square Garden show. Yoko attended the performance and afterward came backstage. "And somebody said, 'Well, there's two people in love . . . There was just that moment when we saw each other and like, it's in the movies, you know, when time stands still? And there was silence, everything went silent, y'know, and we were just sort of lookin' at each other . . . Oh, oh like the Indica Gallery scene again."

So the lovers were reunited, and nature itself was enlisted to testify that the Lennons meant it. The postcard John sent friends portrayed pregnancy as a group activity, "Here's a hard one for you to take: not only are John and Yoko back together. They're pregnant." Their son, Sean, was born in October 1975, a stroke of near-miraculous good fortune given Yoko's age—she was forty-two—and her history of miscarriage.

Not long after, Yoko is reported to have told John, "I've carried the baby for nine months and brought him into the world. Now it's your turn to look after him." Much had changed since the early days of their romance, when they saw themselves as partners: two artists, two virgins. Now, they felt the necessity for a more efficient distribution of labor: a need they satisifed and (so they believed) finessed by switching traditional gender roles—without, apparently, questioning or modifying the strict divisions that has brought so much unhappiness to so many couples. John threw himself into his new job as house-husband and full-time father, a burden presumably lightened by the Lennons' staff of servants. And Yoko bravely opened her mind to the spiritual aspects of high finance. "When John and I decided that I would be a businesswoman, I told myself that in order to attract money and do the new job well I'd have to reconstruct my psyche. My old attitude of not wanting to get into money just wasn't going to do. I meditated on it. I visualized all the materially good things in the world—diamonds, silks, velvets, art— and tried to see those things in my mind with love, which I never did before."

Overcoming her "inverted snobbery" and learning to "enjoy the things that were positive about money" was a bit of a hardship, but Yoko rose to the challenge. She purchased, as investments, five apartments in the Dakota and four farms (with hefty income-tax benefits) in upstate New York, Vermont, and Virginia; one of her cows, a prize Holstein, brought $265,000 at auction at the New York State Fair. By the late 1970s, additional real estate holdings in Florida and Long Island boosted the Lennons' worth to over $150 million—a tidy sum for a Liverpool lad and a former Fluxus artist. "We tried to reverse the trap that artists fall into—because we didn't want to be miserable when we had money and possessions. After all, being miserable is a pretty high price to pay for being an artist!"

A high price, indeed. In her strenuous efforts to reconfigure her psyche, Yoko had apparently forgotten the quaint downtown folk-superstition warning that the business of amassing wealth might prove incompatible with the demands of artistic creativity. The new labor contract negotiated between John and Yoko had somehow failed to allot time, or make provisions, for either to make art.

This voluntary or enforced holiday from their vocations seemed, at first, a blessing. ("It was great . . . I would sit around

thinking what does this remind me of . . . It reminds me of being fifteen. I didn't have to write songs at fifteen. I wrote if I wanted to. I
didn't have to do it, I didn't have some imaginary standard set up by
me or some group of critics or whatever.") John's last few albums—
Some Time in New York City, *Mind Games*, *Walls and Bridges*, and *Rock 'n'
Roll*—were thin efforts, heavily diluted mixtures of abject love
songs, nostalgic tributes to rockabilly touchstones, and political an-
thems in which fans and critics could hear Lennon struggling for
some vestige of authenticity, focus, or direction. Cut off from her
roots in conceptual and performance art, Yoko found her own
career at a different sort of dead end. Faced by the experience of
aesthetic and commercial failure, and by the fear of an equally
unsatisfactory future, what artist hasn't entertained the seductive, self-erasing fantasy of surrender, of simply giving up and
leading a "normal" life?

Unfortunately, creative stagnation—the time-consuming, potentially soul-destroying labor of *not* making art—generally brings
out the least attractive aspects of an artist's personality. During the
late 1970s, John retreated into reclusiveness, eccentricity, and
health-food faddism; his embrace of cozy domesticity began to
resemble clinical depression. He had trouble waking up in the
morning and getting through the day. And he reported being unable
to listen to the radio for fear that he would be enraged by bad—and
envious of good—music. Yoko's flirtation with the occult intensified, as did her involvement with variously well-meaning or shady
psychics, spiritual and financial advisers.

Though John and Yoko had ceased creating and collaborating,
they hadn't stopped competing. The fact that neither was making
art doubtless created a certain free-floating frustration that, because of their isolation, tended to collect around one another and to
surface in testy exchanges like this one, about John's culinary abilities: "I learned to make bread, which I was thrilled with. I took a
Polaroid of my first bread.

"Yoko interjected, 'In a good old macho tradition, he had to record it in history.'

" 'I was thrilled. It's not macho anybody,' John said. 'It was the first bread. It looked great, and it tasted good . . . I was so excited that I could do it, that I would bring all the staff in to eat lunch.'

" 'He makes the bread, and if they don't eat it, it's a personal insult,' Yoko said. 'We went through that one.' "

By the time they decided to go back to work and together make *Double Fantasy*, these frictions had, in theory, been resolved. John had reversed his position on the question of who should get the "A side": "I'm really pleased for Yoko. She deserves the praise. It's been a long haul. I'd love her to have the A side of a hit record and me the B side. I'd settle for it any day." But Yoko's prickly description of their process acknowledges the obstacles and the inertia that had yet to be overcome. "And we went through sort of paradoxical feeling of half-resisting, you know, well I don't want to hear a song now, I'm very tired . . . but I, well, I mean, I've heard yours, all right well, let's hear it then . . . I went through that." Heading into the studio, Yoko worried, "It's going to be like we're both pig-headed people and so maybe we're going to fight like crazy over remix or this and that because we both have very definite ideas . . . John must have thought well, can we really work together, you know?"

Regardless of such misgivings and despite the five-year hiatus, John's account of this period accurately describes—insofar as such accuracy is possible—the experience of making art: "My joy is when you're possessed like a medium, you know, I'll be sitting round and it'll come in the middle of the night or at the time when you don't want to do it—that's the exciting part . . . So I'm lying around and this thing comes as a whole piece, you know, words and music, and I think well, you know, can I say I wrote it? I don't know who the hell wrote it. . . . You're like driven and you find yourself over on a piano or guitar and you put it down because it's been given to you or whatever it is that you tune into."

How unfortunate that what Lennon was *tuning into*—that what was possessing and inspiring him—was *Double Fantasy*. The album represents yet another collaboration, more carefully orchestrated than the free-form duet of *Two Virgins*. It's fifty-fifty, more or less. John and Yoko take turns. "It's the first time we've done it this way. It's a dialogue, and we have resurrected ourselves, in a way, as John and Yoko—not as John ex-Beatle and Yoko and the Plastic Ono Band. It's just the two of us, and our position was that, if the record didn't sell, it meant people didn't want to know about John and Yoko—either they didn't want John anymore or they didn't want John with Yoko or maybe they just wanted Yoko, whatever. But if they didn't want the two of us, we weren't interested."

In theory, it *should* be possible: a successful work of art created to help save a marriage. Works of genius have been produced for stranger reasons, under less hospitable circumstances. Yet such pressures seem unlikely to facilitate the making of great music, and the strain of such an attempt seems far from the less willed and self-conscious process that Lennon described: *something being given*.

Double Fantasy is a conceptual piece, but the concept doesn't work. John's song, then Yoko's, John's song, then Yoko's, we can't keep making the necessary transitions and adjustments, it doesn't function as dialogue or harmony or counterpoint, so what we're left with is the jumpy unease one gets around a couple who keep interrupting each other.

Something's very wrong from the start: Yoko's little peace bell, so whispery and fey, so many feathery octaves above the stentorian death knell of the church bell tolling the introduction to *Imagine*. The first cut on the album—the theme-setter, so to speak—is "Starting Over," which John apparently intended as a joke, several levels of irony deep, not only about his love life but about his musical roots: "To me, it was like going back to fifteen and singing à la Presley . . . I was referring to Elvis Orbison. It's kind of 'I Want You,' 'Only the Lonely,' you know—a kind of parody, but not really parody ... When I was doing it, I was cracking up ... Some people took it seriously, you know."

Yet if listeners took it seriously, it may not have been because they were humorless or dim. For the song not only evoked the brokenhearted rockabilly outpourings of Elvis and Roy Orbison, but also the numerous times that fans had heard John spout, in all seriousness, the sort of platitudinous psychobabble on the subject of personal growth with which "Starting Over" begins. John seemed to have turned into something no longer recognizable as the bad boy possessed (or cursed) with the integrity generated by clear-sightedness, intelligence, alienation, and rage—the John Lennon who would never allow one note of his to appear on the same recording as the song that follows "Starting Over," Yoko's "Kiss Kiss Kiss."

Yoko's contributions to *Double Fantasy* are so awful and disingenuous that they make you long for the yowling of her earlier compositions, which at least seemed sincere. It's not merely that they suggest bad disco versions of bad Japanese pop music (we get the low-culture references, but it's still hard to listen to) but that they seem calculated to please, to amuse, and more important, to sell. Yoko's songs appear to have been composed by someone who deconstructed the work of currently popular musicians—Blondie, the Talking Heads, Patti Smith—and tried to figure out why they were so successful. John seems also to have been apprised of the commercial potential of Yoko's new songs. " 'Kiss Kiss Kiss' is getting a lot of rock-club, new-wave, whatever you call it, disco exposure. So we made a special kind of disc for them, and Yoko came up with the idea, 'Why don't we give them something they don't have?' And we made a kind of discoesque long six-minute version of 'Walking on Thin Ice' which will go out. There's a separate disco or rock-club mix, and it'll go out to them."

"Kiss Kiss Kiss" is the muse's porno siren song. It begins with the subarticulate cooing of sexual invitation one can hear on cable

TV channels featuring ads for escort services, especially those specializing in Beautiful Oriental Girls. The payoff is the orgasm Yoko faked in the studio and which inspired this exchange between Yoko and John, revealing (among other things) the sexual tension that underlies the sexual boasting, the desperate competition for individual attention that belies the mutual adoration suffusing *Double Fantasy*.

"John: Tell them how you recorded it in the pitch dark, hidden behind these big walls here.

"Yoko: I started to do it, and then I suddenly looked and all these engineers were all looking, and I thought, 'I can't do that.' So I said, 'Well, turn off all the lights and put the screen around me.' And so they put the screen around me, and I did it that way.

"John: We were all sitting there saying, 'What's she doing?' She was having an orgasm and nobody was there . . .

"Yoko: It's called acting, you know.

"John: Oh, very good, dear, very good, yes, Ziggy Stardust!

"Question: Do you get embarrassed in the studio, Yoko? Doing something like that?

"John: Sorry to interrupt, but there was John—me—Jack, and Lee, the engineer, and a few people. We were all in there."

If "Kiss Kiss Kiss" recalls the famous Meg Ryan coffee shop scene in *When Harry Met Sally*, though without the punchline, it's even more like Serge Gainsbourg's notorious 1969 international hit, "Je T'Aime . . . Moi Non Plus," banned in Britain and condemned by the Vatican because of the sighs and moans emitted by Gainsbourg's lover, the young British actress Jane Birkin. "Kiss Kiss Kiss" is the soundtrack you mute when you're actually watching a porn video.

Though it's possible that, again, we're missing the joke *and* the message, that it's a political performance piece, insisting on a woman's right to be heard, a precursor of the fierce claims that would soon be made by artists like Karen Finley. Yoko herself argued something along those lines. " 'Kiss Kiss Kiss' is what it is, and the song will explain itself . . . It's mainly sort of a feminine and Asian vulnerability that women are not scared of exposing now. It's all right to show vulnerability and in a way it's saying, 'Well this is woman.' "

Unfortunately, Yoko fails to distingush between vulnerability and the geisha-like submission commonly marketed as one attraction of Beautiful Oriental Girls. It's unconvincing, we feel that the singer is trying to have it both ways, and in the process producing something as unsavory and assaultive as a political lecture and porn sound track set to a disco beat.

A similar inauthenticity leaches into John's songs. The best of them seem recycled. "I'm Losing You," is the heavy hitter, partly because of the honesty that keeps ripping through the song's seductively bluesy fabric, erupting in lines that cast a dark shadow on the rest of the album. And yet underneath it all are chord progressions reminiscent of earlier Beatles songs.

Certain critics have claimed that our discomfort with so many of *Double Fantasy*'s lyrics is a by-product of our unreconstructed collective machismo. ("When John sang, 'Woman, you understand/ The little child inside the man,' a cry of dismay arose: this was 'infantilization,' and it was not acceptable, at least not from this white man with whom critics identified.") In fact, the point is not that the music is "infantilized" but that it is dull, without surprises, or anyway, pleasant surprises; it's neither strong nor moving nor fun. Everything is familiar, airless, programmatic, poisoned by the adoption of various unpersuasive attitudes, from the oxymoronic Zen defensiveness of "Watching the Wheels" to the equally contradictory, rollicking joylessness of "Cleanup Time." According to Lennon's assistant, Frederic Seaman, John was aware of the album's aims—and its failings. " 'Starting Over' was certainly designed to capture the market. As John told me, he crafted it along a certain formula, using bits of Elvis, Roy Orbison, and others, to write a familiar-sounding song people would find catchy. So the album itself was a compromise for John, and he was aware of it, but he knew that it would be a big hit—it couldn't miss."

In its own way, *Double Fantasy* is as tough to listen to as *Two Virgins*. What makes it additionally painful is the fact that it was John Lennon's last album. Because there's never any telling what an artist will do. Some artists make one slip and keep falling, while others regain their footing and launch miraculous new leaps forward. There's no saying what would have happened, and now we will never know what Lennon might have created if things had gone differently on that December night on which he and Yoko returned home from recording her song, "Walking on Thin Ice"—which would later be a successful rock video, and a disco hit.

AND SO LENNON'S MUSE became his widow, during an era of great widows. Like Jacqueline Kennedy and Coretta King, Yoko served as a dignified, heroic figure of calm amid the tempest of the world's sorrow. The great widows showed us how to mourn, they kept their husbands' spirits nearby, and when necesssary even ventured opinions on what the dead would have wanted. "Whenever I do something now, I feel my first concern is, 'Do you think John is liking this?'"

Muses who outlive their artists may find that they have no choice but to change roles yet again, from lovers and inspirers to repositories of history and information. In cases such as Suzanne Farrell's, they *can* keep an artist's work alive, or, in that of Lou Andreas-Salomé—whose past associations with Nietzsche and Wagner shielded her from the Nazis—the dead artist can protect the living muse.

To her credit, Yoko has kept going—running a business, raising a son, representing her dead husband, and all without losing her admirable determination to do her own work and to be recognized for her own self, her own art. And yet there's something about the preceding statement that inspires a twinge of foreboding about what that art might be like.

On the twentieth anniversary of John Lennon's murder, Yoko was everywhere, interviewed in newspaper stories about the pilgrims who traveled to Central Park to hold a vigil outside the Dakota, and featured in TV programs documenting the history of the Beatles and of Lennon's final years. Perhaps coincidentally, Yoko was also, that winter, the subject of a major exhibition "Yes Yoko Ono" at the Japan Society in New York (a show that traveled to Minneapolis, Houston, Cambridge, Toronto, San Francisco, and Miami) and of a handsome art book, also titled *Yes Yoko Ono*, which included, along with biographical and critical essays, a new CD of Yoko's music.

The show was well received. Michael Kimmelman praised it in the *New York Times*, while, in *The Nation*, Arthur C. Danto called Yoko "one of the most original artists of the last half century. Her fame made her almost impossible to see. When she made the art for which her husband admired and loved her, it required a very developed avant garde sensibility to see it as anything but ephemera. The exhibition at Japan Society makes it possible for those with patience and imagination to constitute her achievement in their minds, where it really belongs. It is an art as rewarding as it is demanding."

Such sentences made you want to cultivate those qualities—imagination and patience—and to let them be the light that guided you through the sleek, comprehensive exhibition of Ono's art. How pleasant it would have been to see her instructional paintings as Danto did, as a sort of Zen Viagra for the imagination. Considering the painting that instructs us to "Let a vine grow. Water every day," Danto asks, "So how are we to comply? Well, we could trudge over to the hardware store, buy a shovel, pick up a vine somewhere, dig a hole, plant the vine, and water it daily . . . Or we can imagine all this."

The show offered much that was intriguing and engaging, especially the videos and films—for example, the shots of Ono's 1965 "Cut Piece." It was hard to turn away from the upsetting spectacle of the artist, passively kneeling onstage after having invited the audience to cut away portions of her clothing with scissors, instructions the participants obeyed all too enthusiastically until a man slit her bra strap—and at last she responded, covering her breasts. The performance succeeds, as she described it, as "a social commentary on the quiet violence that binds individuals and society, the self and gender, alienation and connectedness." "Bottoms" retains an odd jolly beauty, and "Fly"'s extreme closeup tracking of an ordinary fly making its trembling, creepy peregrinations around a woman's nude body, pausing on her nipple to rub its awful little legs together, then disappearing in her pubic hair, is also extraordinary—utterly compelling.

But Yoko made it a challenge for viewers to lose themselves in her work, strangely, because her narcissistic desire to be noticed appeared unsatisfied even when one was actually looking at her art. The first thing one registered on arriving at the Japan Society show was the sound of the 1961–63 "Cough Piece," an audiotape, playing constantly, of Ono coughing—a dry, repetitive, nervous hacking— that followed visitors through the instructional paintings, a sound track interposing itself between them and whatever was on the wall. It would have taken superhuman powers of concentration to ignore the coughing, to completely shut it out in order to contemplate the Japanese calligraphy and the spidery handwriting urging viewers to "Drill two holes into a canvas. Hang it where you can see the sky." The grating soundtrack of "Fly"—Yoko's eerie, high-pitched humming—made it nearly impossible not to flee after a few minutes, though the power of the images could have kept one's attention focused for a good while longer.

It may be that, as Danto claims, "we do not know if it is the voice of the fly, or the suppressed voice of the woman, or the weeping voice of an outside witness to what feels like—what is—a sexual violation." In fact, we are *instinctively* aware of the element of violation; it's not rocket science to swat at the fly about to invade our personal space. The sound track evokes the voice of a giant insect in a horror movie, comical but nonetheless off-putting, and its maddening persistence gives it an edge of the mosquitoesque, of some unseen winged pest dive-bombing us in the darkness. A wall text offered a variant interpretation: "Ono's voice suggests the unconscious, otherworldly life of the woman's knocked-out state, a life that is oblivious yet omnipresent to the activities that occupy the flies in search of the sugared water that her flesh has been prepared with for their delection." (sic) Other artists' work—Bruce Nauman's *Clown*, for example—might seem equally abrasive, yet our response to Nauman's art is affected by its more genuine irony and sharper humor, and by the fact that the pieces are personal but never about *himself*, never unabashedly narcissistic.

Much of Ono's art is, to put it bluntly, annoying—and surely annoyance must be fairly low on any conceivable hierarchy of responses to art. Daily life provides enough friction without seeking more in high culture. Yet Ono seems convinced that getting negative attention is a productive form of communication; her work appears to revel in its power to irritate—which is not the same as provoking disquiet or discomfort, reactions that move us toward a revealing confrontation with the question of what exactly is making us so uneasy.

It's rare to find an art piece more passive-aggressive, more literally in your face than Yoko's "Amaze," a clear plastic labyrinth that would require the sonar of a bat to navigate without banging one's nose on its oddly angled walls. On the day I visited, a guard—a pleasant, matronly woman—was assigned to stand outside the maze and talk visitors through it before their inability to find an exit and the escalating level of anxiety and injury caused them to panic, and perhaps sue the museum.

If, as Kafka suggested, art is an ax with which to break up the frozen sea within us, Ono's art suggests that the water is colder than we'd thought. To stumble through "Amaze" is like being condemned to a hell in which you are constantly late and constantly missing your train by seconds. The artist's clamor for attention—the raking intrusive cough redirecting one's consciousness from her painting to herself—mimics the experience of trying to talk on the phone over the call-waiting signal.

And where was John Lennon in all this? Present, but hardly dominant, an occasional muse onstage for just over a decade of the artist's forty-year career. The Japan Society show included photographs of "the best-known of Yoko's advertising works"—John and Yoko's 1969 antiwar posters ("War is Over! If you want it"). The wall text for "Painting to Hammer a Nail In" quoted Lennon's account of the electricity generated by the piece when it appeared at the Indica show. Video monitors showed "Smile," the couple's 1968 film of John's face taking 52 minutes to brighten, and footage of the "Bed-Ins for Peace," scenes of the couple dressed in virginal white, greeting reporters and exchanging cuddly intimate chat:

John (holding imaginary microphone and speaking in mockserious tones): "What effect do you think you're going to have on the world?"

Yoko (snuggling suggestively against John): "I don't know what effect I'm going to have on the world. I know what effect I'm going to have on my husband. . . ."

Yes Yoko Ono—the book—acknowledges Lennon's contribution to Ono's work: "Ono's marriage to Lennon gave new dimension to her deeply philosophical art." An essay by Murray Sayle claims that "the preoccupations of Yoko Ono's vivid Tokyo adolescence had captured Lennon's energy, given his aimless life new direction." An article on Yoko's music credits John for ratcheting up its pitch ("I would hear his guitar and think, 'Wow, I can answer that.' Ono was forced to scream louder than ever against amplified instruments.")

and examines the influence of Lennon's death and its aftermath on his widow's subsequent recordings: "Ono was hurt, angry, confused, nostalgic, and afraid—and her new songs let the world know it."

Visiting the exhibition and reading through the book make the sheer unfairness of death seem doubly exasperating. History is, as we all know, written by the survivors, and in the case of John and Yoko, the surviving artist gets more opportunity to persuade us that the dead artist was important principally as the living artist's helper, companion, and muse.

And yet, despite everything, Yoko inspires a certain sympathy and admiration—a respect for her dogged endurance, for the un-flagging determination that's kept her making avant-garde art for so many years, for her fierce insistence on her right to be an artist. The passage of time has made it possible to overlook the damage that she may have done to Lennon's work (the chilling scene in *Gimme Some Truth*, the hard evidence of *Double Fantasy*) and to appreciate her contribution to such albums as *Imagine* and *Plastic Ono Band*. And finally, what she says about the ways in which the larger society views and treats her has come to seem regrettably accurate.

Almost from the time they met, John and Yoko insisted that the toxic reaction Yoko provoked in so many critics and fans was the consequence of a cultural allergy to her gender and race. John stated it plainly: "She's a woman, and she's Japanese; there's racial preju-dice against her and there's female prejudice against her. It's as sim-ple as that." Yoko made similar claims, while at the same time eliminating any possible confusion as to the true nature of her and John's relative social status: "The world looked on me as the oppor-tunist Oriental. They felt he was marrying down, though in his mind he was the pauper, a Liverpool boy, and I was the princess, a New York sophisticate."

In fact, the Lennons' analysis of the situation was not some six-ties paranoid fantasy. A 1969 *Esquire* piece about Yoko bore the shockingly unenlightened title, "John Rennon's Excrusive Gloupie."

Yoko recalls specific instances of racist slurs leveled by the press. In 1974, a New York newspaper "wrote in their review something like 'shaking her boobs, with her slanted eyes, thinking she's sexy' . . . In 1981 a London newspaper referred to 'sloe-eyed songstress Yoko Ono.' It's always 'slant-eyed' this and that." Not long ago, at a dinner party, when I mentioned that I was writing about Yoko Ono, a former member of a famous eighties rock group volunteered the story of how *his* band was almost broken up by the machinations of another musician's Japanese girlfriend. Mention Ono to artists, and sooner or later someone will compare her work with that of Yayoi Kusama, with whom Yoko has little in common, ultimately, except the fact that both are ambitious, female, and Japanese. The mental hospital outside Tokyo in which Kusama lives is a long way from the Dakota.

If Yoko Ono's work and her public persona possess a certain childishly demanding insistence, if the subtext of her self-presentation and so many of her interviews seems to be "Look at me, look at me, don't look at him, look at me," it is, no doubt, partly characterological. One can imagine her—an indulged, privileged girl from the merchant aristocracy—behaving that way. Yet it's also an understandable and not entirely unreasonable response to her actual situation, to the threat of invisibility, to the obstacles that our culture strews so liberally in the path of Asian and women artists, and to the fact that, as she claimed, it would have calmed the media's anxiety to have been able to call her *Mrs. Lennon*. What makes it so tricky to dismiss the keening and screeching, the droning whine of "Fly," the intrusive onstage presence is our awareness (however unwilling, intermittent, and vague) that our culture has put Yoko Ono in a place from which she has to scream twice as loudly as anyone else, simply to be heard.

It's no accident that the 1970s—the decade during which the Lennons tried to redistribute and share the roles of artist and muse but finally gave up and "got in touch" with their feelings of competition and territoriality—was a decade in which the whole culture was getting in touch with its feelings, when, with dizzying rapidity, our attention was being shifted from exterior to interior, from the Bed-In for Peace to the Primal Scream. In an era that functioned like a petri dish for narcissism of all sorts, the gods gave us yet another muse created in our own image. Once again, a society had selected and nurtured a living avatar of the divine on whom to project its most profound hopes and fears, its deepest instincts and most abstract ideas about men and women, Eros, creativity, mythology and power, and its endless need to revise the ever-changing story of its troubled and rhapsodic love affair with art.

AFTERWORD

PERHAPS WE SHOULD END where we began, in Columbia University's Low Library, where, in 1932, Alice Pleasance Liddell Hargreaves came to receive her honorary doctorate for having inspired Lewis Carroll. Decorated with white flowers, the rotunda was crowded with people, some of whom must have been obliged to suppress an attack of anxious laughter when university president Nicholas Murray Butler confidently parked himself on the flowered throne meant for Alice. Who were these people? What could they have thought? And how much did they know or care about the elderly, self-possessed woman who stood before them?

Possibly the ceremony was attended exclusively by large souls, wise enough to comprehend and accept the mystery of time which, with a single swipe, the most facile sleight of hand, had transformed the little fox in the beggar's rags into a tidy dowager in a brown suit and corsage. More likely, they were ordinary men and women, college professors, administrators, political and cultural figures, at least one reporter from the *New York Times*, who (like most people) were naturally so confounded by this unfathomable mystery and by the related impossibility of holding the ten-year-old and the eighty-year-old simultaneously in their minds that they could only retreat into metaphor and abstraction. The difficulty of connecting the woman before them with the little girl whom Mr. Dodgson had adored was so daunting that it would have been easier for the audience to imagine themselves in the presence of a living goddess, a muse still trailing her gossamer wings from her flight down from Mount Olympus.

As President Butler praised Alice for being the moving cause of one of the great works of English literature, did any of his listeners wonder what he could have meant? Were any of them confounded by the chasm between that golden afternoon and a masterpiece, between Charles Dodgson's desire to entertain and please a child and the actual words and sentences he invented and employed to constuct a parallel and coherent world, a riotous landscape of doggerel-spouting animals, manic rabbits, spacey insects, and hilarious, violent monsters masquerading as human adults? Even if he sat down at his desk with Alice's image in mind, his vision of her must soon have given way to more colorful, complex, and anarchic fanatasies, more necessary for his purpose. The distance between these two points—between the golden afternoon and the book—is in fact so immense that any sensible person would reasonably conclude that the whole concept of the muse is, after all, an abstraction.

But no one's life is an abstraction; rather it is the sum of one highly specific, concrete, and unrepeatable event after another. The facts and details of Alice Liddell's biography shaded the context and the meaning of her presence in Low Library in ways that few members of her audience probably knew or noticed. Did they register the irony of Alice having come full circle back to the milieu in which she had spent her girlhood, back to enjoying the attention and approval of a group of academics whose applause, on that spring day in 1932, might have sounded very much like the polite clapping that filled Dean Liddell's parlor when she and her two sisters performed their party pieces?

Of course, the witnesses to Alice's moment of glory would not have thought to imagine her in the company of her sister muses, of the women who preceded and followed her. They would not have noticed certain things that by now will seem quite clear to us—for example, the fact that Alice Liddell never wrote her memoir, never gave in to the tempting prerogative to which so many muses have succumbed for reasons ranging from personal ambition to resentment to the need to tell their side or to pay tribute.

Another of Charles Dodgson's child-friends, Isa Bowman, had written such a book, a fairly scandalous memoir of the mathematician's ardent kisses. But Isa was an actress, ambitious, a public personality, whereas Alice—either through reticence or delicacy, self-doubt or scruples relating to breeding, gender and class—hesitated to tell the world about the events that led up to her mother's banishing Charles Dodgson from their home when Alice was eleven. Though, it should be noted, neither modesty nor reserve prevented her from repeatedly stating that her importunings on that golden afternoon were what had caused a masterpiece to be written, nor from suggesting, at the Columbia ceremony, that Mr. Dodgson was with them in spirit, observing and rejoicing in their recognition of his muse.

Thus Alice's attitude toward musedom was in many ways the ideal one—or in any case, the ideal advanced by Étienne Gilson and Robert Graves. She was the muse who had been content to inspire without demanding to be thanked, or to marry her artist, or to become an artist herself. How gratifying the Columbia audience must have found it to applaud a muse who carried out her responsibilities so gracefully and so well!

But to consider the lives of the muses is to realize that there is no ideal, no single way of performing a muse's duties. There are as many kinds of muses as there are individual women who have had the luck or misfortune to find their destiny conjoined with that of a particular artist. It's hard to imagine personalities or biographies more dissimilar than those of Alice Liddell and Lee Miller, Lizzie Siddal and Lou Andreas-Salomé, Charis Weston and Gala Dalí, Suzanne Farrell and Yoko Ono. Each responded differently to the dilemmas that have traditionally confronted women, to the obligations, obstacles, and options that customarily surround questions of family, children, work, and so forth. In each case, the terms in which these choices were formulated and resolved reflected the historical and social climates in which these women lived, as well as their determination to resist the prevailing mores and the pressures of their own times—a resolve for which many of the muses paid dearly.

Of the nine muses whose stories appear in this book, two were writers, and—beginning with Mrs. Thrale—wholly or partly supported themselves on the proceeds from their work. Four were artists. All but three had children, though only one, Yoko Ono, had a child with her principal artist. (Gala Dalí had Cecile with Paul Eluard.) As with any group of mothers, some were better at it than others.

Like most of us, they had ambitions. Though Gilson and Graves might have warned them about the dangers of this sort of unruly and unproductive thinking, many of these muses sought answers to the sensible question of why their artists were permitted and encouraged to be artists, while they themselves were relegated to the less enviable position of muse. Yoko asked, and kept asking. Perhaps to her detriment, Lee Miller behaved as if it were beneath her dignity to ask, and as if everything would be all right if she just could keep her courage, which was demonstrably greater than that of most men she knew. Suzanne Farrell was lucky enough to work in an art form that encouraged men and women to collaborate, a field in which both choreographer and dancer could function as fellow artists.

Other muses caved in, with only the briefest struggle. The comforts of opium and worries about her husband's infidelities consumed the energy and time that Lizzie Siddal might otherwise have devoted to work. Or else the muses confined themselves to recreating the concept of musedom—and to channeling their own creative impulses into furthering their artist's career. On one especially anxious day preceding her hospitalization, Gala may have distracted herself by making Surrealist sculpture, but for the most part she directed her talents toward putting the most marketable public face on that disturbing duo, Gala-Dalí.

If the muses resented, or even noticed, the sacrifices they were called upon to make, there were measures they could take, especially when they outlived their artists. Like Hester Thrale, they could publish books that reflected their own ambivalence; like Charis Weston, they could author memoirs that expressed their fears and doubts about their artist's loyalty and love. Or like Lou, they could preemptively reject their smitten artists and write volumes of criticism that included negative assessments of their artist's concerns and methods. Other muses were simply grateful. By the time that Alice Liddell collected her degree from Columbia University, her role in the creation of her old friend's book seems to have remained the most memorable and meaningful event in her long and finally rather sad life.

What, then, do these nine muses have in common, aside from the fact that all of them were beautiful, either classically lovely, like Lee Miller and Charis Weston, or sexy (Gala Dalí), or gifted with a still more unconventional (Hester Thrale, Yoko Ono) appeal? Perhaps the most important thing about these nine lives is also the most obvious—namely, the fact that all these muses loved and were loved by their artists.

Arlene Croce has suggested that Virginia Woolf's muse was not an individual but rather a group of like-minded women. But the easy pleasures of friendship and companionability were not what, after all, seems to have motivated the artists whom these nine women inspired. Something more intense was required, something closer to Eros, though—as we have seen—only a small minority of these couples shared anything remotely resembling the "norm" of mature, consenting, requited love between two heterosexual adults.

And so, once more, we return to the Greeks and to the various examinations and definitions of love and Eros considered in Plato's *Symposium:* the search for the long-lost half of the self, the desire for good and for beauty, the need to procreate, and to create. For these artists, the love of—and for—their muses provided an essential element required for the alchemy of invention, or the fire under the vessel in which talent and technique were melded to produce the gold of art.

Lewis Carroll and Alice Liddell are now long dead, but the books and the photographs survive, physical evidence of the erotic current that we can still feel running between the eccentric photographer and the seductive, transfixed beggar child. Underneath the speeches, the ceremony, the public fuss, the president's gaffe, the challenge of seeing the child muse in the elderly woman, underneath all that is what Alice's doctorate really honored and what the crowd applauded: love, and that rare and precious spark ignited by genius and passion.

ENDNOTES

INTRODUCTION

PAGE:

2 "Awakening with her . . ." Florence Becker Lennon, *Victoria Through the Looking Glass*, Simon & Schuster, New York, 1945, p. ix.

2 "Mrs. Dodgson knows . . ." Ibid., p. x.

4 "Happy he whomsoever . . ." Hesiod, *The Works Of Hesiod Callimachus and Theognis*, translated by Reverend J. Banks, Henry G. Bohn, London, 1856, pp. 6–7.

8 "devastating to modern . . ." "Is the Muse Dead?" Arlene Croce, *The New Yorker*, February 26–March 4, 1996, pp. 164–69.

10 "Denys had a trait . . ." Isak Dinesen, *Out of Africa*, Random House, 1938, p. 225.

13 "Designers Marc Jacobs . . ." *New York* magazine, January 1, 2001, p. 12.

14 "She is either Muse . . ." Robert Graves, *The White Goddess: A Historical Grammar of Poetic Myth*, Noonday Press/Farrar, Straus & Giroux,

1997, p. 446–47.

15 "It may prove . . ." Étienne Gilson, *A Choir of Muses*, translated by Maisie Ward, Sheed and Ward, New York, 1953, p. 177.

15 "The reason why remarkably . . ." Graves, *White Goddess*, p. 449.

17 "only too easily . . ." Gilson, *Choir*, p. 133.

19 "the nostalgic luxury . . ." Ibid., p. 15.

19 "I climbed the ladder . . ." Jann S. Wenner, *Lennon Remembers*, Verso, New York, 2000, p. 38.

HESTER THRALE

PAGE:

27 "the horrible condition . . ." L. B. Seeley, *Mrs. Thrale, Afterwards Mrs. Piozzi*, Scribner and Welford, New York, 1891, p. 24.

28 "His conversation does . . ." *Johnsonian Miscellanies*, edited by G. B. Hill, Oxford, 1897, ii., pp. 169, 374.

28 "such dead . . ." Victoria Glendinning, *Rebecca West: A Life*, Knopf, New York, 1987, p. 156.

28 "a roughness in his manner . . ." *Johnsoniana*, Carey and Hart, 1842, p. 110.

29 "I felt excessively . . ." *Johnsonian Miscellanies*, Hill, ed., vol.1, pp. 234.

30 "To the assistance . . ." *Johnsoniana*, pp. 107–8.

31 "I am perpetually thinking . . ." *Johnson and Boswell in Scotland, A Journey to the Hebrides*, edited by Pat Rogers, Yale University Press, New Haven, 1993, p. 19.

31 "Nothing puts . . ." Ibid., p. 65.

32 "a gentle Puke." Mary Hyde, *The Thrales of Streatham Park*, Harvard University Press, Cambridge, 1977, p. 82.

32 "Although Education . . ." James L. Clifford, *Hester Lynch Piozzi (Mrs. Thrale)*, Columbia University Press, New York, 1987, p. 9.

33 "This was a strange thing . . ." Ibid., p. 22.

33 "barrel of porter . . ." *Mrs. Thrale*, Seeley, p. 18.

33 "all my assurances . . ." Ibid., p. 18.

33 "leaving me to conciliate . . ." Ibid., p. 19.

34 "Autumn came . . ." Ibid., p. 22.

34 "I was now a married . . ." *Hester*, Clifford, pp. 50–51.

34 "Driven thus on . . ." *Mrs. Thrale*, Seeley, p.22.

35 "a heart void . . ." *Hester*, Clifford, p. 79.

35 "almost before it became . . ." *Mrs. Thrale*, Seeley, p. 41.

36 "I count . . ." *Hester*, Clifford, p. 74.

36 "Within prescribed . . ." Christopher Hibbert, *The Personal History of Samuel Johnson*, Harper & Row, New York, 1971, p. 213.

37 "Madmen . . ." Ibid., p. 212.

37 "*De pedicis* . . ." Ibid., p. 213.

37 "Says Johnson a . . ." Ibid., pp. 212–13.

37 "this he knew . . ." Ibid., p. 213.

37 "How many Times . . . a dreadful . . ." Ibid., p. 213.

37 "Johnson's padlock . . ." Ibid., p. 213.

38 "What Care can I promise . . ." Ibid., pp. 213–14.

39 "more famed . . ." *Hester,* Clifford, p. 98.

39 "He is heavy . . ." Mary Hyde, *The Thrales of Streatham Park*, Harvard University Press, Cambridge, 1977, p. 85.

39 "In working up . . ." John Wain, *Samuel Johnson*, Viking Press, New York, 1974, p. 318.

40 "I hear Harry has had . . ." *Hester,* Clifford, p. 115.

41 "Oh how this dreadful . . ." Ibid., p. 125.

41 "It is the horrible . . ." Ibid., p. 127.

41 "I think you shall never run away . . ." Ibid., p. 128.

41 "Mr. Thrale, both . . ." Ibid., pp. 136–37.

42 "So ends . . ." Ibid., p. 138.

42 "one of the most dreadful . . ." *Samuel*, Wain, p. 342.

42 "It is many Years . . ." *Hester*, Clifford, p. 145.

42 "Do not remit . . ." Ibid., p. 146.

43 "one of the best . . ." *Samuel*, Wain, p. 352.

43 "the discussions . . ." *Hester*, Clifford, p. 197.

43 "*Your* note . . ." *Hester*, Clifford, p. 152.

43 "venereal at last . . ." *Thrales*, Hyde, p. 174.

44 "I had scarcely . . ." *Personal*, Hibbert, p. 194.

44 "the black dog . . ." *Mrs. Thrale*, Seeley, p. 129.

45 "Scott and I . . ." *Hester*, Clifford, p. 200.

45 "My dearest darling . . ." *Samuel,* Wain, p. 355.

45 "an eminent . . ." *Hester*, Clifford, p. 99.

45 "If an Angel . . ." *Hester*, Clifford, p. 201.

45 "till I am . . ." Ibid., p. 209.

45 "amazingly like . . ." Ibid., p. 187.
46 "His hand . . ." Ibid., p. 189.
46 "I fancied . . ." *Samuel*, Wain, p. 357.
46 "fiddler . . ." *Thrales*, Hyde, p. 236.
46 "like Puppies . . ." Ibid., p. 236.
46 "Where are you going . . ." Ibid., p. 236.
46 "Adieu to all . . ." *Hester*, Clifford, p. 218.
47 "I perceived . . ." *Samuel*, Wain, p. 359.
47 "We have no Time . . ." *Thrales*, Hyde, p. 239.
47 "Indeed, my dear . . ." *Samuel*, Wain, p. 363.
47 "Madam . . ." Ibid., p. 363.
48 "Till you have changed . . ." Ibid., p. 363.
48 "Whatever I can contribute . . ." Ibid., p. 363.
48 "Piozzified Marriage . . ." *Samuel*, Wain, p. 373.
48 "Mrs. Thrale is fallen . . ." Ibid., p. 231.
49 "No. Nor write . . ." *Samuel*, Wain, p. 373.
49 "I drive her quite . . ." *Hester*, Clifford, p. 239.
49 "Do not neglect . . ." Ibid., p. 239.
49 "I am afraid . . ." Ibid., p. 239.
49 "Of Course . . ." Ibid., p. 245.
50 "Poor Johnson!" Ibid., p. 241–42.
50 "I am aware . . ." Johnsoniana.
51 "very conversant . . . He suddenly . . ." Ibid., p. 18.
51 "another story . . ." Ibid., p. 19.
52 "I had been crossed . . ." Ibid., pp. 106–7.
52 "Veneration . . ." Ibid., pp. 106–7.
52 "Conversation . . ." Ibid., p. 101.
54 "Calling upon some . . ." *Hester*, Clifford, p. 407.
55 "We will see . . ." Ibid., p. 391.
55 "He is so kind . . ." Ibid., p. 421.
55 "made twenty years . . ." Ibid., p. 425.
56 "astonishing elasticity . . ." *Thrales*, Hyde, p. 310.
56 "indulging in . . ." *Mrs. Thrale*, Seeley, p. 323.

ALICE LIDDELL

PAGE:

60 "All in the golden afternoon. . . ." Lewis Carroll, *Alice's Adventures in Wonderland* and *Through the Looking Glass*, Penguin Books, 1998 (Alice's), p. 5.

62 "Full many a year . . ." *Alice's*, Carroll, p. 295.

63 "I rowed *stroke* . . ." Morton N. Cohen, *Lewis Carroll, A Biography*, Knopf, New York, 1995, p. 91.

63 "Near all . . ." *New York Times*, May 1, 1932.

64 "Next Wednesday . . ." *Cornhill magazine*, July 1932.

65 "artist of Agnes Grace . . ." *Carroll . . . Bio*, Cohen, p. 158.

65 "has addressed one sonnet . . ." Ibid., p. 158.

65 "Both the children . . ." Ibid., p. 159.

65 "beautiful little Hallam . . ." *The Diaries of Lewis Carroll*, edited by Roger Lancelyn Green, Oxford University Press, New York, 1954, p. 144.

65 "Tennyson told us . . ." Ibid., p. 146.

69 "Usually . . ." *The Selected Letters of Lewis Carroll*, edited by Morton N. Cohen, Macmillan, London, 1982, p. 195.

70 "My child-friends . . ." *Carroll . . . Bio*, Cohen, p. 469.

70 "You know I can't stand . . ." Ibid., p. 532.

70 "The friendship of children . . ." *Letters . . . Carroll*, Cohen, p. 272.

70 "When a little girl . . ." *Carroll . . . Bio*, Cohen, p. 227.

71 "Their innocent . . ." *Letters . . . Carroll*, Cohen, ed., p. 97.

71 "That is all I want . . ." Ibid., p. 109.

71 "I think all you say . . ." Ibid., p. 244.

72 "I probably bored . . ." *Carroll . . . Bio*, Cohen, p. 466.

72 "For hours on end . . ." *Diaries . . . Carroll*, Green, ed., pp. xxiv–v.

73 "We used to sit . . ." *Carroll . . . Bio*, Cohen, p. 86.

73 "Any one that has ever loved . . ." *Carroll . . . Bio*, Cohen, p. 105.

74 "There was an old farmer . . ." *The Complete Works of Lewis Carroll*, introduction by Alexander Woollcott, Vintage Books, New York, 1976, p. 781.

75 "I am glad you liked . . ." *Letters . . . Carroll*, Cohen, ed., p. 26.

76 "just in time . . ." *Diaries . . . Carroll*, Green, ed., p. 94.

76 "I found . . ." Ibid., p. 95.

77 "Though for my own part . . ." Ibid., pp. 110–11.

77 "a young lady . . ." *Complete . . . Carroll*, p. 1,089.

77 "a thick-built man . . ." Ibid., p. 1,096.

78 "I am the Dean . . ." Anne Clark, *The Real Alice: Lewis Carroll's Dream Child*, Stein and Day, New York, 1981, p. 44.

78 "Oh, time was young . . ." *Complete . . . Carroll*, p. 975.

79 "a long letter . . ." *Carroll . . . Bio*, Cohen, p. 101.

79 "had a good deal of conversation . . ." Ibid.

79 "we tried the game . . ." *Diaries . . . Carroll*, Green, ed., p. 185.

80 "It was delightful . . ." Ibid., p. 193.

80 "I began . . ." Ibid., p. 194.

80 "Child of the pure . . ." *Complete . . . Carroll*, pp. 135–36.

80 "Alice was in an unusually . . ." *Carroll . . . Bio*, Cohen, p. 96.

80 "I met the children . . ." *Diaries . . . Carroll*, Green, ed., p. 196.

81 "About 10 o'clock . . ." Ibid., p. 199.

81 "Wrote to Mrs. Liddell . . ." Ibid., p. 200.

81 "Mrs. Liddell and the children . . ." *Carroll . . . Bio*, Cohen, p. 100.

82 "The nominal object . . ." *Real*, Clark, p. 85.

82 "I suppose you . . ." *Carroll . . . Bio*, Cohen, p. 103.

83 "She does not look . . ." Ibid., p. 188.

83 "Agnes Hull . . ." Ibid., p. 228.

83 "They let me bring . . ." Ibid., p. 185.

83 "I would very much like . . ." Ibid., p. 187.

83 "if I may regard myself . . ." *Letters . . . Carroll*, Cohen, p. 267.

83 "The why of this book . . ." *Carroll . . . Bio*, Cohen, p. 135.

84 "I kissed her on her false . . ." *Complete . . . Carroll*, p. 973.

84 "In the gray light . . ." Ibid., pp. 963–64.

85 "Speak roughly . . ." *Alice's*, Carroll, p. 54.

86 "writing the fairy-tale . . ." *Diaries . . . Carroll*, Green, ed., p. 188.

86 "During these last few days . . ." Ibid., Green, p. 219.

86 "Met Alice . . ." Ibid., p. 230.

87 "Her face . . ." *Alice's*, Carroll, p. 136.

87 "I shouldn't know you . . ." Ibid., p. 192.

88 "I do *not* admire . . ." *Letters . . . Carroll*, Cohen, ed., p. 234.

88 "Will you draw for me . . ." Rodney Engen, *Kate Greenaway,* New York: Schocken Books, 1981, pp. 93–94.

88 "Perugino . . ." *Real*, Clark, p. 102.

89 "I am sure . . ." Ibid., p. 152.

89 "The planet Saturn . . ." Ruskin, *Praeterita,* Rupert-Hart Davis, London, 1949, pp. 470–71.

90 "Out of focus . . ." *Carroll . . . Bio*, Cohen, p. 181.

93 "More than a commonly . . ." *Real*, Clark, p. 214.

94 "My Dear Mrs. Hargreaves . . ." *Letters . . . Carroll*, Cohen, ed., p. 140.

94 "At the Aquarium . . ." *Diaries . . . Carroll*, Green, ed., p. 464.

95 "It is very pleasant . . ." *Real*, Clark, p. 214.

95 "Skene brought . . ." *Diaries . . . Carroll*, Green, ed., p. 465.

96 "My Dear Mrs. Hargreaves . . ." *Letters . . . Carroll*, Cohen, ed., p. 213.

97 "But her sister . . ." *Alice's*, Carroll, pp. 290–91.

ELIZABETH SIDDAL

PAGE:

102 "If I recover . . ." Dante Gabriel Rossetti, *Letters*, edited by Oswald Doughty and John Robert Wahl, Clarendon Press, Oxford, 1965–67, vol. 2, p. 712.

102 "The book in question . . ." *Three Rossettis: Unpublished Letters to and from Dante Gabriel, Christina, William*, collected and edited by Janet Camp Troxell, Harvard University Press, Cambridge, 1937, p. 129.

103 "And didst thou . . ." from "*Dantis Tenebrae*" by Dante Gabriel Rossetti, *The Collected Works of Dante Gabriel Rossetti*, edited by William M. Rossetti, Ellis and Elvery, London, 1897, p. 299.

105 "parading . . ." Stanley Weintraub, *Four Rossettis*, Weybright and Talley, New York, 1977, p. 60.

105 "while her friends . . ." *Four*, Weintraub, p. 60.

106 "Miss Siddal . . ." Dante Gabriel Rossetti, *His Family-Letters with a Memoir by William Michael Rossetti*, Ellis and Elvery, London, 1895, vol. I, p. 173.

106 "He had his defects . . ." Jan Marsh, *The Legend of Elizabeth Siddal*, London, Quarter Books, 1989, p. 60.

106 "Rossetti's ignorance . . ." Evelyn Waugh, *Rossetti: His Life and Works*, Norwood, London, 1976, p. 56.

106 "Have so little . . ." Ibid.

107 "like a monomania . . ." Gay Daly, *Pre-Raphaelites in Love*, Collins, London, 1989, p. 55.

107 "Rossetti's innumerable portraits . . ." Oswald Doughty, *Dante Gabriel Rossetti: A Victorian Romantic*, Yale University Press, New Haven, 1949, p. 119.

107 "I feel puzzled . . ." Ibid.

107 "meek unconscious . . ." Brian Dobbs and Judy Dobbs, *Dante Gabriel Rossetti: An Alien Victorian*, MacDonald and Jane's, London, 1977, p. 88.

108 "thinner . . ." *Gabriel Rossetti: An Alien*, Dobbs, p. 104.

108 "Her character . . ." *Family-Letters with Memoir*, Rossetti, pp. 173–74.

108 "she knew how to . . ." *Four*, Weintraub, p. 60.

108 "On leaving your boat . . ." *Legend*, Marsh, pp. 60–61.

110 "grace, loveliness . . ." *Family-Letters with Memoir*, Rossetti, p. 175.

110 "He feeds upon . . ." *Pre-Raphaelites in Love*, Daly, p. 71.

111 "That she was sincerely . . ." *Family-Letters with Memoir*, Rossetti, p. 173.

111 "Rossetti once told me . . ." *Legend*, Marsh, p. 142.

111 "Her fecundity . . ." *Family-Letters with Memoir*, Rossetti, p. 176.

112 "I wish you and Lizzie . . ." *Gabriel Rossetti: An Alien*, Dobbs, p. 136.

112 "The plain *hard fact* . . ." *Four*, Weintraub, pp. 83–84.

112 "Although far from blind . . ." *Family-Letters with Memoir*, Rossetti, p. 184.

112 "I really do . . ." Ibid.

112 "I should be very glad . . ." *Pre-Raphaelites in Love*, Daly, p. 60.

112 "Why does he not . . ." *Legend*, Marsh, p. 90.

113 "I still trust to God . . ." *Pre-Raphaelites in Love*, Daly, p. 80.

113 "Lizzy has made a perfect wonder . . ." *Letters*, Rossetti, Doughty, and Wahl, eds., vol. 1, p. 17.

113 "Tell Christina . . ." Ibid., p. 183.

113 "I love him . . ." Ibid., p. 249.

113 "Lizzie is a sweet companion . . ." Ibid., pp. 194–95.

114 "It seems hard to me . . ." Ibid., p. 209.

114 "Her lungs . . ." *Four*, Weintraub, pp. 85–86.

114 "That a girl . . ." Ibid., p. 86.

114 "*phthisis* . . ." *Family-Letters with Memoir*, Rossetti, p. 221.

115 "he had known her to take . . ." Ibid., p. 223.

115 "Laden autumn . . .", poem by Siddal, *Poems and Drawings of Elizabeth Siddal*, edited by Roger C. Lewis and Mark Samuels Lasner, Wombat Press, Wolfville, Nova Scotia, 1978, p. 8.

115 "Miss Sid complains . . ." Ford Madox Brown, *The Diary of Ford Madox Brown*, edited by Virginia Surtees, Yale University Press, New Haven, 1981, p. 174.

115 "Rosetti and Miss Siddall . . ." *Diary*, *Brown*, Surtees, ed., p. 149.

116 "Rossetti is every day with his . . ." *Pre-Raphaelites in Love*, Daly, p. 65.

116 "Hunt stayed . . ." *Diary*, *Brown*, Surtees, ed., p. 181.

116 "Emma called on . . ." Ibid., p. 182–83.

116 "I arranged . . ." Timothy Hilton, *The Pre-Raphaelites*, Oxford University Press, New York, 1970, p. 92.

117 "Gabriel has forsworn . . ." *Diary, Brown,* Surtees, ed., p. 187.

117 "Last night a misunderstanding . . ." *Letters*, Rossetti, Doughty, and Wahl, vol. 1, pp. 319–20.

118 "If my reader chooses . . ." *Family-Letters with Memoir*, Rossetti, p. 201.

118 "He met her . . ." Ibid., p. 202.

118 "He put my head . . ." *Rossetti: Victorian Romantic*, Doughty, p. 252.

119 "He paints it all . . ." *Diary, Brown*, Surtees, ed., p. 106.

119 "Miss Sidall has been here . . ." Ibid., p. 195.

120 After that, she determined . . ." Ibid., pp. 195–96.

120 "Of course, I am very glad . . ." Ibid., p. 196.

120 "All day with Gabriel . . ." Ibid., p. 195.

120 "The kissed mouth . . ." *Pre-Raphaelites in Love*, Daly, p. 78.

120 "More stunning . . ." *Four*, Weintraub, p. 106.

122 "I am too blind . . ." Ibid., p. 98.

122 "Lizzy and I are going to be . . ." *Letters*, Rossetti, Doughty, and Wahl, eds., p. 363.

122 "Till yesterday . . ." Ibid., pp. 363–64.

122 "I have been, almost without respite . . ." *Letters,* pp. 364–65.

123 "All hail from Lizzie . . ." *Letters*, Rossetti, Doughty, and Wahl, eds., p. 366.

123 "Paris seems to agree . . ." Ibid., p. 368.

123 "It appears she . . ." *Four*, Weintraub, p. 110.

123 "As he was not a little . . ." *Family-Letters with Memoir*, Rossetti, p. 207.

125 "O God, forgive me . . ." *Legend,* Marsh, p. 208.

125 "And turn away . . ." *Four*, Weintraub, p. 91.

126 "I care not for . . ." *Pre-Raphaelites in Love*, Daly, p. 79.

126 "My brother . . ." *Family-Letters with Memoir*, Rossetti, p. 208.

126 "In fact, I may almost say . . ." *Rossetti: Victorian Romantic,* Doughty, p. 263.

127 "She was compelled . . ." *Family-Letters with Memoir*, Rossetti, p. 212.

127 "an impression . . ." *Four*, Weintraub, p. 112.

127 "I am most sorry . . ." *Pre-Raphaelites in Love*, Daly, p. 83.

128 "I feel surer . . ." *Four*, Weintraub, p. 114.

128 "We have got our rooms . . ." *Letters*, Rossetti, Doughty, and Wahl, eds.,vol. 2, pp. 392–93.

128 "Lizzie is pretty well . . ." Ibid., p. 393.

129 "My dear Mother . . ." Ibid., p. 397.

129 "Lizzie has just . . ." Ibid., p. 397.

129 "Swinburne and I . . ." Ibid.

129 "Hush, Ned . . ." *Legend,* Marsh, p. 65.

129 "Hollow hearts . . ." *Pre-Raphaelites in Love*, Daly, p. 88.

130 "Mr. Rossetti stated . . ." *Family-Letters with Memoir*, Rossetti, pp. 223–24.

131 "My life is so miserable . . ." Violet Hunt, *The Wife of Rossetti*, Bodley Head, London, p. 305.

131 "Don't let her . . ." *Letters*, Rossetti, Doughty, and Wahl, eds., vol. 2, p. 410.

132 "On the second or third day . . ." *Family-Letters with Memoir*, Rossetti, p. 224.

132 "Oh Lizzie . . ." Ibid.

132 "With sobs and . . ." *Four*, Weintraub, p. 124.

133 "I have often been writing . . ." *Family-Letters with Memoir*, Rossetti, p. 225.

133 "Well, the feeling . . ." Ibid.

133 "I mean him to clean . . ." *Four*, Weintraub, p. 130.

134 "It is not at all . . ." *Pre-Raphaelites in Love*, Daly, p. 94.

136 "the poor thing . . ." *Family-Letters with Memoir*, Rossetti, p. 222.

136 "And with her . . ." Ibid.

LOU ANDREAS-SALOMÉ

PAGE:

141 "What attracted . . ." Lou Andreas-Salomé, *Looking Back, Memoirs*, translated by Breon Mitchell, Marlowe and Company, New York, 1995, p. 10.

141 "People who are not 'faithful' . . ." *Freud Journal of Lou Andreas-Salomé*, translated by Stanley A. Leavy, Basic Books, New York, 1964, p. 124.

142 "woman who perhaps never attains . . ." *Freud Journal*, p. 118.

142 "For men fight . . ." *Freud Journal*, p. 130.

143 "In it I saw a pleasant . . ." *Looking Back*, Andreas-Salomé, p. 45.

144 "Greet this Russian . . ." Angela Livingstone, *Salomé, Her Life and Work*, Moyer Bell Limited, Mt. Kisco, New York, 1984, p. 37.

145 "From what star . . ." *Looking Back*, Andreas-Salomé, p. 38.

146 "The most enchanting . . ." Lou Andreas-Salomé, *Nietzsche*, University of Illinois Press, Chicago, 2001, p. xiv.

147 "Picture arrived . . ." Letter from Paul Rée to Lou Andreas-Salomé, translated by Peter Gay.

148 "a grandfather . . ." *Looking Back*, Andreas-Salomé, p. 2.

148 "feeling of a deeply shared . . ." Ibid., p. 10.

148 "Activated by Eros . . ." Ibid., p. 19.

149 "She has a childlike . . ." H. F. Peters, *My Sister, My Spouse: A Biography of Lou Andreas-Salomé*, Norton, New York, 1962, p. 66.

150 "I wonder . . ." Salomé, Livingstone, p. 46.

150 "I think the only difference . . ." *My Sister*, Peters, p. 120.

150 "I have thought of you . . ." *The Selected Letters of Friedrich Nietzsche*, edited and translated by Christopher Middleton, University of Chicago Press, 1969, p. 188.

151 "If you have no more . . ." *My Sister*, Peters, p. 96.

151 "That poem . . ." *Selected Letters . . . Nietzsche*, Middleton, ed., p. 186.

152 "dirty design . . ." William Beatty Warner, *Chance and the Text of Experience: Freud, Nietzsche, and Shakespeare's Hamlet*, Cornell University Press, Ithaca, New York, 1986, p. 170.

152 "If I ask myself . . ." *Looking Back*, Andreas-Salomé, p. 50.

152 "dark dungeons . . ." Peters, *My Sister*, p. 121.

152 "From time to time . . ." *Selected Letters . . . Nietzsche*, Middleton, ed., p. 196.

152 "Do not be upset . . ." *Selected Letters . . . Nietzsche*, Middleton, ed., p. 198.

153 "A cat . . ." *My Sister*, Peters, p. 141.

153 "this dry, dirty . . ." *Salomé*, Livingstone, p. 54.

153 "So the defamation . . ." *Chance and . . .*, Warner, p. 175.

153 "I would like to erase . . ." Ibid. p. 189.

153 "This last morsel of . . ." *Selected Letters . . . Nietzsche*, Middleton, ed., pp. 198–99.

154 "After the trauma . . ." *Chance,* Warner, p. 203.

154 "Woman is not yet capable . . ." Friedrich Nietzsche, *Thus Spoke Zarathustra*, translated by R.J. Hollingdale, Penguin Classics, 1969, p. 84.

154 "Are you visiting . . ." *Thus Spoke*, Nietzsche, p. 93.

155 "meant to last forever . . ." *Looking Back*, Andreas-Salomé, p. 54.

155 "I warn . . ." *My Sister*, Peters, p. 70.

156 "Irresistible . . ." *Looking Back*, Andreas-Salomé, p. 125.

157 "What seemed . . ." Ibid., p. 126.

157 "physical . . . pass" Ibid., p. 125.

157 "I so seldom . . ." Ibid., p. 129.

157 "a reunion . . ." Ibid.

157 "He could never finish . . ." Ibid., pp. 118–19.

158 "The first time . . ." Ibid.

158 "would rather simply stab . . ." Ibid., p. 130.

159 "could indeed . . ." *Nietzsche*, Lou Andreas-Salomé, p. 3.

159 "Come to Leipzig . . ." Ibid.

159 "I want to see the world . . ." Hans Egon Holthusen, *Portrait of Rilke: An Illustrated Biography*, translated by W. H. Hargreaves, Herder and Herder, New York, 1971, pp. 39–40.

160 "A path through the forest . . ." *Looking Back*, Andreas-Salomé, p. 70.

160 "If I was your wife . . ." Ibid., p. 85.

161 "You wanted to remind me . . ." Ibid., p. 86.

161 "We were thinking about our stars . . ." Ibid., p. 86.

161 "All that I am . . ." Rilke, *Uncollected Poems*, translated by Edward Snow, Farrar, Straus & Giroux, New York, 1996, p. 15.

161 "When You asked . . ." *Rilke, Diaries of a Young Poet*, translated by Edward Snow and Michael Winkler, Norton, New York, 1997, p. 77.

162 "Woman's way . . ." *Diaries of a Young Poet*, Rilke, p. 66.

163 "had been one of oppression . . ." *Looking Back*, Andreas-Salomé, p. 46.

164 "We took leave . . ." *Letters of Rainer Maria Rilke, 1892–1910*, translated by Jane Bonnard Greene and M. D. Norton, Norton, New York, 1945, p. 42.

164 "splinters . . ." Ralph Freedman, *Life of a Poet: Rainer Maria Rilke*, Farrar, Straus & Giroux, New York, 1996, p. 116.

165 "No, no!" *Looking Back*, Andreas-Salomé, p. 88.

165 "Now it was necessary . . ." Ibid., p. 90.

165 "Then came the influence . . ." *Portrait . . . Rilke*, Holthusen, p. 38.

165 "Standing before . . ." *Looking Back*, Andreas-Salomé, p. 71.

166 "Everything that is truly seen . . ." *Life . . . Poet*, Freedman, p. 126.

166 "Thoughts of . . ." Rainer Maria Rilke, *Sonnets to Orpheus*, translated by Stephen Mitchell, Simon & Schuster, New York, 1985, p. 57.

167 "They grope . . ." Rilke, *The Lay of the Love and Death of Cornet Christopher Rilke*, translated by M. D. Herter Norton, Norton, New York, 1932, p. 55.

168   "tragic guilt . . . ripeness . . ." *Salomé*, Livingstone, p. 120.

168   "A good marriage . . ." *Letters . . . Rílke*, p. 57.

169   "awkward and beautiful . . ." Ibid., p. 108.

169   "O Lou, I was so tormented . . ." Ibid., p. 111.

169   O Lou, in one of my poems . . ." Ibid., p. 121.

171   "Only plunged . . ." Rainer Maria Rilke, *Uncollected Poems*, Farrar, Straus & Giroux, New York, 1996, p. 13.

171   "all that I . . ." Ibid., p. 15.

171   "God knows . . ." *Letters . . . Rílke*, vol. 2, p. 35.

171   "I am thinking . . ." Ibid., p. 34.

172   "Please tell Herr . . ." *Sigmund Freud and Lou Andreas-Salomé, Letters*, edited by Ernst Pfeiffer, Norton, New York, 1985, p. 28.

173   "No, do not misinterpret . . ." *Sigmund Freud and Lou Andreas-Salomé, Letters*, Pfeiffer, ed., p. 51.

173   "While a successful . . ." *My Sister*, Peters, p. 284.

173   "I was very pleased . . ." *Sigmund Freud and Lou Andreas-Salomé, Letters*, p. 198.

173   "I have not yet done so . . ." Ibid., p. 7.

174   "I would never dream . . ." Ibid., p. 8.

174   "If I understand . . . kept for you . . ." *Freud Journal*, p. 44.

175   "their busy-busy grabbing . . ." *Freud Journal*, p. 130.

175   "That you should have permitted . . ." *Sigmund Freud and Lou Andreas-Salomé, Letters*, Pfeiffer, ed., p. 19.

175   "the most unconditionally . . ." *Freud Journal*, p. 57.

175   "the whole tragedy . . ." Ibid., p. 166.

176   "He is deceiving . . ." Ibid., pp. 167–68.

176   "It may seem boring . . ." *Sigmund Freud and Lou Andreas-Salomé, Letters*, Pfeiffer, ed., p. 44.

176   "I am particularly anxious . . ." Ibid., p. 45.

176   "You are an understander . . ." Ibid.

177   "Every time . . ." Ibid., p. 32.

177   "You are always able . . ." Ibid., p. 172.

177   "I am delighted . . ." Ibid., p. 185.

178   "If I should be in a position . . ." Ibid., p. 61.

178   "all too personal . . ." Ibid., p. 193.

178   "It is the finest . . ." Ibid., p. 195

178   "She was of an unusual . . ." *Salomé*, Livingstone, p. 236.

179   "Anna is splendid . . ." *Sigmund Freud and Lou Andreas-Salomé, Letters*, Pfeiffer, ed., p. 125.

179 "Altogether Anna . . ." Ibid., p. 115.

179 "What Daughter-Anna . . ." Ibid.

180 "You are right . . ." Elisabeth Young-Breuhl, *Anna Freud*, Summit Books, New York, 1988, p. 118.

180 "I am stretching . . ." *Sigmund Freud and Lou Andreas-Salomé, Letters*, Pfeiffer, ed., p. 164.

180 "How wonderful . . ." Ibid., p. 165.

180 "Such a series . . ." Ibid.

181 "I had feared . . ." Ibid., pp. 165–66.

181 "For me it . . ." *Salomé*, Livingstone, p. 200.

182 "The very thing . . ." Ibid.

182 "Poor Tausk . . ." *Sigmund Freud and Lou Andreas-Salomé, Letters*, Pfeiffer, ed., p. 98.

182 "What you write . . ." Ibid., p. 99.

183 "Don't you have any pangs . . ." *My Sister*, Peters, p. 270.

183 "She had the gift . . ." Ibid., p. 271.

183 "a feeling of purest . . ." *Salomé*, Livingstone, p. 199.

183 "No matter how busy . . ." *Looking Back*, Andreas-Salomé, p. 134.

184 "I don't know how many hells . . ." Ralph Freedman, *Life of a Poet: Rainer María Rilke*, Farrar, Straus & Giroux, New York, 1996, p. 549.

184 "claims he is a famous man . . ." Ronald Hayman, *Nietzsche: A Critical Life*, Weidenfeld and Nicolson, London, 1980, p. 318.

185 "She contracted personal . . ." Rudolph Binion, *Frau Lou: Nietzsche's Wayward Disciple*, Princeton University Press, Princeton, N.J., 1968, p. 171.

GALA DALÍ

PAGE:

189 "I tried on . . ." Salvador Dalí, *The Secret Life of Salvador Dalí*, DASA Editions, S.A., 1986. Dial Press, New York, 1942, translated by Haakon M. Chevalier, p. 228.

190 "Caesar or nothing . . ." *Secret*, Dalí, p. 207.

190 "What else could I do . . ." Ibid., p. 227.

191 "Professional . . ." Ibid., p. 226.

191 "the rigor . . ." Ibid.

191 "a poet of the category . . ." Ibid.

192 "that slithering . . ." Jimmy Ernst, *A Not-So-Still-Life: A Memoir*, St. Martin's/Marek, New York, 1984, p. 19.

192 "You don't know . . ." Ibid.

193 "She was . . ." *Investigating Sex*, edited by Jose Pierre, Verso, London, 1994, p. 117.

193 "I should have liked . . ." *Secret*, Dalí, p. 228.

193 "Thus, I was ready . . ." Ibid., p. 229.

193 "Served as an infinitely svelte . . ." Ibid.

194 "a mere pathological . . . purity . . . honesty . . ." Ibid., p. 231.

194 "scatology . . ." Ibid.

194 "catastrophic . . ." Ibid.

195 "My little boy! . . ." Ibid., p. 233.

195 "I threw myself . . ." Ibid., pp. 14–15.

196 "how to dress . . ." Ibid., p. 317.

197 "It is mostly . . ." Ibid., p. 301.

198 "I was destined . . ." Ibid., p. 4.

198 "he had been impotent . . ." Brassai, *The Artists of My Life*, translated by Richard Miller, Viking Press, New York, 1982, p. 28.

198 "I would sometimes see . . ." *Secret*, Dalí, p. 125.

200 "I don't like . . ." Paul Eluard, *Letters to Gala*, Paragon House, New York, 1989, p. 35.

201 "This morning . . ." Ibid., p. 66.

202 "It's impossible . . ." *Vanity Fair*, December 1998, p. 192.

203 "Gala's fantasy . . ." *Secret*, Dalí, p. 246.

203 "my work . . ." Ibid., p. 250.

203 "The alcohol . . ." Ibid., p. 249.

204 "One maxim . . ." Ibid., p. 251.

205 "irrevocable . . ." Ibid., p. 253.

206 "The image . . ." *Shameful*, Gibson, pp. 348–49.

206 "The most ambitious . . ." *Secret*, Dalí, p. 251.

206 "Gala understood . . ." Tim McGirk, *Wicked Lady: Salvador Dalí's Muse*, Hutchinson, London, 1989, p. 62.

207 "This period has . . ." *Secret*, Dalí, p. 263.

208 "Gala is a true . . ." *Secret*, Dalí, p. 370.

208 "It is the duty . . ." *Shameful*, Gibson, p. 187.

209 "paranoiac critical . . ." Robert Descharnes, *The World of Salvador Dalí*, Viking Press, New York, 1968, p. 159.

211 "In 1936 . . ." *Secret*, Dalí, p. 20.

213 "emptied her . . ." *Wicked*, McGirk, p. 126.

214 "With an avid . . ." *Artists*, Brassai, p. 29.

216 "This is the press . . ." *World . . . Dalí*, Descharnes, p. 154.

218 "organizational powers . . ." Meryle Secrest, *Salvador Dalí*, Dutton, New York, 1987, p. 180.

220 "You may be . . ." *Wicked*, McGirk, p. 111.

220 "mean and petit . . ." Ibid., p. 112.

220 "morally and . . . She's got the idea . . ." *Letters to Gala*, Eluard, p. 267.

221 "predatory feline . . . involvement." *Not-So*, Ernst, pp. 152–53.

222 "Those who defend . . ." *Wicked*, McGirk, p. 130.

222 "The boy . . ." Ibid., p. 129.

223 "I am the source . . ." *Dalí*, Secrest, p. 207.

225 "The truth is . . ." *Shameful*, Gibson, p. 640.

225 "Dalí is an indestructible . . ." *Dalí*, Secrest, p. 241.

LEE MILLER

PAGE:

236 "The images . . ." Antony Penrose, *The Lives of Lee Miller*, Thames and Hudson, New York, 1989, p. 38.

237 "modeling sessions . . ." Ibid., p. 29.

238 "I had given up . . ." *Art in America*, Mario Amaya, May–June 1975, p. 55.

239 "He had an economy . . ." Ibid., p. 58.

239 "Man put . . ." Ibid., p. 60.

239 "Something crawled . . ." Ibid., p. 56.

240 "I had already . . ." Ibid., p. 55.

240 "I was dressed . . ." *Self-Portrait*, Man Ray, Bullfinch Press, Boston, 1998, p. 168.

241 "We must have used . . ." *Art in America,* May–June 1975, p. 59.

241 "I have loved . . ." *Lives*, Penrose, p. 38.

242 "With an eye . . ." Ibid., p. 40.

243 "A painter needs . . ." Arturo Schwarz, *Man Ray: The Rigour of Imagination*, Rizzoli, New York, 1977, p. 206.

243 "I had a metronome . . ." *Man Ray . . . Rigour*, Schwarz, p. 331.

244 "We had quarreled . . ." *Art in America,* May–June 1975, p. 56.

244 "Cut out the eye . . ." *Lives*, Penrose, p. 42.

246 "Lee is happy . . ." Ibid., p. 61.

247 "We appeared among an elegant . . ." Roland Penrose, *Scrapbook, 1900–1981*, Rizzoli, New York, 1981, p. 104.

248 "whose splendid . . ." Ibid., p. 106.

248 "For years . . ." Ibid., p. 118.

250 "Feeling like a soft-shelled . . ." *Lives*, Penrose, p. 108.

252 "Applying . . ." *Scrapbook, 1900–1981*, Penrose, p. 130.

252 "Apart from this brief taste . . ." Ibid., p. 132.

253 "I'm extremely irritable . . ." *Lee Miller's War*, edited by Antony Penrose, Bulfinch Press, Boston, 1992, p. 195.

253 "A bad burn case . . ." *Vogue*, September 15, 1944, p.138.

253 "one hundred operations . . ." Ibid., p. 139.

254 "Operating room . . ." Ibid., p. 141.

254 "the ingestion . . ." *Lee Miller's War*, Penrose, p. 11.

254 "Dearest . . ." Ibid., p. 47.

255 "I won't be the first woman . . ." Ibid., p. 65.

255 "the air is blown . . ." Ibid., p. 71.

255 "Somehow it was intended . . ." *Scrapbook, 1900–1981*, Penrose, p. 136.

256 "Germany is beautiful . . ." *Vogue*, June 1945, p. 102.

256 "the adrenalin . . ." *Vogue*, May 1945, p. 143.

256 "burned bones . . ."*Vogue*, June 1945, p. 103.

257 "orderly furnaces . . ." Ibid.

257 "This is Buchenwald . . ." *Vogue*, June 1945, p. 105.

258 "I was living in Hitler's . . ." *Lee Miller's War*, Penrose, p. 188.

259 "It was comfortable . . ." Ibid., p. 199.

259 "The war had disrupted . . ." *Scrapbook, 1900–1981*, Penrose, p. 138.

259 "gay little country . . ." *Vogue*, August 15, 1945.

259 "Who else can get in . . ." *Lives*, Penrose, p. 146.

259 "a new and disillusioning . . ." Ibid., p. 147.

260 "I was not attracted . . ." Ibid., p. 160.

260 "drawn towards a permanent . . ." Ibid., p. 174.

261 "People who knew or had heard . . ." Ibid., p. 176.

261 "The sense of freedom . . ." *Scrapbook, 1900–1981*, Penrose, p. 140.

261 "Physically, it's heavy . . ." *Lives*, Penrose, p. 182.

263 "By 1955 . . ." Ibid., p. 194.

263 "The sudden entry . . ." *Scrapbook, 1900–1981*, Penrose, p. 241.

264 "It means Never . . ." *Lives*, Penrose, p. 196.

264 "There is nothing wrong . . ." Ibid., p. 188.

265 "Lee's cuisine . . ." *Scrapbook, 1900–1981*, Penrose.

265 "Photography had been a passion . . ." Ibid., pp. 186–87.

265 "Those who knew her circumstances . . ." *Lives*, Penrose, p. 203.

266 "rapprochement." Ibid., p. 209.
267 "After her death . . ." *Lee Miller's War*, Penrose, p. 204.

CHARIS WESTON

PAGE:
273 "something of a fanatic . . ." Charis Wilson and Wendy Madar, *Through Another Lens, My Years With Edward Weston*, North Point Press, Farrar, Straus & Giroux, New York, 1998, p. x.
274 "My eyes keep . . ." Ibid., p. 3.
275 "the first important person . . ." Edward Weston, *Daybooks*, George Eastman House, 1961–66, December 29, 1925.
275 "She is invaluable . . ." Theodore E. Stebbins, Jr., Karen Quinn, and Leslie Furth, *Edward Weston: Photography and Modernism*, Boston: Museum of Fine Arts, Boston, in association with Bulfinch Press, Little, Brown and Co., 1999, p. 33.
275 "poor Flora." *Daybooks,* E. Weston, March 21, 1924.
275 "direct proximity . . ." *Edward Weston*, Stebbins, p. 55.
275 "see important forms . . ." Ibid., p. 56.
276 "Close up . . ." *Through Another . . .*, Wilson, p. 3.
276 "She was a small . . ." Ibid., p. 5.
276 "I felt as though . . ." Ibid., p. 6.
277 "When I agreed . . ." Ibid., p. 7.
277 "knowing perfectly well . . ." Ibid., p. 344.
277 "As I drove slowly . . ." Ibid., p. 9.
277 "You know I dislike . . ." *Edward Weston*, Stebbins, p. 14.
278 "the Mexican sun . . ." *Daybooks*, E. Weston, January 30, 1924.
278 "I have been photographing our toilet . . ." Ibid., October 21, 1925.
278 "Under cool reconsideration . . ." Ibid., November 13, 1925.
279 "our tastes . . ." *Through Another . . .*, Wilson, p. 11.
279 "I half-expected . . ." Ibid., p. 11.
279 "I realized that his reputation . . ." Ibid., p. 13.
279 "in the kind of social activity . . ." Ibid., p. 32.
281 "low self-esteem . . ." Ibid., p. 33.
281 "Meeting Edward changed . . ." Ibid.
281 "The pleasure he took . . ." Ibid., p. 44.
282 "Edward's view . . ." Ibid., p. 67.
282 "That he and I could spend . . ." Ibid., p. 66.

282 "When I knew him . . ." Ibid., p. 40.
283 "standing in the kitchen . . ." Ibid., p. 68.
283 "In the cooler . . ." Ibid., p. 216.
283 "a new series of nudes . . ." Ibid., p. 90.
284 "How sad when my only thought . . ." Ibid., p. 112.
284 "The fine, soft sand . . ." Ibid., p. 253.
285 "We sat together to draft . . ." Ibid., p. 107.
285 "eccentricity . . . to oust . . ." Ibid., p. 126.
285 "It seemed the practical thing . . ." Ibid., p. 206.
286 "Ever since the first party . . ." Ibid., p. 151.
286 "Edward hadn't heard . . ." Ibid., p. 152.
286 "With a picnic tomorrow . . ." Ibid., p. 217.
286 "My eyes would need . . ." Ibid., pp. 83.
286 "I avoided . . ." Ibid., pp. 95–96.
287 "Even if I had been strongly tempted . . ." Ibid., p. 87.
287 "Particularly disconcerting . . ." Ibid., p. 88.
288 "My refusal of Edward's offers . . ." Ibid., p. 275.
288 "My goal . . ." Ibid., p. 192.
288 "He thought . . ." Ibid., pp. 293–94.
290 "last regular entry . . ." Ibid., p. xix.
290 "tall, beautiful girl . . ." *Daybooks*, E. Weston, December 9, 1934.
290 "I left . . ." Ibid.
290 "The first nudes . . ." Ibid.
290 "I felt like one . . ." *Through Another . . .*, pp. 203–4.
291 "Edward didn't want . . ." Ibid., p. 122.
291 "the success . . ." Ibid., p. 226.
291 "I was about to remind . . ." Ibid., p. 255.
291 "Edward often mentioned . . ." Ibid., p. 324.
292 "Ten years ago . . ." *Daybooks*, E. Weston, April 22, 1944.
293 "as overwhelming . . ." *Through Another . . .*, Wilson, p. 344.
293 "became active . . ." Ibid., p. 352.
294 "His eloquent eyes . . ." Ibid., p. 359.
294 "My awareness of the world . . ." Ibid., p. xi.
294 "my refuge . . . about to be banished . . ." Ibid., p. 343.
296 "She was not amused . . ." Ibid., pp. 332–33.
296 "So I am not exactly surprised . . ." *Edward Weston*, Stebbins, pp. 101–2.

SUZANNE FARRELL

PAGE:

300   "We know . . ." "Is the Muse Dead?" Arlene Croce, *The New Yorker*, February 26–March 4, 1996, p. 166.

300   "I was called . . ." Suzanne Farrell with Toni Bentley, *Holding On to the Air*, Summit Books, New York, 1990, p. 103.

300   "He saw her . . ." transcribed from *Suzanne Farrell, Elusive Muse*, Video, directed by Anne Belle and Deborah Dickson, distributed by Winstar.

302   "one of the great . . ." Ibid.

303   "Cincinnati . . . I told her . . ." Ibid.

304   "I wanted the company . . ." *Holding*, Farrell, p. 27.

304   "Dear Diary . . ." transcribed from *Suzanne Farrell, Elusive Muse*, Video.

305   "Big fish . . ." *Holding*, Farrell, p. 34.

305   "a domino . . ." Ibid.

305   "I just . . ." transcribed from *Suzanne Farrell, Elusive Muse*, Video.

305   "confused . . ." Ibid.

305   "in terms of health . . ." Bernard Taper, *Balanchine*, Times Books, New York, 1984, p. 35.

306   "I don't know . . . I've decided . . ." transcribed from *Suzanne Farrell, Elusive Muse*, Video.

307   "Mr. B.'s . . ." *Holding*, Farrell, p. 78.

307   "Then a wonderful thing . . ." transcribed from *Suzanne Farrell, Elusive Muse*, Video.

308   "Igor . . ." Ibid.

308   "It's all in the programs . . ." *Balanchine*, Taper, p. 324.

309   "I remember very well . . ." transcribed from *Suzanne Farrell, Elusive Muse*, Video.

309   "I think how you dance . . ." Ibid.

309   "You just hold . . . You're riding . . ." *Holding*, Farrell, p. 13.

309   "The stage is dark . . ." Ibid., p. 9.

310   "She was astonished . . ." *Balanchine*, Taper, p. 215.

311   "Through langour . . . light to lift," *Holding*, Farrell, p. 12.

311   "Over time . . ." Ibid., p. 15.

311   "There's something really daunting . . ." transcribed from *Suzanne Farrell, Elusive Muse*, Video.

312   "We danced entirely for each other . . ." *Holding*, Farrell, p. 115.

312 "we broke one rule after another . . ." Ibid., p. 110.

313 "It was as if our lives . . ." transcribed from *Suzanne Farrell, Elusive Muse,* Video.

314 "I'm sure . . ." Ibid.

314 "When he was dancing . . ." Ibid.

314 "He was in the habit . . ." Ibid.

314 "There was that list . . ." Ibid.

315 "Many of his works . . ." Ibid.

315 "Woman is the goddess . . ." *Holding,* Farrell, p. 115.

315 "Each new epoch . . ." *Balanchine,* Taper, pp. 212–13.

316 "That Balanchine spent his life . . ." *Holding,* Farrell, p. 163.

316 "to try and put a little distance . . ." Ibid., p. 171.

316 "This was made most apparent . . ." Ibid., Farrell, p. 171.

317 "I loved Balanchine . . ." Ibid.

317 "Because I couldn't give . . ." transcribed from *Suzanne Farrell, Elusive Muse,* Video.

317 "The physical side . . ." Ibid.

317 "The age difference . . ." Ibid.

318 "Curious as it may sound . . ." *Holding,* Farrell, p. 182.

319 "way too early . . . tonight . . ." transcribed from *Suzanne Farrell, Elusive Muse,* Video.

320 "Dear George . . ." Holding , Farrell, p. 213.

321 "He was sweet . . ." transcribed from *Suzanne Farrell, Elusive Muse,* Video.

321 "there was no place . . ." Ibid.

322 "Finally, he suggested . . ." *Holding,* Farrell, p. 226.

322 "At each performance . . ." Ibid., p. 237.

323 "I knew the surest way . . ." Ibid., p. 240.

323 "Our conversation that night . . ." Ibid., p. 242.

324 "I was getting older . . ." transcribed from *Suzanne Farrell, Elusive Muse,* Video.

324 "I was walking on the vibrating . . ." *Holding,* Farrell, p. 252.

324 "He had not just made a ballet . . ." Ibid., p. 256.

325 "never again be understood . . ." Ibid., p. 265.

325 "I was looking out . . ." Ibid., p. 267.

325 "After it passed . . ." transcribed from *Suzanne Farrell, Elusive Muse,* Video.

325 "The trumpets . . ." Ibid.

326 "My whole existence . . . physically . . ." Ibid.

326 "I almost feel like . . ." Ibid.

YOKO ONO

PAGE:

329   "Only when a woman . . ." Jon Wiener, *Come Together, John Lennon in His Time*, University of Illinois Press, Urbana and Chicago, 1991, p. 184.

331   "But there was another piece . . ." Jann S. Wenner, *Lennon Remembers*, Verso, New York, 2000, p. 38.

331   "She'd only heard . . ." Ibid.

331   "John Dunbar . . ." Ibid.

331   "Yoko was a . . ." Carolee Schneeman, unpublished interview by author.

332   "Why not have . . ." Yoko Ono, *Yes*, Japan Society, New York, and Harry N. Abrams, 2000, p. 286.

332   "Max Ernst is . . ." Ibid., p. 287.

333   "The whole avant-garde . . ." Ibid., p. 26.

333   "Let a vine . . ." Ibid., pp. 79–80.

333   "So I just went . . ." *Lennon Remembers*, Wenner, p. 38.

334   "That 'YES' . . ." *Yes*, Ono, p. 100.

334   "When Hammer a Nail . . ." Ibid., p. 104.

334   "That's when we really met . . ." Ibid., p. 31.

334   "Imagine two cars . . ." Ray Coleman, *Lennon*, McGraw-Hill, New York, 1984, p. 328.

335   "Dance . . ." *Lennon Remembers*, Wenner, p. 39.

335   "Hide . . ." Yoko Ono, *Grapefruit*.

335   "I'm a cloud . . ." *Lennon*, Coleman, p. 341.

335   "And I said to her, Why don't you sell . . ." *Lennon Remembers*, Wenner, p. 39.

336   "me in drag." *Come*, Wiener, p. 59.

338   "I admire Fluxus . . ." *Lennon Remembers*, Wenner, pp. 139–40.

339   "It's no fun . . ." Ibid., p. 106.

339   "Drugs . . ." *Come*, Wiener, p. 145.

340   "I started from the Mother . . ." Editors of *Rolling Stone, The Ballad of John and Yoko*, Dolphin Books, Doubleday, New York, 1982, p. xix.

341   "We're all responsible . . ." Ibid., p. 57.

341   "Peace . . ." Ibid., pp. 68–69.

342   "If I was a Jewish girl . . ." *Come*, Wiener, p. 94.

342   "Working people . . ." Geoffrey and Brenda Giuliano, *The Lost Lennon Interviews*, Adams Media Corp., Holbrook, Mass., 1996, p. 51.

342 "There must be a line . . ." Ibid., pp. 118-19.

342 "Before meeting John . . ." *Yes*, Ono, p. 37.

343 "In England . . ." *Lennon*, Coleman, p. 615.

343 "In New York . . ." Ibid., p. 467.

343 "I did rhythm and booze . . ." Ibid., p. 466.

343 "When the exhibition opened . . ." *Yes*, Ono, p. 57.

344 "I don't think the poor bastard . . ." *Lennon Remembers*, Wenner, p. 139.

344 "But in general . . ." Ibid., p. 143.

344 "Ike Turner . . ." *Ballad of John*, p. 188.

345 "I learned everything . . ." Ibid., p. xviii.

345 "He was definitely . . ." *Come*, Wiener, p. 34.

345 "There is no reason . . ." *Lennon Remembers*, Wenner, p. 41.

345 "Whatever happened to us . . ." British Broadcasting Corporation, *The Lennon Tapes*, BBC, London, 1981, p. 59.

345 "She has a musical . . ." *Lennon Remembers*, Wenner, p. 5.

346 "What do you mean . . ." transcribed from Video of *Gimme Some Truth: The Making of John Lennon's Imagine Album*, directed by Yoko Ono and Andrew Salt, 2000.

348 "How can they be about you . . ." Ibid.

348 "She's so Heavy . . ." *Lennon Remembers*, Wenner, p. 83.

348 " 'Woman' came about . . ." *Ballad of John*, p. 189.

348 "actually that should be credited . . ." *Lennon Tapes*, p. 43.

349 "When he was alive . . ." Giuliano, *Lost Lennon*, p. 165.

349 "Yoko and I have clashed . . ." *Ballad of John*, p. 115.

350 "This is a Beatles wife . . ." transcribed from Video of *Gimme Some Truth*.

351 "John looked to her as a sorceress . . ." *Ballad of John*, p. 168.

352 "I'm the one who's supposed to know . . ." *Lennon*, Coleman, p. 514.

352 "And somebody said . . ." *Ballad of John*, p. 150.

352 "Oh, oh like the . . ." *Lennon Tapes*, p. 64.

352 "Here's a hard one . . ." *Lennon*, Coleman, p. 517.

352 "I've carried . . ." Ibid., pp. 521–22.

353 "When John and I decided . . ." Ibid., p. 526.

353 "inverted snobbery . . . enjoy the . . ." Ibid., p. 531.

353 "We tried to reverse the trap . . ." Ibid., p. 530.

354 "It was great . . ." *Lennon Tapes*, p. 59.

355 "I learned to make bread . . ." *Come*, Wiener, p. 287.

355 "I'm really pleased . . ." *Ballad of John*, p. 187.

355 "And we went through sort of paradoxical feeling . . ." *Lennon Tapes*, p. 59.

355 "My joy is when . . ." Ibid., pp. 59–60.

356 "It's the first time . . ." *Ballad of John*, p. 187.

356 "To me, it was like going back . . ." *Lost Lennon*, Giuliano, p. 142.

357 "Kiss Kiss Kiss . . ." Ibid., p. 143.

358 "John: Tell them how . . ." Ibid.

359 " 'Kiss Kiss Kiss' is what it is . . ." Ibid., p. 144.

359 "When John sang . . ." *Come*, Wiener, p. 300.

359 "Starting Over was certainly designed . . ." *Lost Lennon*, Giuliano, p. 208.

360 "Whenever I do something . . ." Ibid., p. 165.

361 "one of the most original artists . . . So how are we . . . ?" Arthur C. Danto, *The Nation*, December 18, 2000, pp. 34–36.

363 "we do not know . . ." Ibid.

363 "Ono's voice . . ." *Yes*, Ono, p. 32.

365 "the preoccupations . . ." Ibid., p. 54.

365 "I would hear his guitar . . ." Ibid., p. 235.

365 "Ono was hurt . . ." Ibid., p. 237.

365 "She's a woman . . ." *Lennon Remembers*, p. 143.

366 "The world looked on me . . ." *Come*, Wiener, p. 319.

366 "referred to 'sloe-eyed' . . ." Ibid.

BIBLIOGRAPHY

BOOKS

Andreas-Salomé, Lou. *The Freud Journal,* translated by Stanley A. Leavy. New York: Basic Books, 1964.

———. *Looking Back, Memoirs,* translated by Breon Mitchell. New York: Marlowe & Company, 1995.

Baldwin, Neil. *Man Ray, American Artist.* New York: Da Capo Press, 1988.

Belford, Barbara. *Violet Hunt.* New York: Simon & Schuster, 1990.

Binion, Rudolph. *Frau Lou: Nietzsche's Wayward Disciple.* Princeton, N.J.: Princeton University Press, 1968.

Brassai. *The Artists of My Life,* translated by Richard Miller. New York: Viking Press, 1982.

British Broadcasting Corporation. *The Lennon Tapes.* London: BBC, 1981.

Brown, Ford Madox. *The Diary of Ford Madox Brown,* edited by Virginia Surtees. New Haven: Yale University Press, 1981.

Carroll, Lewis. *Alice's Adventures in Wonderland* and *Through the Looking Glass.* New York: Penguin Books, 1998.

_____. *The Diaries of Lewis Carroll*, edited by Roger Lancelyn Green. New York: Oxford University Press, 1954.

Clark, Anne. *The Real Alice: Lewis Carroll's Dream Child*. New York: Stein & Day, 1981.

Clifford, James L. *Hester Lynch Piozzi (Mrs. Thrale)*. New York: Columbia University Press, 1987.

Cohen, Morton. M. *Lewis Carroll, A Biography*. New York: Alfred A. Knopf, 1995.

Cohen, Morton M., ed. *The Selected Letters of Lewis Carroll*. London: Macmillan, 1982.

Coleman, Ray. *Lennon*. New York: McGraw-Hill, 1984.

Collingwood, Stuart Dodgson. *The Life and Letters of Lewis Carroll*. London: T. F. Unwin, 1898.

Daly, Gay. *Pre-Raphaelites in Love*. London: Collins, 1989.

Dinesen, Isak. *Out of Africa*. Random House, 1938.

Dalí, Salvador. *The Secret Life of Salvador Dalí*, translated by Haakon M. Chevalier. Dial Press, New York: 1942; DASA Editions, S.A. 1986.

Dante Alighieri. *The Portable Dante*, edited by Mark Musa. New York: Penguin, 1995.

Descharnes, Robert. *The World of Salvador Dalí*. New York: Viking Press, 1968.

Dobbs, Brian, and Judy Dobbs. *Dante Gabriel Rossetti: An Alien Victorian*. London: MacDonald and Jane's, 1977.

Doughty, Oswald, *Dante Gabriel Rossetti: Victorian Romantic*. New Haven, Conn.: Yale University Press, 1949.

Editors of *Rolling Stone, The Ballad of John and Yoko*. New York: Dolphin Books/Doubleday & Co. Inc., 1982.

Eluard, Paul. *Letters to Gala*. New York: Paragon House, 1989.

Engen, Rodney. *Kate Greenaway: A Biography*. New York: Schocken Books, 1981.

Ernst, Jimmy. *A Not-So-Still-Life: A Memoir*. New York: St. Martin's/Marek, 1984.

Farrell, Suzanne, with Toni Bentley. *Holding On to the Air*. New York: Summit Books, 1990.

Freedman, Ralph. *Life of a Poet: Rainer Maria Rilke*. New York: Farrar, Straus & Giroux, 1996.

Gabrial, Jan. *Inside the Volcano, My Life with Malcolm Lowry*. New York: St. Martin's Press, 2000.

Gibson, Ian. *The Shameful Life of Salvador Dalí*. New York: W.W. Norton and Co., 1998.

Gilson, Etienne. *A Choir of Muses*, translated by Maisie Ward. New York: Sheed and Ward, 1953.

Giuliano, Geoffrey, and Brenda Giuliano. *The Lost Lennon Interviews*. Holbrook, Mass.: Adams Media Corp., 1996.

Gold, Arthur, and Robert Fizdale. *Misia, The Life of Misia Sert*. New York: Alfred A. Knopf, 1980.

Goldman, Albert. *The Lives of John Lennon*. Bantam Press, London, 1988.

Graves, Robert. *The White Goddess: A Historical Grammar of Poetic Myth*. Noonday Press/Farrar, Straus & Giroux, 1997.

Hayman, Ronald. *Nietzsche: A Critical Life*. London: Weidenfeld and Nicolson, 1980.

Hesiod. *The Works of Hesiod, Callimachus, and Theognis*, translated by Rev. J. Banks. London: Henry G. Bohn, 1856.

Hibbert, Christopher. *The Personal History of Samuel Johnson*. New York: Harper & Row, 1971.

Hill, G. B., ed. *Johnsonian Miscellanies*. Oxford, England: 1897.

Holthusen, Hans Egon. *Portrait of Rilke: An Illustrated Biography*, translated by W. H. Hargreaves. New York: Herder and Herder, 1971.

Hyde, Mary. *The Thrales of Streatham Park*. Cambridge, Mass.: Harvard University Press, 1977.

Johnson, Samuel. *Johnsoniana*. London: Carey and Hart, 1842.

Lennon, Florence Becker. *Victoria Through the Looking Glass*. New York: Simon & Schuster, 1945.

Livingstone, Angela. *Salomé, Her Life and Work*. Mt. Kisco, N. Y.: Moyer Bell Limited, 1984.

Marsh, Jan. *The Legend of Elizabeth Siddal*. London: Quarter Books, 1989.

McGirk, Tim. *Wicked Lady: Salvador Dalí's Muse*. London: Hutchinson, 1989.

Nietzsche, Friedrich. *The Selected Letters of Friedrich Nietzsche*, edited and translated by Christopher Middleton. Chicago: University of Chicago Press, 1969.

Nietzsche, Friedrich. *Thus Spake Zarathustra*, translated by R.J. Hollingdale. New York: Penguin Classics, 1969.

Ono, Yoko. *Yes*. New York: Japan Society, and Harry N. Abrams, Inc., 2000.

———.*Grapefruit: A Book of Instructions and Drawings*. New York: Simon & Schuster, 2000.

Penrose, Antony, ed. *Lee Miller's War*. Boston: Bulfinch Press, 1992.

Penrose, Antony. *The Lives of Lee Miller*. New York: Thames & Hudson, 1989.

Penrose, Roland. *Scrapbook, 1900–1981*. New York: Rizzoli, 1981.

Peters, H. F. *My Sister, My Spouse: A Biography of Lou Andreas-Salomé*. New York: W.W. Norton & Co., 1962.

Petrarch, Francesco. *Petrarch's Songbooks*, verse translation by James Wyatt Cook. Binghamton, N.Y.: Pegasus Paperbacks, 1996.

Pfeiffer, Ernst, ed. *Sigmund Freud and Lou Andreas-Salomé, Letters*. New York: W.W. Norton & Co., 1985.

Pierre, Jose, ed. *Investigating Sex*. London: Verso, 1994.

Ray, Man. *Self-Portrait*. Boston: Bulfinch Press, 1998.

Rilke, Rainer Maria. *Diaries of a Young Poet*, translated by Edward Snow and Michael Winkler. New York: W.W. Norton & Co., 1997.

_____. *The Lay of the Love and Death of Cornet Christopher Rilke*, translated by M. D. Herter. New York: W.W. Norton & Co., 1932.

_____. *Letters of Rainer Maria Rilke, 1892–1910*, translated by Jane Bonnard Greene and M. D. Herter. New York: W.W. Norton & Co., 1945.

_____. *The Sonnets to Orpheus*, translated by Stephen Mitchell. New York: Simon & Schuster, 1985.

_____. *Uncollected Poems*, translated by Edward Snow. New York: Farrar, Straus & Giroux, 1996.

Rogers, Pat, ed. *Johnson and Boswell in Scotland, A Journey to the Hebrides*. New Haven: Yale University Press, 1993.

Rossetti, Dante Gabriel. *Letters*, edited by Oswald Doughty and John Robert Wahl. Oxford: Clarendon Press, 1965–67.

_____. *His Family—Letters with a Memoir by William Michael Rossetti*. London: Ellis and Elvery, 1895.

_____. *The Collected Works of Dante Gabriel Rossetti*, edited by William M. Rossetti. London: Ellis and Elvery, 1897.

Ruskin, John. *Praeterita*. London: Rupert-Hart Davis, 1949.

Salomé, Lou. *Nietzche*, translated and edited by Siegfried Mandel. Chicago: University of Illinois Press, 2001.

Schwarz, Arturo. *Man Ray: The Rigour of Imagination*. New York: Rizzoli, 1977.

Seeley, L. B. *Mrs. Thrale, Afterwards Mrs. Piozzi*. New York: Scribner and Welford, 1891.

Secrest, Meryle. *Salvador Dalí*. New York: E.P. Dutton, 1987.

Siddal, Elizabeth. *Poems and Drawings of Elizabeth Siddal*, edited by Roger C. Lewis and Mark Samuels Lasner. Wolfville, Nova Scotia: Wombat Press, 1978.

Stebbins, Theodore E., Jr., Karen Quinn, and Leslie Furth. *Edward Weston: Photography and Modernism*. Boston: Museum of Fine Arts, in association with Bulfinch Press, Little, Brown & Co., 1999.

Taper, Bernard. *Balanchine*. New York: Times Books, 1984.

Troxell, Janet Camp, ed. *Three Rossettis: Unpublished letters to and from Dante Gabriel, Christina, William*. Cambridge, Mass.: Harvard University Press, 1937.

Wain, John. *Samuel Johnson*. New York: Viking Press, 1974.

Warner, William Beatty. *Chance and the Text of Experience : Freud, Nietzsche, and Shakespeare's Hamlet*. Ithaca, N.Y.: Cornell University Press, 1986.

Waugh, Evelyn. *Rossetti: His Life and Works*. London: Norwood, 1976.

Weintraub, Stanley. *Four Rossettis*. New York: Weybright and Talley, 1977.

Wenner, Jann S. *Lennon Remembers*. New York: Verso, 2000.

Weston, Edward. *Daybooks*. Rochester, N.Y.: George Eastman House, 1961–66.

Wiener, Jon. *Come Together, John Lennon in His Time*. Urbana and Chicago: University of Illinois Press, 1991.

Wilson, Charis, Wendy Madar. *Through Another Lens: My Years with Edward Weston*. New York: North Point Press, Farrar, Straus & Giroux, 1998.

Young-Breuhl, Elisabeth. *Anna Freud*. New York: Summit Books, 1988.

PERIODICALS

Amaya, Mario. "My Man Ray: An Interview with Lee Miller Penrose." *Art in America*. May–June 1975.

Croce, Arlene. "Is the Muse Dead?" *The New Yorker*, February 24–March 6, 1996.

Miller, Lee. "USA Tent Hospital in France," *Vogue*, September 15, 1944.

――――. "Out of the German Prison," *Vogue*, May 1945.

――――. "Half-Way to Victory," *Vogue*, June 1945.

――――. "Germans Are Like This," *Vogue*, June 1945.

――――. "Believe It," *Vogue*, June 1945.

Danto, Arthur C. *The Nation*, "Life in Fluxus." December 18, 2000.

Hargreaves, Caryl. "Alice's Recollections of Carrollinian Days, as Told to her Son," *Cornhill Magazine*, July 1932.

Liddell, Alice. "The Lewis Carroll That Alice Recalls," *New York Times*, May 1, 1932.

VIDEOS

Ono, Yoko, and Andrew Salt, directors, EMI, *Gimme Some Truth: The Making of John Lennon's Imagine Album.* EMI/Capitol Records, DVD release 2000.

Belle, Anne, and Deborah Dickson, directors, *Suzanne Farrell, Elusive Muse.* Wellspring Media, theatrical release 1990, DVD release 2001.

INDEX

Page numbers in *italics* refer to illustrations.

Abbey Road (Beatles), 348
Abridged Dictionary of Surrealism (Eluard and Breton), 213
Accommodations of Desire (Dalí), 203
Adams, Ansel, 277, 286
Adams, Diana, 305
Adler, Alfred, 173–75
After Dark, 320
Agape, 4–5
Albert Edward, Prince of Wales (later Edward VII), 79–80, 81
Alethea (Cameron), 91
Alexandra, Princess of Wales, 79–80, 81
"Alice on the Stage" (Dodgson), 62
Alice's Adventures in Wonderland (Carroll), 1, 59, 62, 79, 83, 84, 85, 87, 96–98, 243
origins of, 61–64
poetic preface to, 60
Alice's Adventures Underground (Carroll), 63–64, 93
Allingham, William, 113, 123, 128
All Year Round, 78
Amaya, Mario, 238, 266
"Amaze" (Ono), 363–64
Andalusian Dog, The (Buñuel/Dalí), 189

Andreas, Friedrich Carl, 139, 145, 155–58, 162, 163, 168, 176, 183
Andreas-Salomé, Lou, 16, 18–22, 137–85, *138*, *146*, 196, 201, 207, 271, 273, 280, 283, 287, 292, 360, 372–73
Andreas's marital relationship with, 155–58
feminist views of, 142
Freud's friendship with, 7, 11, 139–43, 171–82, 231
in journey to Russia, 162–66
Lucerne photograph of, 143, *146*, 147–48, 149, 154, 162
Nietzsche's friendship with, *see* Nietzsche, Friedrich Wilhelm
Rée's friendship with, 143–47, *146*, 149, 150–53, 155–56, 161–62, 175–76, 179, 182–83
Rilke's friendship with, *see* Rilke, Rainier Maria
traits and beliefs of, 140–42, 144, 148, 149, 177–78, 183
writings of, 141, 148, 151, 155, 156, 157, 158–59, 163, 165, 178, 181, 332

Anecdotes of the Late Samuel Johnson (Thrale), 28, 32, 33, 50–52
Angelus of Gala, The (Dalí), 209
Ansonia Hotel, 305
Apfel, Alice, 199
Apollo, 3, 4
Apotheosis of the Dollars (Dalí), 210
Aragon, Louis, 192
Art in America, 266
Artists of My Life, The (Brassaï), 214
art wives, 272, 277, 314
Atget, Eugène, 276
Athena, 4
Auden, W. H., 10
Awakening Conscience, The (Hunt), 105, 116, 119

Baiser, Le (Magritte), 246
Balanchine, George, 9, 17, 18, 19, 21, 299–326, *307,* 349
   ballets of, 17, 22, 243, 300–303, 306–13, 317–26
   Farrell as unattainable muse of, 312–16, 321, 324
   Farrell fired by, 319–20
Ballet du XXème Siècle, 320
Ballet Russe de Monte Carlo, 306
Balzac, Honoré de, 13
Bardossy, Laszlo, 260
Barney, Natalie, 10
Beata Beatrix (Rossetti), 107, *134,* 135
Beatles, 20, 331, 334–37, 339–42, 346, 350, 361
Beatrice, 5–7, 14, 17, 21, 61, 103, 104, 134–36, 154, 198, 271, 282, 299, 329
Beatrice Meeting Dante at a Marriage Feast, Denies Him Her Salutation (Rossetti), 107
Becker, Paula, 167
"Bed-Ins for Peace" (Lennon/Ono), 364
Beethoven, Ludwig van, 339
Béjart, Maurice, 320, 322
Belle, Anne, 309
Beloved, The (Rossetti), 136
Benet, William Rose, 280
Bernays, Paul, 179
Berry, Chuck, 338
Beuret, Rose, 16, 272
Bey, Aziz Eloui, 242, 245–46, 248, 262, 265
Bey, Nimet, 242

Beyond Good and Evil (Nietzsche), 153
Bice, 6
Biederman, Alois, 149
Binion, Rudolph, 14, 185
Birkin, Jane, 358
Bjerre, Poul, 172, 183
Black Sun, 215
Blakemore, Edith, 69
Bleeding Roses, The (Dalí), 210
Blixen, Karen (Isak Dinesen), 10–12
Blondie, 357
Blood of a Poet, The (Cocteau), 236, 241
"Blue Stocking Circle," 43, 54
Bocca Baciata (Rossetti), 120, 127
Bodman, Emanuel von, 168
Boethius, 35
Bonnard, Marthe, 18
Bonnard, Pierre, 18
Book of Hours, The (Rilke), 166
Boswell, James, 31, 36–38, 40, 45, 48, 53
Boule de Neige (Ray), 238
Bow, Clara, 234
Bowles, Paul, 13, 221
Bowman, Emma (Emsie), 94
Bowman, Isa, 94–95, 371
Brassaï (Gyula Halész), 198, 213–14, 215
Braun, Eva, 259
Brenner, Anita, 278
Breton, André, 192–93, 211, 213, 217
British Synonymy (Thrale), 54
Brockhurst Gallery, 286
Brooklyn Museum, 197
Brooks, Albert, 8
Brooks, Louise, 234
Brooks, Romaine, 10
Brown, Emma, 115–16, 120
Brown, Ford Madox, 106, 107, 108, 111–12, 113, 115, 119, 123, 129
Buchenwald, 230, 257–58
Bulow, Frieda von, 159
Buñuel, Luis, 189, 198, 204–5, 208, 219–20
   works of, 189, 208
Burch, Irene, 83
Burne-Jones, Edward, 105, 117, 129, 131
Burne-Jones, Georgiana, 119, 127
Burney, Dr. Charles, 43
Burney, Fanny, 36, 40, 43, 46, 49
Butler, Nicholas Murray, 1, 369–70

Cadell, Thomas, 50
Cadmus, 3
Cage, John, 332
California and the West (Western), 291
Calliope, 3, 5, 289
Cameron, Julia Margaret, 90–91, 262
    photo portraits by, 91
Canzoniere (Petrarch), 14
Carmel, Calif., 276, 277, 295
Carrington, Leonora, 248
Carroll, Lewis, *see* Dodgson, Charles
Cassavetes, Zoe, 13
Cavett, Dick, 320
Chaconne; Union Jack (Balanchine), 322, 326
Chandler, Flora May, 275, 285
Chanel, Coco, 215, 218
Charis Weston (Weston), 274
Charlotte, Mary, 74
Chataway, Gertrude, 70
Chicago Sun-Times, 314, 316
Chien Andalou, Un (Buñuel/Dalí), 189
Chirico, Giorgio de, 193
Choir of Muses, A (Gilson), 15
Christianity, 4–5
Cincinnati Conservatory of Music, 304
Civilian Defense (Weston), 294
Claudel, Camille, 16, 272
"Clean Up Time" (Lennon), 359
Cleaver, Eldridge, 341
Clio, 3, 229, 289
Clown (Nauman), 363
Cocteau, Jean, 236, 241, 255
Cohen, Morton, 83
Condé Nast Publications, 261
Cooke, Helen, 280
Cornell, Joseph, 245
Cornforth, Fanny (Sarah Cox), 118–20,
    123–24, 131, 133, 135, 136, 289
Cornhill, 64
Corpus Hypercubus (Dalí), 210
"Cough Piece" (Ono), 362
courtly love, 5
Cox, Kyoto, 333, 343, 351
Cox, Tony, 332–33, 343, 351
creativity, 5
    and Eros, 10, 23
    experience of, 2–3
Crick, Francis, 223
Crime and Punishment (Dostoevsky), 62

Croce, Arlene, 8–9, 300, 302, 373
Crosby, Caresse, 215–16, 218
Crosby, Harry, 215
Crucifixion, 5
Cunningham, Merce, 332
"Cut Piece" (Ono), 362

Dachau, 257–58
Dada, 331
Dalí, Ana Maria, 197, 205
Dalí, Gala, 5, 7–8, 10, 16, 20, 22,
    187–226, *188*, 271, 280–82, 286,
    372–73
    editorial help given by, 203
    illness of, 210–11, 213, 225
    social celebrity of, 196–97, 207,
        214–18, 223
Dalí, Salvador, 5, 10, 20, 22, 187–226, *188*,
    244, 281–82
    early life of, 197–99
    eccentricities of, 190–91, 193, 195, 207,
        211–12, 216, 223–24
    memoir of, 189
    paintings of, 194, 200, 203, 207, 208,
        209–10, 219
    scatological obsession of, 191, 194–95
    sexuality of, 198, 202
    social celebrity of, 196–97, 207,
        214–18, 223
    in war era, 218
Daly, Gay, 129
d'Amboise, Jacques, 300, 302, 304,
    306–7, 315, 321, 324
"Dance of the Happy Shades, The" (Bal-
    anchine), 326
Dancing for Mr. B., 301, 303
Dante Alighieri, 5–7, 14, 17, 21, 61, 103,
    104, 106, 134–35, 282, 329
Dante Drawing an Angel (Rossetti), 107
*Dante's Dream at the Time of the Death of Beat-
    rice* (Rossetti), 107, 116
"Dantis Tenebrae" (Rossetti), 103
Danto, Arthur C., 361
Davidsbündlertänze (Balanchine), 323–24
Davis, Miles, 347
Daybooks (Weston), 275, 278, 287–90,
    292, 296
Déjeuner sur l'Herbe (Manet), 294
Delacroix, Eugène, 13

de la Falaise, Loulou, 13
Delap, John, 29
Deriaz, Diane, 263–64
desire, creativity and, 17
Deverell, Walter, 105, 106, 108, 111
Diaghilev, Sergey, 10, 306
Diakonovna, Helena Deluvina, *see* Dalí,
    Gala
Diamond, Hugh, 86
Dickens, Charles, 78
Dickson, Deborah, 309
Dictionary of the English Language, A (John-
    son), 27
Dinesen, Isak (Karen Blixen), 10–12
*Discovery of America by Christopher Columbus,
    The* (Dalí), 209–10
Disney, Walt, 218
Divina Commedia (Dante), 17, 103
Dodgson, Charles (Lewis Carroll), 10, 11,
    12, 17, 18, 19, 21, 59–98, 101, 114, 146,
    154, 161, 196, 207, 369–71, 374
    Alice as unconsummated passion of, 68
    child-friends of, 69–73, 78–79, 83–84,
        93–96, 371
    Mrs. Liddell and, 76–78, 81–82,
        86–87
    nude child subjects of, 71–72
    photographs by, 18, 66–68, 77–78, 79,
        86
    poems of, 60, 74, 78, 80, 84
    prose works of, 1, 59, 62, 63, 77, 79, 84,
        87, 90, 91, 93, 243
    see also Alice's Adventures in Wonderland
Dodgson, Edwin, 79
Dodgson, Mary, 71
Dodgson, Wilfred, 79, 82
Donkin, Alice, 78–79, 82
Don Quixote (Balanchine), 22, 300–304,
    308–13, 317, 325
Don Quixote (Cervantes), 33
Double Fantasy (Lennon/Ono), 348,
    355–60, 365
Doughty, Oswald, 107
Drozhzhin, Spiridon, 162, 164
Dubuffet, Jean, 262, 266
Duchamp, Marcel, 233, 331–32, 336,
    338–39
Duckworth, Robinson, 61, 63
Duino Elegies (Rilke), 170

Dunbar, John, 331–32
Dylan, Bob, 340

Echo, 4
Ecumenical Council, The (Dalí), 210
Edward Weston Print of the Month
    Club, 286
Eliot, T. S., 289
Elle, 225
Elopement (Dodgson), 79
Eluard, Cecile, 189, 192, 200, 204,
    219–20, 225, 372
Eluard, Paul, 189, 191–94, 199–204, 208,
    210, 213, 220, 247–48, 255, 372
    writings of, 201
"Epithalamium" (Boswell), 45
Erato, 3, 289
Ernst, Jimmy, 221–22
Ernst, Max, 192–93, 200, 247–48, 261,
    332
Eros, 18, 140, 148, 367, 374
    Agape vs., 4–5
    creativity and, 10, 23
Esquire, 365
Euterpe, 3
Evans, Walker, 276
Everson Museum, 343

"Faces in the Fire" (Dodgson), 78
Fair Rosamund (Rossetti), 126
Farley Farm, 262–63, 266
Farrell, Suzanne, 9, 16, 17, 18, 21, 22, 139,
    297–326, 307, 349, 360, 372
    Balanchine's artistic collaboration
        with, 301–3, 308–12, 314, 317,
        321–22
    Balanchine's firing of, 319–20
Faucigny-Lucinge, Prince, 214, 215, 220
Federal Art project, 282
Fellini, Federico, 222
Fellowes, James, 56
feminism, feminists:
    Andreas-Salomé and, 141–42
    Balanchine and, 302, 316
    Lennon and, 330
    musedom as viewed by, 8–9, 299–300
Fenholt, Jeff, 223–24
Ficker, Robert, 303
Fillmore East, 343

Finley, Karen, 358
First View (Penrose), 247
Fitzgerald, F. Scott, 9
Fitzgerald, Zelda, 9
Florence Diary (Rilke), 161–62
Fluxus, 331–32, 338, 343–44, 353
"Fly" (Ono), 362, 366
Fonteyn, Margot, 251
Ford, Ford Madox, 110, 335–36
Ford, Parson, 51
Fornarina, La (Raphael), 219
Found (Rossetti), 119, 124
Frau Lou: Nietzsche's Wayward Disciple (Binion), 14
Freud, Anna, 139, 179–80
Freud, Sigmund, 7, 11, 13, 139–43, 151, 171–82, 231
   Andreas-Salomé's friendship with, 7, 11, 139–43, 171–82, 231
   Freudian psychology, 8, 205, 281
Freud Journal (Andreas-Salomé), 141, 142

Gabrial, Jan, 283
Gainsbourg, Serge, 358
Gala and "The Angelus" of Millet before the Imminent Arrival of the Conical Anamorphoses (Dalí), 209
Garbo, Greta, 218
Garcia Lorca, Federico, 191, 198, 202, 204–5
Garrick, David, 27
Gast, Peter, 151
Gauguin, Paul, 13
Gebsattel, Emil von, 175
Genealogy of Morals, The (Nietzsche), 153
Genthe, Arnold, 234, 237, 252, 280
"Germans Are Like This" (Miller), 256
Gilchrist, Alexander, 129
Gillot, Henrik, 149, 176
Gilson, Étienne, 15, 17, 19, 371–72
Gimme Some Truth, 346–48, 350, 365
Giotto Painting the Portrait of Dante (Rossetti), 107
"Glass Onion" (Beatles), 340
Gluck, Christoph Willibald von, 326
"God" (Lennon), 340
Godstow, 62, 64
Goemans, Camille, 189, 205
Goemans Gallery, 208

Goldsmith, Oliver, 27
Good Shooting (Peurose), 247
Goya y Lucientes, Francisco, 345
Grapefruit (Ono), 335, 343, 348
Graves, Robert, 14–15, 17, 371–72
Gray, Euphemia, 88
Great Masturbator, The (Dalí). 203
Greek-English Lexicon (Liddell and Scott), 61, 91
Greeks, ancient, 3–5, 12, 374
Greenaway, Kate, 88
Guggenheim Foundation, 285

"Half a Wind" (Ono), 335
"Half-Way to Victory," 256
Halmi, Bela, 260
Hamsun, Knut, 158
"Happiness Is a Warm Gun" (Beatles), 340
Hargreaves, Alan, 92
Hargreaves, Alice Pleasance Liddell, *see* Liddell, Alice
Hargreaves, Caryl, 59, 64, 92, 93
Hargreaves, Leopold, 92
Hargreaves, Reginald Gervis (Regi), 91–93, 95, 96
Harmonia, 3
Harris, Neil, 293
Harrison, George, 346, 350
Harry, Deborah, 13
Hartford Atheneum, 216
Harvey, Lilian, 245
Hatton, Denys Finch, 10–11
Hauptmann, Gerhart, 158
Hayden, Melissa, 301
Hearn, Lafcadio, 13
Hector, Edmund, 40
Helicon, 3
hell, circles of, 5
Hesiod, 3, 4, 14
Hicks, Michelle, 13
Hitchcock, Alfred, 218
Hitler, Adolf, 249, 258–59, 267, 342
"Hitleriana" (Miller), 259
Holding On to the Air (Farrell and Bentley), 300, 322
Homer, 5
Hope, Bob, 251
Horst, Horst P., 235, 237, 242, 252

"Hot Coffee," Mojave Desert (Weston), 285
Houdini, Harry, 2
"How Do You Sleep?" (Lennon), 346
Howell, Charles, 102, 110
How They Met Themselves (Rossetti), 121, 123, 124
Hoyningen-Huene, George, 235, 237, 242, 252
Hull, Agnes, 83
Human All Too Human (Nietzsche), 144, 154
Hunt, Violet, 110, 114, 131
Hunt, William Holman, 105, 106, 116–18
Hyacinthus, 4
"Hymn to Life" (Andreas-Salomé), 151, 153, 181

Imagine (Lennon), 20, 346–48, 350, 365
"I'm Losing You" (Lennon), 359
Imperial Ballet school (St. Petersburg), 305
Imperial Monument to the Child-Woman Gala; Memory of the Child-Woman (Dalí), 209
"In an Artist's Studio" (Christina Rossetti), 110
Indica gallery, 331, 334, 352
Inside the Volcano (Gabrial), 283
inspiration, mystery and unpredictability of, 2, 30
Institute of Contemporary Art (London), 263
In the Service of the People (Penrose), 256
Investigating Sex (Eluard), 192
Invisible Man, The (Dalí), 207
Isle of Wight, 65
"Is the Muse Dead?" (Croce), 8–9

Jacobs, Marc, 13
James, Edward, 217–18, 219
Japan Society, 361–62, 364
Jesus, 4–5, 210, 341
Jesus Christ Superstar, 223
"Jesus the Jew" (Andreas-Salomé), 158–59
"Je T'Aime...Moi Non Plus" (Gainsbourg), 358
John, Elton, 352
"John Rennon's Excrusive Gloupie," 365
Johns, Jasper, 332

Johnson, Samuel, 7, 17, 19, 20, 22, 27–56, 69, 273, 281, 292
  eccentricities of, 28–30, 56
  masochism of, 36–38
  medical and psychological disorders of, 27, 29–31, 36–38
  Thrale's friendship with, 27–32, 34–38, 40–43, 45–46, 52
  Thrale's rift with, 31–32, 47–49
  Thrale's view of, 31, 37, 50–52
  works of, 22, 27, 31, 39, 42, 43
Johnson, "Tettie" (Elizabeth Porter), 32
Johnson's Court, 29
Joukowsky, Paul von, 151
Journey to the Western Isles of Scotland (Johnson), 22, 39
Joyce, James, 201

Kallman, Chester, 10
Kapurthala, Maharajah of, 215
Karp, Ian, 332
Kennedy, Jacqueline, 360
Kennedy Center, 326
Kent, Allegra, 301
Kesey, Ken, 341
Kiki of Montparnasse, 199, 234, 238, 244
Kimmelman, Michael, 361
King, Coretta, 360
King Cophetua and the Beggar Maid (Burne-Jones), 105
Kirstein, Lincoln, 306
"Kiss Kiss Kiss" (Ono), 357–59
Kistler, Darci, 301
Kockashinski, Madame, 233–34
Kusama, Yayoi, 366

La Cour, Marian, 304–5
Lady Clare (Siddal), 125
L'Age d'Or (Buñuel/Dalí), 208
la Touche, Rose, 88
Laura, 14, 271, 299, 329
Lawrence, Gertrude, 245
Lay of the Love and Death Cornet Christopher Rilke (Rilke), 166–67, 172
Lear, Amanda (Alain Tap), 224
Lebedour, George, 158
Le Clercq, Tanaquil "Tanny" 301, 310, 314, 317
Lee Miller's War (Scherman), 251

Leiris, Michel, 262
Lennon, Cynthia, 335–36
Lennon, Florence Becker, 82
Lennon, John, 9, 16, 19–22, III, 231, 302,
   329–67, *328*
   creative stagnation of, 354–55
   documentaries of, 346–48, 364
   Ono's competition with, 343–44,
     349–51, 354–55
   paintings of, 338–39, 364
   recordings of, 207, 336–37, 338,
     346–49, 354–60
Lennon, Sean, 352
Leonardo da Vinci, 345
Leopold, Prince, 59, 91, 93
Let It Be (Beatles), 339
Letters to and from the Late Samuel Johnson,
   L.L.D., 53
Letters to Gala (Eluard) 201
Levet, Robert, 48
Levy, Julien, 215, 217
Lewis, Sinclair, 280
Liddell, Albert Edward Arthur, 80
Liddell, Alice, 7, 10, II, 16–17, 21, 57–98,
   66, III, 146, 154, 196, 207, 369–374
   beauty of, 66–67
   as Dodgson's Beggar Child, 18, 66–68,
     77–78, 86
   as Dodgson's unconsummated passion,
     68
   fictional Alice compared with, 85
   press and, 2
   Ruskin's friendship with, 88–90
Liddell, Edith, 61, 76, 80, 84, 86, 88, 89,
   93
Liddell, Harry, 75–76
Liddell, Henry George, 61, 64, 75, 89, 93,
   114
Liddell, Lorina (Ina), 61, 76, 82, 84, 86,
   87, 88, 91
Liddell, Lorina Reeve, 65, 75–78, 84,
   89
   Dodgson and, 76–78, 81–82, 86–87
Life, 196, 197, 218, 251, 315
Life of Congreve, The (Johnson), 43
Life of Pope, The (Johnson), 31
Life of Savage, The (Johnson), 27
"Life's Pleasance" (Dodgson), 80
Limbour, Georges, 266

Linus, 4
Lisson Gallery, 335
Lives of Lee Miller, The (Penrose), 235
Lives of the Poets (Johnson), 17, 31, 42
Looking Back (Andreas-Salomé), 140, 148,
   156, 157, 163, 165, 183
Lopez-Willshaw, Arturo, 215
Los Angeles County Museum of Art, 266
Lovers Listening to Music (Siddal), 124
Lowry, Malcolm, 283
Lugubrious Game, The (Dalí), 194, 200
Lyon, Ninette, 264
Lysons, Samuel, 49

McCartney, Paul, 339, 346
McGirk, Tim, 222
Madar, Wendy, 290
Maddow, Ben, 273
Madonna of Port Lligat (Dalí), 210, 220
magic, art vs., 2
Magritte, René, 189, 246
Mahler, Alma, 19, 139
male muses, 9–11
Mammy's Cupboard, Natchez (Weston), 285
Man Ray, *see* Ray, Man
Man Ray Shaving (Miller), 237
Manucci, Count, 42
Marriage at Cana, The (Veronese), 123
Marsyas, 4
Martins, Peter, 323
Marx, Harpo, 218
Maryinski Ballet, 306
Mason, James, 251
Mather, Margarethe, 275, 287
Matisse, Henri, 13
Mdvani, Prince, 215
Meditation (Balanchine), 17, 243, 300,
   308–12
Mejia, Paul, 318–19. 323
Melpomene, 3, 229
Melville, Herman, 289
Meninas, Las (Velázquez), 214
Meysenburg, Malwida von, 143
Michael X., 341
Millais, John, 88, 105, 106, 124
Miller, Annie, 116–18, 119, 123, 124, 126,
   131
Miller, Erik, 242, 245–46, 265
Miller, Henry, 218

Miller, Lee, 7, 15, 16, 18, 22, 227–67, *228,*
    232, 271, 273, 280, 283, 349, 372–73
    education in photography, 230, 237,
        239
    Man Ray's relationship with, 229, 231,
        235, 237–38, 240, 241–45, 247, 248,
        254, 261, 262, 265
    as model and photographer, *228,* 235,
        237–40, 249, *250,* 256–57
    personality and talent of, 230–31, 254
    portrait business of, 240, 245
    wartime photojournalism of, 230,
        249–57, 259–61, 267
    writings of, 256–57, 263
Miller, Mafy, 246
Miller, Theodore, 231–37, 258
Milton, John, 5
Mind Games (Lennon), 354
Mintz, Elliot, 351
Miró, Joan, 190, 218, 266
misogyny, 14–15
Mitchell, Arthur, 300, 318
Mnemosyne, 3
*Model Preparing for a Millinery Salon after the
    Liberation of Paris, 1944* (Miller), 235
Modotti, Tina, 275, 277–78, 287
Moe, Henry Allen, 290
Montague, Mrs. Elizabeth, 43, 48, 49
Monte Sacro, 145, 147, 154, 179, 207
Moore, Henry, 262
Morris, Jane, 133, 135
Morris, William, 128, 133
Morse, Robert, 221
Mostyn, John, 54
"Mother" (Lennon), 340
Mouis, Marie-Christine, 326
Movements for Piano and Orchestra (Balan-
    chine), 306–8, *307*
Mozartiana (Balanchine), 308–9, 323–25
Mrs. Thrale and Her Daughter Hester
    (Reynolds), *26*
Munro, Alexander, 116
Murphy, Arthur, 27
Muse, The (Brooks), 8
muses:
    as art wives, 272, 277, 314
    characteristics of, 299–301
    child, 73
    fashion industry and, 13

feminism and, *see* feminism, feminists
free art-education benefits of, 230–31
function of, 195
history of, 5–23
Ideal Child Friend as, 12–14
Ideal Woman as, 12
independent development of, 229
male, 9–11
mythical, 3–5, 229, 282
origin of word, 3
same-sex, 10
in Victorian Literature, 62
Museum of Modern Art, 13, 216
My Little Gray Home in the West (Weston),
    294–96, *295*
My Thanks to Freud (Andreas-Salomé), 178

Nast, Condé, 234
Nation, 361
National Museum (Mexico), 275
Nemesis, 128
Newhall, Nancy, 292, 296
New Poems (Rilke), 169, 170
New York, 13
New York City Ballet, 21, 305–6
New Yorker, 8
New York Times, 8, 63, 361, 370
Nietzsche, Elisabeth, 144, 151, 155
Nietzsche, Friedrich Wilhelm, 7, 18, 22,
    139–56, *146,* 162, 173, 175–76, 179,
    181, 183–85, 201, 207, 231, 360
    Andreas-Salomé as viewed by, 151,
        153–54
    Andreas-Salomé's view of, 150
    writings of, 144, 153, 154
Night and Day (Penrose), 247
Nijinsky, Vaslav, 10
Nin, Anais, 218
"No. 4 Bottoms" (Ono), 333, 362
Noailles, Vicomte de, 200, 208
Noguchi, Isamu, 332
Nonconformist Chapel (Miller), 249, *250*
Noskowiak, Sonya, 276–77, 281, 287, 290
Notebooks of Malte Laurids Brigge (Rilke), 171
Nusch, 199, 201, 220
Nutcracker, The (Tchaikovsky), 304

Obiols, Juan, 225
Object to be Destroyed, (Ray), 243

Observations and Reflection Made in the Course of a Journey Through France, Italy, and Germany (Thrale), 54
"Observatory Time" (Ray), 229, 243–44
Olympus, 3
Ono, Yoko, 7–9, 16, 19–21, 207, 231, 302, 316, 327–67, 328, 372
  art works of, 331, 332, 333–34, 335, 364
  Beatles' reaction to, 337, 339–40, 346
  books of, 335, 343, 348
  early career of, 331–35
  films of, 333, 345–47
  Lennon's competition with, 343–44, 349–51, 354–55
  recordings of, 336–38, 352, 355–56
Oppenheim, Meret, 249
Orbison, Roy, 357, 359
Orpheus and Eurydice (Gluck), 311, 326
Orwell, George, 199
Out of Africa (Dinesen), 10
"Out of the German Prison" (Miller), 256
Overbeck, Franz, 153, 155
Owen, Atty, 83

paganism, 5
"Painting to Hammer a Nail In" (Ono), 334, 364
Pang, May, 351
Paradiso (Dante), 6
Parkes, Bessie, 107, 134
Parnassus, 3
Parsifal (Wagner), 140
"Passing of Love, The" (Siddal), 125
Patroclus, 3
Pegasus, 4
Penrose, Antony, 236–37, 251, 260, 262–67
Penrose, Roland, 247–49, 252, 254–55, 259–66
  works of, 247–49
Petrarch, 14, 329
Picasso, Pablo, 19, 204, 218, 222, 248, 255, 262, 265, 315
Pierus, 4
Pineles, Friedrich, 160
Piozzi, Gabriel, 31, 43, 45–46
Piozzi, John Salusbury, 55–56
Pippa Passes the Loose Women (Siddal), 125

Plastic Ono Band (Lennon), 20, 340, 356, 365
Plato, 374
Polignac, Princess Marie-Blanche de, 215
Polyhymnia, 3
Pomona (Cameron), 91
Pongs, Herman, 165
Pope, Alexander, 33
Portinari, Folco, 6
Portrait of Alice Liddell as the Beggar Child (Dodgson), 18, 66–68, 77–78, 86
Portrait of Galerina (Dalí), 219
Prendergast, Bea, 295
Pre-Raphaelites, culture of, 7, 21, 101, 104–7, 108, 116, 118, 131, 132
Pre-Raphaelites in Love (Daly), 129
Presley, Elvis, 357, 359
Prickett, Miss (Liddell's governess), 76, 80
Proust, Marcel, 205

Raphael, 219
Rasselas (Johnson), 27
Rat Tails (Miller), 240
Rauschenberg, Robert, 332
Ray, Juliet Man, 261
Ray, Man (Emmanuel Radnitsky), 7, 19, 22, 197, 229–52, 254, 258, 261–62, 265–66, 283, 349
  Miller's relationship with, 229, 231, 237–38, 240, 241–45, 247, 248, 254, 261, 262, 265
  works of, 229, 238, 243, 266
Rée, Paul, 143–47, 146, 149, 150–53, 155–56, 161–62, 175–76, 179, 182–83
Reinhardt, Max, 158
Remington Silent (Miller), 249
Renaissance, 14, 73
Retrospection (Thrale), 55
Reynolds, Sir Joshua, 26, 27, 105
Richmond, William, 88
Rilke, Rainer Maria, 7, 18, 20, 21, 22, 139, 140–41, 155, 159–71, 176, 184, 196, 231, 283, 292
  poetics theory of, 169
  writings of, 159, 161–62, 166–67, 169–72
Rivera, Diego, 275

Road is Wider Than Long, The (Penrose), 248–49
Robert Fraser Gallery, 338
Rock and Roll Circus (Rolling Stones), 345
Rock 'n' Roll (Lennon), 354
Rodin, Auguste, 16, 169, 272
Rolling Stones, 345
Romanoff, "Prince" Mike, 245
Rosenbach, A. S. W., 93
Ross, David, 343
Rossetti, Christina, 107, 110, 111, 113
Rossetti, Dante Gabriel, 7, 21, 101–36, 121, 154, 230, 289, 349
    eccentricities of, 133, 136
    paintings and watercolors of, 107, 119, 120, 124, 126, 136
    poems of, 103, 126
Rossetti, Gabriele, 103
Rossetti, Helen, 131
Rossetti, Maria, 103
Rossetti, William, 20, 104–5, 110–14, 118, 120, 122–24, 126–28, 131–33
Rotlein, William, 222
Roumeguére, Pierre, 225
Rowell, Ethel, 83
Ruggles of Red Gap (Wilson), 280
Ruskin, John, 59, 87–90, 91, 105, 111–13
Ryan, Meg, 358

Sabater, Enrico, 224
St. Laurent, Yves, 13
St. Peter's Cathedral, 145
Salusbury, John, 33
Salusbury, Thomas, 39
Sayle, Murray, 364
Scheherazade, 11
Scherman, Dave, 251–52, 254, 258, 260, 267
Schiaparelli, Elsa, 215, 218
Schill, Sofia, 164
Schneeman, Carolee, 331
Schnitzler, Arthur, 158
School of American Ballet, 305–6
Schumann, Robert, 323
Scott, Bell, 118
Scott, Robert, 61
Scott, W. B., 116
Scrapbook, 1900–1981 (Penrose), 247, 259, 261

Sculpture in Window (Miller), 239
Seaman, Frederic, 359
Seasons, The (Glazunov), 305
Secret Life of Salvador Dalí, The (Dalí), 189, 198
Self-Portrait (Miller), 228
Self-Portrait (Ray), 266
Sert, Misia, 139, 215
Shadow of a Dante, A (M. Rossetti), 103
Shakespeare, William, 348
Sheeler, Charles, 275
"She's So Heavy" (Beatles), 348
Siddal, Elizabeth Eleanor (Lizzie), 7, 16, 20, 21, 29, 99–136, 99, 154, 230, 271, 273, 289, 349, 372–73
    art works of, 124, 125
    character of, 108–9
    death of, 129–33
    exhumation of, 102–3, 136
    illnesses and addictions of, 106–7, 113–15, 120–23, 127–29
    poems of, 125
    Rossetti's marriage to, 112–13, 117, 120–23
Sinclair, John, 341
Sirens, 4
Sistine Chapel, 2
Skeffington (Dodgson's uncle), 79
Skene, W. B., 91
Slaughter on Tenth Avenue (Balanchine), 318
Sleeping Beauty (ballet) 304
"Smile" (Lennon/Ono), 364
Smith, Patti, 357
Smothers Brothers, 351
Some Time in New York City (Lennon), 354
"Song of the Bower, The" (Rossetti), 126
"Sonnets to Orpheus" (Rilke), 166, 170
Southey, Reginald, 75
Spanish Civil War, 218
Spector, Phil, 346
Spellbound (Hitchcock), 218
Spencer, Edmund, 5
Sphinx, 4
Sprouse, Stephen, 13
Stalin, Joseph, 291
Starr, Ringo, 331
"Starting Over" (Lennon), 356–57, 359
Steichen, Edward, 234, 237, 253
Stein, Gertrude, 10

Steinberg, Saul, 262
Stephens, Frederic, 117
Stevens, Enid, 72
Stieglitz, Alfred, 275, 276–77
"Stolen Waters" (Dodgson), 84
Stone, Sharon, 8, 12
Strand, Paul, 275
Stravinsky, Igor, 306–8, 310
Stravinsky, Vera, 19
Streatfield, Sophia, 44
Streatham Park, 27, 28, 30, 34–37, 46, 51, 54, 56
Strindberg, August, 158
Struggling for God (Andreas-Salomé), 155
sublimation, as motivation for art, 13
Suggestions for the Committee Appointed to Consider Senior Studentships (Dodgson), 90
Summer Sunshine (Weston), 274
Surrealism, 5, 187–226, 230–31, 233, 237, 247–48, 285
Suzanne Farrell: Elusive Muse (documentary), 300–301, 302, 304, 309, 326
Svirsky, Zizzi, 241
Swan Lake (ballet) 304, 320
Swinburne, Algernon Charles, 110, 126, 129, 131–32
Symphony in C (Balanchine), 319–212, 325
Symposium (Plato), 374

Talking Heads, 357
Tallchief, Maria, 301, 310, 323
Tanguy, Yves, 192, 212
Tanning, Dorothea, 261
Taper, Bernard, 315
Tate Gallery, 265
Tausk, Victor, 175, 182
Tchaikovsky, Peter Ilyich, 310
Teixidor, Ramon Vidal, 225
Tell, William, 205
Tennyson, Alfred Lord, 64–66. 125
Tennyson, Hallam, 65, 75
Terpsichore, 3
Thalia, 3
Thamyris, 4
Theater-Museum, 224
Theogeny (Hesiod), 3, 4
There Are Fairies in the Grotto of My Garden (Weston), 275

"There Was an Old Farmer of Readall" (Dodgson), 74
This Quarter, 244
Thompson, Gertrude, 88
Thomson, Virgil, 245
Thrale, Cecilia, 53, 54–55
Thrale, Frances Ann, 35, 41
Thrale, Harriet, 46–47
Thrale, Harry, 40, 41
Thrale, Henry, 27–44
    illness and death of, 43–44
    infidelities of, 33, 44
Thrale, Hester (Lynch Salusbury), 7, 16, 17, 19, 20, 22, 25–26, 26, 69 139, 273, 281, 292, 372–73
    children of, 34, 35, 39, 40–41, 45–47, 53, 54–55
    domestic worries and responsibilities of, 32, 36, 38–39, 41–42
    Henry Thrale's marriage to, 33–34, 39, 43–44
    Johnson as viewed by, 31, 37, 50–52
    Johnson's friendship with, 27–32, 34–38, 40–43, 45–46, 52
    Johnson's rift with, 31–32, 47–49
    in London society, 27–28, 43, 48–49, 53–56
    Piozzi's marriage to, 45–46
    Piozzi's separation from, 47
    writings of, 28, 32, 33, 42, 45, 49, 50–52, 53, 54, 55
Thrale, Hester Maria (Queenie), 34–35, 40, 41, 45–47, 53, 54
Thrale, Ralph, 39, 40–41
Thrale, Sophy, 47, 53, 54
Thrale, Susan, 54
Thraliana (Thrale), 33, 42, 45, 49
Three Apparitions of the Visage of Gala (Dalí), 219
Through Another Lens (Weston), 273, 280–81, 290, 292
Through the Looking Glass (Carroll), 84, 87
Thus Spake Zarathustra (Nietzsche), 153
Time, 197, 238
Times (London), 93
Titus, Edward, 244
Toklas, Alice B., 10
Tolstoy, Leo, 162, 163–64
Toshi, Ichiyanagi, 332

Turner, Ike, 344
Turner, Joseph Mallord William, 112
Turner, Tina, 344
Twelfth Night (Deverell), 105
Two Virgins (Lennon/Ono), 21, 207, 336, 338, 352, 356, 360
Tzigane (Balanchine), 305–9, 322

Urania, 3
U.S.A. Tent Hospital...in France (Miller), 253

Valse, La (Balanchine), 320
van Dyke, Willard, 286
Van Gogh, Vincent, 29, 339
Victoria, Queen, 59, 91
Victorian attitudes and mores, 68, 72, 74, 82, 92
Victoria Through the Looking Glass (Becker), 82
Vienna Waltzes (Balanchine), 302, 322, 325
Vietnam, 341
Violin d'Ingres, Le (Ray), 238
Visible Woman, The (Dalí), 203
"Visions of Christ" (Rilke), 159
Vita Nuova, La (Dante), 5–7, 136
Vogue, 231, 234–35, 249, 251, 253–57, 259, 261, 263

Wagner, Cosima, 151
Wagner, Richard, 140, 144, 151, 154, 360
Wain, John, 39
"Walking on Thin Ice" (Ono), 360
Walls and Bridges (Lennon), 354
War and Peace (Tolstoy), 62
Warhol, Andy, 196, 223, 244, 347
Warner, William Beatty, 154
"Watching the Wheels" (Lennon), 359
Watson, James, 223
Waugh, Evelyn, 106, 125
"We Are Seven" (Wordsworth), 106
Wedding Album (Lennon/Ono), 339
Wedekind, Frank, 158
Weimar Psychoanalytic Congress, 172
Weld, Agnes Grace, 65
"Well, Well, Well" (Lennon), 340
West, Rebecca, 28

Westhoff, Clara, 167–69
Weston, Brett, 282–83
Weston, Charis, 16–18, 139, 269–96, 274, 301, 372–73
  as memoirist, 272–73, 280–82, 289, 290, 296
  E. Weston's rift with, 291–93
Weston, Cole, 282
Weston, Edward, 16, 18, 272–96, 274, 312
  domestic routines of, 282–83
  nude subjects of, 277–78, 283–85, 290, 294–95
  photography of, 274–75, 277–78, 285, 291, 294, 295
Weston, Neil, 282, 286
When Harry Met Sally, 358
"Whirlwind, The" (Charlotte), 74
Whistler, James McNeil, 135
White Album, The (Beatles), 20, 337, 340
White Ball, 233, 240, 247
White Goddess, 15
Wife of Rossetti, The (Hunt), 110
Wilde, Oscar, 131
Williams, Llewellyn, 102–3, 110
William Tell and Gradiva; The Old Age of William Tell (Dalí), 209, 210
Wilson, Harry Leon, 280
"Winterplan" commune, 144, 151, 152, 160
Winter Zero Swatzel's Bottle Farm (Weston), 285
Withers, Audrey, 255, 258
Woeful Victory (Siddal), 124
Woolf, Leonard, 9
Woolf, Virginia, 9, 28, 373
Wordsworth, William, 106
"Working Guest" (Miller), 263
"Workingman's Hero" (Lennon), 340
World War II, 218
  photojournalism in, 230, 249–57, 259–61, 267

"Yes Yoko Ono" (Ono), 361
"You Are Here" (Lennon), 338
Zappa, Frank, 343
Zeus, 3
Zodiac Club, 215, 286

Picture Credits

Mrs. Thrale and Her Daughter Hester	Gift of Lord Beaverbrook, The Beaverbrook Art Gallery, Fredericton, N.B., Canada.
Portrait of Alice Liddell as the Beggar Child	Photograph by Lewis Carroll (Charles Lutwidge Dodgson). Gilman Paper Company Collection.
How They Met Themselves.	Fitzwilliam Museum, Cambridge University UK/Bridgeman Art Library.
Beata Beatrix.	Tate Gallery, London/Art Resource, NY.
Lou Andreas Salomé.	Roger Viollet/Getty Images.
Salomé, Ree, and Nietzsche.	Roger Viollet/Getty Images.
Salvador and Gala Dalí.	Estate Brassai.
Lee Miller Self-Portrait.	Photograph by Lee Miller © Lee Miller Archives, Chiddingly, England.
Lee Miller and Her Father.	Photograph by Man Ray courtesy of the Lee Miller Archives, England © 2002 Man Ray Trust/Artists Rights Society (ARS), NY/ADAGP, Paris.
Nonconformist Chapel.	Photograph by Lee Miller © Lee Miller Archives, Chiddingly, England.
Charis Weston.	© 1981 Center for Creative Photography, Arizona Board of Regents.
My Little Gray Home in the West.	© 1981 Center for Creative Photography, Arizona Board of Regents.
Balanchine and Farrell.	Martha Swope/TimePix.
Yoko Ono and John Lennon.	© 1980 Lilo Raymond.

Perennial

Fiction by Francine Prose:

BLUE ANGEL: *A Novel*
ISBN 0-06-095371-3 (paperback)
NATIONAL BOOK AWARD FINALIST

Deliciously risqué, *Blue Angel* is a withering take on modern academic mores. This scathing tale vividly shows what can happen when academic politics crashes head-on with political correctness—and reveals the fates of the innocent (or not so innocent) men and women caught in the wreckage.

GUIDED TOURS OF HELL: *Novellas*
ISBN 0-06-008085-X (paperback)

A daring and transgressive pair of short novels whose characters—less-than-innocent Americans in Europe—find their lives changed forever when the shocking pleasure tours of hell on which they embark reveal the difficulty of feeling the "appropriate emotions" about the greatest historic tragedy or the smallest personal sorrow.

PRIMITIVE PEOPLE: *A Novel*
ISBN 0-06-093469-7 (paperback)

The primitive people in this darkly hilarious novel are not where one might expect. Their native habitat is upstate New York's bucolic Hudson Valley, where they enact the barbaric rituals that pass for social and family life in decaying mansions and at malls, trendy weddings, and dinner parties.

WOMEN AND CHILDREN FIRST: *Stories*
ISBN 0-06-050728-4 (paperback)

Bright and entertaining tales that display Prose's special gift for revealing the mysteries and contradictions at the heart of contemporary life.

HOUSEHOLD SAINTS: *A Novel*
ISBN 0-06-050727-6 (paperback)

Set in New York's Little Italy in the 1950s—a community closely knit by gossip and tradition—this is the story of the extraordinary Santangelo family: Joseph, the butcher, who cheats in his shop and at pinochle; his mother, who sees the evil eye everywhere; his wife, Catherine, who's determined to raise a modern daughter; and Theresa, their daughter, whose astonishing discovery of purpose moves the novel toward its unpredictable conclusion.

■ HarperCollins*Publishers*

Nonfiction by Francine Prose:

THE LIVES OF THE MUSES: *Nine Women & the Artists They Inspired*
ISBN 0-06-055525-4 (paperback)

In her first nonfiction book, Prose offers a brilliant, wry, and deliberately provocative examination of the complex relationship between the artist and his muse. In so doing, she illuminates with great sensitivity and intelligence the elusive emotional wellsprings of the creative process.

Juvenile Fiction by Francine Prose:

THE DEMONS' MISTAKE: *A Story from Chelm*
ISBN 0-688-17565-1 (Greenwillow hardcover)

The mischievous demons of Chelm, the legendary town in Poland where only fools live, wreak havoc on a daily basis. Then they hear about an irresistible new place called New York City—a mayhem-loving demon's dream! When they get there, though, the big city is more than they bargained for.

YOU NEVER KNOW: *A Legend of the Lamed-vavniks*
ISBN 0-688-15806-4 (Greenwillow hardcover)

The town of Plotchnik hasn't had a drop of rain in forty days. But the town's humble shoemaker, Poor Schmuel, has the power to command rain and much more. What makes him so extraordinary? Nobody, including the town elders, can explain it until one night the Rabbi has a very strange dream . . .

AFTER: *A Novel*
ISBN 0-06-008081-7 (Joanna Cotler Books hardcover)

A chilling novel about the aftermath of a high school shooting, and what happens when personal freedoms are extinguished in the name of security.